Policing Twentieth Century Ireland

The twentieth century was a time of rapid social change in Ireland: from colonial rule to independence, civil war and later the Troubles; from poverty to globalisation and the Celtic Tiger; and from the rise to the fall of the Catholic Church. Policing in Ireland has been shaped by all of these changes. This book critically evaluates the creation of the new police force, an Garda Síochána, in the 1920s and analyses how this institution was influenced by and responded to these substantial changes.

Beginning with an overview of policing in pre-independence Ireland, this book chronologically charts the history of policing in Ireland. It presents data from oral history interviews with retired gardaí who served between the 1950s and 1990s, giving unique insight into the experience of policing Ireland, the first study of its kind in Ireland. Particular attention is paid to the difficulties of transition, the early encounters with the IRA, the policing of the Blueshirts, the world wars, gangs in Dublin and the growth of drugs and crime. Particularly noteworthy is the analysis of policing the Troubles and the immense difficulties that generated.

This book is essential reading for those interested in policing or Irish history, but is equally important for those concerned with the legacy of colonialism and transition.

Vicky Conway is a senior lecturer in Criminal Law at the University of Kent. With degrees in law and criminology she completed her PhD on accountability in the Irish police at Queen's University Belfast in 2008. She has previously held positions at the University of Leeds, University of Limerick and Queen's University Belfast. She has published extensively on policing and the Garda Síochána and regularly contributes to humanrights.ie.

Routledge SOLON Explorations in Crime and Criminal Justice Histories
Edited by Kim Stevenson
University of Plymouth
Judith Rowbotham
Nottingham Trent University
David Nash
Oxford Brookes University

This series is a collaboration between Routledge and the SOLON consortium (promoting studies in law, crime and history), to present cutting-edge interdisciplinary research in crime and criminal justice history, through monographs and thematic collected editions which reflect on key issues and dilemmas in criminology and socio-legal studies by locating them within a historical dimension. The emphasis here is on inspiring use of historical and historiographical methodological approaches to the contextualising and understanding of current priorities and problems. This series aims to highlight the best, most innovative interdisciplinary work from both new and established scholars in the field, through focusing on the enduring historical resonances to current core criminological and socio-legal issues.

Shame, Blame and Culpability
Crime and violence in the modern state
Edited by Judith Rowbotham, Marianna Muravyeva and David Nash

Policing Twentieth Century Ireland
A history of an Garda Síochána
Vicky Conway

Policing Twentieth Century Ireland

A history of an Garda Síochána

Vicky Conway

Routledge
Taylor & Francis Group

LONDON AND NEW YORK

First published 2014
by Routledge
2 Park Square, Milton Park, Abingdon, Oxon OX14 4RN

Simultaneously published in the USA and Canada
by Routledge
711 Third Avenue, New York, NY 10017

Routledge is an imprint of the Taylor & Francis Group, an informa business

British Library Cataloguing in Publication Data
A catalogue record for this book is available from the British Library

Library of Congress Cataloging-in-Publication Data
Conway, Vicky.
  Policing twentieth century Ireland : a history of an Garda Siochana / Vicky
Conway.
    pages cm. – (Routledge SOLON explorations in crime and
    criminal justice histories)
  1. Ireland. Garda Síochána. I. Title.
  HV8198.A2C663 2013
  363.209417–dc23   2013006149

ISBN: 978-0-415-69194-9 (hbk)
ISBN: 978-0-203-07000-0 (ebk)

Typeset in Times New Roman
by Deer Park Productions

Printed and bound by CPI Group (UK) Ltd, Croydon, CR0 4YY

Dedicated to my parents, Rory and Jean

Contents

Figures

Tables

Acknowledgments

First and foremost, I would like to thank those retired gardaí who permitted me to interview them. They happily gave of their time, welcomed me into their homes and shared with me their breadth of experience. They were honest and encouraging, and often followed up with additional material for me. Theirs is a story not often told but an important one to hear. I hope this book does justice to the lives they shared. I am also grateful to those persons who put me in touch with these retired gardaí. I'm sorry for hounding you!

This research has received financial support from a number of sources. I could not have completed this work without assistance from the British Academy, the Department of Education and Libraries (Northern Ireland) and the University of Kent. I am grateful to the staff at the Garda Museum in Dublin Castle who facilitated my presence, and answered my queries over many visits. Their expertise helped me find much information, which I would otherwise have missed. I also had research assistance in later stages from Lucy Welsh, University of Kent, which greatly enabled this work.

This project began as a PhD and I was exceptionally lucky to have Phil Scraton and Graham Ellison as supervisors. I'm very grateful for their insight and support. They worked me hard, challenged me intellectually and believed in my ability, even when I didn't. Many of the comments of my examiners, Professor Shadd Maruna and Professor Scott Poynting greatly assisted the development of the PhD into this book.

Since my days as a PhD student at Queen's University Belfast I have worked at the University of Leeds, the University of Limerick, Queen's and now at the University of Kent. I have had excellent colleagues at each of these institutions and have been exposed to inspiring and challenging research cultures. A number of people deserve particular thanks for their guidance, support and encouragement. Dermot Walsh, Peter Manning and Aogán Mulcahy have all made an immense impression on me as a researcher and have generously given of their time to read and comment on my work. Thanks to Dean Wilson for comments on draft chapters, Sinead Ring for sharing her expertise and to the anonymous reviewers for their helpful comments on the proposal. Thank you to both the University of Victoria and Northeastern University for providing a friendly space to work on this project while I visited. Thanks also to all of those at Routledge for their help and guidance throughout the writing of this book. Particular thanks to Nicola Hartley for her endless patience and understanding. Unfortunately, I cannot blame any of these people for any mistakes or inaccuracies in the text. These are my own.

I am indebted to my parents, Rory and Jean, for their love and endless belief in me. A huge thanks to my siblings, their partners and their beautiful children for bringing so much laughter and so many smiles into my life. Thanks also to Louise, Richard, Michelle, Elaine, Sara, Anna, Edel, Ciaran, Camilla, Liz, Alex, Máiréad and Emilie. Darren, your support and proofreading has got me here. Your tolerance, whether my head was stuck in the 1930s or the 1970s, has been invaluable.

Vicky Conway, Canterbury

Abbreviations

ACA	Army Comrades Association
AG	Attorney General
AGSI	Association of Garda Sergeants and Inspectors
CPAD	Concerned Parents Against Drugs
CPF	Community Policing Forum
DE	Dáil Éireann
DMP	Dublin Metropolitan Police
DPP	Director of Public Prosecutions
ECHR	European Convention of Human Rights
ECPT	European Committee for the Prevention of Torture and Inhuman or Degrading Treatment or Punishment
EEC	European Economic Community
EU	European Union
GAA	Gaelic Athletic Association
GPAS	Garda Public Attitude Survey
GPO	General Post Office, Dublin
GRA	Garda Representative Association
GSCB	Garda Síochána Complaints Board
GSOC	Garda Síochána Ombudsman Commission
ICCL	Irish Council for Civil Liberties
INLA	Irish National Liberation Army
IRA	Irish Republican Army
IRP	Irish Republican Police
JPC	Joint Policing Committee
MP	Member of Parliament (Westminster)
NYPD	New York Police Department
OASA	Offences Against the State Act
RIC	Royal Irish Constabulary
RUC	Royal Ulster Constabulary
SE	Seanád Éireann
SMI	Strategic Management Initiative
SO	Station Orderly
TD	Teachta Dála, member of Dáil Éireann

Introduction

The Irish police force, an Garda Síochána ('Guardians of the Peace'), is a relatively young police force, just 90 years old. It was born in the early days of Irish
independence, in a country brutally damaged by the War of Independence of
1919–21 and hurtling towards civil war. It was tasked with replacing the Royal
Irish Constabulary, a British colonial force that had become despised in the final
years of Irish union with Britain. These factors, which made the creation of a
police force all the more challenging, simultaneously made it all the more necessary. Since the force's creation the country has faced repeated threats and difficulties, all of which changed what it means to do the job of policing in Ireland:
from the IRA to the pseudo-fascist organisation the Blueshirts, to the Troubles,
from low crime to drug epidemics and so-called 'gangland feuds', and from bust
to boom and back to bust again. As the twenty-first century began, the force was
consumed in a scandal of unparalleled scale, which threatened its legitimacy and
internal morale.

> The short history of independent Ireland is littered with failures, missed op-
> portunities and institutional inadequacy. One thing the new State got right,
> however, was policing. The creation of an unarmed, democratically account-
> able police force that could win the consent of the vast majority of the popu-
> lation in the shadow of a brutal civil war stands as an extraordinary achieve-
> ment. The loss of public confidence in the Garda would therefore be not just
> an alarming development in itself, but the final step in a long and desperate
> process.
>
> (O'Toole, *IT*: 09/11/02)

O'Toole was writing in the wake of the decision to create a tribunal to investigate
allegations of serious police misconduct. The Morris Tribunal went on to document serious corruption and misconduct in the North West of Ireland. The year
2002 was also the year that this research began and in many ways that quotation
captures a central concern of this book. An Garda Síochána has been seen by
many as an achievement and as an institution of which Irish people can be proud.
The events considered by the Tribunal threatened this conception of policing in
Ireland. But what do we actually know or understand of the impact of those

transitions on policing in Ireland? This book analyses the history of the force in the hope of providing a fresh understanding of how it currently operates. Kilcommins contends that 'implicit in any methodology of policing history ... should be the need to take account of the "total context of conditions" when mapping the contours of policing systems rather than adopting an over deterministic approach' (1998: 51). With this in mind this work contextualises policing in Ireland, examining how those contexts have impacted on policing. This chapter will set the theoretical context of the work, explore the aims of the book and outline the structure adopted.

Post-conflict, post-colonialism, post-communism: post-transitional policing

Much of policing literature has been dominated by Anglo-American perspectives on policing. There are problems with the dominance of this literature and its applicability more broadly, primarily because in these countries mass social upheavals have not occurred since the creation of structured policing. For much of the world this is not the shared experience. Many countries have emerged from colonialism, dictatorship, communism, conflict and civil war and have faced the challenge of reforming or rebuilding policing. This experience generates a context of policing with which the Anglo-American analyses fail to engage. For instance, people in transitional countries may be less trusting of the police because of past experience or they may trust a new force more because it is a part of what they struggled to achieve. They may conceive of policing as more about order and security than responding to and preventing crime, and associate policing with the continuance of particular political orders.

Invariably, contends Ghandi (1998), the aftermath of colonialism involves an overpowering need on the part of the newly independent state to strike out in a different path, move away from and attempt to forget its colonial past (Whelan 2003; Young 1991). By engaging with the very issues that the state has sought to leave behind, 'post-colonialism can be seen as a theoretical resistance to the mystifying amnesia of the colonial aftermath' (Ghandi 1998: 4). This is not simply an academic exercise of dwelling on the past, for 'the triumphant subjects of this aftermath inevitably underestimate the psychological tenacious hold of the colonial past on the post-colonial present' (Ghandi 1998: 6).

If this is true, if most states that have emerged from colonialism suffer from a 'historical condition' of underestimating the psychological impact of the colonisation, then such analysis is both relevant and necessary in the case of Ireland. Given that the police put in place by the British in Ireland became the model for colonial police across the world, it is of particular interest here to determine the impact of 'the psychological tenacious hold' of that history. Internationally, Ireland does not receive much attention in post-colonial studies (Young 1991), due to a continuing debate over whether Ireland was in fact a colony. Caroll and King (2003) argue that Ireland was the first colony and in this way became a training ground for other colonies. This is accepted in relation to colonial police forces, all of which trained in Dublin under the Royal Irish Constabulary (RIC) in the early twentieth century (Lowe 2002). In the 1880s police in Queensland used the RIC's manual and the influence of the Irish force has been noted in New Zealand, Africa, and Canada among other places (Anderson and Killingray 1991). The defining features of the RIC that permeated these other forces included its paramilitary nature, centralised control and the disconnect between members and the public. Many officers chose to work in the colonies for those police forces when the RIC disbanded, stretching that influence further (Herlihy 1997).

Much has been written about the nature of colonial policing, but less has been said about how a colonial policing experience shapes post-colonial policing. This is a significant gap in the literature given how much of the world these debates engage. Cole (1999) has outlined how trends can be identified between French, Portugese and Spanish post-colonial policing on the one hand and British post-colonial policing on the other. Across each it tended to be the case that colonial policing systems were 'preserved, practically in their original state' (1999: 96). So post-European colonies, such as North Africa, Brazil and Mexico adopted complex, decentralised policing with separate forces at the federal and state level. Former British colonies on the other hand, such as in Africa and India, are notable for having a national police force with centralised control. Unsettled political climates in the early days of independence lent this approach great attraction, 'as an indispensable means for ensuring the political unification and the survival of the new states' (1999: 97). This is, of course, in direct contrast to the approach Britain adopted in its 'home' policing. This lingering colonial influence is also seen in countries where revolutionary attitudes have continued to play a role post-independence, such as Chilé where policing has continued to be paramilitary and political irrespective of transition. Cole concludes, on the basis of this review, that 'political policing appears to be the most obvious colonial legacy' (1999: 98), evidencing that in certain parts of Africa 'political leaders have been able to continue in the colonial tradition of using the police and police chiefs for political ends' (1999: 98). Further, there is no democratic involvement in local policing, and there is 'no political platform upon which policing issues are debated or even challenged' (1999: 99).

There are other transitions that can have such impacts on policing: transitions from communism to democracy as seen across Eastern Europe from 1989 onwards or transitions from conflicts such as in West Germany or Japan after World War Two, or, in more recent decades, Northern Ireland and South Africa (Mawby 2001). In all of these pre-transitional regimes the police had a core function to play in maintaining the status quo and defending the existing political regime. Politicisation, paramilitarism, centralisation and a lack of accountability were common themes in policing in those states. It is unsurprising then that in the wake of transition the police would be identified as a site of reform. Mawby has argued that efforts at police reform in transitional states have been largely ineffective, save for processes of lustration (the replacement of personnel associated with the previous regime). Functions, structures and legitimacy of the police remain fundamentally unaffected. Public confidence in the police tends to remain low, although Mawby found that confidence tended to rise where there had been direct contact with the police, suggesting that the perception of policing was more negative than reality. Increased crime rates have also been a feature in many of these countries, post-transition.

This book explores these issues of policing and transition through the lens of Ireland where, it will be shown, colonialism has shaped a range of core aspects of the police, including structure, function, increased centralisation, political involvement, democratic governance, accountability and public attitudes. This analysis is necessary and important for a number of reasons. Firstly, despite the publication of a number of collections that consider policing in post-colonial (Anderson and Killingray 1991), transitional societies (Kadar 2001) or those more generally trying to enhance democracy (Haberfeld and Cerrah 2007), there is a lack of knowledge and assessment of the Irish experience. Ireland's post-colonial status is disputed for a number of reasons and this may have distracted from the importance of this analysis. There are those who question whether the country was ever colonised (Kennedy 1992/1993). There are those who suggest that given the continuing situation in Northern Ireland it would be incorrect to claim that Ireland is 'post'-colonial (Young 1991). And there are those who argue that even if it was, the recent successes of the country indicate that this is no longer relevant. It is submitted that a post-colonial understanding is in fact relevant and appropriate and that it has played a significant role in shaping policing in the twentieth century. When it came to decolonisation, memory played a vital role in shaping the new, emerging state. Given the length of colonisation in Ireland, 'remembering' what came before was a difficult task. Added to this was the 'nationalistic project', which had emerged in the 1880s. Throughout the century preceding independence and beyond, literature and media had developed an image of Romantic Ireland, based in rural, Gaelic Ireland (Hutchinson 1994; Boyce 1982). People were at that time told that their traditional values were being torn apart by colonialism, and the public began to identify and define themselves in this way (Howe 2000). Whelan points to authors such as 'Cusack, Hyde, Pearse, Yeats and Corkery – who created the Gaelic Athletic Association, the Gaelic League, the Irish Literary Revival, the Abbey Theatre, and a Catholic nationalist version of Irish history' (2003: 94). The process of decolonisation, which began in earnest in 1922, focused on this perspective, and strove to create an Ireland which reasserted these romantic notions. For this work, this is a central point. As Cleary asserts:

> Colonialism was not simply a remote historical phenomenon but something that remained critical to the development of Irish society until the twentieth century and the consequences of which continued to shape developments in the post-partition period in both the Northern and the Southern states.
>
> (Cleary 2007: 17)

An Garda Síochána, as it emerged in the 1920s, can be seen as emblematic of this nationalism, being created in the image of this decolonising romanticism.

The Republic of Ireland has moved from colonialism to civil war to democracy in the last 100 years, with that democracy repeatedly threatened. Not only does

Ireland provide an opportunity to explore in depth how those transitions can shape policing, but it enables us to consider the extent to which these experiences continue to impact in the long-term. It can take time for the full consequences of colonialism, conflict and transition to emerge. For instance, while Mawby's documentation of scepticism towards the new police was apparent in Ireland in the first decades of the new force's life, this was overcome within the space of 30 years. The police in Ireland have since enjoyed unusually high levels of public confidence. This, it will be argued in the book, could also be a legacy of colonialism. As Manning has said, 'the Garda are both sacred and legitimate as a result of their connections to the origin of the state and this insulates them from the usual vagaries and variations in public opinion even in the face of scandal' (2012: 2). In this way, Ireland can provide an understanding of those effects of the colonial and post-colonial experience on contemporary policing that might not immediately be apparent.

The twentieth century was a time of rapid social change in Ireland: colonial rule, the nationalist movement, the attainment of independence through a divisive treaty and partition, civil war, poverty, mass emigration, the Northern Irish Conflict, and more recently the Celtic Tiger, the impact of globalization, Europeanisation and the collapse of the Catholic Church. Each created substantial challenges for policing, effectively redefining the role of the police in Ireland. The last decade has been one of particular controversy, with the Morris Tribunal producing eight damning reports on the state of discipline, governance and culture within the force. This scale of criticism had not previously been endured by the largely popular force. Substantial legislative reforms have been introduced but questions exist as to their ability to address the underlying causes.

Objectives of the book

The objective of this work is to provide a new, socio-historical understanding of the Irish police that can contribute both to international questions of policing post-transition and to national questions of policing in Ireland. Brady (2000), Allen (1999) and McNiffe (1997) have provided excellent historical accounts of the early decades of policing in Ireland. Criminological analyses of policing in Ireland, on the other hand, has been somewhat absent. Walsh offers an in-depth legal analysis of the constitutional status and accountability of the force (1998), as well as the impact of human rights (2009b) and through a plethora of articles continues his important and critical legal analysis. Vaughan and Kilcommins (2008) and Hamilton (2007) have insightfully focused on different aspects of the criminal justice system, with much to say about the role of the police and the way in which they interact with the system. Mulcahy has produced criminological analyses of community policing (2008) and the policing of travellers (2012). Most recently, Manning has written on trust and accountability in the Irish police (2012). Empirical research of the gardaí has not been conducted by many academics, due in part to the still nascent state of criminology in Ireland and to an unwillingness on the part of the police to engage in such research. Data of this type could provide an innovative understanding of policing in Ireland, of prevalent cultures, of how social changes have changed the nature of policing, and of the lived experience of policing.

It is in this way that this book makes its most substantive contribution. Oral history interviews have been conducted with 42 retired members of the Irish police, 41 male and 1 female, who have provided honest and open accounts of policing in the period 1952–2006.[1] These were lengthy interviews averaging at close to two hours, with some stretching for much longer. Interviews were conducted in eight different counties and participants had policed in all counties and major cities. There was a spread of experience in terms of ranks, ranging from Garda to Assistant Commissioner. Participants were asked to speak on all aspects of their careers, from background and why they decided to join, right up to the decision to retire. This rich narrative is combined with analysis of government debates, reports, legislation, case-law and in-depth newspaper archival searches to present for the first time a cultural understanding of the Irish police. Lacking still, however, are published studies of serving police, particularly of the ethnographic variety that have been so informative in other jurisdictions (Manning 1977; Bittner 1990; Van Maanen 1982; Brewer and Magee 1991; Loftus 2009).

Structure of the book

The book provides a chronological history of policing in Ireland. Chapter 1 traces the origins of policing, focusing in particular on the development of formal policing structures under British rules in the eighteenth and nineteenth centuries. This will establish that policing in Ireland in this time, through the RIC and DMP, was primarily focused on social control and preventing disorder and uprising. These concerns shaped the nature, structures and functions of policing, as well as how the police interacted with the public. As nationalism grew towards the end of the nineteenth century the police were targeted, attacked and ostracised for their role in maintaining British control. The colonial dimension is central to this analysis. The Irish version of policing, so different to that implemented in Britain, became a model for policing throughout the colonies. But in Ireland, it became a hated model and breaking with this policing past was key when independence came.

The establishment of a new police force in the wake of Irish independence is the focus of Chapter 2. In a country where policing symbolised colonial control, where the entire infrastructure of a state had to be developed and where civil war was imminent, this was an enormous challenge. Substantive efforts were made to break with the past: members of the RIC were not permitted to join an Garda Síochána and Eoin O'Duffy as Commissioner attempted to embed the force in a culture of Irish nationalism. The chapter argues, however, that in substance little changed in Irish policing following independence and, in fact, a marked increase in police violence can be identified, possibly linked to the lack of experience and the politicised nature of policing.

Chapter 3 centres on the 1930s and 1940s when DeValera, who had opposed the Free State and its institutions, including the gardaí, came to power. His first few years in office were something of a crisis for the gardaí with their functions now heavily embroiled in political machinations. The chapter explores how politicised policing became, as two opposing organisations, the IRA and the Blueshirts, regularly came into violent conflict on the streets. This became a defining moment for the gardaí who, through their acceptance of the new leadership, won the support of all political parties. In the meantime however, much damage was done to public relations with regular use of violence to police these groups. With the 1940s came a time to repair some of these wounds and the emergency of World War Two provided an opportunity to interact more positively with the community.

The 1950s and 1960s, examined in Chapter 4, have been presented by other writers as the most peaceful decades in Irish policing. In some ways this is true: recorded crime was low and the threats of previous decades had dissipated. A new generation of police, including for the first time women, were recruited and the experiences of the IRA and the Blueshirts became memories and folklore. However, concerns as to dreadful living and working conditions rose to the fore, leading to protests and government enquiries. These experiences exposed the failure of governments to provide the forms of support desired by gardaí. Drawing on interviews, this chapter explores in original detail the difficulties of policing in Ireland at this time. Newspapers are used to explore the issue of use of force by an Garda Síochána during this period. The combination of this data challenges previous representations of this time as the golden age of policing in Ireland.

Chapter 5 focuses on an area overlooked in the literature on Irish policing, the impact of the Northern Irish Troubles on policing in Ireland. The chapter first considers the response of the government to the Troubles, which consisted of expanding police powers and increasing garda strength. The intention appeared to be the criminalisation of paramilitary activity and the extent to which this happened will be analysed. Data from interviews is used to explore what policing the Troubles involved, from attending protests, to protection work at prisons and the attending and investigation of bombings. For the first time since 1942, gardaí were killed in Ireland. For this generation of police this was the first time such dangers had been faced and so their perception of the role fundamentally altered. The second part of the chapter looks in particular at the lived experience of policing the border with Northern Ireland. This generated a further range of specialist tasks such as checkpoints, weapons searches and engagement with the police of another jurisdiction. Most striking is the extent to which policing in this part of the country differed from elsewhere and in fact through the creeping nature of the Troubles, it bore more in common with policing in Northern Ireland. Gardaí were neither sufficiently trained nor supported through this and the chapter calls for a greater acknowledgement of the difficulties endured in this time.

Chapter 6 considers the role of the Special Branch in policing the Troubles. During this period allegations of police brutality emerged in relation to the policing of paramilitaries. The response to these allegations from government is analysed and the argument is developed that through a failure to investigate, a particular attitude towards accountability emerged. As politicians clamoured to express their support for the force, an ability to act without question developed.

Chapter 7 examines how the gardaí engaged with the changing nature of Irish society in the 1970s, 1980s and 1990s. The arrival of drugs, dramatic rises in crime, the changing economic climate, cultural diversity, globalisation and secularisation changed both the work of the police and how they interacted with society. Changes in conditions of policing, including pay, technology and the experience of women are also discussed. While respect for other institutions such as the Church and politicians began to fall in the 1990s, the gardaí maintained high levels of public confidence as a result, it is contended, of the legacy of post-colonialism reasserted by the Troubles. The chapter will explore how subsequent scandals failed to impact on public confidence.

Chapter 8 presents an assessment of where policing in Ireland is today. As the twentieth century came to a close, a scandal developed which would bring the gardaí into question in a way that had not occurred previously. The chapter examines the Morris Tribunal, which substantiated serious allegations of corruption in Donegal, concerning the framing of two men for a murder which had not been committed and the planting of hoax IRA bomb finds by gardaí. The government response was the Garda Síochána Act 2005, which introduced reforms to accountability mechanisms and government control of the force. These reforms are analysed and it is argued that they do not address the problems of policing in Ireland, which have been considered throughout this book. However, as will be explored, the impact on public confidence has been minimal. Further, the chapter considers how a new language of managerialism has come to dominant official policing discourse and how the current recession is impacting on policing.

The conclusion draws the foregoing analysis together, providing a coherent assessment of the changing nature of policing in Ireland through a century in which the state itself has changed enormously. I will argue that the legacy of transition still haunts Irish policing in a largely unacknowledged way. Throughout the book a number of core themes repeatedly emerge; that policing in this jurisdiction has been highly political and politicised; that use of force and violence has been perennial and often excessive; that trust has been high and accountability weak; that the day-to-day concerns of police have been neglected to a point that is detrimental to morale; and that members have experienced enormous challenges and difficulties to which they have been expected to adjust. A three-way disjuncture is apparent in what politicians say, expressing deep-rooted support for gardaí, what politicians then do, often not effectively addressing the needs of police, and what gardaí have done to prompt such expressions of support, which often come in response to allegations of abuse or misconduct. It is argued in this book that this disjuncture can be traced to transition and that it has serious repercussions for police morale, legitimacy, governance, accountability and overall effectiveness. The Irish experience may be instructive for other countries recently emerged from such dramatic transitions.

Notes

1 A full methodology is presented in Appendix 1.

1 Colonialism and politicised policing

The British invasion of Ireland involved, naturally, control and reform of the legal system, replacing the Irish Brehon system with its feudal legal system. As formalised watch systems developed in England, they were replicated in Ireland. In time, Ireland became a site of experiment for structured policing as concerns and objections were raised in Westminster to proposals for England. The result was the Royal Irish Constabulary (RIC), a force which held an awkward position in Irish society and whose demise was inevitable following the bitter War of Independence. From its ashes emerged an Garda Síochána. A central argument of this book is that modern policing in Ireland was fundamentally shaped by pre-independent policing in two conflicting ways. On the one hand a desire existed in the 1920s to differentiate policing in independent Ireland from the RIC and colonial policing that had been used politically to control and suppress. On the other hand, when the country achieved independence, time constraints and a lack of alternative experience led to the retention of many of the core features of colonial policing. Therefore, twentieth-century policing was defined by efforts to be ideologically different but practically similar to the RIC of the nineteenth century. Appreciating that legacy and why it developed as it did is, therefore, essential to our understanding of modern policing, as much as an understanding of the colonial context underpins an understanding of the desire for change in the 1920s.

This chapter explores what colonial policing meant in Ireland. What such a study reveals is a policing experiment in a society where the predominant concern is order maintenance and suppression of nationalism rather than law enforcement and crime control. The chapter will trace the erosion of an indigenous justice system and the imposition and consolidation of British, structured, professional policing. But more than this, the chapter will examine that experience of policing to argue that policing in Ireland is historically highly centralised and politically directed, a theme which continues through independence. Simultaneously, the chapter will consider how difficult and trying policing was in Ireland in this period as the force lurched from social crisis to social crisis, performing functions more akin to an administrative body than a crime control organisation. The final decades of the force, the descent into a policing crisis in the War of Independence, will be scrutinised to contextualise the public understanding of policing at the time independence was achieved in 1922. What emerges is that the colonial nature of the state and its police force are essential to that context, and that they shaped policing in independent Ireland irrevocably both in terms of the structures and nature of policing and public perceptions.

Early policing in Ireland

The eighteenth century was a watershed in Europe in terms of policing and social control. It brought the first attempts to construct organised police forces but this was not the first experience of policing in Ireland. For centuries Brehon Law (Kelly 1988) provided a system whereby brehons, or judges, investigated crimes and imposed punishments, usually fines. Laws developed through custom over time and were passed down orally until the seventh century, when they were first written down. Brehon Law has been considered progressive law, with an emphasis on restitution rather than punishment. A thorough and developed body of law, it dealt with criminal law, family law, personal injury and contract law, among other areas (Ginnell 1917). It permitted divorce, espoused gender equality and was not bound by the then powerful Canon law. Neither courts nor police were required, such was the respect for this law, as communities and kinships enforced decisions. In essence it was a self-policing system. From the twelfth century the English attempted to supplant Brehon Law but it was not for another five or six centuries that it could be said that English law prevailed. The development of policing in Ireland, in terms of persons being delegated policing functions, was inextricably linked to the spread of the English legal system throughout Ireland.

For centuries following the Anglo-Norman invasion the spread of English law was limited to Dublin, or the Pale as it was known. From the fourteenth century, this system involved justices of the peace, petty constables and night watchmen. Enforcement by the community was central, as in the Brehon system, with Boyle describing 'collective involvement' as 'the lynchpin of social organisation' (1972: 118). Hue and cry, whereby community members would shout to alert those responsible that a crime had occurred, as well as collective fines, emerged as central features, both placing responsibility on the wider community. While this was community-based, because Protestants dominated the professions of magistrates, judges, lawyers and watchmen, Catholics continued to trust in local methods of justice (Malcolm 2005: 18).

Developments in the eighteenth century brought the domination of English law throughout Ireland. In the early 1700s churchwardens[1] in Dublin appointed part-time constables who in turn were charged with appointing night watchmen. However in 1715 legislation secularised this task, giving this role to the Dublin Corporation (O'Sullivan 1999: 12). Magistrates fulfilled this role in the rest of Ireland. The position of watchman became paid during the eighteenth century due to the incompetence and corruption of post-holders and as citizens became less willing to volunteer (Henry 1994). A distinctive feature of the organised watch system was a clear division of organisation between day and night policing, with resources being directed toward the latter. In 1778 there were two-dozen daytime police in Ireland whereas night-time numbers ranged from 350 to 400 (Palmer 1988: 97).

Over time this system was deemed insufficient to maintain order. In addition to the growth of cities and the impact of urbanisation, there were outbreaks of social unrest with the growth of the United Irishmen in the late eighteenth century. From the 1760s the Whiteboys, a secret organisation, used violent tactics to uphold the agrarian rights of tenants. Legislation was passed to address riots and uprisings, the number of constables was increased and the army was regularly drafted in to provide supplementary support. Indeed, Boyle argues it was the problems generated by having the army so embedded in Ireland that 'stimulated the search for alternatives to regular soldiers' (1972: 15). Westminster was at this time discussing the establishment of a police force in England, and the unrest in Ireland made the need all the more pronounced. What would emerge was the first formal system of policing in the British Isles.

The Dublin Police Act 1786

The legislation that created the Dublin Police in 1786 was initially drafted for the purpose of creating a police force for London. A variety of factors in the English capital drove the movement towards organised police:

> All of these forces (i.e. rapid urbanisation, increases in disorder, the prohibition on collective violence as a means of equalising power relations, the impetus provided by men such as Patrick Colquhoun and Sir Robert Peel, increased anxiety about thieftaking as a method of law enforcement, the onset of lawyerisation, the burgeoning system of private prosecution, and the 'common matrix' of rationalism) consequenced themselves, in a broad sense, in the movement from a paternalistic, particularistic and spasmodic model of law enforcement to a new homogenised and disciplinary agency of social control.
>
> (Kilcommins 1998: 45)

The Bill for London was defeated in Westminster as an invasion of liberties (Philips 1980: 172) but was considered appropriate for transference to Dublin. The concerns in swelling urban populations in England, which centred on increasing crime and class power conflicts, differed wildly from Ireland where British concerns related to controlling the agrarian disturbances of the 1760s in rural areas and threats of nationalism. Transposing the Bill from one jurisdiction to another when 'the attached "twins" exhibited very different personality characteristics' and when the concerns arose from different foundations should have raised grave concerns (Palmer 1988: 36). Large sections of the Irish population voiced concerns with the Bill. Henry Grattan, a leading nationalist Irish politician, described the Bill as 'the most obnoxious and alarming that ever, perhaps, arrested the attention of an Irish senate' (Grattan 1822: 291). Dublin newspapers decried the development particularly in light of its rejection in London. The Irish Parliament enacted the Bill, creating the first professional police force in Great Britain, in spite of these concerns. The vote took place though at a time of year when many MPs were absent from Parliament due to assizes where they served on juries or participated in cases.

The Act divided Dublin into four districts, each with a Chief Constable, ten petty constables and one hundred night watchmen, all Protestant, salaried, uniformed and armed. Three Commissioners of Police were appointed by government, one of whom served as Chief Commissioner. Policing in Ireland was centralised from the beginning and the political involvement went further. While the London Bill had barred MPs from assuming the role of Commissioner, this was not the case in Dublin. Not only could the head of the police be a political appointment but they could indeed by a politician, with all the attendant concerns.

While crime in Dublin fell in the force's first year, those who had opposed the Bill continued to challenge the Dublin Police after their creation. A campaign was launched and 'after a decade of agitation, riots, inquiries, petitions and repeal bills, opposition to the police establishment was to triumph, and the Dublin Police Act was abolished' (Boyle 1973a: 104). Complaints concerned abuse of powers, detention without cause and improper treatment of detainees though it was the expense of the system that enticed the government to repeal the Act within a decade. For four years Dublin reverted to a reduced watch system under the control of the Lord Mayor (Herlihy 2001: 8). The argument that it was inefficient and expensive meant a return to the Dublin Police in 1799, even though it was lingering debt from the original Dublin Police that had immobilised the system. It was at this time that there developed 'a conception of police as a separate department of government authority, subject to government control and responsible for executing government policy' (Boyle 1973b: 342). The dissolution of the Irish Parliament, via the Act of Union 1800, brought an end to any domestic discussions of policing matters for over a century. All further legislation on policing stemmed from Westminster and so any Irish concerns were silenced.

Establishing the Royal Irish Constabulary

Initial developments for a police force for the rest of the island occurred at the same time as the Dublin Police was created. The Preservation of the Peace Act 1787 created baronial police forces, rather than a general police force for which Thomas Orde, the Chief Secretary of Ireland, had advocated. Robert Peel extended this in 1814 into a Peace Preservation Force. Initially this comprised just 400 men but within eight years it had grown to over 2300 men (Palmer 1988: 21). This was a reactive system of policing: once the Lord Lieutenant deemed an area 'troubled' a squad comprising of a Chief Magistrate, a Chief Constable and 50 constables was dispatched (Curtis 1871: 3). This system was expensive and, as it was paid for locally, unpopular. Nor was it sufficiently numbered to provide support and control. An Irish Militia had been introduced in 1793 and two years later a Yeomanry was added, indicating the perceived limitations of the Peace Preservation Force.

Following crop failures and attendant agitation, the Constabulary Act 1822 created a County Constabulary to supplement the Peace Preservation Force.

The Peace Preservation Force dealt with disorder and riots, while the Constabulary orientated itself towards crime prevention and investigation. The Irish Constabulary Act 1836 consolidated the force into one body, the Irish Constabulary, centrally controlled by Dublin Castle, numbering nearly 8000 men and with a rigid hierarchical structure. Perhaps due to the abiding British concern for order in Ireland there was a strong connection between the military and the Constabulary. Curtis documents how many generals and officers of the army were drafted into senior positions, though this tended to be problematic as the work was so different in nature (1871: 45). In 1842 a national training depot was built in Phoenix Park in Dublin, bringing an end to separate, provincial police training. From 1846 responsibility for payment for policing rested with government, rather than local authorities, eradicating many objections while solidifying centralised control.

Structurally little changed in the coming decades. Reforms related either to increases in pay or a redistribution of numbers, often following disorder such as the Belfast riots of 1864, which led to the creation of a force for the city of Belfast. An inquiry was held in 1865 into pay and conditions. Two years later, when the Constabulary defeated a rebellion by Fenians in various parts of the country, the Constabulary was renamed the Royal Irish Constabulary (RIC). The men involved were financially rewarded for the 'gallantry and fidelity which had been displayed' and became a talking point in Westminster (Curtis 1871: 179).

As its purpose was to maintain order in a country where social, political and agrarian unrest was common, the RIC was a large force with 14,000 men in the 1880s, larger than an Garda Síochána today, although the size altered dependent with the unrest. This was particularly evident during the Famine, the Land War of the 1880s and in the final days before independence during which times the numbers swelled. At all times, numbers were far greater than in England. In 1851 Ireland and England had the same number of police officers, though the population of Ireland was 6.5 million compared to 18 million in England. There was also a reserve force, which could be deployed rapidly. Malcolm (2005: 59) estimates that 100,000 men served as policemen in Ireland between 1822 and 1922, most of whom were Catholic Irishmen.

The RIC inhabited some 1400 barracks, a huge number. There are two obvious reasons for this: first, transport being as it was, in order to be able to respond to emergencies quickly police needed to be widely spread, and second, such omnipresence supported the British efforts at control. Unsurprisingly, given the volume, barracks were not large and usually comprised a sergeant and four constables. There was a rigid, hierarchical structure to the RIC, with parallels to an army structure. Barracks were grouped into 250 districts in the country, and were presided over by a district inspector. Districts were further organised by county, with each county having a county inspector, assisted by a head constable. Disparity in county sizes meant that some county inspectors presided over scores of stations while others had just a dozen or so under their command. Above the rank of county inspector were the four provincial police commissioners above whom sat the Inspector General, aided by a deputy and assistant. The Inspector General reported directly to the Chief Secretary of Ireland. This structure created a somewhat top-heavy situation: in 1913 there was one officer for every 3.1 men (Malcolm 2005: 47).

Until 1922, therefore, two separate forces, the Dublin Metropolitan Police (DMP) and the RIC, co-existed in Ireland. The size, militaristic style and central-ised nature has been described as a combination of a rural gendarmerie, a civil police and a basic civil service (Brady 2000: 2). This was in stark contrast to the system that developed in England, where the first police force came in the form of the Metropolitan Police Service in 1829 (Emsley 1996). Increasing civil disor-der finally outweighed the civil liberties concerns of the 1780s. Peel, who intro-duced the legislation for the Metropolitan Police, had served as Chief Secretary in Ireland from 1812 to 1818. In difference to the Irish experience, in order to address lingering hostility, the first constables in England were directed to be civil and polite to win over the public. Their uniforms (blue) were purposefully clearly distinguishable from the military (red). These police officers were unarmed, save for wooden truncheons. Beat patrols dominated their work and their stated purpose was to prevent crime. Proven efficiency in tackling crime helped over-come much hostility. Over the coming decades similar police forces were estab-lished in other urban areas such as Manchester, Birmingham and Bolton. In 1856 every county was required to establish a police force. An Inspectorate of Constabulary was created and central government agreed to contribute 25 per cent of the cost of policing. Within a short space of time over 200 police forces existed throughout England and Wales, each with its own Chief Constable. Brogden (1987) has argued that in spite of this quick proliferation animosity continued, particularly among the working classes who perceived the police as an organisa-tion of control.

The distinctions between policing in both countries are clear. Ireland had a centralised, hierarchical structure entirely funded and directly answerable to government. In England policing was locally organised, only partially funded by government with an oversight body to ensure a certain level of professionalism was maintained. In Ireland the police function was to maintain order, while in England it was to prevent crime. Boyle comments that,

> In the final result the divergence of the systems of the police when finally established in the nineteenth century, as between England and Ireland, is to be explained not in terms of different conceptions of police, but in the different conditions, social, economic and political obtaining in the two societies.
>
> (Boyle 1973a: 95)

Ireland was a colony ruled from Westminster while England was emerging as a democratic state. From a British perspective the policing needs were completely different. But this discussion tells us little about the nature of policing, what the job entailed or how the police were perceived. Using various biographical accounts and social studies of the RIC, these issues will now be considered.

Life in the RIC

Malcolm conducted an in-depth study of life in the RIC, which, combined with a number of autobiographical accounts from the nineteenth century, reveals the nature of policing in Ireland at that time. From the 1850s onwards a dispropor-tionately high number of new recruits came from Munster and Connaught. These were largely rural areas so recruits had previously been labourers or farmers and so were accustomed to hard work for low wages. Such men were familiar with certain sets of social relationships, effectively class based: 'social relationships based on traditional divisions and forms of deference were thus preserved and, indeed, reinforced' (Malcolm 2005: 55). Recruits were male, between the ages of 19 and 24 and mostly Catholic, though this was not reflected in the officer ranks. Married men were not permitted to join and recruits had to serve seven years before permission to marry could be sought. Until the 1860s only 20 per cent of the force was permitted to be married. All policemen, even those married with children, resided in the barracks unless permission to live outside was granted, which would only be due to limitations of space.

As to why they joined, for many it was the promise of a job, particularly for rural men where farming prospects were limited and a lack of education excluded other occupations. Brewer cites one man who joined the RIC: 'Well, in Donegal there's nothing but farming and small farms at that, and a lot of them had big families and the only thing if you didn't join the police you went to America' (1990a: 33). In addition to avoiding emigration, and the permanency that tended to involve, the job offered a stable wage, a pension, social respectability, enhanced marriage prospects, camaraderie and a sense of importance within the community. Malcolm does not address, presumably due to a lack of data, whether the distrust and even animosity felt towards the force at certain times factored in decisions to join. One can imagine that the need for gainful employment may have outweighed any such concerns for potential recruits.

Officers were separately recruited and trained and many had a military back-ground. These men generally came from the east of Ireland and tended to be middle class and Protestant. They were invariably men without many career opportunities who, just as the Catholic members, decided against immigration. In later decades, Catholics achieved officer rank through promotion.

Training was for a period of six months and after 1842 all training took place at the Phoenix Park depot. Training was highly regimented and discipline was severe. The depot was militaristic in nature with a heavy emphasis on drill. Reading, writing and accounting also featured. Criminal law and barrack regula-tions were learned by rote. In discussing the nature of weaponry training Malcolm comments: 'Like so much of the depot drill, it was far more appropriate to wartime conditions than to routine policing' (2005: 77). The depot embedded a sense of discipline that would not easily be shaken: 'it took the recruit abruptly out of his previous milieu, isolated him from society and sought to control every aspect of his waking day: not only what he did, but even what he thought'

(Malcolm 2005: 92). Boyle states that '[i]t [the RIC] was built on the lines of an army and embodied much of the military experience gathered in policing duties in rural Ireland in the preceding years' (1972: 117).

During the lifetime of the RIC there were particular periods of great unrest, which would have consumed their work including the Famine, the Land Wars and the War of Independence. Certain parts of the country were also more regularly captured by unrest. This was difficult work for the RIC, presumably even more so for Catholic members as this unrest stemmed from British rule and so loyalties may have been divided. By current standards this was dangerous work. Lowe shows that between 1843 and 1845, 133 police officers died on duty (1994: 67). As discussed further below, the final decades of the force's life were particularly dangerous for its members. During the Famine of the 1840s, tasks included the protection of clerks distributing wages and food convoys as well as aiding evictions, work that made them hugely unpopular. Lowe describes, however, how they also ran food-distribution points and soup kitchens during the Famine, which made them simultaneously indispensable to communities (1994: 16). As crime rose during the famine, primarily the theft of food, animals and weapons, so too did requests for help made of the police, demonstrating the extent to which people had come to accept the RIC as a source of protection. Indeed numerous petitions were made to Dublin Castle calling for increased numbers of police. They were, however, greatly exposed to death and disease: between 1847 and 1849, 600 police officers died, mostly from disease contracted through working conditions.

In less disturbed times there were a range of tasks performed by constables. They investigated crime, with licensing laws and the distillation of poteen receiving particular attention. Court work was a regular feature of policing at this time both in terms of prosecuting and giving evidence. But in reality crime was a minor function and their time was consumed with numerous other tasks, many of which appear benign and administrative, but had a central information-gathering function for the government. A wide variety of books and journals had to be kept on matters such as licensed public houses, fees collected, licences granted and hotel accommodation. Men were required to know the locals and the features of their district. They conducted the census, gathered information on animals and crops, food, weights and measures, attended fairs and meetings, checked the safety of boats and transferred persons to workhouses and lunatic asylums. They walked the beat every day. They attended public meetings and marches that were likely to produce riots, including both nationalist events and Orange Order marches. All of these functions provided opportunities to gather information about local communities. Malcolm writes, 'probably no other arm of the state was quite so ubiquitous, so intrusive or so rigidly controlled' (2005: 128). For British authorities in Dublin this was essential, particularly given that while there were small detective units within the RIC, they had limited success in rural, close-knit communities. The need for political intelligence grew and the Crime Branch Special was created in 1882, which utilised networks of surveillance and spies. In spite of these developments the policeman on the beat continued to provide some of the most essential information. Given this broad range of duties Malcolm concludes that Ireland during the operation of the RIC could be described as a police state (2005: 128).

RIC men were never really off duty. As we have already noted they lived in the barracks and were expected to respond to calls received at any time. The RIC Code of Regulations dictated all aspects of life in a very strict way, including matters such as whether they could keep animals or grow food on barracks land. Uniforms were worn at all times. Marriage was restricted and for those who secured permission, the lives of their wives and children were equally controlled. Wives were directed as to what rooms they could enter in the barracks and what work they could do. Children, who received better education than they would otherwise have had, nonetheless faced difficulties in having a 'peeler' for a father. One account by a man who grew up in a barracks tells of being beaten up regularly on the way to school while being called an English spy and a traitor following the Easter Rising (Brewer 1990a: 73).

Although the secure wages was a draw to the job, throughout the life of the RIC pay, promotion and pensions all proved to be sources of contention. Inquiries into pay and conditions were neither unusual nor irregular. Indeed, three occurred between 1866 and 1882. Concerns were also rife that promotions were difficult to come by and occurred on unfair grounds. Evidence presented to some of those inquiries testified to the belief among constables that promotion was reserved for those favoured by officers. Class, religion and politics were all relevant factors in promotion. Discontent produced unrest and agitation in Limerick in 1882, in Belfast in 1907 and in Kerry in 1920 where a mutiny occurred, linked to their role in the War of Independence.

As has been shown, there were difficult times for members of the RIC, such as the Famine and the Land Wars, which brought them into conflict with the public. Their relationship with the public was complex however. Walsh describes how

> [t]he close identification of the police with a government in Dublin which was remote and alien to large sections of the population throughout the country meant that the close association between police and public, which was a hallmark of English policing, never really emerged in Ireland prior to independence.
>
> (Walsh 1998: 7)

On the other hand, in times of peace, as Brady outlines, there was a difference in how the men and the force were perceived. As individuals, members of the force tended to be well respected and popular in their local communities. As a force, the majority were Catholic Irish men, meaning that they could not be considered an entirely foreign force. Officially they were an armed force but unless there was a particular disturbance in an area, officers did not carry weapons. However, accompanying this was always the knowledge that during crises their loyalty remained to the Crown, and the RIC lurched from crisis to crisis. This was not softened by the fact that Protestants held a disproportionately high number of senior positions. Brady explains that '[t]hey were acceptable when things ran smoothly in the district, but when there was a whiff of disaffection in the air they were the Castle's men and that basic fact underlay their affability' (2000: 12). The end of the nineteenth century, and the first decade or so of the twentieth century were among the more peaceful that the RIC had experienced. Nonetheless Brady quotes from the memoirs of District Inspector George Garrow Green who, while having had a good reception in Kerry, knew that the residents 'still looked forward to the near future and when they would have a police force of their own making' (2000: 12).

Of course, not all problems with the police related to their policing of political disturbances. In 1872, in what became known as the Maam Trasna murders, a family of five were murdered. Eight men were found guilty of the crime, three of whom were hanged, on the basis of testimony from witnesses which was later proved to have been falsified at the behest of the government and the police who wished to frame certain people for the crime. An inquiry was conducted into the event after some public uproar. While in England an Inspectorate of Constabulary was created under the County and Borough Police Act 1856 no method of accountability existed for the Irish forces. This was presumably not deemed necessary for a colonial force with the primary aim of maintaining law and order. No doubt this increased public scepticism and distrust.

The job of the policeman in Ireland then was not one that men aspired to but chose over emigration and for the security of the pension. It was a highly disciplined, regulated and all-consuming life. Day to day it could be benign work involving highly administrative tasks relating little to crime, although this generated a varied and enjoyable career. On the other hand, in times of unrest in the country it was a difficult and dangerous job. The final and most dangerous decade of the force's existence will now be considered.

The growth of nationalism and the demise of the RIC

The Easter Rising of 1916 brought the police and the public into direct conflict for the first time in decades. Indeed, turn-of-the-century policing in Ireland had been relatively peaceful, save for the Dublin Lock Out of 1913, one of the largest trade union disputes in Ireland. The DMP policed many of those rallies and in August when they attacked a rally two men died. But it would be the Easter Rising that would have greater repercussions for policing in Ireland. While the rising did not have the widespread support of the people, the subsequent executions of the leaders garnered support for the nationalist movement. Lowe describes how the Defence of the Realm Act 1914 was thereafter used to conduct searches, arrests and disrupt nationalist activities on a scale that had very negative effects for community relations (2002: 81).

From 1914, given British entanglement in a war overseas and the fact that the Home Rule Bill had been presented, the Irish administration was instructed to do little and to conserve finances. This extended to the police who, Bowden contends, were not permitted to take action without approval. This had severe consequences for morale within the force. One military leader at the time described the consequences for RIC men: 'This once magnificent body of men had undoubtedly deteriorated into what was almost a state of supine lethargy and had lost even the semblance of energy or initiative when a crisis demanded rigorous and resolute action' (Bowden 1977: 42).

In January 1919 the leaders of the political uprising convened in the form of Dáil Éireann, a self-proclaimed government, to issue the Declaration of Independence. The War of Independence, a guerrilla war, commenced at this time with the killing of two RIC men at Soloheadbeg in Co Tipperary. The Dáil called for an immediate boycott of the RIC, knowing that they had to be the first target for elimination if they were to successfully terminate British rule in Ireland as they were the very symbol of it. DeValera, a leading republican who became leader of the Dáil in 1919, referred to them as 'spies in our midst … the eyes and ears of the enemy' (Lowe 2002: 85). Notices issued by the IRA, and reported in *The Irish Times*, stated that 'interaction of any kind whatsoever is strictly forbidden between citizens of the Irish Republic and that portion of the Army of the Occupation known as the Royal Irish Constabulary' (*IT*: 18/06/20). Any person who failed to comply with the boycott would themselves be boycotted. *The Irish Times* referred to this as 'the War on the Police' and documented how in June 1920 railwaymen were refusing to work trains on which policemen and soldiers were travelling (*IT*: 26/06/20). In the same month it reported that Roscommon traders refused to serve police officers to the extent that the threat of force was used to obtain basic supplies such as milk:

> In one shop where they were met with a refusal the police seized a milk can. Meanwhile a large crowd assembled outside and the police drew their revolvers. Then a party of soldiers in a motor car came on the scene and were placed on duty in the streets. Infantry and cavalry were drafted into the town at night and patrolled the streets and roads.
>
> (*IT*: 26/06/20)

People moved if a member of the RIC sat on their pew at mass. Undertakers refused to handle policemen's bodies. Girls who dated policemen had their hair cut off. It was a total social boycott. In some areas they smuggled food from friends in secrecy. In addition to the personal distress this caused, it also prevented the police from performing basic aspects of criminal investigation. Nationalist forces attempted to avail of this by using part of the IRA as a Republican Police. District courts were established and by 1920 these were effectively operational in 28 counties. The power and authority of the RIC was significantly undermined by this parallel legal system.

While talks with London began, violence gripped the country with the RIC at the receiving end of much of this (O'Halpin 1999: 2). Between 1919 and 1922, 493 RIC members were killed violently, 18 went missing (presumed dead), 77 died mistakenly or in accidents connected to the fighting and a further 700 were injured. Some of these deaths could be described as assassinations[2] while others occurred in the course of violent encounters between volunteers and police.[3] An assassination attempt was made in June 1920 on the Assistant Inspector General, the third highest-ranking officer in the RIC (*IT*: 26/06/20). Members of the RIC were effectively marked men and as Hawkins states, 'it's much denounced "military training", an abbreviated form of that given to the Regular Army, was similarly fifty years out of date and quite unrelated to the type of fighting which actually ensued' (1966: 174).

Between the violent attacks and the social boycott many perceived their position in Ireland untenable and it was stated in Westminster in 1922 that 1200 RIC men had left the country (Sheills 1991: 144). Lowe further documents that between March 1920 and December 1921, 2690 offences had been committed against the RIC. By August 1920 'about half the police stations in Ireland had been vacated or destroyed' (2002: 89), many having been burned out by nationalist forces. Sixty-nine attempts were made to seize active police stations in that 22-month period. Further, weapons of the RIC were often seized and barracks regularly destroyed. Police were warned and trained for attacks on police stations and in 1919 stations began to be closed in the west of the country, and in November of that year all 'vulnerable' stations were immediately shut (Lowe 2002: 83). The military protection that became required only estranged them further in the public's mind. The opening months of 1920 saw dozens of attacks on police stations. Baton rounds occurred as the police became increasingly militarised. For some police it was not a simple case of walking away: IRA leaders requested some men to remain within the force to assist in encouraging others to leave. Ferriter quotes the words of a constable from Meath who said 'I wanted to resign from the force, but General Boylan of the IRA would not allow me … I was more useful where I was' (2005: 207).

The situation was aggravated by the RIC killing of the Republican Lord Mayor of Cork, Tomás MacCurtain, the death by hunger strike of his successor Terence MacSwiney while in prison and the hanging of 18-year-old Kevin Barry in Dublin. Each made international headlines. *The Irish Times* reported the 'terror' that had infiltrated cities throughout the country to the extent that when independence was secured it instructed its readers that '[t]he Provisional Government has many urgent duties but its first and most urgent duty is the restoration and maintenance of public order' (Brady 2000: 35). Unsurprisingly, unrest in the force grew, to the extent that in June 1919 the Commissioner of the DMP issued a warning to members of both forces that if they failed to perform their duties they would be dismissed, losing their pension (*IT*: 07/06/19).

Bowden outlines in detail how the intelligence services, clearly essential in such a time of crisis, were in a poor state of array (1977: 44). Different sections of men in different divisions were given tasks that duplicated the others' work. Even when information was available, such as in relation to the 1916 Easter Rising, action was not taken by superiors. This can only have compounded the work and experiences of members of the RIC.

The Chief Secretary of Ireland declared the support of the British Government for the RIC: 'we will loyally abide by you and give you every help and every support' (*IT*: 07/06/19). Core to this was the issue of pay, given the enhanced dangers being faced by members. Resignations from the RIC rose from 85 in 1903 to 299 in 1913.[4] Between June 1920 and July 1921 there were 1200 resignations (Lowe 2002: 106). Working conditions and long-term career prospects were clearly very poor and the sentiment grew that men were not being paid sufficiently for the work. In 1918 the *Constabulary Gazette* derided that the force took the approach to 'use two men for one man's work and underpay both' (Bowden 1977: 29).

A Viceregal Committee chaired by Sir John Ross was tasked with examining the structure of the two forces and considering matters of pay. It reported in December 1919, addressing many of the concerns previously outlined here. It advised a reduction in the number of sergeants and some structural reforms, including the abolition of the mounted division and full dress uniform. In terms of pay it recommended the adoption of pay rises granted in England under the Desborough Committee and provided for a retirement allowance. A White Paper adopting these recommendations was issued by the government in May 1920 and came into effect late in 1920 (O'Sullivan 1999: 344).

A further method of support from the government was to increase police numbers, given that resignations were so high and local recruitment had come to a standstill. Two supplementary police forces were added to the RIC at this point, the Black and Tans and the Auxiliaries. In March 1920 the first recruits from England arrived to supplement the RIC, men who would become known as the Black and Tans due to their uniform. Most were men who had served in World War One. They were untrained in policing and did not have the attention to discipline that RIC men had. Bennett contends that their violent behaviour in Ireland strengthened the cause against the British, as they became a particularly hated force (1959: 38). They engaged in reprisals and retaliations for attacks made on the RIC, often directed at civilians rather than nationalist forces: 'there had been cases of wild shooting in Limerick and the bombing and burning of houses in Thurles and Bantry as reprisals' (Bennett 1959: 56). Military generals were placed in command of both the RIC and the DMP, as well as these supplementary forces, pushing them further towards paramilitaries rather than police. They were armed with rifles and machine guns and Bennett reports that one commander stated 'the more you shoot the better I will like you'. Following the killing of a head constable in the town of Balbriggan, the Black and Tans conducted a raid, seizing alcohol, setting fire to dozens of homes and businesses and shooting people (Bennett 1959: 93). There were reports that the Black and Tans harassed citizens, shooting the poultry of local people and claiming it for themselves (Ferriter 2005: 233). The sacking of villages after the killing of RIC men was not a one-off either. In December 1920 numerous buildings in Cork city, including the City Hall, were set on fire. Five acres of the city were burned to the ground and the current equivalent of over €94 million worth of damage was caused. While initially denied, it was determined by a British Army Inquiry, the Strickland Report, that the fire was started by members of the Auxiliaries (*IT*: 16/02/21). At one point the Black and Tans issued a proclamation stating that for every policeman shot, five or six Sinn Fein leaders would be killed (Bennett 1959: 98). On Bloody Sunday, 21 November 1920, after Michael Collins had 14 British agents assassinated, the Black and Tans opened fire at a football game in Croke Park, killing 14 and injuring many more, though instructions had simply been to search all those in attendance. One week later, 18 members of the Auxiliaries, who had been conducting raids in nearby towns, were killed in an ambush in Kilmichael, Co. Cork. In contrast to the RIC all the Auxiliary men were British drafted into Ireland: they were indeed a foreign, violent entity that quickly became deeply hated. A priest in Limerick witnessed the following incident:

> In one house the Black and Tans found a young family, the wife rocking the cradle. They ordered them out on the street while they sprinkled the house with petrol. The young husband, who was not an active 'Sinn Féiner', muttered something about his house being destroyed. A 'Black and Tan' fired point blank at him and as the young man screamed with the pain of the bullet, they lifted him and threw him into his blazing house.
>
> (Ferriter 2005: 234)

Nor was their venom reserved for republicans and civilians. A number of ex-RIC men who gave evidence to the American Commission on Conditions in Ireland 1921, testified that once they had resigned they had been attacked and threatened by Black and Tans. Some were beaten, shot and then left the country, fearing for their safety (Breathnach 1974: 90). A crime wave set in as no police force had authority or legitimacy in Ireland and after the events at Kilmichael martial law was imposed. McNiffe notes that '[p]erhaps the greatest difficulty for the Irish Republican Police (IRP) was the fact that they themselves were on the run from the British army, the DMP and the RIC, as well as the Auxiliaries and the Black and Tans' (1997: 9). O'Halpin contends that the IRP was successful solely in terms of propaganda (1999: 3). The DMP remained alienated from the public in Dublin as a result of violence during the 1913 Lock Out. O'Sullivan states that the DMP 'was perceived by the strikers and the general public to have acted totally on the side of the employers, and it took a number of years for the wounds connected with this to heal' (1999: 16).

As early as June 1920, as the Home Rule Bill was being debated in Westminster, the question of whether the RIC would survive or be disbanded was appearing in newspapers (*IT*: 04/06/20). As the Bill progressed there was much debate over which government would have control of the police force(s). It was clear from early on that the British government intended to financially secure the police so as to ensure that men who had given their loyalty to the state should not suffer for that loyalty, though this was while it was planned to retain the existing forces for three to six years. It was Edward Carson, the Unionist politician, who suggested that for political reasons retention would be untenable and the forces should be disbanded (*IT*: 04/06/20). This approach was further supported by the representative associations of the RIC who issued a statement saying: 'all men claim disbandment and refuse to serve any government other than that of the British Parliament' (*IT*: 01/12/21).

A truce ended the War of Independence in July 1921 and that December the Anglo-Irish Treaty was signed, proposing the Irish Free State and partition of the island. The days of the RIC seemed numbered.

Conclusion

There are many things to be said about policing in Ireland under the RIC. It was to begin with an experiment, one which appears to have been viewed as a success by the British administration given its expansion throughout the island and its replication throughout the British colonies. It was not desired by the Irish, but resistance had only a temporary effect. The structures put in place were different from those later implemented in London and England, primarily in being more centralised and hierarchical. Their orientation was largely to prevent public disorder and to that end training was highly militaristic. They performed roles more akin to an administrative agency that had an effective information-gathering function. All of these elements indicate the extent to which this was a colonial force imposed by a government in another country concerned with maintaining order. This was aggravated in the final years by the imposition of the violent Black and Tans. Policing therefore was seen as a controlling arm of government, not as a protective service, upholding the rights of individuals.

At the same time it has to be acknowledged that the role of the RIC was difficult and dangerous. Policemen lurched from exceptionally trying times like the Famine or the Land Wars to quite boring administrative work. Bowden argues that the RIC was a 'creature of crisis' (1977: 38). Death rates were high. Public attitudes towards them could change rapidly. In the final decades it must have been unbearable to perform those functions. Pay was poor. Life was regimented. Discipline was strict. They had to live in barracks cut off from society. Promotion prospects for Catholic members were low. Structures were weak: 'The RIC ... changed very little during its existence in terms of its organizational structure. Such inertia was in fact one of its principle weaknesses ... For eighty-five years it remained in a condition of suspended animation' (Bowden 1977: 27). Indeed, it is hard to imagine how the security of wages and pension compensated for all of the difficulties. But for the British state these were not matters of real concern and few of these were addressed.

The next chapter will explore the birth of the police in the new Free State. In the context of the creation of all the apparatus of a state little time or effort was dedicated to the creation of the police. Resultantly, much of what has been outlined above unfortunately carried over. For this reason this detailed understanding of the RIC has been required. Indeed, as we move forward to the later chapters, where the accounts of men and women who joined an Garda Síochána in the 1950s and 1960s are examined, we will see how the influence of the RIC on policing in Ireland continued even then.

Notes

1 Of the Church of England, not the Roman Catholic Church.
2 For instance the 'dastardly' murder of a sergeant and a constable by six armed raiders of a train in May 1924 (*IT*: 24/05/19) or the shooting dead of District Inspector Lea Wilson in Limerick in June 1920 (*IT*: 19/06/20).
3 Constable Doogue was killed in an encounter where stones were thrown at police (*IT*: 26/06/20).
4 All resignations and retirements were subsequently suspended for the period of the war.

2 An Garda Síochána

An ill-conceived birth

Our country is on the threshold of a new era. For better or for worse, Ireland's destinies are in Irish hands, and the future will be of our own making. If the new Ireland is served by a force which will uphold the best traditions of the Royal Irish Constabulary she will be fortunate, indeed.

(*IT*: 18/08/22)

You now have a police force of your own, who are not out to force law and order down your throats with a gun like their predecessors, but to cooperate with you in the protection of life and property.

(Eoin O'Duffy, *II*: 20/11/22)

The year 1922 saw the disbandment of the RIC and the creation of a new police force. This was a defining moment in Irish policing, a reality captured in the above quotes. Emerging from both colonialism and conflict, on the verge of civil war, the challenge of forming a police force that could express an ideological statement of the role of the public police in the new nation was immense. The context outlined in Chapter 1 meant that the new Irish police force would be formed on the basis of what it was not. O'Duffy's words capture the core of that ideology, that Ireland could move from policing by coercion and force to policing by consent and cooperation, and from a focus on social control to one of upholding liberties. But as Chapter 1 explored there was much more to British policing in Ireland. These were not the factors that led Malcolm to the conclusion that Ireland in the nineteenth century was a police state: instead it was the barracks, the omnipresence, the information-gathering functions. As we will see in this chapter, the rhetoric of the time indicated that it was the final years and the brutality that would define what Irish policing had to be different from, thus determining what Irish policing would be.

This chapter will explore the birth of the new police, focusing on the context of its emergence, in particular the fact that all the institutions of the new state had to be created when the country was on the brink of civil war. Limited time was spent planning the new force, a fact that backfired within months when a mutiny broke out among recruits. Beyond these structural and organisational factors, the chapter will then explore the experience of policing in Ireland in the first decade of the new state. In some ways this was a surprisingly stable time for the country, with William Cosgrave leading a government for ten years. Similarly, the police were led by the former army general Eoin O'Duffy for a decade. Through his stable leadership a philosophy of policing developed as a performance of Irish nationalist values and ideals. Yet a continuing threat from the IRA exposed deficiencies in the new force, the politicised nature of policing in the new Ireland and the influence of violence.

The Anglo-Irish Treaty

The failure of the British forces to defeat the IRA and the loss of control throughout the country heightened the need for a political solution to the War of Independence. A truce was agreed in the summer of 1921 and in December representatives of Dáil Éireann, including Michael Collins, the Chief of Staff for the IRA and an MP, signed the Anglo-Irish Treaty in London. The Treaty was much contested. It would create the Irish Free State, but also partition the country, keep Ireland within the Commonwealth with Dominion status and require members of the new Irish Parliament to swear an oath of allegiance to the British monarchy. Not even the cabinet of Dáil Éireann could agree,[1] recommending it to the Dáil by a vote of four to three. After heated and lengthy debate in the Dáil it was ratified on 7 January 1922 by a vote of 64 to 57. De Valera immediately resigned as President of Dáil Éireann.

This was a bitter period in Irish history. The Treaty was ratified by a slim minority and large sections of the population vehemently opposed it and the institutions created thereunder. A Provisional Government, chaired by Michael Collins and separate to Dáil Éireann, was created to oversee the implementation of the Treaty and to organise all aspects of the administration of the new Free State in the context of its own disputed existence. A general election was scheduled for June 1922, effectively serving as a referendum on the controversial treaty. There was genuine fear that the country could tip towards civil war.

The country was partitioned with 26 counties forming the Irish Free State, and the other six, which had a predominantly Protestant and Unionist population, forming Northern Ireland. During treaty negotiations, it was decided to disband the RIC. The force had become so despised that its retention was not viable and a new force would be needed. The DMP, however, had not been so fatally wounded and was retained. In Northern Ireland, a committee was appointed to consider the establishment of a new police force. The result was the creation of the Royal Ulster Constabulary in June 1922, which was similar in many ways to the RIC (Ellison and Smyth 2000). A date of disbandment in the Free State was set during negotiations for 20 February 1922. In December Collins asked all parties to contribute to a Committee of Public Safety but the other parties refused to cooperate (DE: 09/01/22). In the end, it was not until after ratification in January that any action was taken about a new police force.

In terms of policing the challenge was clear. Despite the existence of the RIC, the DMP and the IRP, there was, as detailed in Chapter 1, no effective police force operating on the island in 1922. The replacement of the RIC necessitated both the creation of a new force, including recruitment and training, and the removal of the RIC while maintaining security. Violent attacks on the RIC continued and so there were justifiable concerns as to their safety. The delay in commencement of planning the new force complicated the disbandment process further. The army was directed to provide the necessary support until the new police force was created. Perhaps out of frustration in August 1922 members of the Cork City Corporation were tasked with the formation of a police force to assist the army. Interviews were held in the courthouse and those recruited began work for the Cork City Police[2] in August 1922. They were unarmed and tasked with conducting traffic, arresting looters, enforcing licensing laws and enforcing curfews that were in existence.

Changing the Guard

It was not until February 1922, weeks before disbandment was due to occur, that Collins convened a committee to plan a replacement police force. The first meeting of the committee, chaired by future Commissioner Michael Staines, a Sinn Féin MP, took place on 9 February 1922 in the Gresham Hotel in Dublin. The committee included Patrick Walsh, a former RIC District Inspector who had been loyal to the nationalist movement and had been asked to remain in the force. Four sub-committees, comprising only of RIC and DMP men, were formed which met throughout February and examined organisation, recruitment, training and conditions of service (Allen 1999: 15). The influence of colonial policing was inevitable.

The report of the committee was submitted on 27 February and the structure it proposed was accepted in its entirety by the Provisional Government. There were a number of core distinctions from the RIC. The Civic Guard (the People's Guard was the name recommended by the Committee) would replace the RIC, a change of name being essential. It would be organised around 21 divisions rather than the county structural basis of the RIC. A new uniform would be issued, including a change from the green of the RIC to blue. The basic rank would be renamed garda, rather than constable. In the core visual and symbolic ways this would be a different force. It would comprise up to 4300 men, less than half the size of the RIC. Such a reduction in numbers was highly significant, earmarking that the function was no longer the maintenance of order. In reality numbers were only reduced by a quarter: in 1926 the total police numbers outside of Dublin were 6005 while the total for the RIC in 1914, excluding the Northern counties, was 7852 (DE: 30/04/26).

But in other structural, and perhaps less visible ways, it would be little altered from the RIC. While the name of the basic rank would change, individuals in that position would retain the same powers and functions. It would be a unified, national force as with the RIC. Significantly, the force would be armed with revolvers, waist belts, truncheons and whistles. While a move away from a paramilitary force was desired, both the Committee and the government envisaged that all policemen would carry lethal weapons. At this point, it was not intended to move away from the militarised policing of Ireland. The Committee also made recommendations on recruitment, recommending the use of former RIC men where suitable and possible. Any materials from the old force, from forms to bedding, were to be used.

There are two further features of RIC policing that were retained which have had a lasting effect on policing in Ireland: the number of police stations and the centralised structure. Old RIC barracks were to be used by the new force. It was envisaged that two-thirds of the barracks (roughly 800) would be utilised, which on the basis of the planned recruitment meant six members per station. The new force would have a wide presence in the country, often in sparsely occupied stations, just as the RIC. This is in marked contrast to England and Wales, which currently has an average of 100 police officers per station (Home Office 2012). Maintaining such a high number of stations is operationally demanding and restrictive, as each station will create administrative demands. There may have been a desire to have the new police embedded in communities at a local level, fears as to the volatility of the country may have created a desire to maintain the strong information-gathering network as the RIC had done, or there simply may not have been time to consider alternatives.

The Civic Guard would be controlled by a Commissioner – a name change from District Inspector – who would be directly accountable to government. This decision to have the Commissioner report to the government, and not a local policing authority or watch committee, as was the case in England, retained a central feature of colonial policing which excluded local people from policing debates. Kevin O'Higgins, Minister for Justice, argued that 'countries which had not a centralised police force very much wished that they had' but did not explain the disadvantages he perceived with locally run forces (DE: 29/09/22). A suggestion to establish a police authority found little political support (DE: 03/02/25).

On this basis, it is difficult to contend that the Civic Guard represented a break from the colonial police force in anything more than symbolic ways. Context arguably mitigated against any other approach. The creation of a police force was just one task facing the Provisional Government. The entirety of the state administration had to be dissolved and recreated, financial arrangements with Great Britain had to be resolved, the Constitution had to be drafted and the border settled. State finances were non-existent and some 130,000 people were unemployed (Kissane 2005: 68). Disbandment was scheduled for February 1922. Time permitted little else and there was no policing experience beyond the RIC.

But it may not simply have been a case of circumstances: Allen maintains that Collins would have retained the RIC if it had been possible (1999: 13) but the Treaty could not be altered. It was he who appointed so many RIC men to the organising committee. He also left the planning to the last minute. Examples from other jurisdictions could have been considered. Policing in England for instance provided a clear blueprint for an alternative version based on local control, strong oversight, democratic involvement as well as a broad recruitment base, which had included women since 1914. Ireland did not even need to look abroad: the Dublin Metropolitan Police had operated effectively as a local police force since the end of the eighteenth century. There was a clear example of how that could and did work, but in the end it was the RIC and not the DMP that 'most influenced the development of the Civic Guard' (O'Halpin 1999: 4). Perhaps it was the tumultuous condition of the state in which security was not assured and crime had risen dramatically, that led to a belief that centralised control was to be preferred. Perhaps some approved of the RIC policing model, as per the *Irish Times* quote which opened this chapter. Collins, through the War of Independence, had displayed an appreciation for paramilitary-style policing and the gathering and use of intelligence. Early in 1922, before the organising committee had conducted its work, Collins created a Criminal Investigation Division, known as the Oriel House men due to the location of their offices, within the Free State Army. This unit comprised men who had previously served in IRA intelligence, DMP intelligence and the IRP. Two further forces, the Protective Officers Corps, which provided protection for politicians and officials, and the Citizens' Defence Force, which conducted secret intelligence gathering, were also created. These were absorbed into CID in time. The Oriel House men soon became synonymous with extra-judicial killings and abuse of prisoners, and following the truce in the civil war they were disbanded in November 1923. When a proportion of these men joined the DMP, in the new Special Branch, the intelligence division C3 was created. The military, which continued to do much of the intelligence work relating to the IRA's activities, transferred this work and some 24,000 files to the Special Branch in 1926. The volume of files indicates the extent of dedication to intelligence work. The location of this work within the police justified secrecy around policing and avoidance of accountability. The decision to largely replicate the structure of the RIC would shape policing in the twentieth century, detracting from accountability and democratic influence. The evidence analysed above indicates that this may have been by design.

The Auxiliaries and the Black and Tans disbanded and returned to Britain on 18 February. The large-scale departures had some negative consequences; some left without paying bills while some towns had grown dependent on the financial benefits of the men in the barracks (Ferriter 2005: 249). For the RIC the process was slower and staggered. Evacuations of stations began in March (*IT*: 10/03/22). The IRA took over barracks as the RIC left and assumed policing duties on an interim basis as the Civic Guard was not yet in a position to begin work. By 11 April 1922, 2332 men had left the RIC. Full disbandment was stalled after the killing of two ex-RIC men generated fears for the safety of the remaining British officers in Ireland. The RUC replaced the RIC in Northern Ireland in June; 47 per cent of that new force's membership had served in the RIC (Malcolm 2005: 218). The Constabulary Ireland Act 1922, passed on 4 August of that year, legislated for the disbandment of the RIC. Every member would retire and receive compensation from the British state. On 17 August 1922 the last 100 RIC men left Dublin Castle and 380 men of the Civic Guard, just 70 in uniform, took control of policing in Ireland. *The Times* in London reported that 'the loss is Ireland's' (*IT*: 16/08/22). *The Irish Times* commented on the lack of a ceremony and, contrary to the tide of sentiment in Ireland, stated that 'many of the onlookers regarded the proceedings with a feeling of regret at the passing of what was admittedly the finest police force in the world' (*IT*: 18/08/22). On 31 August the last of the RIC left the Phoenix Park depot.

The first recruit to the Civic Guard was attested on 20 February (Brady 2000: 41) before the final report of the organising committee was even submitted. Publicly advertised recruitment was unsafe given that anti-Treaty sections of the public rejected the new institutions of the state. Instead, recruitment was on the basis of personal contacts and on some occasions recruits did not know why they were going to Dublin. Brady quotes one man who remembered a police officer calling at his house at 2 a.m., under the cover of dark, instructing him to be on the train to Dublin in the morning. Only on the train was he told why (2000: 47). The force emerged with an air of uncertainty and uneasiness, its legitimacy and authority challenged from inception.

In March the *Irish Independent* revealed that a new police was being formed, interestingly using the name an Garda Síochána even though the force would not be called that until 1923 (*II*: 08/03/22). Following this announcement recruits faced the wrath of anti-Treaty protestors. Protection was required on some trains transporting recruits. The Royal Dublin Society, a temporary home while the military and police evacuated, was attacked in March (Brady 2000: 48). Recruiting officers were arrested by the IRA (*II*: 15/03/22) with one being forced to sign a statement that 'he had been guilty of conduct calculated to cause disaffection amongst the IRA' (*II*: 16/03/22). Austin Stack, a former Minister for Home Affairs, wrote to the *Irish Independent* stating that 'the setting up of this new force is not calculated to promote order, but rather suspicion, discontent and disorder' (*II*: 08/03/22). As O'Duffy, then IRA Chief of Staff, stated, '[t]he object was to strangle the infant Garda at its birth' (1929: 331). The Provisional Government was questioned about the force in the Dáil on 28 February, the day after the report of the organising committee was received, but maintained secrecy over both the force and the report.

When government acknowledged the force, the commitment to policing by consent was emphasised. Michael Collins, in the first official mention, told a crowd in Dublin, '[i]t will be a people's guard for the protection of all classes and parties' (Brady 2000: 43). The Minister for Home Affairs announced that 'it will be the duty of the new force to protect the lives and property of all Irish citizens irrespective of their political views and in their recruiting and training this end will be kept in view' (*II*: 08/03/22). Policing would not be politicised around Treaty politics. Recruits would be drawn from the IRA and the IRP, men who had all fought for Irish independence. Nationalism should be the defining feature. The first Commissioner was named as Michael Staines, a Sinn Féin MP. Staines, whose father had been in the RIC, had served as acting chair of the police organising committee. Allen quotes a sergeant explaining that a new recruit,

> must also be made to fully understand that he is now enforcing laws made by his own countrymen who have the welfare of their country at heart, and that the utmost loyalty, obedience and devotion to duty will be demanded.
>
> (Allen 1999: 24)

The new police, adopting this policing by consent approach, was linked fundamentally to the nationalist imagery of Ireland, developed in the late nineteenth century by politicians and authors such as Pearse, Connolly and Yeats (Whelan 2003).

In terms of practicalities, recruits were unmarried and aged between 19 and 27. They had stipulated height and chest measurements and underwent medical examination. There were examinations in reading, writing from dictation and arithmetic, and testimonials from clergymen were required. Initial pay was £3 10s. a week (*IT*: 07/10/22). Irish language was not initially a requirement though if a recruit spoke Irish other requirements could be eased. But most significant was the role given to former RIC men. By the end of April there were 1500 men based in the RDS, 97 per cent of whom were ex-IRA members, who had fought for the independence of Ireland (Brady 2000: 47). Only 3 per cent of new recruits had served in the RIC, and these were the only men in the Civic Guard with structured policing experience. RIC men were only permitted to join if they had been dismissed or had left for political reasons and if Collins trusted them implicitly.[3] Complete absorption was not practically possible: in 1920 the strength of the RIC had been almost 14,000 and in 1922 the Civic Guard comprised just 4000, although obviously serving a smaller country. By the end of 1922 a total of just 160 former RIC men had been absorbed into the Civic Guard, 14 at officer level, with 20 more joining in the next ten years (Herlihy 1997). Denying entry to members of the RIC, or lustration, is a common feature in transitional states whereby employees of the previous regime are expunged from the new institutions. The removal of these people leaves a substantial vacuum in the staffing and experience of affected institutions (Boed 1999; Capoccia 2001; Kritz 1996). Not only does this create a serious, practical problem but it can also be perceived as a form of punishment, where no crime has actually been committed (Schabas 2001). None of the 12,000 who had been serving at the time of disbandment were allowed to join (Lowe 2002), a decision of Collins' which provoked no debate. Instead they received a pension for which the British government provided over £1,350,000 (Fedorowich 1996: 93). All were Irish men. Had they been English, like the Black and Tans, it would simply have been a case of returning home but the animosity felt through the country made home an unattractive prospect, particularly given that killings and attacks continued in spite of disbandment. The impact for those officers who had remained in the RIC was profound:

> For practically every one of them, there was no returning to their native place or any place close to it. Many of them had been threatened and death sentences had been passed on some of them by IRA elements. In many cases their families had been threatened, and some had been shot at while home on holidays or while paying visits to elderly parents.
>
> (O'Sullivan 1999: 374)

Even in 1922 men who had resigned were still being murdered (*II*: 11/04/22). By April, 314 had travelled to England and 2000 more had expressed their intention to do so. *The Irish Times* declared that 'the future safety and welfare' of these men was the British government's responsibility (*II*: 13/04/22). A week later advertisements appeared advising men that the Deputy-Inspector General in Dublin Castle would advise on the accommodation that would be supplied in Britain (*IT*: 24/04/22). By early August, 763 ex-members, 87 married couples and 2171 children had been provided with accommodation in England (*II*: 02/08/22). Over 1400 RIC men emigrated to Australia, Canada and America between 1919 and 1923 (Fedorowich 1996: 105). Many joined other police forces: 1350 joined the RUC in Northern Ireland and almost 500 joined the police in Palestine. Forces in Britain, America and Australia resisted recruiting them due to the style of policing of which they had experience (Malcolm 2005: 221).

The majority remained in Ireland and little is known of what became of them or how they coped with the hostility. Malcolm found that most who left the country in that period eventually returned. Their children, often bullied in school, were instructed not to mention their father's previous careers. Indeed, Noel Browne, a high-profile politician in the mid-twentieth century, did not mention his father's RIC career in his autobiography. No support for these men was provided in Ireland; they were Britain's responsibility. Not only did they and their families suffer but Irish policing was denied their experience, which could, with training, have been modified to suit the new circumstances. The justification was discontinuity, to break absolutely with the past (Kertesz and Szikinger 2000). The Irish people wanted a force that was their own. Men who had served in the RIC were, by 1922, viewed as traitors and as part of the decolonisation process, and it was believed that they needed to be removed from policing institutions.

Training

The vast majority of the force had little policing experience but there was little time for training before the men were sent to the community at which point the poor communications network throughout the country inhibited training while on the job. This affected the appointments and promotions processes, which had to operate swiftly. In the earliest days men were stationed in the RDS showgrounds in Dublin where initially they lived quite 'a regular military life'. Training consisted of drill and class though the *Irish Independent* declared that training 'will be carried out on lines totally different from the methods used to turn out members of the RIC' (*II*: 08/03/22). Two hours a day were spent learning Irish. There was physical and firearms training as well as instruction on law enforcement. The pre-existing RIC Policeman's Manual was used in training until 1942 when the Garda Síochána Manual was first published. Gerard Lawlor, later of the Garda Technical Bureau, recalled that legal instruction was so poor that the Judges' Rules, which regulated criminal investigation, were largely ignored (Allen 1999: 25). Day-to-day matters like book keeping, report writing and presentation of cases in court were not attended to.

The Kildare Mutiny

In April 1922 most of the Civic Guard moved from the RDS to an army barracks in Kildare while some used another army barracks at Collinstown (*II*: 21/11/22).

There were at this point over 1500 recruits and close to 1000 were transferred to Kildare. Tensions were high in Kildare as the ex-IRA men viewed the ex-RIC men as traitors. Commissioner Staines was advised of this problem but took no action as 'Collins was adamant that an Garda Síochána should accept the leadership of the men whom he had used in his intelligence network' (Brady 2000: 55). When five RIC officers were promoted to Deputy Commissioner in mid-May, mutiny erupted with just a dozen of the recruits in the depot pledging loyalty to the Commissioner. The situation grew in seriousness when the mutineers secured control of the armoury, still fully stocked from the prior presence of the army (Allen 1999; Brady 2000). Civil war appeared imminent at this point, the Four Courts in Dublin having been seized.[4] Needing a stable police force, Collins met with the leaders. Six weeks after the mutiny began it was agreed that the officers in question would be re-employed as civilian advisors and Commissioner Staines resumed command (McCarthy 2012). At this point weapons were cleared from the barracks and the men remained suspended for a period of eight weeks. When the men received delayed wages, celebrations occurred during which a recruit from Leitrim was accidentally shot dead.

An inquiry established into the mutiny, chaired by Kevin O'Sheil, began in July. It collapsed when one of the instigators refused to be cross-examined, though O'Sheil nonetheless reported (O'Halpin 1999). While he found that on the whole the force was loyal and able, there existed 'a state of grave insubordination and lack of discipline' (cited in Allen 1999: 50). Senior officers had failed to appreciate the nationalist sentiment of new recruits. The barracks was heavily armed and most of the men there had spent years resolving disputes by recourse to force. Following the inquiry most of the principal actors and about 350 others involved left the force, removing the strongest nationalist sentiment.

O'Sheil recommended that politicians should not serve as Commissioner and so on 18 August Michael Staines resigned as the first commissioner. A number of constructive recommendations were made which were not acted upon. While agreeing that centralised control should be maintained, O'Sheil advocated that 'it would be a good thing if a local council had the power to hold the local police body directly responsible for certain local duties'. This was not acted upon. Perhaps most significantly the inquiry recommended that the force be disbanded and reconstituted as an unarmed force, which has become a defining feature of Irish policing. As Commissioner Staines stated, in what has become a motto for an Garda Síochána, '[t]he Civic Guard will succeed not by force of arms, or numbers, but on their moral authority as servants of the people'. McNiffe (1997) contends that Government's decision to enact this recommendation truly marked the Civic Guard apart from the RIC. Not arming them was a symbol of Irish freedom, and set them apart from the violent policing that preceded independence. This was undoubtedly a bold and innovative move in the face of the violence and crime that had become endemic in the country, even if it only occurred to prevent further mutiny. However, the RIC were not always armed and, it is submitted, it was the centralised nature and the broad range of functions that demarcated them as a police force.

The leadership of Commissioner O'Duffy

General Eoin O'Duffy was selected to replace Staines as the Commissioner. The first choice for the position had in fact been Sean Ó'Muirthuile who had worked with Collins previously but who opted for an army posting. O'Duffy had been an active leader in the IRA and had been involved in seizing RIC barracks. He was repeatedly elected to the Dáil, imprisoned a number of times and in January 1921 he became the IRA Chief of Staff. This background made him suitable to help mark the Civic Guard apart from the RIC but equally it meant that his experience was of paramilitary, not civil policing. O'Duffy would lead the Guards for 11 years, a time-span which has only been matched by two subsequent Commissioners. Later he would lead the 'Blueshirts' in an attempted fascist coup of the state, before becoming involved in the Spanish Civil War (McGarry 2005). O'Duffy was a very important choice for the leadership of the Civic Guard at this point. Brady believes that he,

> at thirty years of age, was precisely the man to organise and direct the novel and ambitious undertaking of creating an unarmed native civil police for a country whose experience of justice administration had been the contrary of this ideal. He had a natural flair for organisation and imagination ... In addition, he had a keenly developed sense of nationalism and idealism. The ideal of giving the Irish people their own unarmed police which would be "Irish in thought and action" appealed to that sense. If anybody could give an Garda Síochána zeal and purposefulness, it would be O'Duffy.
>
> (Brady 2000: 73)

This 'keenly developed sense of nationalism' would ensure that the Civic Guard would become a living image of the ideals espoused by those who had fought for independence and who convinced the country to boycott the RIC. But it was not just about directing the force; his task was to make them legitimate in the eyes of the public. Given recent events this would not easily be done. He recognised in his acceptance letter that the Civic Guard 'stands very low in the estimation of the people. It will be difficult to retrieve its position' (cited in O'Halpin 1999: 9). O'Duffy managed to use his leadership qualities to build a strong system of honour and belief within the force. He epitomised the sentiment of those who had fought for an independent Ireland and aimed to bring these ideals to fruition. He had charisma to which the members responded and built a strong level of authority on that basis.

In June 1922, Kevin O'Higgins became Minister for Justice. O'Higgins was charismatic, determined and able. For him, establishing 'normal' policing was central to the transition of Ireland. Previously stable and peaceful areas had been overrun by lawlessness during conflict and transition. This was to be worsened by the Civil War of 1922–3. Townsend maintains that 'the Irish Free State was almost mortally wounded at birth' (1992: 117) by the Civil War. O'Higgins and O'Duffy together worked to develop a coherent philosophy that would underpin the Civic Guard to enable it to be a mechanism for restoring order. After what had been experienced with the RIC they agreed that accountability to the public was important, but believed that this could be achieved through the elected representatives. O'Higgins and O'Duffy attempted to ensure that the police would be both emblematic and protective of democratic ideals. A message from O'Higgins to all members shows his dedication to those principles:

> The internal politics and political controversies of the country are not your concern. You will serve with the same imperturbable discipline and with increasing efficiency any Government which has the support of the majority of the people's elected representatives ... you will remain steadfast and devoted in the service of the people, and of any government which it may please the people to return to power.
>
> (*Garda Review*, December 1927: 3)

It was for this reason that gardaí were not given the vote until 1951, as exercising that right would involve declaring partiality towards one politician or another. Expressions of that commitment to accountability centred on internal regulations, rather than external oversight. Gardaí were not allowed to serve in the area they were from. Should a member marry a woman from the locality in which he served he automatically had to be transferred.

Other structural matters were soon legislated for. The Garda Síochána (Temporary Provisions) Act 1923 provided the first legislative provisions and structure for the force. It changed the name of the force to an Garda Síochána, guardians of the peace. It dealt with issues such as appointments, distribution, pay, allowance and pensions, a reserve force, disciplinary enquiries, resignation and dismissal and the formation of representative bodies. For continuity it also stated that any mention of the RIC in statute was to be replaced with Garda Síochána. There was a stated maximum number of 5520 in the force, a 20 per cent increase on the initial plans. The Reserve Force would have less than 230 men. These temporary provisions were made permanent by the Garda Síochána Act 1924, at which point the force could be said to have a clear legislative framework. By 1924 there were some 6300 men in the force: 4918 gardaí, 1200 sergeants, 150 inspectors and superintendents, 27 chief superintendents and 5 supervising officers.

Given the fact that 75 per cent of RIC stations had been destroyed and had not been repaired legislation was passed to aid the acquisition of premises. O'Higgins stated in June 1923 that the Civic Guard had acquired 400 stations and that it was intended that the total would be 807 (DE: 23/06/23). Powers were created enabling the government to acquire any premises for the purpose of a police station, at one month's notice. These powers were renewed annually until 1932. In 1928 it was reported that the power was exercised in 85 cases and in 40 cases the gardaí had since vacated the premises. Two hundred stations remained unsuitable for occupation (DE: 09/05/28). Even with these provisions conditions in stations were often appalling and the Garda Representative Bodies regularly complained of the illness caused. Damp and rot led to tuberculosis in many stations. Hardly any stations had telephones and many suffered from poor and irregular postal services. This combined with the attacks on stations led to some men leaving the force and moving to England (Brady 2000: 95).

The first structured disciplinary regulations were issued in 1924 (Garda Síochána Designations, Appointments and Discipline Regulations 1924), which set out clearly the code of discipline. It is difficult to know how frequently these measures were used; the Regulations required a Disciplinary Report Book be kept at both District and Divisional Level, recording every complaint made, but these are not publicly available and there were no reports published at the time indicating levels of complaints. This research identified two incidents where calls were made for the establishment of an inquiry,[5] and only in one of these was an inquiry held. As shall be seen, there is evidence of serious breaches occurring in many other instances.

The question of garda welfare arose early on. The 1924 Garda Síochána Act specifically stated that members were not permitted to join trade unions, but the Act permitted the establishment of representative bodies to enable members to 'bring to the notice of the Commissioner and of the Minister matters affecting their welfare and efficiency, other than questions of discipline and promotion affecting individuals' (s.13(1)). The 1927 Regulations permitted one representative body for the rank of garda and another for the ranks of sergeant and inspector. The formation of these bodies caused quite a bit of unrest as members of the DMP felt that their particular interests would not be adequately addressed by national bodies (Allen 1999: 123). The DMP had survived independence and included men who had served during the Dublin Lock Out of 1913, the Easter Rising and the War of Independence. Their concerns were vastly different to those men who joined in 1922. Issues of pay superseded their concerns, as in 1924, just two years after the Desborough rates of pay had been adopted, the pay of recruits was reduced by £1. Later that year it was announced that the pay of gardaí and sergeants was to be reduced by 12 per cent and the bicycle allowance was reduced by over 10 per cent. Objections by the representative bodies were lodged. The cuts were introduced without any concession to the concerns of the members. This early encounter set a tone for many such discussions in future years: gardaí feeling unappreciated and somewhat ignored, government feeling gardaí were particularly well paid in the national context. In 1929 boot allowances were withdrawn and the bicycle allowance was cut again, a move that was perceived harshly given that both items were compulsory. In those early years then, the gardaí faced difficulties. While they were well paid, particularly in the context of the economic situation in the state as a whole, the reduction of wages came at a time when the job was difficult due to the poor working conditions and ongoing attacks from the IRA, discussed below.

Policing the Civil War

The new force became operational in September 1922, in the midst of civil war. Its first public appearance in uniform was at the end of August at Dublin Castle for the funeral cortege for Michael Collins, who had been killed in an ambush in County Cork. By the end of September there were over 1500 men on duty throughout the new state (*IT*: 30/09/22) and by the end of the year there were 2000 men in the community with 2000 more in training. Five hundred men were initially sent to 20 different stations but in a defining move, the Civic Guard was not tasked with policing activities relating to the civil war. Indeed, until 1924 the gardaí were shielded from the reality of policing as the army, swelled to a size of 50,000, conducted most policing duties. Instead early tasks included protective duties in counties such as Kildare, Carlow, Laois and south Dublin and providing cover for railway lines, reservoirs and signal boxes, but not directly engaged with the IRA. O'Halpin describes the army 'as a surrogate police force' even after the end of the civil war (1999: 41). Kevin O'Higgins told the Dáil that the function of the Civic Guard was 'the protection of the rights and of the property of the people, of all the people' (DE: 29/11/22). He also stated that while they were being dispatched unarmed this was an experiment.

This decision to exclude the police from civil war clashes had a number of implications for the development of policing in Ireland. Firstly, it shielded them from attack by anti-treaty forces. In the course of the Civil War there was only one fatality within the Civic Guard,[6] which was surprisingly low given the high levels of animosity towards the force as an institution of the Free State. The anti-Treaty forces were specifically instructed by Liam Lynch, the Chief of Staff, that while they were permitted to intimidate members of the new force they were not to injure any of them (Brady 2000), both because they were unarmed and because they were not participating in the war. Intimidation, however, did occur. In November 1922, for instance, two weeks after arriving the six men in Blessington station were raided by 15 armed men who took their uniforms and equipment (*II*: 14/11/22). In the year from September 1922 there were approximately 200 attacks on Civic Guard stations throughout Ireland and approximately 400 gardaí were personally attacked in some way (Brady 2000).

> Under cover of darkness, bands of armed Irregulars attacked isolated police units and burned or bombed the improvised barracks, the flames engulfing furniture and bedding, station records, and the bicycles and other private property of the men.
>
> (Allen 1999: 58)

Enough hardship was inflicted on the members to merit the sympathies of the public, but not so much physical violence as to require that they be armed. Had there been more violence, the result may have been the arming of the Civic Guard with a possibly deleterious impact on community relations. As it was, O'Duffy used these attacks to engender pride in the force. After a number of men in Wicklow withstood an attack from IRA members he proclaimed:

> I feel elated as they do, and have the same pride and confidence in the Guard and in their future when I receive the modest reports which cover heroism of the highest kind. This is why on occasion, as now, I feel impelled to address

the Guard as a whole and to say how much I appreciate their courageous stand and firm attitude.

(O'Duffy, January 1923, cited in Allen,1999: 63)

Secondly, the nascent and inexperienced force did not have to take responsibility for intelligence gathering. For this purpose, Collins had established the Oriel House men. It would not be until 1924 that the gardaí would engage in this work. When farm labourers caused unrest, and strikes spread through the country during the summer of 1923, it was the army and not the police who responded. The combination of these points meant that the Civic Guard was completely detached both from politics and the hardship and bitterness imposed by the civil war. That they did not engage in the war gave them the opportunity to build relationships with their communities.

Entering the community

In spite of these attacks the general reaction of the public to the arrival of the Civic Guard was positive and comments were soon made in the Dáil of how 'since the force went out there is a greater feeling of security' (DE: 22/06/23). The men were, as we have noted, subject to some attack by anti-Treaty forces, but others often made up for it through welcoming gestures. In one town in Monaghan the local Orange Order turned over the Orange Hall for use by the Civic Guard after their station was destroyed (Brady 2000). Parish priests often publicly welcomed the men, which, given the powerful status of priests in Irish towns, was a significant gesture. In Dublin six women were employed. They did not have powers of arrest: 'they are a kind of patrols [sic], semi-official patrols, for the protection of women in the city' (DE: 28/11/22).

The lack of telephones and an adequate postal service saw O'Duffy relying on the force magazine *Iris an Ghárda* to publicise his instructions and orders. Even in 1926 telephones were still being installed in police stations. At that point the force had a total of 50 vehicles (DE: 30/04/26). A Cadet system and an accelerated promotion scheme came into operation in 1923. Gradually it began to be seen as an attractive career, with a steady wage, pension and promotion prospects. This is evidenced in the growth of applications to the force, a marked difference from the initial recruitment campaign, which could not be publicised (McNiffe 1997: 31).

In terms of their functions, a primary focus was tackling the disorder that had taken hold. Crime statistics are difficult to come across for the time period[7] but *The Irish Times* (03/12/23) gives an indication of the work conducted by the Civic Guard by the end of October 1923:

Indictable offences reported:	6,345
Convictions:	1,685
Summary prosecutions:	17,451
Convictions:	15,127.

This would suggest 0.14 indictable crimes per 1000 population compared with 2.4 in England and Wales at the same time (Hicks and Allen 1999). This presumably relates to the low numbers of inexperienced police in the country, recording difficulties and perhaps a public hesitancy to report crime. Garda reports for late 1924 indicate that in certain parts of the country, such as south Leitrim, 'complete lawlessness prevails' (Kissane 2005: 95). That said, over the coming years, crime rates did not increase significantly. Further, conviction rates were high (see Table 2.1).

This ability to tackle crime soon won them praise. In November 1923 gardaí were commended in the Dáil for protecting rivers and the fishing industries from poachers (DE: 21/11/23). A particular problem in the early days was the illegal poteen trade, which had expanded in the previous three years with stills being found in inner-city Dublin. Both the high proof and the unhygienic conditions of its production made this a dangerous substance, not to mention its effect on family and community life. Raids and finds were regularly conducted, with one such raid yielding 500 gallons of poteen and nine stills (*IT*: 02/05/23). Success in relation to this problem engendered the police to communities which began to turn to the Civic Guard with other local problems (O'Halpin 1999). The police themselves were required to abide by a strict rule of abstinence in line with the belief of O'Friel, the Minister for Home Affairs, that drinking on or off duty 'would deprive an Garda Síochána of all their public usefulness in the enforcement of the Licensing Laws, apart from the breach of discipline' (cited in Allen 1999: 85). In November 1922 O'Duffy stated:

> Guns will not smash the Civic Guard. Humiliation will not smash you but want of self-respect and self-control will. Once you allow yourselves to give way to drunkenness or any of the evils that follow in its train, you will go from bad to worse until your future career will be blasted.
>
> (*II*: 21/11/22)

In 1924 it formed part of the disciplinary regulations that a garda was not to be under the influence of intoxicating liquor on or off duty. Even more forcefully the regulations of 1926, disciplined 'the slightest departure from strict sobriety'. That is not to say that these efforts were effective. Breathnach (1974: 119) cites the report of an Assistant Commissioner who conducted an inspection of a station in the West of Ireland and found that most of the contents of a poteen still, which

Table 2.1 Offence and conviction rates 1927–31.

Year	Indictable offences	Conviction rate
1927	7476	63%
1928	6862	70%
1929	6724	70%
1930	6640	74%
1931	6497	71%

had been seized the previous day, had been consumed and there were women hidden in the cells.

But the efforts in this regard were part of a view that the police had an important role to play in personifying the image of independent Ireland. This was replicated in other areas such as sport, religion and language. An Garda Síochána became keenly involved in sports, both in the Gaelic Athletics Association (GAA – the Irish sports of football and hurling) and in athletics. That most members came from farming backgrounds meant they had good strength and fitness. The GAA had been a major facet of the nationalist movement. 'In the organisation and training of football and hurling teams and the formation of boxing clubs, the Civic Guard contributed immeasurably to the healing of the wounds of the civil war' (Allen 1999: 99).

In future years this would link them strongly to important sections of the community, as the GAA became the largest organisation in the independent state. Garda sports days (Aonach an Gharda) drew enormous crowds and gardaí were internationally successful at boxing and tug-of-war (Allen 1999). In the first decade tournaments were held in Dublin hosting teams from Scotland (*IT*: 04/04/25) and France (*IT*: 14/07/26). In a similar way the force was used to promote and teach the Irish language. Combined with the national Irish language revival movement O'Duffy had visions of all police business being conducted in Irish (Communication to Department of Justice, 1927). Simultaneously, government was attempting to reintroduce the language to schools. O'Duffy's efforts were not particularly effective however. The most proficient Irish-speaking gardaí were sent to Gaeltacht areas, and given the view of such places as 'backward', men were often slow to reveal language aptitude (Allen 1999). Over time the place of the Irish language within the gardaí diminished.

Another important point in their legitimation process was their pronounced religious inclination. In 1928, 250 gardaí visited Rome where they were received in a special audience with the Pope who declared that 'Ireland was the most crimeless country in the world'. According to *The Irish Times*, it was the first time a foreign, uniformed police force marched through Rome (*IT*: 19/10/28). The delegation also met with Mussolini, who praised the order and security they had secured in Ireland, an interesting occurrence given that O'Duffy would later lead a quasi-fascist movement in Ireland. The pilgrimage was at the men's own expense. A further pilgrimage went to Lourdes in 1930. The state was dedicated to the importance of Catholicism, which had infiltrated core facets of government policy such as strict censorship, bans on contraception and divorce, and the unique constitutional status given to the Catholic Church (Inglis 1998). This symmetry of policy affirmed to the public that the police as an institution reflected their beliefs, a key step in the legitimation process and in the decolonisation project the state was embarking on:

> The prodigious creativity of the 1880–1920 generation shrivelled as it was formalized in the new state into a reified command culture, with an officially approved version of Irish history and identity. This artificially constructed

identity – Roman Catholic not Protestant, rural not urban, Celtic not Anglo-Saxon, agrarian not industrial, religious not secular – was imposed in the name of tradition.

(Whelan 2003: 96)

In this variety of ways the Civic Guard aligned themselves early on with an ideal and a belief system which was being dogmatically imposed across the country. In an emerging post-colonial state, they presented evidence that the country could live up to these Irish ideals for which the nationalist movement had been clamouring for decades. This viewpoint, this idealised vision of the police, has been clung to, leading to an unwillingness to criticise or question the force. In reality the Civic Guard did not always live up to that vision, and violence has been a feature of policing in Ireland since these early days.

The use of force: the Special Branch and the IRA

By early 1924 the army withdrew and the Civic Guard was given responsibility for all crime. Reductions in army numbers meant that in fact a great deal of crime was being committed at this time by ex-soldiers. At the same time some 12,000 republican prisoners were released after the Civil War. While government policies prevented a mass outbreak of republican activity, enhanced by an increasing public acceptance of the institutions of the Free State (including the police), an element within the republican movement continued their campaign. They targeted the Civic Guard, four of whom were killed in 1923 (Allen 1999). In response, some gardaí armed themselves and there were also reports of severe abuse of prisoners. O'Duffy himself later admitted it was a problem and acknowledged that 'some individual members had not sufficient strength of character, willpower and moral courage to control their tempers and to display that restraint and moderation so essential in the disciplined and thoughtful policeman' (Brady 2000: 115). He continued, declaring strongly that abuses would not be tolerated:

The fullest vigour of the code and of the law will be enforced for transgressions of this nature … no plea of extenuating circumstances, over-zealousness in the discharge of duty, or meritorious past service will be considered, and while the Garda is protected by law in all authorised acts, if they overstep the legal boundary of their duty in the slightest degree, they are then answerable to the law, both civil and criminal.

(Brady 2000: 115)

In contrast to these sentiments, Brady notes that not only was police brutality tolerated by the force and by the community but on many occasions it was welcomed. Petty crimes could often be dealt with by a 'good thrashing', rather than involving the individual in criminal prosecutions. Brady contends that this approach was necessary if the Civic Guard was to be accepted by the people. It must also be accepted that these men had no policing experience, limited training and would have witnessed violent policing in the decade prior to independence. But the fact that they were resorting to the use of force in order to assert their authority indicates that they were not succeeding by moral authority.

This would be compounded by the birth of the Special Branch. The Police Force Amalgamation Act 1925 amalgamated the DMP and the Garda Síochána, expanded police powers, and created the Special Branch, an armed detective squad. The debate on the legislation revealed concerns over the centralised nature of the force. Members of the Dáil accused Minister O'Higgins of recreating the centralised system of the RIC (DE: 03/02/25). More localised control was proposed but was not adopted due to a fear that the country was not ready for decentralisation. This was a missed opportunity to increase democratic accountability and limit the politicisation of policing that would occur in coming years.

Instead the force became more centralised than it had been under British rule as all national security and intelligence came within the one force. A detective unit was established comprising two sections, crime ordinary and crime special. The latter was known as Special Branch and replaced the Oriel House men. The intention was that Special Branch, who could carry weapons when necessary, could deal with subversive elements leaving unarmed policeman to deal with ordinary crime. O'Halpin (1999: 65) contends that this division ensured that the odium which would soon attach to Special Branch would not taint the rest of the gardaí. This was arguably an extension of the principle applied during the Civil War of excluding gardaí from those politics. However, it also meant that national intelligence was within the force and could be used to shroud policing activity in secrecy. The new unit soon had 200 recruits, chosen under rigorous criteria and trained especially for six months. In the years that followed, the Special Branch:

> was to become perhaps the most controversial element in the security policy of the state. Its members were to be regarded on the one hand by government supporters as the saviours of democracy and order, a terror to evildoers, good men performing a thankless and dirty task; conversely, they were to become the object of vilification and hatred by the large dissident minority which still opposed the Free State and everything it stood for.
>
> (Brady 2000: 141)

In 1925 Éamon de Valera established a new political party, Fianna Fáil, which refused to recognise the legitimacy of the government of the Free State and did not enter the Dáil. His departure from Sinn Féin, the political wing of the IRA, left them without any direction but members of that party continued aimlessly to target their frustration toward an Garda Síochána. This became a bitter campaign, which lasted until 1932. One incident, where the IRA raided 12 garda stations to secure arms, resulted in the deaths of two unarmed gardaí in November 1926. Special Branch retaliated, rounding up senior IRA officers. In Waterford it was alleged that on hearing of the police deaths republicans in custody were beaten for hours by gardaí. A sworn inquiry into the events was held during which O'Duffy argued for leniency due to the provocative circumstances. He threatened to resign rather than take action against the men in question. O'Higgins was insistent on dismissal. The gardaí involved were not expelled but made to pay a portion of the costs awarded to the men in question (Brady 2000: 147). Accountability was not living up to O'Duffy's rhetoric. It may be that his experience of paramilitary policing and reprisals influenced his thinking.

O'Higgins, the proponent of accountability, was killed in July 1927. His murder had an immediate and significant impact on criminal justice in Ireland. For one, de Valera led his party into the Dáil. But it also sent the state into a position of 'institutional repression' (Townsend 1992: 129) as a resurgence of the IRA campaign was feared. Under the Public Safety Act 1927 habeas corpus was temporarily suspended and the right to trial by jury was qualified. The government became more conservative. The Special Branch took advantage of the climate and stepped up efforts against the IRA, with the full support of the government. Cumman na mBán, the women's republican paramilitary organisation, produced a series of anonymous pamphlets designed to produce disaffection among gardaí:

> Soldiers of the Free State Army, Members of the Free State Police. Where do you stand now? Remember England with all her might and money cannot uphold its Government in this country without the assistance of Irish Police and Soldiers. Are you willing to do her Infamous work for her? … resign now …
>
> (Bowyer Bell 1997: 75)

The IRA appeared to be disarming however. Between 1925 and 1927, the gardaí found large volumes of dumped arms: 629 rifles, 767 revolvers, 2475 shotguns and 815 bombs (Kissane 2005: 167). Nevertheless, disputes between gardaí and the IRA were frequent and violent:

> In certain parts of the country, notably in Co. Clare resentment against An Garda Síochána was rapidly assuming extremely dangerous proportions. Criticisms in the Dáil and Senate became more frequent, newspaper eulogies of the Garda Síochána became a thing of the past, and local bodies and representatives became increasingly concerned at what they considered to be the employment of the police in the wrong manner and on the wrong problems.
>
> (Brady 2000: 148)

After a detective was killed by an IRA booby trap in County Clare in July 1929 it was discovered that some Special Branch men had a plan to murder the local IRA leader, T. J. Ryan. De Valera in opposition subsequently gave a statement to the Dáil detailing his findings of police brutality on a trip to Clare to visit Mr Ryan:

> On refusing to give an account of his movements (he had already been held up three times on the journey from Sallins), Mr. Ryan was pushed against a wall, threatened, and struck repeatedly on the stomach and chest. He was then ordered into the car, and, as he was entering, one of the detectives rushed at

him and kicked him. When in the car he was again assaulted, one detective, taking hold of the iron starting handle of the car, struck him with it on the legs, severely wounding him on the shin. The other detective rushed at him and struck him with his fist on the right eye, blackening it. Before he was let go threats of all sorts were made by the detectives, including threats to murder Mr. Ryan.

(DE: 31/07/29)

These claims were denied by the government. However, the frequency of such allegations and the unwillingness of the government to establish a tribunal to resolve the issues (DE: 31/07/29) raised suspicions that such behaviour continued.

In 1929 there were an increased number of prosecutions for involvement of any kind with the IRA. The following year the Superintendent of Tipperary was murdered after making plans to prosecute IRA members for drilling (Breathnach 1974). This scared many members of the force who now saw themselves as legitimate targets in what they perceived to be an effort by the IRA to overthrow the Free State. Between 1922 and 1931, 12 gardaí were killed on duty. Most of these men were shot, sometimes in direct attacks on stations, often in situations where it was unexpected. Gardaí felt powerless and it would appear that out of frustration they resorted to violence. Numerous civil actions were taken against gardaí by the IRA for harassment (Brady 2000).

In late 1931 a state of emergency was declared. A constitutional amendment was passed, which enabled government to suspend trial by jury in favour of tribunals staffed by army officers. The IRA and a number of other groups were proscribed. On the one hand, this enabled gardaí to secure the arrests of many high-profile IRA members, driving the group underground, and reducing violence in everyday community life. On the other hand, the operation of the section had very negative effects on community relations and certain areas of the country were deemed no-go areas for the police. Within ten years in the community the position of the gardaí had become highly precarious.

Conclusion

For many the first decade of the Free State represented incredible achievement. From the depths of the War of Independence and the Civil War emerged a police force which, save for the Special Branch, was largely popular and had brought order to society, all while unarmed. And this from men who had been politically handpicked with limited policing experience. Only small sections of the IRA persisted in their efforts. While this was impressive there were also foundations laid in this time which would develop into problems later: the force was thoroughly centralised with no local input; it had no democratic accountability or oversight mechanisms in place, unlike forces elsewhere which were already developing these; and it came to house state security, giving sections of its work an air of secrecy. It retained a widespread basis in nearly 800 barracks and conducted such a range of administrative functions that it could be seen to be gathering a great deal of intelligence about local communities. What is also evident, if not understandable in the context, is the prominence of violence in policing in the 1920s. Policing in this period was challenging, in poor conditions with repeated pay cuts.

Many of these problematic elements stemmed from the features of the RIC that were retained. Practically speaking, the Garda Síochána was not in any fundamental way different from the previous colonial force. Efforts to differentiate policing focused on image and rhetoric. Gardaí played a significant, performative role in the decolonisation project, which saw them embody nationalist values and, until the creation of the Special Branch, maintain a distance from political policing tasks. A myth was created at this time that the gardaí were different from the RIC, while in reality many of the core problems with the RIC remained.

Notes

1 Indeed it is believed by many that de Valera sent Collins to negotiate and sign the Treaty because he would not personally sign for anything less than full independence and knew that would not be offered.
2 Sometimes referred to as the Cork Civic Patrol (O'Halpin 1999).
3 O'Halpin describes: 'he valued them for their service, for their practical police experience, and – probably – because he could rely on their personal loyalty to him' (1999: 6).
4 For a full account of how the country moved towards civil war, see Kissane (2005: Chapter 4).
5 The abuse of detainees in a station in Waterford (discussed later in this chapter), and the killing of a young man at an auction in Cork (discussed in Chapter 3).
6 A 20-year-old named Harry Phelan was killed in an entirely unprovoked attack in County Tipperary on 28 October 1922 when he was mistaken for his brother who had been in the RIC (Allen 1999; Brady 2000).
7 Brewer *et al.* (1997) provide a brief section on crime rates after partition, which gives some detail for Northern Ireland but none for the Free State.

3   The 1930s and 1940s

Transition and political policing

Introduction

The 1920s, while challenging, has rightly been credited for the emergence and predominant acceptance of an unarmed police force. The challenges of the 1930s were as fundamental as those of 1922. In 1932 Éamon de Valera and Fianna Fáil came to power, where they would stay until 1948. Having challenged the Treaty, the Free State and all its institutions, the questions of how he would engage with the police and whether the police would support his leadership were not without warrant. Within a year, he dismissed Eoin O'Duffy, commissioner of ten years. This chapter will explore the consequences of these dramatic political transitions. O'Duffy went on to lead a quasi-fascist organisation, known as the Blueshirts, which regularly clashed with the IRA. Indeed, this would bring what is arguably the most challenging time for policing in Ireland as the government directed limited policing of the IRA and gardaí resorted to regular and intense uses of force. The Blueshirt crisis will be considered in detail to explore how the gardaí were utilised in and responded to a violent political crisis. When this abated further challenges emerged from the IRA. The 1940s involved policing the Emergency, as World War Two was known in Ireland. Finally, the chapter will consider the conditions of policing as well as efforts toward modernisation across the two decades.

It will be seen that this period in Irish policing had a number of important effects for the future. In some ways it is impressive that policing survived from this crisis period as stable and intact as it did, with internal morale damaged by dramatic changes and challenges as well as ongoing pay concerns. The fact that men simply continued to perform their functions as directed during a change of government and the Blueshirt crisis, won the gardaí near universal political support on a scale which would in future shield them from criticism and rebuke. Further, even as the force matured into its second and third decades, violence became embedded with very limited accountability for this. If anything, the broadened political support basis meant that there were fewer audible criticisms.

De Valera comes to power

In January 1932 an election was called in the context of international recession. It was a bitter campaign during which a garda in Leitrim was killed while providing protection to a Cumann na nGaeladh (the ruling party) candidate. In a true test of the democracy of the still fledgling state the result heralded the first change of government as Fianna Fáil, De Valera's party, entered into a coalition with the Labour Party. De Valera, who had fought against the Treaty, the government and every associated institution, including an Garda Síochána, was now President of the Executive Council.[1] This was a highly significant transition: the state was barely ten years old and in effect its political opponents were now in power. Fears of coups and civil war proved ill-founded. A clear-out of an Garda Síochána was anticipated given Fianna Fáil's constant criticism of the institution. Those now in government were those who, in the preceding years, the gardaí 'had tracked down, persecuted, arrested and imprisoned' due to their political allegiances with the IRA (Brady 2000: 162). Initially, however, rather than changing police personnel or attempting to directly influence policing, de Valera used alternative legal mechanisms to prevent the policing of the IRA. He brought an end to the constitutional proscription of the IRA, meaning people could no longer be arrested or prosecuted for membership. Political prisoners were released. The Attorney General was replaced with a Fianna Fáil supporter, Maguire, who made clear that he was unwilling to proceed with prosecutions relating to the IRA. The new Minister for Defence declared that Fianna Fáil's policy was to 'kill violence by kindness': 'We want to get willing obedience to the law and we also want willing loyalty to the state' (cited in Brady 2000: 171). In reality however, the IRA provided a strong base of support for the government and it seems much more likely that de Valera was trying not to alienate this support. It is likely that he did not trust the gardaí and wanted to keep the IRA on side should he need to call on them. Many of the actions he took in the coming years – abolishing the oath to the monarch and replacing the Governor-General with a 1916 veteran – also aligned with the IRA perspective. The Minister of Defence's stated desire to secure obedience to the law would be much easier to achieve if the law was altered to omit certain political offences.

De Valera's assumption of power gave the IRA room to engage in its activities without fear of prosecution, as long as it did not carry arms or attempt to import weapons (O'Halpin 1999: 108). For the gardaí this posed numerous difficulties: IRA men were overtly drilling and parading as well as attempting to intimidate gardaí who could do little as the Attorney General would not prosecute. Reports surfaced that IRA men attempted to direct gardaí on policing priorities and instructed them to leave various towns stating that de Valera would soon replace the police (Brady 2000: 164). Equally, gardaí could not provide police protection at meetings and gatherings of opposition parties fearing that this would be perceived by government as action against the IRA, who regularly protested such meetings. Without directing policing de Valera had altered the policing landscape.

A number of incidents would, however, force the government's hand in this respect. In Kilrush, County Clare IRA men were openly drilling and parading. On 15 August 1932 they clashed with gardaí over posters. That evening, two IRA men[2] were arrested for the attempted murder of two Special Branch detectives during the dispute. Both IRA men were suffering from serious injuries, including gunshot wounds. Two days later the charges were dropped and the gardaí involved were suspended pending an investigation. For both gardaí and the opposition this incident served to cement beliefs that the IRA had some hold over government and that policing was highly politicised. The government announced a public inquiry into the affair, headed by the barrister Patrick Lynch, a future Fianna Fáil Teachta Dála (TD) and Attorney General. In a controversial, though not unexpected, ruling the inquiry found in favour of the IRA men, determining that the detectives had not been provoked into attack. Fitzgerald-Kennedy TD, speaking in the Dáil stated:

> These men are being treated with gross injustice. Of course, there has been a finding against them. Everyone who saw the personnel of the Commission knew that there would be a finding against them. Everyone knew that the Commission was set up for the purpose of finding against them.
>
> (DE: 2/11/32)

The government had engaged in the motions of accountability, as they would have called for while in opposition, but in a way that was perceived to lack independence. Importantly, in a report to government that was not made public, the inquiry stated that the Special Branch was:

> in a very anomalous position. They have no written or printed rules to guide them or regulate discipline … [they are] victims of circumstances, of a system established without proper safeguards for discipline and conduct.
>
> (Cited in McGarry 2005: 194)

Nelligan, Head of the Special Branch, supported the men, accepting that they had acted excessively but arguing that they had been strongly provoked and to that end he organised a collection for the suspended men, with the consent of O'Duffy. For this act, he was suspended from his position by government and later moved to a different department (Allen 1999: 103). Both the outcome of the inquiry and the treatment of Neligan angered gardaí, and suggestions were made that high numbers should resign in response. The government used these findings to announce its plan to reduce and restructure Special Branch. De Valera's leadership was, as many had predicted, causing difficulties for many in the police, sending mixed messages as to how policemen should behave.

O'Duffy's dismissal

In January 1933, de Valera called a snap election and three weeks later Fianna Fáil secured a sole majority in the Dáil. As a result Fianna Fáil was no longer reliant on the support of the IRA and could look to break those ties. De Valera also had more freedom to implement his policies. Within one month O'Duffy was dismissed as Commissioner. The reason was never clearly explained by government, leaving others to speculate. Conflicting accounts have emerged. Breathnach (1974) attributes it to his outspokenness and the political needs of Fianna Fáil. Brady (2000) suggests that O'Duffy attempted to encourage people to join him in a military coup. Allen (1999) proposes an alternative version of events, which involved Nelligan assisting an academic in gathering pamphlets on communism in Ireland. When O'Duffy informed government of this work a number of persons were arrested under the Official Secrets Act 1911 and within a week O'Duffy had been dismissed, replaced by Broy.

The dismissal was a public scandal, a 'sensational announcement' (*IT*: 23/2/33) that would 'startle the country' (*II*: 23/2/33). O'Duffy was praised in the national media as 'an outstanding figure in the public life of the country' who, as Commissioner, had ensured the 'success of the force' which 'has won unstinted praise on all sides for its efficiency and impartiality' (*II*: 23/2/33). O'Duffy called on the gardaí to maintain the 'high standard of discipline, loyalty and self-respect which has characterised the force up to now' (*IT*: 24/2/33). Even though, he said, he had remained stoutly apolitical while in office he believed he was penalised for enforcing 'the people's law' (*IT*: 16/03/33).

When de Valera was forced to explain, he admitted there was no specific charge against O'Duffy but spoke more generally of how '[w]e want a chief of police of whom no section of the community can say that that man is deliberately and politically opposed to us, and is likely to be biased in his attitude because of past affiliations' (DE: 14/03/33). *The Irish Times*, described how in 'one of the most dramatic debates' in the Dáil, de Valera was enraged, 'thundered' of how indiscipline was 'condoned', while thumping the table, and how government had a right and it was in the public interest to position a supporter of their party in the post (*IT*: 15/03/33). When pushed by opposition members to state what Broy had that O'Duffy did not, de Valera tellingly stated that Broy had not served the previous administration for ten years. A motion of censure by the opposition was narrowly defeated, though not before reference was made to a letter from the Pope in praise of O'Duffy. De Valera's explanation of his actions reveals overt politicisation of the force and frustration at efforts to prevent him from acting in this way. However, he may have felt that he was simply rectifying the previous politicisation of the police: those who joined the police in the early 1920s had been handpicked for their support and O'Duffy had been a political appointment.

O'Duffy's departure was part of an overhaul of key personnel as the leadership of Special Branch also changed. An attempt two years later to move six Special Branch men back to uniform was reversed following legal action (Brady 2000: 182). Paddy Ruttlege became Minister for Justice and Chief Superintendent Broy, a former DMP man Collins had trusted, took over as Commissioner, the first to have served in an Garda Síochána. He was promoted by de Valera ahead of all Deputy and Assistant Commissioners, indicating a lack of trust in those men. If de Valera no longer intended to court the IRA he could expect to become a target and would need a police force he could trust. Broy would be both loyal and malleable (Allen 1999: 109).[3] The change of personnel had far-reaching consequences as O'Duffy found a new role in Irish society.

The Blueshirt crisis

De Valera offered O'Duffy alternative posts, such as ambassador to Washington, but he turned these down. What he chose to do instead challenged the gardaí for years to come. In 1932 the Army Comrades Association (ACA) was formed to protect the interests of ex-army men, to address the concern of the growth of communism, and to defend against the perceived threat of Fianna Fáil and the IRA to the free speech of Cumann na nGaedheal (Manning 2006: 30). The ACA, aligned to Cumann na nGaedheal, acted as stewards at their political meetings, which gardaí had been hesitant to police. Conflicts with the IRA regularly led to riots and brawls. At one event in October 1932, the ACA had to be escorted out of Limerick by the military when they assisted a garda cordon against IRA protestors at a Cumann na nGaedheal meeting and fighting broke out. The gardaí responded at these meetings by using force. In Cork, in December 1932, nearly 4000 people gathered outside a Cumann na nGaedheal meeting. Police used repeated baton charges after the crowd began throwing stones and sticks. In a subsequent prosecution one defendant stated in court that 'if the Guards behaved as they did on that day it was the right of everyone to arm himself' (*IT*: 14/12/32).

Support for the ACA grew substantially when de Valera's government withheld £5 million in land annuities owed to Britain for sums advanced for land purchases by tenants, beginning the Anglo-Irish Trade War, often known as the Economic War. The British response, to impose a 20 per cent duty on Irish livestock exports, hit the industry hard: within a month exports had fallen by nearly £2 million and cattle trade was down nearly £1 million. Simultaneously a 'red scare' hit Ireland with regular violent protests at communist meetings. When a snap election was called in January 1933, it was marked by conflict and violence with the ACA heavily involved. At a campaign meeting in Dublin 50 people were injured in garda baton charges. By the end of the election the ACA, who had adopted a uniform of a blue shirt, had become a significant body, much despised by the IRA and Fianna Fáil. This was an unsettled time for gardaí. On the streets protests and clashes were regular, while the political context changed with dramatic implications for their leadership.

In July 1933, O'Duffy, now dismissed, accepted an invitation to lead the ACA: for gardaí, their leader of ten years was now leading an organisation with which they were regularly in conflict. He renamed the ACA the National Guard, though they became known as the Blueshirts due to their uniform which generated scepticism, if not fear, as fascism spread across Europe. Their stated aim, however, was to provide strength and a voice to the political right, to promote the values of Catholic Ireland, to support the legitimacy of the Free State and to support farmers. Inherently, this meant that they supported the gardaí and abided by the law. Numbers swelled under O'Duffy. His leadership of the gardaí influenced his approach, including a focus on drilling and publishing a newspaper. Blueshirt parades and meetings were frequent, large, processional affairs. One procession included 41 horses, 2600 Blueshirts and 3 marching bands (McGarry 2005: 244).

O'Duffy may have hoped, and the government certainly feared, that having been Commissioner for so long gardaí would be loyal to him, but this was not the case.[4] Blueshirt numbers swelled to 30,000 (*IT*: 26/07/33) and O'Duffy planned a commemorative march to Glasnevin ceremony, where Michael Collins and other nationalist heroes were buried, in August 1933. De Valera feared a coup would be attempted and responded in a number of ways. He banned the march, increased garda strength at government buildings, and in an effort to disarm the Blueshirts, instructed gardaí to enforce the Firearms Act 1925, recalling weapons from O'Duffy, former ministers and Blueshirt supporters throughout the country. Gardaí were being politically directed and complied without protest. This is somewhat surprising, not just because of O'Duffy's position but also because 97 per cent of those who joined the force a decade prior were pro-Treaty, ex-IRA. Brady questions why gardaí did not mutiny given the difficulty of their position and such changes in leadership and hostility on the ground. Geographically most gardaí were divided and isolated and this militated against organised protest. Many had young families making revolt unappealing as job security would be lost. Brady argues that O'Duffy and O'Higgins' efforts to convince gardaí to serve government, whoever was in power, prevented dissent. However, it could be that the men were not politically motivated, that they were practically rather than normatively attached and possibly disenchanted. Without accounts from members at this time it is not possible to know why such action was not taken, but it is feasible that in the previous ten years they had adjusted to being politically directed.

The government remained sceptical of garda loyalty and augmented the force with its own supporters. Seventy nine members were hand-picked and attested in the three days before the march. All were active supporters of Fianna Fáil and many were former members of the IRA who had clashed with gardaí in recent years. About 80 per cent were over the legal age of recruitment, almost half were married, which was forbidden at the time for new recruits (McNiffe 1997: 43) and some had been dismissed previously from the force (Allen 1999: 111). Known as the Broy Harriers,[5] training involved a ten-minute lecture before being issued with weapons. Not only were the gardaí being used politically but they were perceived as political, in need of rebalancing.

Once banned, O'Duffy, who had a stated commitment to obeying the law, cancelled the parade. Small parades were instead held across the country a week later. After minor disturbances in Limerick, Cork and Wexford, de Valera banned the National Guard and reconstituted military tribunals. Now not only were the Blueshirts clashing with the IRA, but they were an illegal organisation and as such, were in direct conflict with the gardaí. Gardaí were now required to take action against O'Duffy and the Blueshirts, but not the IRA. The Minister for Justice created a Special Armed Unit, which would be supplied with military equipment including armoured cars. In January 1934, these men were photographed training in uniform (armed men were, to date, plain clothes detectives) with Lee-Enfield service rifles (*IT*: 23/01/34). This was in addition to the fact that in 1931, following the murder of a superintendent, all divisional and district offices had been issued with additional weapons. The unarmed nature of the force was being seriously undermined in light of the perceived threat by the Blueshirts. Both law and policing were being politically twisted, this time against the Blueshirts rather than the IRA.

Opposition parties, including the Blueshirts, merged to form a new political party, Fine Gael, with O'Duffy as party leader. The Blueshirts were renamed the Young Ireland Association, sidestepping proscription and the special powers. The following months saw sustained violence by gardaí in the face of resistance. The IRA was engaged in a Boycott British campaign and baton charges occurred when republicans attacked supplies of Bass, public houses which sold Bass and Bass employees (*IT*: 27/09/33). The trials of men for these offences regularly descended into violence, with baton charges (*IT*: 09/09/33) and the military being called in (*IT*: 06/09/33). When O'Duffy addressed a gathering in Limerick, violence broke out, baton charges occurred 'every other minute', police fired shots and gardaí were seem beating up prisoners behind the police station (Brady 2000: 208). Thirty people were hospitalised, including a garda who was stabbed (*IT*: 25/09/33). The same week in County Clare shots were fired at the garda station after a riot and the military had to provide support. Prior to one Fine Gael meeting in Cork in early October soldiers wearing gas masks and carrying rifles walked the streets (*IT*: 02/10/33). Between September and October nearly a dozen incidents resulted in baton charges: the default response of the police appears to have been to use violence and force.

In early October a particular dangerous riot occurred in Tralee when O'Duffy attended a Fine Gael convention. A dozen gardaí were seriously injured, O'Duffy was attacked and his car destroyed (Brady 2000: 210). A grenade was thrown into the crowd but failed to detonate. A bus carrying police reinforcements was attacked. Baton charges occurred. The military arrived, tear gas was used and shots were fired. Early the next morning a machine gun was fired at the garda station (*SI*: 08/10/33). Over a dozen people were treated in hospital, including one man for broken arms and legs. An unexploded bomb was found at the back of the meeting hall. O'Duffy attacked the government, claiming that mob law ruled (*SI*: 08/10/33).

What is a real feature of this period of time is recurring and frequent clashes between the Blueshirts and the IRA. Brady (2000: 210) states that the gardaí were quite stymied in these circumstances. There was no point arresting anyone who started trouble as there was hesitancy on the part of the Attorney General to proceed with any prosecutions of the IRA. He also maintains that they were slow to use force as allegations of police brutality would not be well received by the government, which had led the Kilrush inquiry. In the Dáil it was suggested that the hands of the gardaí were tied in the handling of these disturbances and it was joked that had a superintendent carried out his duties properly he would be sacked (DE: 11/10/33).

However, a review of newspapers of that time suggests an alternative analysis. Firstly, there were in fact a wide range of powers that could be used. The Dublin Police Act 1842 made it an offence to throw a stone or other missile to the damage or danger of any person. The Summary Jurisdiction (Ireland) Amendment Act 1871 criminalised offensive or riotous behaviour. The Public Meeting Act 1908 specifically made it an offence to act in a disorderly manner for the purpose of disrupting a lawfully held meeting, or inciting another to so do. Additionally, policemen possessed a common-law power of arrest for breach of the peace. With sufficient manpower it would therefore have been possible to use these powers to intervene at the first sign of trouble at such events. There is evidence to suggest that these and the special powers that were introduced were being used. Manning (2006: 32) cites that in 1934 there were 451 convictions before the military tribunals: 359 for Blueshirts and 102 for the IRA. The imbalance indicates that police attention was focused on the Blueshirts, which does suggest politicisation but also indicates that the police were not powerless. Further, contrary to what Brady contends, gardaí actively resorted to the use of force. From October 1932 and October 1934 there are reports of over 25 incidents at which gardaí used baton charges (*IT*; Brady 2000; Breathnach 1974). On some occasions guns were fired, tear gas was occasionally used and the military sometimes called in. This was not just active use of force; it was paramilitarised policing. Riots and disorder innately 'encourage excessive use of force' (Waddington 1987: 40) but any force used should be commensurate to the level of force used by protestors, which is belied by the regularity of the baton charges and the frequent evidence that unarmed persons were batoned. In Britain at this time the prevailing public-order policing tactic was to win by appearing to lose and thereby generate sympathy (Reiner 2000: 53). Gardaí, it seems, preferred to use force. McNiffe (1997: 155) documents that between 1922 and 1931, 500 men (close to 5 per cent of the intake) were dismissed, the vast majority for either indebtedness or drunkenness, and few for serious criminal offences. Not only did assault not lead to dismissal, but it was arguably actively supported by government, which was increasingly arming gardaí and militarising these situations. Nor was the government declaring that force should be used sparingly. In a debate on the Tralee riot, Minister for Justice Ruttledge explicitly stated:

> No member or officer of the Civic Guards [sic] has been interfered with in any way so far as the carrying out of instructions is concerned, or called to task afterwards for carrying out those instructions. We have made it perfectly clear to the officers of the guards and to the guards as a whole that this government is behind them and prepared to back them up fully in the carrying out of their duties to ensure the right of free speech for political parties in the country.
>
> (DE: 11/10/33)

Within two years of coming to power the government was expressing its full support for the gardaí, even when they were using this level of force. In opposition de Valera had actively criticised police violence. Now the police had the support of all sides of parliament and were free from accountability for how they used their powers. Efforts to create a police force that was unarmed and impartial, succeeding by its moral authority, were being seriously eroded as policing was fundamentally politicised. Given the clear potential for fatalities in the Tralee riot the government finally supported the trial of IRA men, despite criticism from some TDs. The IRA and not just the Blueshirts could be policed. Two months later 14 men were convicted before a military tribunal.

Early in December, in the wake of this violence, the government proscribed the Young Ireland Association. Once again O'Duffy renamed the organisation (the League of Youth) to evade the prescription. De Valera was making every effort to stretch constitutional mechanisms but if anything his efforts were strengthening the Blueshirts and giving O'Duffy a standing he may not otherwise have had. An attempt to arrest him within a week of the ban was deemed unlawful by the Supreme Court as the name change meant it did not apply to the organisation he represented.

Violence and clashes continued into 1934: two Blueshirts died from attacks (*II*: 01/02/34) and tear gas was again used by police. De Valera attempted to outlaw the uniform but was defeated in the Senate (Manning 2006: 118). Local elections were announced in June and the campaign was violent. Support for the Blueshirts grew in particular among farmers, who were suffering from the impact of the land annuities. Government seized cattle from farmers who refused to pay the government in 1934, provoking dreadful scenes as protestors carrying pitchforks burned garda vehicles and police fired shots. The auctions for the seized cattle were equally bitter and the Blueshirts supported the farmers. At one auction in Cork in August 1934, a 22-year-old unarmed man was shot dead by police. The detective in charge had requested additional men to deal with anticipated trouble but instead his men were issued with revolvers. Relations with the police in Cork deteriorated. Later in the year the Minister for Justice admitted in the Dáil that the two men involved in this shooting had since been promoted to sergeant (*II*: 19/12/34). In certain communities around the country gardaí were no longer welcome (Brady 2000: 223). In Limerick their presence could cause a riot, meaning that they only entered certain areas in absolute necessity.

Calls for an inquiry into the shooting were ignored. The victim's father sued members of an Garda Síochána. The judgement blamed the events on the Broy Harriers, but not the force as a whole. Mr Justice Hanna declared:

> I am satisfied on the evidence that these men [Broy Harriers] were selected mainly for their skill and experience with the gun ... they were uncontrolled and left to their own undisciplined judgement in the use of firearms ... These 'S' men are not real Civic Guards. They are an excrescence upon that reputable body.
>
> (Lynch v. Fitzgerald and Others [1938] IR382 at 390/391)

He found that the gardaí in question fired upon the crowd with the intention to kill. Having been shot in the stomach, the deceased hid behind a tar barrel into which a further three shots were fired. Justice Hanna concluded that some police endeavoured to kill him. This judgement also asserted a need for greater discipline and accountability. Brady (2000: 219) asserts that the order to shoot came from an assistant principal officer in the Department of Justice.

There can be no doubt that this was a difficult time for the police. Brady reflects that:

> there were signs that the Guards were beginning to crack under the strain of two years' constant struggle to maintain peace between two organised, armed and often violent groupings, each with its own claim to legitimacy and each demanding of the government and the police the uncompromising liquidation of the other. And there was the sheer physical strain of more than two years of raids, street fights, baton charges and political meetings with guards on duty without a break for anything up to fourteen or fifteen hours at a time. There were long cold and wet nights of checkpoint duty, followed after perhaps a few hours' sleep, by seizure raids or more political meetings.
>
> (Brady 2000: 217)

Morale, it seems, could not have been lower within the force. Violence continued and the opposition complained of improper, partisan policing. It was alleged that in one incident policemen implemented a baton charge supposedly without any provocation or conflict:

> D. Foley, Blakestown, Leixlip, was refused admission to the pound by Superintendent Heron who, catching his walking-stick by the wrong end, said: 'The first man who tries to pass I will split his skull.' That was in the interests of law and order ... Terence McMahon, St. Catherine's, Leixlip, was standing by himself away from the general crowd when Superintendent Heron ran at him, struck him across the head with his stick and badly split his ear ... Mr. Edward Gaynor, Lake View, Collinmore, Mullingar, was getting into his motor car when he received several blows from Superintendent Heron. He had no connection whatever with the crowd. Mr. Hickey, Narraghmore, was standing talking when Superintendent Heron rushed over and struck him across the eye with his stick. Mr. Edward Hyland, did not realise that anything was amiss and did not hear any order to disperse until he was knocked into the gutter by a crack on the head from a Guard's baton. Major North Bomford, on coming out of the Hibernian Bank, was reading a paper while walking down the street when struck from behind by Superintendent Heron. Superintendent Heron eventually broke his walking-stick beating a boy named Hunt of Johnstown, aged from 12 to 14 years, who was standing on the footpath.
>
> (DE: 09/05/34)

Conversely this was a relatively safe period for the police in Ireland. No gardaí were killed from 1931 to 1940 in spite of all the violence that they instigated. Their legitimacy must, however, have been seriously damaged. The re-election of Fianna Fáil saw O'Duffy and other leaders become more extreme in their speeches.

One leading Blueshirt announced: 'We have members of the police earmarked, and when we get into power we will know how to deal with them, to relegate them to their proper place' (Manning 2006: 134). Speeches such as this and a call from O'Duffy for farmers not to pay the land annuities sparked a crisis in Fine Gael, which was dedicated to legal obedience. In September, without any warning, O'Duffy resigned throwing the party, and the Blueshirts, into disarray. The government seized on the fact that the farmers could no longer call on the strength of the Blueshirts, creating a 'flying squad' in the gardaí to aid the collection of land annuities (*II*: 08/10/34). Arrests and prosecutions before the military tribunals reached an all-time high and resistance died off. Agreements with Britain eased the impact of the Economic War in 1935, though it did not formally end until 1938.

The Blueshirt crisis ended suddenly but policing had been fundamentally scarred. The gardaí had become tools of politicians, losing discretion on how to handle conflict and receiving orders directly from government. The concept of the unarmed garda had been seriously wounded. In some communities the police were entirely alienated from the public. This whole episode had been damaging for the Commissioner and so in 1938 Broy was replaced by Kinnane, an Assistant Secretary of the Department of Justice, a change that would politicise the gardaí even further.

With morale low, issues of pay unsurprisingly arose. In 1932 a cut of 5 per cent in unmarried garda wages was planned until the Senate intervened. This aggrieved gardaí more than political direction. An editorial in the *Garda Review* declared that this would generate 'a crisis without parallel in the life of the force' (Allen 1999: 130). The representative bodies wrote to the Department of Justice in 1937 alleging that half of its members were in debt, which could lead to corruption (Allen 1999:131). Months of waiting resulted in a partial restoration of an allowance for boots, considered a somewhat humiliating response (*Garda Review*, January 1938). However, politicians were concerned at the approach of the representative bodies, 'the tone' of which, the Minister for Finance felt, 'shows a failure to appreciate what right standards of discipline require ... and must leave in the public mind the impression that the Garda is an undisciplined force, rather more concerned with advancing its own interests than in doing its duty to the public' (Allen 1999: 134). Teachers secured pay rises but, in spite of all the supportive rhetoric for policing, no progress would be made by gardaí until after World War Two.

The resurgence of the IRA

As the Blueshirts collapsed, the IRA resurged, targeting personnel involved in military tribunal prosecutions. A barrister who had acted for the state was kidnapped and assaulted. In March 1935 armed men fired at gardaí in Dublin (*II*: 04/03/35). In 1935 two murders, suspected to be conducted by the IRA, shocked the public: an admiral who had provided references for men joining the British Navy and a young man who had left the IRA. The response was firm. The Special Branch was reorganised and strengthened. Republican publications were banned. The IRA was proscribed. Special Branch kept a 'cold hard eye on the IRA' (Bowyer Bell 1997: 139). However, de Valera's 1937 Constitution was accepted by the people and with this popular endorsement of his approach, the IRA became an increasingly irrelevant force in Irish politics. Policing of them was eased significantly.

In January 1939, at a time when it was clear that Europe was heading towards war, the IRA began a bombing campaign, the Sabotage Campaign, in England. Bombings were targeted to disrupt the infrastructure of the state, hitting power stations, gas mains, train stations, hotels, cinemas, post-boxes and sorting offices. Seven people were killed, 300 bombs exploded and 96 others were injured. In Ireland the Offences Against the State Act 1939 and the Emergency Powers Act 1940 were hastily passed, allowing for internment without trial, military tribunals and execution of IRA members, all with the aim of dismantling the IRA. De Valera was attempting to maintain a position of strict neutrality towards events in Europe and the actions of the IRA threatened that. A new Minister for Justice, Gerry Boland, was appointed and changes were made to senior personnel in Special Branch. By the end of 1939 it was reported that the whole of the IRA organisation was under surveillance. When in December 1939 the Irish Army's ammunition store was stolen from Phoenix Park, gardaí recovered all of the ammunition and more within days. Between September 1942 and October 1944 the IRA also maintained a campaign in Northern Ireland, along the border, the purpose of which was to gather weapons caches throughout Ireland and move them to the border area to be smuggled over prior to any planned action (Bowyer Bell 1997).

Dozens of IRA men were arrested in the wake of the campaign in Britain, most of whom were sent to the military camp in the Curragh. Conditions were purposefully appalling in the hope that they could not strengthen and regroup while there (Rogan 2011: 56). The combination of intense surveillance and the treatment of prisoners provoked major hostility from the IRA and clashes with the gardaí (O'Halpin 1999: 248). This was one of the most dangerous times in policing in independent Ireland. Between 1940 and 1942 six gardaí were shot dead in ambushes, raids and attacks on garda stations, with others injured and a similar number of IRA men killed or wounded. On one occasion the IRA managed to plant a bomb in Special Branch headquarters in Dublin Castle (Brady 2000: 236). Following the murder of a detective in 1942, a prominent member of the IRA, Charles Kerins, was arrested and tried before the Special Criminal Court, which, upon conviction, sentenced him to death. Despite numerous public protests, which required heavy policing by the gardaí, Kerins was executed in December 1944. Five other men were executed during this period, two of who had shot but not killed gardaí. Detective Garda Mordant, killed in October 1942, was in fact the last member of an Garda Síochána killed in the line of duty until 1970 and the outbreak of the Troubles. This intense period of policing ushered in what would be the quietest period of policing in Ireland.

The gardaí at war

Commitment to neutrality in World War Two generated political and national unity 'unknown since the halcyon days of the Irish Party' (Manning 2006: 192). For those gardaí involved in policing the IRA, the war was a quiet, if not tedious, time. The Emergency generated new forms of crime and work. Duties included supervising of rations and the policing of black markets. Gardaí were praised in the Dáil for their assistance in the large-scale task of issuing the ration books (DE: 27/06/44). Tree-felling licences were withdrawn at the outbreak of the war, due to scarcity of fuel, creating both criminal offences and a new garda licensing regime (DE: 16/12/43). Figures provided in the Dáil indicate that from 1933 to 1938 there was 130 convictions for illegal fellings, while from 1938 to 1943 there were 756. Similarly, theft of turf from bogs was a problem that posed significant organisational difficulties for gardaí given the remoteness of bogs (DE: 21/06/44). A subdivision of Special Branch transformed into a counter-espionage squad with the task of protecting the state from German, British and American agents. The handling of those agents arrested inevitably involved gardaí in international politics. Questions as to Irish neutrality were raised when German agents were detained for the duration of the war, while Allied agents were released.

Ireland was bombed by the Germans six times between August 1940 and July 1941, largely in Leinster. Two of these caused fatalities: three were killed in a bombing of Wexford in August 1940 and in May 1941 four bombs fell in North Dublin, killing 43 people (Ferriter 2005: 387), injuring 90, destroying 300 homes and leaving 400 people homeless. The police and other emergency services were deployed to each of these. Gardaí and emergency services were praised by the coroner for their work at the North Dublin bombings, having attended day and night to a 'gruesome task' (*IT*: 04/06/41). As data presented in later chapters will show, this type of work was especially harrowing for police, particularly given that these men would have had no experience of such scenes. It was not always handled well. In May 1943 a mine washed up on a beach in Donegal and 19 men and boys who went to investigate died. The inquest into these deaths found that they could have been avoided if gardaí had taken greater steps to cordon off the mine after it had first been spotted (DE: 23/04/08).

As men throughout Ireland left to fight in Europe two new reserve police forces were created. The Taca (Irish for support) force, created in 1939, comprised over 300 men to whom the standard entry requirements applied (McNiffe 1997: 45). They patrolled in uniform in Dublin, with the same powers as other gardaí. In May 1940, another reserve body, the Local Security Force, was created to carry out auxiliary policing duties and internal security work. Comprising 25,000 men it conducted, instructed by gardaí, patrol functions throughout the country until the end of the war. In other countries war efforts saw women engaged in domestic policing for the first time but not in Ireland. The impact of involving the local community in policing with gardaí during these times was significant:

> [M]en of all ages volunteered in their tens of thousands, including old republicans who had never before crossed the threshold of a garda station.

While the local sergeant instructed volunteers in basic police duties, the Garda roped in the farming community, bus-drivers, commercial travellers, night workers and, along the coast, volunteers in the fishing industry for observation duties. Citizens living in the vicinity of the garda stations were rostered for station and cordon duties or as messengers. The owners of motor vehicles were put on notice to hold themselves in readiness to provide emergency transport, and the location of every bicycle was listed.

(Allen 1999: 116)

This strengthened relations between the police and the public as they worked together for the security of the state. Superintendents were also tasked with planning and training an army reserve and later provided men on secondment to conduct its administrative duties.

In 1942, nearly 300 of the Taca men were attested to the force. This was the first group of men recruited as policemen in independent Ireland not driven by political considerations. Unlike the recruits of the 1920s or de Valera's men of the 1930s they were not discernible by their political affiliations. Indeed, it is the first time the men were not recruited because of their connection to the IRA. For some time to come preference would be given in recruitment to men who had served in these reserve forces (DE: 16/11/43). Indeed, between 1942 and 1948, over 1000 men were recruited to the gardaí, restricted to men who had served in the defence or auxiliary forces. This waned at the end of the war: in 1946 when 200 recruits were sought only 168 applied with reserve experience. The low pay made opportunities in post-war Britain more attractive for men with defence experience (McNiffe 1997: 56). For the general public however, policing remained a highly sought-after job, with 3300 men applying for just 100 posts in 1942.

The conditions of policing in 1940s Ireland

While the war brought emergency bonuses of seven shillings a week for gardaí it was not until the post-war national pay increases that any substantive improvements were made in pay. A garda who joined in 1922 now earned just two shillings more a week (Allen 1999: 137). The impact was that the garda was a less attractive career prospect for better quality candidates. Given that most of the force was recruited in the early 1920s, this would soon become a pressing issue. Recruitment was halted in 1948 by John A. Costello's government, at which time the strength of the force was 7500. Gardaí received just two days' leave a month, at the discretion of their supervisor and were not paid for overtime. They were never, as it were, off-duty. Days generally involved a 'split shift' with a few hours in the morning and more in the evening. There were no night patrols but the station orderly (rotating between gardaí, generally one night in three, increasing to two in three from the 1940s as numbers dropped) would be on duty 24 hours and men would be roused if needed. They usually lived in barracks: married men could find alternative accommodation but were only permitted to sleep at home on alternative nights. They could be transferred to any part of the country with one week's notice. Half of all barracks needed to be either replaced or majorly renovated and while the Department proposed in 1944 to build 285 new stations, money was only provided for 15 (McNiffe 1997: 101). A garda writing in the *Garda Review* in 1949 described how accommodation had neither electricity nor running water, and slopping out was the sanitation system. Promotion prospects were limited due to the stagnation in both recruitment and retirement. For instance, 60 per cent of the men who served as superintendents in the first 30 years of the force were appointed to that rank before 1926 (McNiffe 1997: 72), most of whom had no previous policing experience. On average, there was one promotion a year for the 130 superintendents between 1925 and 1952. The ageing profile of men who did not start retiring in any large number until the 1950s made this work, the living conditions and the dependency on bicycles harder to bear. In 1950, more than 80 per cent of the force was over 40 years of age.

Duties of the police were divided between what were called police and non-police duties. During these early decades crime rates were low and related to larceny, breaches of licensing laws, property crime, agrarian crime and increasingly crime related to cars. Sexual offences or abuse of children were rarely reported to police and there is some evidence that even when they were little action was taken. Garda days were filled with walking the beat, or cycling in the countryside, issuing and checking licences, monitoring school attendance, security at meetings or other events, escorting prisoners and the mentally insane as well as the station orderly duties. Non-police duties were highly varied including the issuing of licences and certificates for firearms, dogs and gambling, compiling agriculture and commercial statistics, conducting weights and measures inspections, maintaining the voting and juror lists, enforcing school attendance laws, enforcing various laws relating to animals (breeding, dipping and disease), controlling traffic, issuing pension books, signing passport forms and conducting the census. It also appears that police were responsible for allocating places for buses to stop (DE: 13/06/44), for conducting a census of 'tinkers' (DE: 19/09/44), and the Commissioner determined the taxi charges for Dublin and Cork (DE: 26/09/44). A question in the Dáil (DE: 18/04/44) provides an interesting breakdown of the duties performed by gardaí in the Dublin Metropolitan area:

– Members in charge of stations, station orderlies, etc.	111
– Clerical duties, telephone, office, stores, messes, etc.	94
– Duties at courts, serving summonses, collecting fines, enforcing warrants, etc.	57
– Protection duties (public buildings, etc.)	195
– Traffic duties (including carriage office)	45
– Patrol duties (including cycle and motor patrols)	373
– Criminal investigation	44
– L.S.F. administration	13
– Miscellaneous duties	34
– Sick	63
– On leave	213

– On loan to detective branch	78
– On loan to Commissioner's office	7
– Total	1327

Just 3 per cent were involved in criminal investigation, with more involved in traffic duties. Through these duties the gardaí became indispensable to government but these also brought them into regular contact with the entire community. Any query that a member of the public had went to the gardaí. It also gave the police an exceptionally high level of local knowledge, which cynically could be described as an extreme form of surveillance, similar to that engaged in by the RIC. Unquestionably, it made them indispensable to the administration of the state, a factor repeated regularly during pay negotiations.

Public-order disturbances continued to result in the police use of force whether at unemployment rallies (*IT*: 16/05/41) or butchers' strikes (July 1945). Some of these incidents reveal quite poor relations with the community. Throughout the 1930s and 1940s gangs, often referred to as the Animal Gangs, in Dublin had been a growing problem and the use of force by police was a common response. One particular riot in May 1940, known as the Battle of Baldoyle, left one man dead. A sword, knuckledusters, potatoes filled with razor blades, tomahawks and tyres were recovered from the scene (Neary 1985). A similar 'battle', the Battle of Tolka Park, occurred two years later at a football match (*IT*: 24/03/42). In May 1945 on the night that peace was declared in Europe the celebrations on the streets of Dublin descended into a baton charge when some sections of the crowd waved tricolours. In October 1946 a garda attempted to arrest an individual in Edenderry for the trivial point of not giving his name on being asked. When others nearby attempted to prevent the arrest there was a baton charge. That night 100 men attacked the garda station and a further baton charge was ordered. And in November 1949 a baton charge occurred in Dublin during a picket on a Royal Artillery Association dance. The newspaper report of the event indicates that 'on each occasion when the guards drew their batons, loud boos were heard from the crowd'. These examples make it evident that police use of force was not confined to politically motivated incidents. Public dissatisfaction is also apparent in these accounts. So while the joint effort during the war may have aided the police in overcoming lingering anti-Treaty politics, relations with the public were more complex than this.

Advances were made in the pay order of 1947 and the second round of national wage increases the following year. Unsatisfied, some younger members attempted to call a meeting of protest and despite the Minister agreeing to meet with them, 100 men staged an unofficial meeting in Dublin. In addition to seeking a 25 per cent increase in pay they also sought a set 44-hour working week, as opposed to the 54 hours worked in Dublin and the 88 hours worked in rural stations. The high number of stations in operation contributed to these working hours. Barracks were still in poor condition, demonstrated by regular questioning in the Dáil about the securing of new premises and buildings in numerous districts. Indeed, on one occasion the superintendent in Kerry had to move towns, with all his office staff, as no housing for him could be found (DE: 11/07/45). Half of the barracks had been operating on a reduced-strength level of three men, instead of four. Resultantly, if one garda was sick or on leave, weekly hours could increase to over 100 (Allen 1999: 140). The winter of 1948, after national increases did not meet garda hopes, was described by the *Garda Review* as 'the blackest Christmas' in the history of the force (January 1949). Gardaí in Dublin had a greater sense of discontent stemming from DMP days and planned to march through Dublin in protest, however this was banned by the Commissioner. On amalgamation, the DMP had been assured that their band would be retained but in 1938 it was disbanded (DE: 07/12/38). Fears grew that the special status of members of the DMP was being eroded. In September 1949 the Deputy Commissioner with responsibility for the Dublin Metropolitan Area wrote to the Commissioner complaining of insufficient manpower in the city: 'Unless the police force in Dublin is speedily brought up to a strength adequate to its duties, a very serious ... breakdown will shortly occur' (cited in Allen 1999: 141). The process of recruitment and training meant that even if the minister permitted recruitment, no men would be available for 12 months by which time it was anticipated that in Dublin alone, another 100 men would have resigned. In January 1945 it was admitted in the Dáil that two retired policemen had been recruited in Dublin to write summonses for court as neither the courts nor the gardaí could spare the men required to address a backlog (DE: 31/01/45). By the end of the 1940s, poor pay and conditions and the fact that they could not vote or form trade unions meant that garda morale was very low, particularly in Dublin. For all the rhetoric of support of the gardaí that emerged in the 1930s, the problems that mattered to members were not addressed.

Moves towards modernisation

Technology became a feature of policing in Ireland through the 1940s, though much slower than in other jurisdictions. In 1934, 100 men were on permanent traffic control, or point duty, in Dublin, and electronic controls were being considered (*IT*: 19/04/34). In 1945 the force had a total of 38 vehicles (DE: 12/12/45). The Commissioner's Report for 1947 provides a great deal of information about the status of scientific methods within the force. The Technical Bureau provided training both for members of the detective branch and recruits, with an emphasis on preservation of crime scenes. The Crime Investigation Manual was published that year and a copy was issued to all members. In addition to training the Bureau was divided into six subsections: investigation, fingerprinting, photography, mapping, ballistics and wireless. Investigation involved using the services of the state pathologist, the state analyst as well as textile and handwriting experts. In 1947 the fingerprint section held 61,491 records, a figure which grew by 2000 per annum in the coming years. This subdivision also took photographs of suspects, which were circulated to all stations, as well as photographing crime scenes, evidence and bodies in murder cases. The mapping section prepared maps of scenes of crimes for court. Ballistics examined firearms, ammunitions, motorbikes and cars. An example is provided of how in that year glass found at the scene of a hit and run was used to identify the car in question, a fact that was praised by the court during the trial.

Perhaps the most significant advances came in the area of wireless technology in the 1940s. In 1940–1, nine cars had two-way wireless devices and another four had one-way devices. Receiving sets were fixed in 20 garda stations in Dublin and nearby counties. Some two-way systems were available for installation in disturbed areas. Much of this machinery was old and the report states that it was operating at that time at below 50 per cent efficiency. There is also discussion in the 1947 report of the first business in Dublin to install an alarm connected to a garda station.

The 1948 report reveals that new wireless machinery had been received but not yet implemented. It operated at very high frequency so it was only at that point that systems operated without interference from other stations or local electrical installations. In 1949 improvements are documented. A central receiving and transmitting station was now operating in Dublin by remote control. Two-way devices had been installed in nine cars in Dublin. But perhaps most significantly the 999 emergency call system was created for Dublin. Fifty thousand leaflets explaining the system were distributed across Dublin and was receiving 12 calls a day. This system had been implemented in London in 1937 following a parliamentary inquiry into complaints that a woman had been placed in a phone queue when trying to report a fire in which five women were killed. Ireland was, perhaps for economic reasons or perhaps due to a low crime rate, quite slow to move into this technology, most of which was only available in Dublin at this point in time. In the rest of Ireland, police could be contacted through an operated telephone system or by approaching the policeman on the beat, who did not have any means of communicating with the station remotely.

Conclusion

As the 1940s came to a close the first generation of policemen approached mass retirement. Theirs had been a tumultuous period of policing, from the stabilising of the state post-civil war, the transition to Fianna Fáil leadership and the extreme crisis of the Blueshirts. More than a dozen policemen had been killed and community relations for all men had been extreme: hatred in 1922 to acceptance in the mid-1920s, pushed back again to being despised by farmers and republicans but becoming, through the war and Emergency, something of a unifying feature of Irish society.

However, excessive violence and regular baton charges had become commonplace and the unarmed nature of the force had been severely undermined with the issuing of weapons beyond the Special Branch. There are repeated reports of baton charges through the 1940s in circumstances that had no relationship to the politics of the 1930s, suggesting that violence had become a normalised mechanism of control. Many of these instances could have been policed through recourse to the law, not violence. In the first 20 years, 17 members of the gardaí had been killed. This was a generation that knew danger and threat. Policing involves the transmission of knowledge and skills across generations as rookies learn their trade from more experienced police. The next generation of police in Ireland would hear tales of these threats and danger but would experience nothing like it.

But perhaps the most striking feature of this chapter is that policing in these transitional times was highly politicised. Leadership and membership of the Special Branch and the rank and file were politically selected and recruited and operational matters connected to national security were politically directed. Questions were asked and criticisms were made but governments managed to interfere without any lasting political repercussions. While in the 1920s republican politicians had distrusted and criticised the police, the gardaí emerged from this period with the support of all political parties. This is evidenced in a Dáil debate of 1941 on regulations that would permit the Commissioner to force unsuitable or inefficient men (suggested to be no more than a dozen) to resign on partial pension. Those that objected were concerned with the lack of recourse to an appeals mechanism. The debate was filled with praise for the gardaí from all sides of the House, including a statement from Dillon, a Fine Gael TD, that they were one of the 'finest police forces in the world'. Norton, leader of the Labour Party described the force as 'a body which, during the past 20 years, has, certainly, given service to the nation which entitles it to the admiration and respect of all the citizens'. In addressing the fact that there were men to be removed in this way he relied on a bad apples thesis that 'the sins of the few officers or members of the force will not be made a reason for casting a reflection on the Garda ... which should enjoy the highest possible confidence in present circumstances' (DE: 19/06/41).

Nine years previously, de Valera's lack of trust in the gardaí drove him to augment the force with his own supporters, but now Fianna Fáil agreed that they were the best police force in the world. The fact that the gardaí had complied with all orders and not mutinied, particularly when in conflict with their Commissioner of ten years, made them acceptable to Fianna Fáil.

Politicians stated that they supported the gardaí yet when it came to matters that vexed the police, primarily pay and conditions, government did not act supportively. Gardaí lived with the possibility of pay cuts and in substandard accommodation. Government did not act when these concerns were raised. Instead, political support manifested itself in a policy that the police should not be criticised. Force was used with impunity. And while there were mutterings of discontent as gardaí had much to be disgruntled about, there was no large-scale dissent.

Notes

1 Following the introduction of the new Constitution, Bunreacht na hÉireann, in 1937 this position would be renamed an Taoiseach.
2 Including T. J. Ryan, who de Valera had previously argued on behalf of in the Dáil.

3 Broy, as O'Duffy before him, placed great emphasis on sports within the force and served as president of the Olympic Council of Ireland in 1935, while Commissioner. O'Duffy, indeed, had held the post of manager of the Irish Team at the 1932 Olympics in Los Angeles.

4 Brady does suggest that Blueshirts were occasionally permitted to use garda facilities but as government would be hostile, this was limited.

5 This was a derogatory phrase which played both on Commissioner Broy's name and on the old English force, which was known as the Black and Tans. A further 480 men were later admitted in a similar way. The Garda Síochána Act 1937 would later have to be passed to validate their admission as it was felt that they were not actually members of the force.

4 The 1950s and 1960s

A policeman's paradise?

Introduction

The 1950s and 1960s have been presented as a policeman's paradise in Ireland (Brady 1974: 240), as in England and Wales. Certainly there is much to support this conclusion: recorded crime rates were low and threats from groups like the IRA and the Blueshirts, which had dominated the policing landscape for so long, were largely absent. Without those concerns, these decades could in fact be ones of consolidation, where the threats of the past were forgotten and all could support the police. Declarations of political admiration, which emerged in the 1940s, continued. A new generation of police officers replaced the old, politicised guard. Women were recruited for the first time. The nature of work also changed. Isolated stations were closed and radios and cars became commonplace.

But as we will see, this was a period of particularly low morale due to pay and working conditions and despite supportive rhetoric the government was slow to act. While in the past there had been grounds for the police to distrust government, it was now, for the first time since 1922, that a revolt against government would occur. The new generation of men had very different expectations to the previous members. These decades, of mass emigration from Ireland, of austere leadership, did not bring the gardaí the working condition improvements they sought. Instead, they secured expressions of confidence from politicians, even when criticism may have been warranted. The lack of political accountability noted in Chapter 3 became an embedded feature of Irish policing. This, however, did not address grievances. Distrust emerged from the rank-and-file men who felt unappreciated and unacknowledged. Many of the participants in the research joined the force in these decades, and so this chapter draws heavily on those interviews in order to examine policing at that time.[1]

Pay and conditions

As discussed in Chapter 3 by the end of the 1940s recruitment had been halted, men were resigning at an increased rate due to the aging demographic of the force and half of stations were operating at reduced strength. In rural stations men were now regularly working over 100 hours a week with just two days off in the month, at the sergeant's discretion. There were grave concerns for the consequences to the level of policing and in March 1950 the government established an interdepartmental inquiry, chaired by the Minister for Justice, Sean MacEoin, to assess the situation.

The MacEoin Inquiry

The terms of reference were to inquire into the duties, organisation and strength of the force and whether it could be reorganised, reducing cost while not impairing the provision of policing. The terms also referred to recruitment and non-police duties. The MacEoin Inquiry visited nearly 60 police stations in Ireland, and five in Britain to learn their policing methods (DE: 14/03/51). It reported to government in the summer of 1951. It called for the recruitment of 300 men, particularly for Dublin, as a matter of urgency, which government soon did (DE: 06/05/52). The report stated that there could be a reduction in numbers by over 700 men if greater use was made of patrol cars and non-justice roles were scaled back. According to interviewees non-justice work included conducting the census, searching for noxious weeds, checking bulls had been castrated, gathering agricultural statistics, delivering pension books and checking school attendance. The inquiry felt many of these duties could be reallocated. For instance, pension books could be distributed by registered post rather than by hand. Responsibility for enforcing the School Attendance Act could be assigned elsewhere.

Many of these duties brought gardaí into close, non-confrontational contact with members of the community. The school attendance work had previously been highly praised in the Dáil as contributing to changing attitudes to law enforcement:

> It is certainly a pleasure to see the way in which they handle those numbers of children and to see the bonds of affection between the gardaí and the little children as they cross the street. I think that is a great thing, because the tradition in this country was that the people were against the forces of law and order. It is a grand thing that that new spirit of cooperation is developing right from the time at which our city children start going to school.
>
> (Deputy Cowan, DE: 07/07/50)

Authors such as Allen and Brady lament the loss of this positive contact, particularly when economics was the driver. This research suggests that the impact of these functions may be more complicated. Many of those interviewed certainly attributed knowledge of and relationships with the people to these non-justice tasks.

> The area I was doing, I was doing for seven years so at that time I knew every man, woman and child in it and I knew who they were related to.
>
> (16)

However, according to SG3 this was not always non-confrontational work:

> [D]oing the agricultural statistics, which was probably once or twice a year, you met everybody … And the funny thing about it, you went into one house and they said, 'Ah guard, well sure we know all the neighbours around the townland. We'll tell you how many cows they have and how many pigs and sheep.' They told you the truth of what they [the neighbours] had, whether they had six cows and ten pigs and twenty hens … But when you call then to the other house the numbers were always reduced. Instead of the ten pigs they had only five pigs and fifteen hens. Because it was the country, people going back to those times, it was all about what you had in case you'd be taxed on it. Where did this information go? People were very much afraid of declaring what they had.
>
> (SG3)

Police having this degree of knowledge did not inherently enhance police community relations and may have added a layer of fear and distrust into the relationship. Gardaí were, through doing all this work, the eyes and ears of the state so while from the garda perspective this may have generated knowledge of the community there may have been elements of fear and distrust on the part of the residents. A number of interviewees stated that, as children, they feared rather than respected the local gardaí.

In urban areas, that level of local knowledge was not generated. Agricultural statistics were not gathered and the scale of census work was immense:

> [Y]ou had to call to every single house. I remember doing Blarney Street [in Cork], which has 396 houses, one of the longest streets in the country and at that time you had tenements in them, maybe three or four flats.
>
> (SG6)

In this urban context it was impossible for the garda to know everyone, but this work did ensure that all residents had met a garda: 'That would bring you in contact with people, without having conflict with them' (G16). In both urban and rural areas these functions meant police were not simply there to arrest people or deliver bad news; they did however know a great deal about you and in rural areas this may have been feared. Reallocating these functions would reduce the knowledge that police and communities had of each other but this may not have been an entirely negative development.

On the basis of the MacEoin Report and in the name of efficiency some of these duties were transferred, though not all. By the end of the 1950s garda strength had been reduced by 1000 men with a saving of half a million pounds. One hundred and thirty police stations were closed between 1950 and 1970, bringing station numbers from 833 to 703. Between 1958 and 1968 a further 40 stations were reduced to one-man stations (*IT*: 11/12/68), making for difficult and lonely working conditions. The inquiry had proposed these savings if coupled with appropriate investment, such as in technology, but that did not happen quickly. Patrol cars were introduced beyond Dublin but on a limited basis. SG6 was stationed in Cork in 1959:

> And at that time we had no communication, no walkie-talkies at that time. I mean you could be out there and you had no way of contacting your base … And 'twas actually during that time that I remember getting the first radio-controlled cars in Cork. They got two, one on the north side, one in the south side, which is very limited.
>
> (SG6)

Cork city and the suburbs on the north and south side had a total population of 115,689 in 1961. The Commissioner's report of crime for that year also revealed that there were over 1000 crimes recorded in the Cork region, accounting for one-sixth of all crime outside the Dublin Metropolitan Area. Yet there were just two radio-controlled cars.

> If you were on town patrol you were told to keep to a look out for a black Ford, or black Anglia … And nobody came to see you afterwards and you'd be out there and you had no communications whatsoever with base.
>
> (I6)

> When I came to Macroom there was only one car in the whole district. Everyone was on bikes.
>
> (AC2)

The Garda Commissioner report for 1953 indicates that there were 19 cars with radio systems at that point. There does not appear to be any significant increase in the coming decade although vehicle numbers did rise (see Table 4.1). Such increases in vehicle numbers required enhanced driving skills and in 1963 advanced driver courses began in Dublin. Safety was a concern: between 1953 and 1967 seven gardaí were killed in collisions. But even by the late 1960s bicycles remained the main mode of garda transport. Personal radios were not widely available in Dublin for gardaí on foot patrol until 1967, and the following this year this was extended on a limited basis to other cities. In 1967 a mobile crime van was introduced, which could travel to crime scenes and provide supplies and assistance. Despite the reduction in garda numbers on the basis of

Table 4.1 Numbers of garda vehicles 1958–66 (DE: 03/04/62, 24/11/66).

	1958	1962	1966
Cars	94	151	261
Motorcycles	14	50	219

the 1951 MacEoin Report, the investment in technology that had been recommended did not materialise. Instead there had simply been a reduction in garda numbers, stations and functions.

The committee, which had visited numerous stations, also commented on the condition of barracks, which were damp, frugal and showed no signs of improvements since the nineteenth century. In April 1951 one station in Offaly did not yet have electricity (DE: 17/04/51). The committee foresaw consequences for recruitment if new stations were not built and others not refurbished. However the Department of Finance was not willing to provide the money and ignored repeated requests to comment on the report. This was during an economic crisis for the country but nevertheless gardaí were living, not just working, in appalling conditions. SG7 remembered Bruff garda station when he arrived there in 1962:

> There was no heating ... That winter ... there was a Belfast sink, white Delph thing. We used to fill that with water before we got to bed because the taps would be all frozen. We had to break the ice in the morning to get water for a wash, to wash your face.
>
> (SG7)

This was not limited to rural or isolated stations. I5 recalled conditions in Mountjoy Station in Dublin:

> The toilets were outside, there was one toilet inside. If you happened to be living at the top of the house, which was four storeys, if you wanted to wash yourself or have a shower, you went to the very basement ... Some of the rooms held two, three, four and the big room at the top where I started off was seven. In the room were two fireplaces. Now, remember that guys were on shift work. The light in the room was on permanently because fellows were on different shifts. You always knew where the senior fellow was because he was the furthest away from the fireplace ... because we had turf fires and guys were throwing turf on the fire and all the smuts and debris from the turf would come out on top of you in the bed if you were beside the fireplace. So, as you got more senior, you moved further away from the fireplace.
>
> (I5)

> In our case now there were eight young fellas living in the one room ... The last fella in would get the worst bed ... You just had a locker there or whatever ... Make do with working out of a suitcase really ... there were no showers of course, there was no central heating. But what you had was, in all the stations, it was a big responsibility to maintain a good fire. That was usually in the day room. Everyone had to row in there in the morning. Usually there was a person who would come in in the morning, a lady who'd be cleaning the station and she'd put on the fire but during the day you were expected to keep it going.
>
> (G9)

I was in a station 12 miles from the GPO [in central Dublin]. We had to go to a barrel two miles away to get water to wash with and to boil.

(I1)

Men should not have had to live in such conditions. It was, however, attributed with creating bonds: 'we had a snooker room and that kind of thing and it was rough and ready in some ways but there was great camaraderie about the place' (SI5). Of course, this created a willingness to assist colleagues:

I remember whenever things happened there at night, you know you might be upstairs, off duty and you just help out. You just put on your uniform if there was any kind of a serious incident you just helped out.

(G9)

Equally SG5 said:

I lived in Fitzgibbon Station and there were 65 of us, off duty. If there was a problem all the sergeant had to do was shout up the stairs and he had 60 men ... There was no question 'Am I going to get paid extra for it?' You just did it.

(SG5)

In-station accommodation saved a great deal of money. The ability to call on these off-duty men meant it was not necessary to recruit additional gardaí. Rogan notes that at this time the government had reduced its expenditure on prisons (2011: 79). While the camaraderie made the unacceptable conditions bearable, it made gardaí very isolated from the rest of the community. Reiner (2000) explores in detail this phenomenon of isolation and solidarity that policing can generate. While it can assist greatly in coping with the difficulties of the job it can also lead to support of colleagues, even when they have done wrong.

Those who did not live in the stations, usually because the station had been condemned, initially lived in 'digs' (cheap rooms in a house where the landlady would provide meals), often grouped together. G16 was assigned to a large station where the 14 or so unmarried gardaí lived in the same digs. Salaries were not sufficient to purchase or even rent accommodation. SG5 recalled saving up to buy a bicycle; there was no question of owning a car: 'And I used to bring another man home on the bar of the bike. In uniform.' Condemning a station did not always mean that everyone moved out:

V: How long did you live in the station for?
You couldn't. It was condemned. I couldn't begin to describe what it was like. There was actually two or three guys hanging in there. But I think as far as my recollection it was condemned. There were pigeons in the rooms upstairs. It was a terrible place.

(I6)

The Minister reported in 1964 that 23 new stations were being built and 30 houses for married members had been provided (DE: 06/02/64) but the Office of Public Works had identified a need for 130 new stations.

The recommendations of the MacEoin inquiry were implemented in ways which saved money, but the necessary improvements that had been identified were not acted upon, due it seems to conflict with the Department of Finance. The methodology adopted by the committee was encouraging and considered, making its lapse into obscurity most unfortunate. Perhaps what this experience reveals most is the conflict, or at least a lack of communication, between the Justice and Finance Departments (Allen 1999: 146). The problems, however, did not disappear. Gardaí were unquestionably overworked, living and working in unacceptable conditions, with limited equipment and for insufficient wages. The force was also ageing, which made the work harder.

Continuing grievances

One issue that mattered greatly to members where some success was achieved was the outdated and heavy garda uniform. I6 spoke of how awkward the case for the baton was: 'if you needed to take it out you'd be beaten to a pulp by the time you'd get it out and in the summer time they were heavy to wear'. A particular bone of contention was the winter coat, which had to be worn from October to April:

> I thought I would die with the weight, with the pains in my shoulders with the weight of the grey coat … No belt in it, so it all hangs from your shoulders in your neck. Oh jeex, after six or seven hours you know all about it. And you used to try and lean against a wall and press against the wall and go down like that a small bit to get the weight off your shoulders. Banjaxed you'd be. Just walking with the coat on ya. Specially if it rained.
>
> (SG7)

For seven months of the year this was the bane of garda life. The representative associations had long argued for a change of uniform and a lighter shirt option for the summer. Commissioner Costigan and the Minister agreed changes, but again the stumbling block was the Department of Finance.

> We were a long time fighting to get a summer shirt … times like that would have been low in that fellows felt that no one gave a damn about you and you're up for everything that's going on and the guards were getting blamed for a lot of things.
>
> (G16)

To the garda mindset then, this was a simple matter that had a negative impact on their working environment, which was being ignored. Undoubtedly, this was a difficult financial time for the country but the simple ignoring of requests by government aggravated the situation.

Of greatest concern to those interviewed was the working hours and leave. Members worked seven days a week and, nominally, eight hours a day. This could be in one shift or split into two four-hour periods, such as a morning and an evening shift. The length of shifts could easily increase if the work took longer. There was a rotation of months of night duty. The day room (reception area of the station) had to be manned 24 hours by the station orderly (SO). The SO was a rotational post and would involve a 24-hour shift followed by 24 hours off. In small stations this could be performed by each member a number of times a week. In stations that were formally closed at night the front door would be closed at midnight and the SO stayed in the day room to answer any callers. SG7, SI3 and G9 mentioned a mattress being kept in a press, which could be taken out after midnight to have a sleep. Those living in the station would also respond to night calls, with no question of overtime:

> [W]hen you were living in the station then you answered the call at twelve, or one or three o'clock in the morning. If the door knocked you answered it … It was part of the job. You just did it. You got up and there could be an accident. A car accident. And we would be called at three o'clock in the morning and you were off duty in bed. Bang on the door, you'd hear the knocker and you got up and you went down, got dressed, put on the uniform and went up and investigated the accident. You'd to be up again in the morning for nine or ten o'clock for work whatever. You couldn't lie on and say I was up last night for a couple of hours.
>
> (SG3)

Members received just two 24-hour periods of leave in the month, at the discretion of their superiors. Depending on how busy the station was, or the attitude of the superior, these might be granted together or separately. SG1 noted that he was stationed too far from home to visit and he was also required to leave his address and be contactable at all times.

> There was a limit I think of three or four, I forget now, three could be off any one day and seniority counted again. So if you had your name down on a day the two most senior people wanted their days off then you wouldn't get them. You'd be put back to the end of the month, sometimes you wouldn't get them … There were months I probably didn't get my two days off but you're away from home in those days. Where would you be going? Even if it was your day off you'd still be hanging around the station.
>
> (SI5)

> But a lot of the time you wouldn't be going because you wouldn't have enough time, you'd spend most of your day nearly thumbing home and I know Mullingar's only an hour away but still, to get there was awkward enough.
>
> (G16)

The poor transport network in the country meant that in reality members often only got home once or twice a year, arguably no more frequently than if they had emigrated. In this context, particularly when men were living in the station, it was easy to see how the force became like a family: 'You were married to the job really. Compelled as part of routine. Your time off was very limited' (G12).

Some sergeants appeared to be very understanding and attempted to facilitate members:

> I worked with a sergeant at one stage and I was from Galway ... And he put me working early the day before I went home so I was going to finish at six o'clock in the evening. Now the day I came back then he never started me working till six o'clock in the evening. So I had three full days off. Now it might seem very normal today but at that time it didn't. You could have been in work until 12 o'clock the night before your days off with an awkward sergeant, and I seen it, and you could be back at nine o'clock the following after, the day after.
>
> (SG3)

Another longstanding issue was that of location. A national force meant potentially being stationed anywhere in the country and initial postings often placed members in locations they knew nothing about:

> So they called out the names and my name was called out, 'Blarney, Cork'. I head of Blarney anyway but I know nothing about it, you know? And being from Leitrim, it was a long way from Cork. But then some of them said, 'You're going to a nice spot'.
>
> (SG6)

This was just the beginning. Regulations prevented assignment close to home. Promotions and marriage meant automatic transfers. Further transfers could occur if a need arose elsewhere, through another transfer or retirement. There were temporary transfers to troubled areas that required additional men for a time. Those in more senior roles, like inspectors, were expected to do relief duty around their division. Special skills, like riding a motorcycle, could prompt additional transfers. Misconduct or a scandal could result in transfer ('controversy at all, girl pregnant, anything at all, gone', G11). Members could request a transfer, maybe due to family illness, but there was no guarantee that it would be granted.

The possibility of transfer remained for the entire career with the result that a promoted man with a family would often commute, rather than relocate the family, and then seek transfers back. For instance SI6 had seven transfers, due to marriage, promotion and attempting to get back to where his family was based. And, as an inspector, he was sent all over the division to provide cover: 'I served in every district in the borough, I think, bar one.' The unpredictability of it was very difficult. SG7 spent a number of years in Cork city before being transferred on promotion to a rural station. Having prepared himself for the 'culture shock' he arrived at the station to be find a transfer order waiting for him to send him to the border: 'and sure enough, I was down for a transfer to Monaghan the following Monday'. SG5 claimed to know a colleague who was living in his twenty-eighth house. II said: 'The mobility was very disturbing. You could be moved from Donegal to Waterford just like that. It is said of children of such guards that they have no place to call home.'

Among participants for this research, once children were in school the member suffered the brunt of transfers, commuting long distances, on poor roads, to spare their children the disruption. Members had to choose stability of life or progress in the job. Ambition meant mobility. So for instance AC2 who reached the second highest rank in the force spent two years in Cork, one and a half in Waterford, then Cork for ten years, as inspector moved around Dungarvan, Dublin and Kilkenny (while his children grew up in Cork), then Dublin, then finally back to Cork.[2] Some participants managed to spend their whole career in the same district, but were never promoted.

The nature of this system left room for abuse. When SG3 was informed of a transfer having served two and a half years in a station:

> I got a call that some local person wanted to see me … He said, 'I believe you are being transferred'. 'Yes', I says. 'Do you want to go?' 'Well', I said, 'I didn't look for it but I don't mind.' 'Well if you want to stay here you'll stay.' The following day there was a phone call from my boss that I was staying.
> *V: That's a nice endorsement.*
> I: That'll tell you how well I got on with the people. But it also tells you the political pull was there at the time.
>
> (SG3)

It was alleged in the Dáil at one point that 'certain people in the Fianna Fáil organisation can tell guards and sergeants to their faces, "If you prosecute me I will have you sent to the far end of Mayo or Donegal"' (DE: 10/12/68). The implication is a great deal of political interference in policing.

Grievances boil over: the Maculsha Ballroom Affair

> Macushla had to come because we had moved into the twentieth century and we were not a part of the twentieth century … the danger to policemen was becoming greater and the police force wasn't an attractive job anymore. So Macushla had to come … There comes a time when you have to stand up for yourself.
>
> (SG5)

In May 1959 the government approved a scheme of conciliation and arbitration for the gardaí after intensive lobbying by the representative bodies. Sean MacEntee, Minister for Health, argued for an inquiry into the administration and organisation of the force. Commissioner Costigan disagreed, feeling that the force was progressing well and that it would undermine the MacEoin Report, not ten years old. The Minister took the Commissioner's advice. Allen (1999: 161) calls this decision 'in light of subsequent history … one of the greatest tragedies in the history of the Garda Síochána'. Hindsight was not needed: dissatisfaction was intense, vocal and reaching a tipping point.

Dissatisfaction with pay and conditions came to a head in October 1961. The eighth round of national pay increases excluded garda members with less than five years' service. These younger gardaí, totalling some 1500 members and largely based in Dublin, adopted a 'go slow' approach to traffic duty in November. Dublin's traffic was brought to a snail's pace (*IT*: 06/11/61). A mass meeting in the Macushla Ballroom in Dublin was organised. Instructed by government, Costigan banned the meeting but nonetheless 815 men attended. In what has become known as the Macushla Ballroom Affair, a committee of 36 was elected. This committee noted the 'grave dissatisfaction' of all present, called for an inquiry into pay and conditions of service and recorded a lack of confidence in the representative body. *The Irish Times* described the dispute as 'the most serious of its kind to have faced any Government since 1922' noting that men were leaving the force to join the police in England and Northern Ireland (*IT*: 06/11/61). Two of those interviewed for this research attended the meeting.

A hard line was adopted by government and garda authorities. Commissioner Costigan stated, 'I believe what has occurred constitutes a threat to the very existence of the Garda Síochána as a disciplinary force with all the implications that is, for the preservation of law and order' (*II*: 6/11/61). Charges were preferred against the 167 identifiable men. Further meetings of gardaí were held in Limerick, Cork and Waterford calling for the resignation of the representative body (*IT*: 8/11/61). Costigan dismissed the 11 ringleaders, who were given just eight hours to vacate their stations. Protests were quickly planned and hundreds of men throughout the country threatened resignation. The Archbishop of Dublin intervened as a peacemaker and managed to arrange a compromise. The men were reinstated on declaration of loyalty to the force and on promise from government that an inquiry into negotiation machinery would be established. Allen (1999: 171) suggests that Costigan did not want to take these steps and that the incident pushed him close to a breakdown.

Charles Haughey, Minister for Justice, implemented new policies to restore relations between the force and government. A memorial to members killed on duty was financed and Haughey proposed reforms to the promotion system to ensure all members had 'a fair crack of the whip'. This would prevent a situation where 'natural and human disappointment should be transformed into a sense of frustration and injustice leading to discontent' (DE: 16/11/61). He announced a ten-year plan to build new stations and homes for married guards which would cost £3.5 million (Allen 1999: 175). In 1963 gardaí were permitted to vote for the first time. These, however, were not the issues that had sparked the protest. The central issue of pay was not addressed.

This incident reveals much about Irish policing at the time. Firstly, it is noteworthy that it was concerns as to pay and conditions in the 1960s, rather than the politicisation of the 1930s gardaí, which pushed gardaí to protest. Secondly, the Commissioner, a former civil servant, banned the meeting and sacked the

11 men. Whether he desired to do so or not, he did not stand up for his members. For many gardaí this confirmed that Commissioners should come from within the force. The third point is related to this, that it was the intervention of the Church and the Minister for Justice that restored order. Both politicians and the Church had a powerful influence over policing. Finally, the standing of the representative body was badly damaged. A new body, the Garda Representative Association, would soon emerge and be led for some time by Jack Marrinan, one of the sacked men.

Quinn took over as Commissioner after Costigan resigned in 1965, bringing an end to lengthy terms for Commissioners. O'Duffy, Kinnane and Costigan had all served over a decade, but in the next four decades there would be no fewer than ten Commissioners. The 1960s were, in contrast to the 1950s, one of significant prosperity in Ireland. Emigration and unemployment fell. Television arrived in the country. Vatican II in 1967 had a hugely relaxing impact on the country and generally encouraged greater discussion of social, cultural and religious issues. And still the issue of pay went unaddressed. Quinn remained as Commissioner for two years and was replaced by Patrick Carroll, who had also risen through the ranks. He appointed an internal working committee to look into pay and working conditions, which reported in May 1968 and called for significant increases in strength, a request not well received by the Department of Justice. In November 1968 the government finally established a commission of inquiry under Judge Conroy to make recommendations on the remuneration and conditions of service in the gardaí.

The need for the inquiry was reinforced in the summer of 1969 when gardaí in Crumlin, Dublin reacted to the militarily strict style of discipline imposed by their Superintendent (*IP*: 26/07/69). One day 70 men failed to present for morning parade and 28 that afternoon. Internal legitimacy had reached a new low. The *Garda Review* described it as a more 'grave internal crisis' than the Kildare Mutiny (10/69: 3). *The Irish Times* noted that 'among the garda there is a widespread feeling that the civil servants in the Department of Justice are exercising far too much influence over the force' (*IT*: 30/07/69). The reforms heralded by the Conroy Commission will be discussed at the end of this chapter, but there were other changes to the force during these decades.

The changing face of the force

The face of the force changed dramatically in the 1950s and 1960s. In 1952 two-thirds had joined prior to 1926 and were over 45 years of age (McNiffe 1997:159). In the 1950s, over half the manpower, 3500 men, retired, despite continual government efforts, including raising the retirement age from 57 to 63. The result was high levels of recruitment and a shift in the demographics from old to young. Two thousand and eight hundred new members were recruited in the 1950s and 1960s. Twenty-six of those interviewed for this research joined in these decades.[3] For 14 of these men, it was a job, at a time when unemployment and emigration were high. Four out of five people born in Ireland in the 1930s emigrated in the 1950s. Ferriter states that in 1958 alone 60,000 emigrated (2005: 463). The 1950s became known as the 'vanishing decade'.

SG6 stated 'it was that or America' and when asked if he had been excited about joining his response was 'not really'. SI7 stated that 'there wasn't any other job. It was either go to university and get a job teaching or something or emigrate'. For many an unsuccessful application would have meant emigration to America or Britain. For I7 it was a way to return to Ireland having worked in Britain for six years. Another factor in the decision to join was the influence of those around them:

> My mother had encouraged me and the local schoolmaster encouraged me. I wasn't inclined but they kinda pushed me.
>
> (SG7)

> [I remember] my mother beating me across the back to go down to the local sergeant and you know, sign up the papers, which I duly did.
>
> (I5)

While the pay was not particularly good, there was security and a pension, which was more than many jobs in Ireland.

One-third of those interviewed had an ambition to join. I6 said, 'I wanted to join the guards. It was my ambition'. G16 explained: 'I always wanted to be a guard. It was one of my ambitions … you think you would do something good, some good with it.' For some the attraction was the technology: 'I had a big interest in cars from a very early age' (G14). Half of those with ambition towards policing had family in the guards, usually a father. One (SI2) had a granduncle in the RIC. Interestingly, garda fathers often discouraged sons from joining: 'His attitude was, like, that you could end up in a very small station and be there for the rest of your life. But he didn't envisage that there was movement in the guards' (SG3).

So while the unemployment situation in the country was determinant for two-thirds of the men, there remained a significant number who joined out of a sense of vocation. Those that joined did so for financial reasons or a desire to do the job, what could be considered somewhat 'normal' reasons. Gone was the political recruitment that had dominated the history of an Garda Síochána. Recruitment was not driven by a pressing need to defend the state and joining was not a statement of political allegiance.

McNiffe (1997) details that of those who joined up to 1952, 53.45 per cent had worked on a farm before joining. Over half of those interviewed for this research came from farming backgrounds, which in those times was not a particularly prosperous profession. Even as this changed and recruits came more from the cities it was still the sons (and later daughters) of rural families who had moved to the city (McNiffe 1997). Many believed this rural basis was central to the success of the garda in this period:

> They, the gardaí, were coming from the people, they were of the people. In 1964 there were 500 in the training centre and out of those only six were

Dublin fellas … Fellas were joining and then were serving in communities exactly like the ones they had left. That was the secret.

(G1)

Developments in training

The 1950s and 1960s saw a number of changes to the system of recruitment. Admission, previously based on the Commissioner's selection, was amended in 1953 to include a written examination (DE: 05/02/53). Discussions on moving the training centre from Dublin began in 1952 but it was not until 1964, however, that it moved to an eight-acre site in Templemore, County Tipperary. The redevelopment of the old military barracks in Templemore cost a total of £580,000 and provided accommodation for 375 people. It included an indoor-heated swimming pool, expected to enhance national water safety. The *Irish Independent* called it a 'new era' for recruits (*II*: 12/10/63). A year after it opened *The Irish Times* examined the impact on the small town of Templemore, leading with the news that three recruits were engaged to women of the town (*IT*: 16/09/64).

Eleven participants in the current study trained in Phoenix Park, the rest in Templemore. While all had some fond memories of training, they were critical of the strictness, the lack of free time and the lack of preparation for 'real' policing. The view that the training was heavily regimented, strict and disciplined was commonplace: 'It was closer to what would be an army, how an army is run' (DG15). The requirement of tight haircuts was a source of discontent: 'You had to get your haircut three times a week, a week … There couldn't be any hair showing under your cap' (15). SI4 and G16 knew men who left because of this requirement. This, of course, made them highly recognisable: 'Everybody knew the guard with the wee tight haircut. You didn't have to tell the girls … there was no point telling them that you were something else' (17).

The strict regime also extended to limited, regulated free time. Classes were held Monday through Saturday and recruits were required to parade to mass on Sunday morning, after which they were free. Most were too far from home to visit. Mid-week, recruits were permitted to leave the depot in the evening but had to return by 11 p.m. One interviewee recounted stories of one instructor, a 'legend' who,

> would stand at the gate where they signed the book … Now, there was a queue of six or eight people and you just happened to be number eight in the queue and the clock went bong, bong, bong, bong, eleven. He would consider you late and this was the disciplinary offence.

(15)

There were strict inspections of bedrooms:

> [T]he first day we were in, this in-house sergeant [said], 'there are four ways of making your bed, the right way, the wrong way, your way and my way. And while you are here you will do it my way.

(17)

Floors had to be polished but amusement could be found in these tasks: 'we put the polish on the floor. You got a blanket and one of us sat into the blanket. The other two lads at each end pulled them up and down to shine the thing' (G16).

A number of the instructors were renowned for being harsh. 'If the sergeant said boo, you jumped' (DG15). Or as a garda who joined in 1953 recounted:

> [W]hen I joined [X] was drill sergeant. I can still remember him with his cane under his arm. There were 30 in the class and he would shout out 'Gentlemen, my name is Sergeant [X], you will never address me by my Christian name. When you see me you will genuflect and when you write home you will tell your mother you met God. I hold the power of life and death.'
>
> (G2)

The direct result of this approach to instruction was that orders were not disobeyed: 'If you were told to do something, you did it. You might crib and you might complain but you did it' (G16). However, the same garda made a connection between this level of discipline and how they performed their jobs once stationed:

> [I]f you were out there and you had a super[intendent] or a sergeant, whoever, and they said to you 'do something' you did it. You didn't think and you didn't have to think. You automatically complied with what you were told.
>
> (G16)

The strict discipline of the training instilled an unquestioning attitude to orders, for good or bad.

Additionally, all but a few of these men had never lived away from home before and would not previously have been required to fend for themselves: 'A lot of nonsense discipline but it was good training for Catholic young fellas that never had to do anything' (I7). On the other hand, for those who had previously lived away from home the strictness could be difficult to adjust to:

> It was very tight after coming back from England and Scotland where you could come in at any hour of night you like and you could get up any hour of day you liked. But there, there was somebody banging the bell at eight o'clock or nine o'clock and you had to be out and dressed and shaved and up to the depot … spit and polish, uniform had to be toast, shoes had to be shined, hair cut.
>
> (I7)

The training itself involved classes in law, policing, first aid, giving evidence in court and the Irish language. For many it provided the first opportunity to learn to drive a car: 'I was never behind the wheel of a car before that. And that's where I picked up my driving skills' (SG6). There were sports, including running and boxing, and a great deal of drilling: 'But the drill, the drill was the thing. Up for marches, up, run up to Phoenix Park, for miles' (SG7). Most interviewees, when asked about training, mentioned drill, a skill which had little practical relevance to policing and was a hangover of colonial policing.

Those who were stationed in Dublin enjoyed being able to socialise in the city centre: 'there were great events on, a lot of dances on … teachers' dances and there were nurses' dances and you'd be given invitations to go to them … they were very enjoyable nights' (SG6). And although parading to mass on Sunday denied them time off many recounted these parades fondly, mentioning the music of the garda band and the crowds which came out weekly to see them parade: 'The footpaths were full of people, just to see this parade every Sunday morning' (SG6). The Dublin location clearly enhanced interaction with a large and diverse community, an experience that could not be replicated in Templemore.

There were negative comments made about the standard of the training: it was short (these men had either 18 or 22 weeks of training) and the focus on drill had little bearing on the reality of policing. A number of interviewees commented that nominally they were supposed to have supervision after training but this did not happen in their experience.

> [B]ut I felt the regime in Templemore was too strict for the job we were going to be … when you left Templemore you were going to be out on your own, literally standing on your own two feet. You had to make all the decisions and you were treated in Templemore as if you were a schoolboy.
>
> (SG3)

> It was crushed into five months which was too short … When we came out you were supposed to be guided round with an older guard for so long, to get the ropes as the man says. But that didn't really happen … I can honestly say, when I came out first I made an awful lot of mistakes.
>
> (G9)

In the 1950s and 1960s when there was a near complete turnover of the police the majority of the police were young and had not received the necessary supervision. This was compounded by the fact that gardaí were spread so thin on the ground due to the high number of stations. Some were even sent on duty while still training:

> The senior class at the time would be sent to Dublin for the month of Christmas [sic] and then back to Templemore after Christmas to finish off your training … You'd be directing traffic and things like that. And at that time you went out in full uniform. There was no distinctive feature to say that you were a student … and sometimes you might have an established member with you. Other times you mightn't.
>
> (G14)

Recruits at that time were attested as gardaí the day they arrived in the training depot and so had full powers.

In terms of training, while the provision of better facilities at Templemore was excellent, recruits lost the beneficial interaction seen in Dublin. The content of training did not change despite recognised problems by recruits. There must also have been those within the force who questioned the spending of money on training facilities when stations were in disrepair.

Recruiting women

The 1950s was also the decade that saw the recruitment of women for the first time, ending a long campaign. In 1917, four female police wardens were appointed in Dublin, to provide assistance to police. They performed patrols of the streets in the evening and reported on the 'moral state of the streets' (Shephard 2009). The Corrigan Committee on Criminal Law, reporting in 1931, recommended the recruitment of 12 policewomen but this was not done. The matter had been a founding concern for the Joint Committee of Women's Societies and Social Workers and in 1935 the Minister for Justice promised to consider the proposal (Ferriter 2009: 146). The Joint Committee pointed out that 28 countries employed female police. Even 'Turkey, land of the veil and Purdah, has women police'. The Department of Justice was dismissive of the 'utility' of female police (Beaumont 1997: 178). Government letters indicate that it was not felt that the utility justified the 'very considerable expenditure' required (Clancy 2009: 22). In 1948 and 1952 senior police made requests for the immediate appointment of a handful of police for Dublin. The MacEoin Inquiry, discussed above, heard evidence from a variety of groups arguing for female police and recommended women be recruited (Chapter VII of the report). Their recommendations appear to be the basis for the changes that came at the end of the decade.

In 1958 the Minister introduced the Garda Síochána Bill permitting the recruitment of women. Female members were distinguished initially as Ban Ghardaí ('ban' meaning woman). Female recruits had to be older than their male counterparts: 20 as opposed to 18. Deputy O'Malley was not satisfied: 'We hear that one of the main duties will be ... protecting the morals of the young. Who is going to protect the morals of these young girls?' (DE: 21/03/74). They were paid less than men, which was additionally punitive given that it was not possible for a woman to live in the station. They had to retire on marriage due to concerns as to the impact on families, an unsurprising requirement in a country where, in 1959, only 5.2 per cent of married women were in the workforce.

The debate on the legislation permitting women in the force reveals the government's intention that women should focus on 'matters affecting children and young women ... but they will be given general police training and may be required to do any police duties which women would be capable to performing' (DE: 22/05/58). This is similar to many countries where female police are invariably relegated to specific tasks involving women, children and sexual offences (Silvestri 2003). The international trends towards including women were mentioned in the debate as a reason for this development, even though this had occurred in Britain during World War One. The marital ban arose during the

debate with Deputy Sherwin, concerned that recruits would soon leave, expressing the view that 'while recruits should not be actually horse-faced, they should
not be too good-looking; they should be just plain women and not targets for
marriage'. Similarly, a number of years later one TD posed the following question
to the Minister for Justice:

> Is the Minister aware of a recent statement that quite a number of the Ban
> Ghardaí will marry this year? That being the case, does it not demonstrate
> that good-looking Ban Ghardaí should not, in the public interest, be recruited?
>
> (DE: 08/03/62)

This is not perhaps that different from the experience of female police in other
countries (Brown 2000; Martin 1996). Their uniform attracted much attention: a
special committee was established to consider this (*IT*: 24/04/59) and an *The Irish
Times* article discussing the new recruits expressed shock that the women would
be wearing '*flesh coloured!*' nylons but was complimentary of their skirt (*IT*:
10/08/59). Appearance was the focus of discussion on this development.

There were 178 female applicants to join the force; 41 were interviewed and
12 selected (Clancy 2009). They were attested in July 1959 and one year later
three were promoted to sergeant. A decade later there were 26 female members,
five at the rank of sergeant. A sergeant from Liverpool Women's Police Force
came to Dublin to provide classes as part of their training and to act as supervisor.
In October 1959 the *Irish Independent* reported that the 12 female recruits were
threatening to resign unless they achieved wage parity with the male recruits.
While men were given free accommodation during training, women had to pay for
theirs while earning less than men. They availed of the new arbitration procedures
and had the full support of the representative bodies.

There was a great deal of shock and novelty at the posting of those first women.
The first time that a woman conducted point duty in Dublin merited a picture and
article in the *Irish Independent* (05/03/60).

> I was there now when the first lady came to Newcastlewest, which was …
> everyone standing in amazement to see this nice young lady arriving. It was
> a big change. A major change.
>
> (G9)

In February 1970 *The Irish Times* ran a lengthy article concerning a day spent
with a female sergeant. Sergeant Sara McGuiness had applied due to the variety
of the job as she wished for something 'challenging and rewarding'. She admitted
the first year was difficult and she 'often thought of leaving'. Women were not
permitted to do detective work or crime prevention, though a woman was on
probation with the Drug Squad. It was also noted that when investigating a case
women had to travel by public transport, rather than use garda cars. For some
time additional female recruitment only occurred when a female member retired
or married. While the 1960s saw the first women on patrol in Ireland the scale of

social prejudice towards women engaging in this kind of role hampered the extent of its impact for a long time to come.

Policing in a time of little crime

Policing in Ireland became a particularly peaceful experience in terms of work in the 1950s and 1960s due to low crime rates and a lack of threats of the kind experienced in previous decades. Crime rates were low and stable in this period: 1955 produced the lowest level of recorded indictable offences on record. Other institutions, including families, schools and the Church, had a role in this, as they policed and controlled behaviour.

In 1950 there were just 469 men and 69 women in prison (Ferriter 2005: 518) indicating that few of the crimes committed were serious enough to merit imprisonment though as will be discussed below large numbers were detained in other institutions. Analysis of the crime figures for 1960 gives an insight into crime and the related policing tasks at that time. There were over 15,000 indictable crimes recorded that year, 57 per cent of which occurred in the DMA region. The detection rate was 60 per cent and 55 per cent were prosecuted. There were 675 offences against the person (including 2 murders, 45 manslaughters arising from traffic fatalities and 178 sexual offences), almost 3000 offences against property with violence and over 11,000 offences against property without violence. Three-quarters of all recorded indictable crime, therefore, involved non-violent, property offences, half of which involved either thefts of bicycles or larcenies where the value did not exceed £50. There were a further 94,653 convictions for summary offences including minor assaults, dog offences, offences under the School Attendance Act, road traffic offences and intoxicating liquor offences. Almost 550 persons were prosecuted for begging and 60 for noxious weeds. The statistics suggest that the majority of police work relating to crime was, therefore, of a minor nature.

Interviewees spoke of this low crime rate. SG3 stated that in a rural station in the 1960s the biggest crime was when 'young fellas went and ran amuck on a Halloween and they stole tractors and drove them down the village. They damaged, they took gates and people got very annoyed over it'. G4 had a similar experience: 'crime was so light then as well. My first year in Fermoy there were 40 crimes and most of them were stolen bikes'. Even in cities crime was not particularly serious. In Cork in the 1950s SG6 found that '[t]here'd be an odd

Table 4.2 Crime levels 1945–65 (Brewer *et al.* 1997).

Year	Indictable crime
1945	16,786
1950	12,231
1955	11,531
1960	15,375
1965	16,736

larceny or that type of thing but no serious crime. Very few break-ins or anything like that'. He remembered just one reported rape in his time in Cork, but robbing the gas meter and house break-ins were common. He also recalled multiple people on bicycles riding down hills: 'And they'd have one or two on the carrier maybe one behind them and we were supposed to go out and stop them and, prosecute them, which you did when you got a chance at them.'

For many, particularly those stationed in rural areas, the function of police was not crime-orientated and without the threats of the IRA, the Blueshirts or wars it was a pleasant time in terms of the work itself:

> You patrolled the country roads or the city, wherever you were, or the town. And you met people, and you talked to people, you know, the time passed very quickly … There was no crime worth talking about. 'Twas probably easy going, maybe, I won't say a lazy life but it was, it was more easy going. 'Twas nice.
>
> (SG3)

For the new generation of police recruited in these decades, this was the policing that they came to know. SG6 noted a public-order problem, stemming from workers in the larger factories in Cork. The employees would come to Blarney, where he was stationed, on a Sunday night:

> There was one hotel there and three pubs and they packed them in, just sitting, packed into the pubs and anyway it was grand until about closing time and then they came out and the fighting started! And really it was rough. You'd a job trying to get them on the buses, and there was some of them quite treacherous. You could be hit or anything.
>
> (SG6)

Despite the fact that crime was low, when there was a slight rise in the late 1950s it was considered something of a crime wave. A number of high-profile murder cases that remained unsolved did nothing to allay concerns. The *Irish Independent* was not satisfied by the Minister's contention that crime in Ireland was much lower than elsewhere: 'he gave poor comfort to the thousands of aged people living alone who do not know the hour of day or night that they may be beaten or robbed in their homes' (*II*: 24/04/59). Media commentary placed the blame on Commissioner Costigan, a former civil servant, and the recent turnover in staff. The *Evening Herald* criticised his approach: 'Junior Gardaí were suddenly promoted over the heads of senior men in the mistaken belief that youth in itself was a substitute for the skill, astuteness, knowledge and loyalty obtained in years of service.'

It was not however until 1967 that the first mention was made of a 'war on crime' by the Minister for Justice. That year also saw the first concerns being expressed about drug use and a criminal justice bill introduced that year aimed to tackle a perceived problem of flick knives (Rogan 2011: 120). Towards the end of these decades, the idyllic state of crime in Ireland began to change due to factors such as economic growth and the declining influence of the Church on society (Brewer *et al.* 1997: 121). But by then many of the 1950s recruits had experienced over a decade of policing with minimal crime work. This was, for them, policing.

In many places crime was so low police were engaged in a wide range of other duties. Being based on Mountjoy Station, next to the prison, I5 transferred prisoners to courts across the country: 'You would be sent to Donegal. You could be out from six in the morning until, you mightn't get home until eight or nine at night. And there was no money, you just did it.' He also provided security when prisoners were admitted to hospital: 'I often spent 13 weeks or 14 weeks on the trot over in the Mater Hospital, minding prisoners.' SI1 provided security for the visit of President Kennedy from America in 1964. Others provided protection for government buildings. Signing dole forms was another common activity. In rural areas police continued to be engaged in activities such as compiling agricultural statistics, dealing with noxious weeds and checking bulls: 'We would have to go checking the bulls to make sure they had been castrated. You'd get dinner for doing that' (G4). Variety was fundamental to the job:

> [M]e and my partner commented at the end of the day on the variety of people we had dealt with. The biggest knackers in Cork, a judge, solicitors, the Circuit Court, nuns and a reverend Minister, shopkeepers and a bishop.
>
> (CSI1)

Along the border quite particular issues arose. People from Northern Ireland regularly travelled across the border either for shopping or to socialise as the licensing laws were more relaxed in the Republic. SI5 experienced this in Dundalk in the 1960s. It created problems as these were strangers, who might have different attitudes to the police. Prosecutions were impeded as they lived in a different jurisdiction. The border itself could require policing. In 1968, 1000 gardaí were sent to the border when there was an outbreak of foot and mouth disease in the UK (*IT*: 15/01/68).

Policing in Ireland at this time bore all the hallmarks of Bittner's (1974) view of the breadth of activities that could be considered to fall within the functions of policing: 'something-that-ought-not-be-happening-about-which-something-ought-to-be-done-NOW!'

> So many things happen that you're not specifically trained for but you'll have training to deal with things, think on your feet kind of thing, because you could never be trained for every scenario you're going to walk into, that kind of thing. Just for instance, my second day in Dundalk on the beat, a man was driving his car down the street and he died at the wheel of the car and he crashed into two or three cars ... the strange thing about it was that I'd met the man concerned and I'd spoken to him the day before ... So you have to think on your feet and apart from anything else you have to be seen to be

doing something ... I went over and tried to sit him back in, get his tie opened and a few things like that before the doctor arrived or whatever. But if you stand there and do nothing, well the people are going to say, 'Well that's a complete idiot anyway', but you have to be seen to be doing something.

(SI6)

There is, however, the dark figure of crimes like sexual assault, domestic or child abuse, which were either not reported or not recorded by gardaí. Some data in relation to this is beginning to emerge. The McAleese Report, for instance, reveals that gardaí were involved in referring young girls and women to the Magdalene Laundries, where they worked unpaid in laundry rooms, often without the freedom to leave. Garda referrals to the Laundries were for minor infractions of the law or for being 'runaways, vagrant, stranded, deserting or deserted' (2013: 317). Stranded could mean 'money stolen. Unbalanced. Over from England and no place to go. Assaulted' (2013: 317). McAleese documents that gardaí also transferred women to the Laundries once referred there by the courts or from prison. Their involvement in transferring women from psychiatric institutions or hospitals remains unknown. Gardaí were instructed to arrest and return any women who left the Laundries without permission (2013: 305). O'Sullivan and O'Donnell note that in 1951 more than one per cent of the population was confined in some way: in prisons, borstals, reformatory schools, industrial schools, Magdalen laundries, psychiatric hospitals, county homes and private institutions (2007: 35). While, as O'Sullivan and O'Donnell conclude, this was commonly at the behest of families who 'vigorously patrolled' 'the boundaries of acceptable conduct' (2007: 44), the extent of garda involvement is unknown and was not discussed by participants of this study. The only formal mention of this work is in the Garda Code of 1965, which relates to the payment of expenses incurred during these transfers (McAleese 2013: 305). Garda knowledge of the sexual abuse of children by members of the Catholic Church will be discussed in Chapter 7.

The advent of technology

In the meantime efforts were slowly made in advancing the technical side of policing. Most of the Commissioners reports for 1950–69 included a section on scientific aids to the detection of crime. Six divisions fell under this heading:

- The investigation unit: this unit visited crime scenes (mostly house break-ins but sometimes homicides) and employed the services of the pathologist, handwriting and textile experts etc.
- Fingerprints and criminal records: In 1950 the unit held 67,773 criminal records. Records and photographs of criminals were sent to all detectives in booklets. Fingerprints were held centrally for manual searching, which was time-consuming with limited success. In 1963 Haughey pushed for retention of fingerprints from all criminals and when Costigan informed him that records were held for just 15 per cent Haughey declared it a 'farce' (*II*: 30/12/68).

- Photography, including photographs of crime scenes, criminals and repro-
  duction of photographs for court.
- Mapping prepared necessary maps for the department and the courts.
- Ballistics, in addition to examining weapons and ammunition, also examined glass fragments from traffic collisions and cutting instruments used in
  break-ins.
- Radio: A slowly developing aspect was the acquiring and distributing of
  radios to stations, cars and men on foot patrol. This unit also included the 999
  service for Dublin, which increased its intake of calls from 3000 in 1950 to
  82,000 in 1969.

Beyond Dublin then, there was no 999 service, limited cars and radios. As other
countries moved to a fire-brigade style of policing, where police primarily
responded to call-outs rather than preventative patrolling, this was not yet possible in Ireland. Investigations were hindered by the state of records and paperwork
as I6 recalled:

> I remember investigating one hit and run accident in Letterkenny and spent
> the whole day, from around ten o'clock to around half five to get the owner
> of the car. A sold it to B who sold it C … C sold it ten miles down the road,
> back in and we finished about two miles from where we originally went. But
> it was the whole day because it was taxed from January to January or what-
> ever and there was no obligation on them to notify the motor tax office of
> change of ownership.

There were aspects of the job that were distressing for gardaí. Road fatalities
reached high levels: 239 people were killed on the road in 1951 (DE: 27/02/52),
and this continued to rise dramatically over the coming decade (and beyond) to
302 in 1960, 356 in 1965 and 462 in 1969 (RSA 2010), almost nine a week.
Policing fatal crashes is highly traumatic work whether it involves responding at
the scene, investigating or delivering news to families. However, the culture of
policing expected men to deal with these aspects of the job and members developed ways of dealing with the more difficult aspects. I5 spoke of attending a
caravan where it was believed an elderly resident had died:

> We went up there and it was pitch-black like and I said to [my colleague],
> 'I will give you a hootch up into the window of the caravan and force it.' The
> next thing, he goes in the window and the next thing he says 'Ah Jaysus', he
> was a Dub, you know, 'I am after landing on top of the corpse.' [Laughing]
> So, funny stories like that, you know like.
>
> (I5)

As low as crime was, dealing with death was a perennial feature of policing.
As a coping mechanism distressing incidents were normalised and the funny side
found.

The 1960s saw specialisation and the formation of units within the force, including a dog unit in 1960 and a sub-aqua unit in 1966. In 1963 Haughey, the Minister for Justice, announced the creation of a juvenile liaison scheme, which would caution rather than prosecute. The men involved were sent to Britain for training and worked with youth clubs and organisations on their return (*IT*: 23/02/63). Ten men were selected with priority given to athleticism. The 1967 Annual Report reported that the scheme had engaged over 3000 young people and made 32,000 visits to homes. The recidivism rate was just 11 per cent. Two female gardaí were involved in the scheme. A rise of house break-ins prompted the creation of a Crime Prevention Unit in 1963 (DE: 06/02/64). It worked with businesses and cash-in-transit vans to identify prevention options. Members gave lectures, produced leaflets, had material published in newspapers, held exhibitions at various events and had a permanent exhibition room on crime prevention techniques. In 1966 they began hosting a TV programme on the state broadcaster called *Garda Patrol*. Fifteen minutes in length, it provided details of ongoing criminal investigations as well as advice on crime prevention.

By the mid-1960s public order was a serious concern, particularly in Dublin. The 1950s saw violence and more panic over 'Teddy Boys' (*IT*: 23/10/54, 05/08/55), including an account of how 'marauding gangs of Teddy Boys' caused damaged in Dublin on New Year's Eve 1955 (*IT*: 07/01/56). Beyond these gangs there were protests and incidents throughout the 1950s relating to the economic situation of the country, the policing of which appears to have been heavy-handed and suppressive. In April 1952 budget cuts lead to serious violence on the streets of Dublin. Gangs 'roamed O'Connell Street for two hours attacking buses, breaking shop windows, and throwing stones at Civic Guards ... Baton charges followed each other in quick succession' (*IT*: 07/04/52). Seventeen members of the public were treated in hospital, including a 16-year-old woman. Two gardaí were hospitalised, one with a broken nose and a fractured skull.

The Dublin Unemployed Association (DUA), formed in 1953, organised numerous protests including sit-down protests on O'Connell Bridge, which halted the Dublin traffic. Baton charges and scuffles occurred (*IT*: 03/06/53). The police response was to attempt to scupper the organisation. In August marches involving sit-down protests or slow marching were banned. When politicians questioned whether this breached the freedom of assembly, the Minister replied that it was a policing matter. Marches that proceeded resulted in baton charges and clashes (*IT*: 07/07/53). Eight leaders of the DUA were arrested for failing to pay fines and imprisoned for months (*IT*: 09/10/53). Their detention was protested, leading to injuries for 12 protestors and 2 gardaí. The garda strategy was to stifle the organisation by banning marches, arresting leaders and using force on peaceful protests. Indeed, there is evidence that suggests that police use of force was widespread. On New Year's Eve 1954 when revellers spilled over onto the streets in Dublin, garda efforts to clear them involved a baton charge (*IT*: 01/01/55). Five people had to be treated in hospital, two of whom claimed to have simply been walking down the street.

Continuing concerns about inner-city violence led to the creation of a riot squad in August 1964, under the leadership of Sergeant James 'Lugs' Branigan, a garda with a huge reputation for preventing and investigating crime in Dublin or, in the words of Kearns (2006: 55), 'battling bare fisted against gang members'. Lugs was praised by media, senior gardaí and the judiciary for tackling gang problems in Dublin, evidenced in his appointment to the riot squad. He also petitioned many judges not to imprison convicted men, for which many families were grateful. Yet evidence of his violent methods abounds. In an oral history study of Dublin, Kearns (2006: 101) quotes one participant who claims to have seen Lugs hitting people with knuckledusters under gloves. Kearns cites women using Lugs as a threat to abusive husbands: 'I'll get Brannigan and he'll chastise you' (2006: 125). When it came to young boys doing wrong rather than arresting them he slapped them and told them what would happen if he caught them again (2000: 129). Another participant presents a disturbing picture of the policing of unrest:

> They didn't just waltz you down to the station. A fella would be batoned to the ground and I mean with a big baton. Oh, break his skull with them, they would. And when they'd put you down they'd pull your trousers and your long-johns down and twist it to drag you. You were dragged in. And they bashed you on the ground as you were getting pulled. I can guarantee you that this is the gospel truth. They bashed you all the way down … and your head hitting the kerbs and anything. You were 'resisting arrest' whether you were conscious or not. This is the way they done it.
>
> (Kearns 2006: 154)

Violent policing was a normal response to the disorder at the time, a response which was accepted by criminals, the public and the judiciary alike. Senator David Norris later recalled his knowledge of Lugs' years:

> As a university student I recall seeing Garda 'Lugs' Branigan in the Olympic Ballroom. He parted the hordes like the Dead Sea to take three people who were in front of the band stand into the back alley and rendered his own justice. Nobody protested.
>
> (SE: 05/05/93)

Neary, in an account of the life of Branigan, considers the work of the riot squad, which in reality dealt with gangs and public disorder rather that riots. Use of the word riot, however, generated greater fear and concern, justifying the police response. In 1966 hundreds of peacefully protesting farmers were arrested. When Princess Margaret visited Ireland in January 1963, disorder led to baton charges and the scene 'at times resembled a battlefield as men and girls collapsed on the ground bleeding from their heads' (*IT*: 20/01/65). In April 1966 the National Council for Civil Liberties and Labour held a meeting to protest at garda brutality at a republican march where baton charges occurred and nine people were admitted to hospital (*IP*: 28/04/66). Allegations of brutality were made during subsequent trials (*IP*: 06/04/68) and following the policing of protests at the visit of the King and Queen of Belgium to Dublin in 1968 (*IP*: 16/05/68). That year the Dublin Housing Action Committee was established and protests were regularly followed by allegations of brutality. After one protest the Committee released a statement alleging 'an unwarranted amount of physical violence' by gardaí. A week later when the committee protested at an eviction it was alleged that gardaí stood by as bailiffs assaulted protestors while removing them (*IT*: 16/01/68). In May, the garda riot squad attended a demonstration and three persons were hospitalised. Despite these serious injuries no one was arrested. Witnesses stated that one man was 'knocked out by a police sergeant who used a four-foot pole' and *The Irish Times* reporter saw police strike a young woman three times across the face with the stick of a placard (*IT: 07/05/68*). An *Irish Times* editorial concluded:

> A policeman's lot is not a happy one. But there are too many accounts by reliable witnesses of acts of unnecessary roughness and sometimes brutality of individual guards to make the most recent complaint seem frivolous.
>
> (*IT*: 14/05/68)

There is therefore a plethora of evidence to suggest that policing in Ireland was violent in the 1960s and that both the riot squad and the Special Branch were involved. Caution must be exercised not to apply today's standards in analysing policing. We can see however that NGOs and some Labour Party politicians were drawing attention to this. Ireland had at this time signed (though not ratified) the European Convention on Human Rights. Unnecessary violence was a breach of discipline under the Garda Síochána (Disciplinary) Regulations 1924. There was recognition of the inappropriateness of such violence. However, it seems that the police could engage in this violence without fear of repercussion. Complaints against the police were dealt with internally. Political statements at the time acknowledged that force was used, implying that this was appropriate on occasion, but are highly critical of allegations of brutality:

> [W]e should reject the mischievous accusations which have been made by an irresponsible element in the community that gardaí have been guilty of brutality. It is an extraordinary thing that the more force some people are prepared to use to get their unlawful ends the more they are inclined to accuse the Garda of brutality. Those who live by force can hardly expect to be treated with velvet gloves. Those who seek to cause mischief can hardly expect people to sympathise with them when the forces of law and order in our midst endeavour to obstruct their ill-designed aims.
>
> (Deputy Ryan, DE: 26/03/69)

Throughout these decades there was unstinting political support for the gardaí, with even de Valera declaring:

> [H]ow much this state owes to its police force for the quiet, silent and extremely efficient work which that force has done in the past years of its history, will never really be appreciated. It deserves well of the community and it deserves the support of the community in enforcing the peace of the community.
>
> (DE: 14/03/51)

Indeed, this even went so far at times as to ignore the many difficult periods which the gardaí faced in the first decades of the force and proclaim total acceptance by the community:

> It is a force of which we can all feel proud. They are doing excellent work ... one of the reasons why they have been so effective and so successful is because they were accepted from the beginning, right down through the years, by the people of this country as their friends.
>
> (Morrisey, DE: 14/03/51)

> [P]erhaps too few of us recognise that one of the big success stories in this country was the establishment and development of the unarmed Garda force. The country as a whole owes a debt of gratitude to the Garda force.
>
> (Higgins, DE: 26/03/69)

Political dissent for garda behaviour was unlikely. Perhaps this was a trade-off of sorts for not equipping the force appropriately. Were the politicians to criticise the force for how it conducted itself, there may have been a fear of a rebellion of sorts, given that members were angry about pay, conditions and uniforms. Nor did it appear that the judiciary were particularly critical. In the summer of 1967 a judicial inquiry was held into the death of Liam O'Mahony in custody at the Bridewell garda station in Cork. He had numerous injuries on his face and died from internal injuries and bleeding. An inquiry was established but only, according to the Minister, 'to clear away the atmosphere of suspicion that has been created' (DE: 18/07/67). Suspicions were expressed that gardaí hand-selected the jurors and had not supplied all of the available evidence. The inquiry comprised three judges, sat in public, heard 11 days of evidence from 77 witnesses and according to *The Irish Times* cost £40,000. The inquiry found that Mr O'Mahony had died from falling off a stool in a pub, rather than from injuries inflicted by gardaí as a friend had alleged. It is impossible to say from this whether the police in that case had used severe force but the witness who made that allegation was disbelieved. There is no doubt that on many occasions violence was used by police but it did not result in remonstration from the courts or politicians. This may be due to the fact that the individuals alleging this treatment were, in the main, members of gangs, residents of tenement areas, republicans or those engaged in protests against the actions of the state. All of these persons can be dismissed as other in some way. Suppression, either through denial of rights of assembly or use of force, was an accepted response. Indeed, there is some evidence to suggest that police were acting under political instruction when it came to policing some of this unrest. Writing in *The Irish Times* Conor Brady quoted a garda who had policed milk protests in 1966 and felt they had been politically directed:

> I do not see why the force should be used by the Government in its squabbles with anybody; if things had been right, we would have handled the situation

as we saw fit, just as the British police do in cases like this. Instead, we found ourselves being 'instructed by the Department' to ignore this law and enforce that law just as it suited the conditions.

(Brady, *IT*: 21/08/69)

One can easily imagine the political impetus to suppress many of the groups who alleged police brutality in this period. The Church had quite a powerful role in policing. As already noted, the intervention of Archbishop McQuaid following the Macushla Ballroom Affair resulted in the reinstatement of 11 men. The Murphy Report on child sexual abuse in Dublin notes that in 1960 photographic film that was submitted for developing by a priest based in a children's hospital was sent to Scotland Yard (2009: 189). A report was submitted to Commissioner Costigan, who passed the matter to the Archbishop of Dublin and did not conduct an investigation into the matter. The police response to child sex abuse will be dealt with in greater detail in later chapters but it is worth noting at this point that the Murphy, Ryan and Fern reports all record allegations of child sex abuse stemming back to the 1960s. Many of those involved told how they did not report to the gardaí for fear of the scandal it would cause to the Church.

The 1956–62 IRA border campaign

In the mid-1950s the IRA conducted arms raids in England and Northern Ireland, effectively stockpiling for the Northern Irish border campaign which ran from 1956 to 1962. The campaign, which commenced in November 1956 with the burning of custom huts on the border, targeted military installations, communications and public property in Northern Ireland. A number of RUC men were killed by explosions near the border and in all there were over 500 incidents (English 2004: 76) and 12 deaths (Moloney 2002: 51). Prior to the campaign the IRA Army Council issued a directive that gardaí were not to be attacked so as not to provoke a response of the Irish government (Moloney 2002: 50). Internment without trial was swiftly introduced in Northern Ireland and the next year in the Republic. The campaign failed to have a political impact and if anything damaged the IRA. By its end in February 1962, the IRA was severely weakened: 'funding had dried up, they were short of weapons and there were not enough Volunteers coming through to replace those who had been imprisoned or killed' (English 2004: 83).

SI1 was in the Special Branch when the campaign began. Prior to this campaign the Branch had conducted protection work of politicians, foreign ambassadors and any magazines that contained explosives. He was relocated to the border in December 1956 and was on duty the night two IRA men, South and O'Hanlon, were killed in a foiled attack on an RUC station. Having heard of the attack SI1 and a sergeant drove to the border, having changed into uniforms so as not to be mistaken for terrorists.

We saw a guy coming out of nowhere. He was in combats with a black face. He was one of the survivors. He asked where he was and [the sergeant] said we were guards and he said 'Thank God'. The men were injured in the house … We took him to the station. We knew there were more. We told him that if they needed help he would have to tell us where they were. So he did. We took him with us. The army were cover. We went in and put him in the door first. I had a gun under each arm. It was like a casualty ward inside.

(SI1)

This was far removed from the nature of the work he was engaged in previously. Nor were they well equipped for the demands of the campaign. I6 was stationed in Donegal during this campaign and recalled the poor radio network:

[Y]ou'd a week on night duty on the border and stopping cars and searching and the usual craic. We had a radio in the car and you could get the stations [on the radio] if you were maybe 20 miles away and then if you were three miles away you mightn't get it at all.

(I6)

One significant consequence for policing in Ireland was the reintroduction of internment. In July 1957, 63 persons were rounded up in one evening and brought to the Curragh. In total 200 persons were interned at the Curragh and were not released until February 1959, unless they made undertakings to the government. One interned individual unsuccessfully challenged this practice before the European Court of Human Rights (Lawless v Ireland 1957–61). De Valera defended the policy of internment, stating that if groups such as the IRA were not stopped then there would be both a war with the UK and a civil war (*II*: 29/07/57). Police gathered intelligence, arrested individuals and provided security at the Curragh, where protests were regular (*IT*: 24/07/57). SG6 was moved to Kildare around this time:

[T]here were a lot of protests…
    V: So a total change from what you were used to?
    Completely, a change yes. The protests were quite rough now. It wasn't local people … They came from Dublin, Northern Ireland and places like that … You were in danger with most of them.
    V: Would they have been quite violent protests?
    Oh they were, quite violent, indeed they were, yes. And that went on for a couple of years and then there were a couple of breakouts, out of the camp, and then there were searches on to get them and they were found in bogs and everything. You could be out, that time, for a couple of days, and you wouldn't be coming in. There were no hours. You just went out and fended for yourself and try and get something to eat some place … you went out and you were forgotten about.

(SG6)

The response to this campaign was fire-brigade in nature, responding to problems as they emerged. Gardaí had not policed the IRA for decades and as SG7 experienced, structurally the force was not sufficiently organised to deal with the threat effectively. The campaign soon died off but this was a taste for gardaí of what was to come.

The Conroy Commission and the advent of change

For most gardaí the 1950s and 1960s were a time of little crime, plenty of extraneous duties and dissatisfaction with pay and conditions. This all changed fundamentally at the close of the decade when crime began to rise sharply and the report of the Conroy Commission heralded a new era for policing. When Morain was appointed as Minister for Justice in 1968 he found the force to be a 'machine that was outmoded, outdated and inefficient':

> I immediately acceded to the Garda Representative Body's request to establish the Conroy Commission. I did this because I was utterly dissatisfied with the lack of efficiency I found in the force ... I am appalled at the number of nuts being released on the public ... and I am amazed that so many of them are left in the force for so long.
>
> (*SI*: 10/10/71)

The Conroy Commission reported in January 1970 having heard evidence from an abundance of parties and having visited police forces oversees. Salmon (1985: 90) describes the report as a milestone 'after which it can truly be said that nothing was quite the same again'. For Breathnach, '[t]hrough dealing with 'bread-and-butter' issues, Conroy succeeded in doing what the first Free State government failed to do, namely change RIC conditions to [Garda Síochána] conditions' (1974: 148). Conroy spent 14 months performing this task whereas the Police Organising Committee in 1922 had just three weeks.

The Commission made 52 recommendations on pay, working hours, conditions, training, recruitment, accommodation and discipline regulations. It determined some garda accommodation was 'sub-standard and not fit to live in' (para. 826). It recommended a 42-hour working week (para. 747) and set out a scheme for the payment of overtime (para. 752). The immediate response of many gardaí was dissatisfaction as the requested pay rise had not been recommended. A 24-hour 'go sick' was threatened (*II*: 26/01/70) though it seems that the intervention of the GRA led to a fuller understanding of the full impact of the report. As if a reminder of the importance of the changes was needed, two weeks after the submission of the report the ceiling of the public office in the divisional headquarters in Waterford collapsed, leaving 30 men operating out of a converted bicycle shed with no radio communications (DE: 06/02/70). By July it was stated that 27 of the 52 recommendations had been implemented although this was perceived by many as a delay that contributed to unrest. Gardaí had threatened action if certain recommendations were not implemented by 1 April (*IT*: 13/03/70). Those interviewed spoke most favourably of Conroy:

> Conroy came at a real low point. It had a dramatic effect and really boosted the internal confidence.
>
> (DSG1)

Conroy changed the whole thing. I remember the following Christmas I got back pay of over £500. That was unreal – you could get a car for that.

(G4)

These changes also helped to make the representative associations popular with younger gardaí (G2). Men could now afford to move out of stations, which did have the effect that 'you lost that community spirit to a degree as well ... call it progress or whatever you like' (SI6).

This, of course, was expensive: in February 1971 the government stated that £250,000 had been requested in overtime payments for the first six months. There were operational difficulties with implementing Conroy: 'I was in administration at the time and it created enormous problems to try and get it implemented because it was brought in overnight really' (SI6). SG3 recounted working with a sergeant who encountered difficulties providing round the clock cover without resorting to overtime.

[W]hat three men did before Conroy, it took four to do after that ... The position became impossible, because there was no increase in the men available for operational duties, and the situation gradually got out of control.

(Devitt 1997: 93)

The GRA attempted to provide assistance by drafting duty rosters, a task in which management were not skilled. The reduction in working hours was connected by some in the media to the growth in crime (*II*: 14/10/70).

While deserved, overtime payments had negative consequences. Men soon became competitive and sought to improve their own pay this way:

For management overtime was a disaster. It made people mercenaries. It created jealousies.

(I1)

Before that, the guards, they did their duty and it had to be done, but now they do it and they know, 'Okay I'm only required to work between X and X hours and if it's anything over that it has to be overtime'. And that was the way they kinda looked at it.

(G14)

I don't know if we had the same kind of morale after it. You'd wonder sometimes were you better off with the flexibility.

(G9)

From this point on members were competing for overtime. Financial rewards replaced a great deal of the vocational aspects of the job.

Conroy concluded with a call for an examination of the role and organisation of the force and in particular the relationship between the force and the

Department of Justice (para. 1266). This hints at the perennial problem of politicisation of the gardaí but, whether due to a lack of will or the pressures created
by the outbreak of the Troubles and a dramatic rise in crime in Ireland, this did
not happen. It would haunt the gardaí in future years that an opportunity to
address this longstanding problem was missed.

Conclusion

The 1950s and 1960s are often presented as quiet, peaceful times for Irish policing, where the sole concerns were pay and conditions. This chapter has explored
how in reality it was much more complex. The personnel in the force changed
almost completely as the first generation retired. Those that replaced them were,
most significantly, not political appointments as the previous generation had
been. These were recruits who were either desperate not to emigrate or had a
vocation towards policing. Women were finally permitted to join the force though
traditional perspectives limited their role for some time to come. This new
generation joined at a time of low crime, diverse tasks, limited technology and
when the force was regularly used to respond to public-order situations. This was
the policing they learned.

Throughout this period gardaí called for improvements to pay and conditions.
While the Conroy Commission heralded substantive change in the early 1970s for
over 20 years their concerns had been repeatedly downplayed and ignored by
government. The MacEoin Inquiry in 1951 had stated that reductions in numbers
could be achieved if technology was invested in: numbers were reduced but the
technology did not develop. On the one hand, politicians defended the police
vociferously against criticism but on the other hand they would not address
fundamental problems with living and working conditions. This may not simply
have been hypocrisy: an economic inability to provide for the gardaí may have
left government constrained from criticising the police for how they responded to
those conditions. Either way, for another generation of police, violence was
normalised without fear of accountability. Conroy did eventually address many
of the garda concerns but not before gardaí felt abandoned by their Commissioner
and politicians. Morale had reached such depths that when overtime and
improved working conditions came, they had attendant negative consequences.
Gone were the days of a sergeant shouting upstairs for additional help; now
gardaí expected overtime.

Notes

1 Interviewees are referred to by rank and order of interview, e.g. G12 was the 12th Garda
  interviewed, SG1 was the first sergeant interviewed. See Appendix 2 for a full list.
2 Or SI2 followed this trajectory: Offaly – Portlaoise – Mayo – Kildare – Roscommon –
  Carlow –Abbeyleix.
3 Four from 1952–4; four from 1955–9; ten from 1960–4 and eight from 1965–9, all male.

5 The Troubles and policing Ireland

Introduction

Previous chapters have charted the history of the policing of the Irish state from colonisation, to partition, through civil war, the subsequent period of stabilisation through to the 1960s. North of the border however, politics and society moved in a very different direction. The partition of the country had been organised to keep those counties of the island with a majority Protestant population within the United Kingdom. Under the Anglo-Irish Treaty of 1922 these counties remained a part of the United Kingdom, and Northern Ireland was given devolved government (McKittrick and McVea 2000). At this point nationalists, most of whom believed in a united Ireland, comprised about 35 per cent of the population of Northern Ireland, and contested the legitimacy of the Northern state (McGarry and O'Leary 1995). The failure of the new state to integrate these nationalists sparked violence and in the first two years of its existence more than 500 people were killed in political and sectarian violence (McKittrick and McVea 2000). The Royal Ulster Constabulary, formed in the wake of the Royal Irish Constabulary, and supported by an auxiliary police force, the B-Specials, was involved in much of this violence, earning a contentious status in the new jurisdiction (Hennessey 1997).

From the 1920s Unionists saw Nationalists as disloyal to the state in which they lived, feared their determination to form a united Ireland, which would be Catholic in nature, as well as their potential population growth (Bew *et al.* 2002). This continued threat was the basis for preferential treatment of Unionists in terms of housing, employment and other benefits. The economic success of the region, in contrast to Ireland's economic struggle, reinforced Unionist belief in the Northern state, while nationalists continued to see it as an illegitimate, corrupt British imposition (McKittrick and McVea 2000). Just as in the Republic of Ireland, occasional trouble flared in the 1940s and the 1950s as the IRA launched bombing campaigns (Hennessey 1997).

In the 1960s organisations emerged which aimed to highlight the discrimination that Catholics were suffering in Northern Ireland. One of these, the Northern Irish Civil Rights Association (NICRA), actively began campaigning for equal voting rights to combat the inequalities and gerrymandering which suppressed

Catholic representation in Parliament (Bew and Gillespie 1999). They also called for equality in public housing and employment, and the disbandment of the B-Specials. In the summer of 1968 the NICRA and the Derry Housing Action Committee staged a series of protests against these issues, which later developed into civil rights marches, leading on occasion to the use of baton rounds by the Royal Ulster Constabulary to disperse the crowds (Ellison and Smyth 2000; Mulcahy 2006). Tensions mounted, marches continued and violent clashes began to result from the stand-offs. The British army was introduced in 1969 to provide back-up and specialised support to the RUC (Bew and Gillespie 1999). Government efforts to address concerns over the franchise, housing and the policing of Northern Ireland throughout 1970 did not manage to displace tensions (Bew *et al.*, 2002). Internment was introduced in August 1971. Protests were held against this practice and at one of these in January 1972 soldiers opened fire killing 13 in what became known as Bloody Sunday (Walsh 2000). Soon after, direct rule from Westminster was imposed. By this point Northern Ireland had entered the most violent period of the conflict, which would last for another 20 years.

An abundance of academic research has analysed the Northern Irish conflict from political, sociological, economic and criminological perspectives. Within the criminological field, this has often looked at the security forces in Northern Ireland and how they responded to the threats they faced (Mulcahy 2006; Ellison and Smyth 2000; Gethins 2010). This chapter aims to analyse the Troubles from another side to understand what it meant for policing in Ireland. It will examine both what it meant to be a garda in Ireland at this time but also what this period tells us about the accountability of the gardaí. Interview data is drawn on throughout.

For many members of an Garda Síochána, the 'relaxed' way of life experienced in the 1950s and 1960s was severely disrupted in the 1970s by the outbreak of the Troubles in Northern Ireland. During the Troubles gardaí dealt with bombs, riots, colleagues being killed in the line of duty, kidnappings, armed robberies, being seconded to duty both on the border between Northern Ireland and the Republic, and to prisons. While the Troubles did not impact on the Republic of Ireland to the extent that they did in Northern Ireland,[1] given how peaceful policing in Ireland had been for the previous 20 years for those gardaí serving at the time the changes to policing which the Troubles brought were substantial, scary and unlike any previous policing experiences.

This chapter will first assess the impact that the Troubles had for policing in Ireland from a number of perspectives: the legislative framework, the strength of the organisation, the crime that related specifically to the Troubles and the range of additional functions which gardaí were required to perform as a result of the conflict. It will be shown how the Troubles significantly altered what it meant to be a garda in Ireland and the dangers that then became an inherent part of the job. It will also be argued that the government response to the Troubles was inadequate in terms of policing. The chapter will then focus on a particular set of gardaí for whom the experiences were particularly intense: those who policed the border regions. Through the interview data we will explore how different policing was in this part of the country and how in fact it had more in common with policing in the North at this time. Again, the theme of how the government responded will be explored to show how the men on the border were left in something of a no-man's land.

From the 1930s policing of the IRA in the Republic been the preserve of the Special Branch with the result that until the outbreak of the Troubles just one, small group of men had experience of the required policing skills (Brady 2000; Allen 1999). This was exacerbated by recruitment cycles. The complete recruitment to the force in the 1920s created near total turn-over of members in the 1950s and 1960s (Allen 1999). By the time the Northern Irish conflict began in the late 1960s the force was almost entirely composed of new, young recruits who had been members during the most peaceful period of the new state. They had not policed Ireland during a time when the legitimacy of the state was being challenged through unlawful and violent means. The force was unprepared in terms of policing experience, training and equipment for what the Troubles would bring. As one interviewee described: 'You had a Garda Síochána who thought that the problems with the IRA were all over and had for a while. Even the Special Branch had lapsed into quiet satisfaction. They were disturbed; they didn't have the appropriate personnel' (G3).

Policing the Troubles: a legislative response

The outbreak of the Troubles placed a great deal of pressure on the government. Not only, as we shall explore, did it bring with it numerous internal security and crime dilemmas but it is also directed British and Northern Irish attention to what the Irish government was doing to eradicate republican activities. Allegations that the Republic was a 'safe haven' for the IRA were regular (Patterson 2013: 7), though at the same time successive governments were acutely aware that heavy policing of the IRA would have been a relatively unpopular move among the Irish electorate and, more worryingly, it might generate more lethal IRA activity in the Republic. The government response primarily involved the vast increase in numbers of the gardaí (which may have occurred anyway, given the significant rise in ordinary crime) and the changing of the legislative framework in order to utilise the criminal justice system in as much of a preventative and controlling way as possible.

In December 1970 the government announced its intention to reintroduce internment in Ireland as a pre-emptive measure following garda intelligence about plans for high-profile kidnappings, armed robberies and possible murders (*IT*: 5/12/70; Davis 2006: 125). The necessary proclamations were, however, never made and internment remained a threat. One of the first legislative moves was the passing of the Prisons Act 1972 which, following riots in Mountjoy organised by republican prisoners, permitted the transfer of prisoners to military custody. Rogan cites that there was just two days between the drafting and the passing of the Bill (2011: 139). Around 40 prisoners were subsequently sent to the Curragh, which was used until 1983 and was the site of hunger strikes and prison escapes. An inquiry into state security and terrorism policies was established after these riots, headed by Justice Finlay (Patterson 2013: 66).

During the debate on the Prisons Bill the Minister for Justice announced that the Special Criminal Court, a three-judge, non-jury court, was being re-enacted to deal with terrorist-related crime as, under Article 38 of the Constitution, 'the ordinary courts are inadequate to secure the effective administration of justice, and the preservation of public peace and order'. The Offences Against the State Act 1939 allowed for such courts and had most recently been briefly used in 1961 during the IRA's border campaign (Davis 2006). The required proclamation was made on 26 May 1972 and four days later an order was made bringing it into effect and appointing judges. The 1939 Act was also amended to make membership of the IRA once again illegal. Under s.30 gardaí could arrest anyone suspected of being involved in an offence against the state, search them and detain them for 24 hours. This was a much-used provision, though only a small portion of arrests translated into charges, (see Table 5.1).

The Offences Against the State Act (OASA) was also amended to permit the statement of a Chief Superintendent to be accepted as evidence of membership of an illegal organisation.[2] Further to this, Cosgrave's government in 1973 made it illegal to broadcast interviews with members of either republican or loyalist paramilitary groups (O'Halpin 1999; Twomey 1998). This ban lasted until 1994.

Following the killing by the IRA of the British ambassador Christopher Ewatt Biggs and an explosion in the vicinity of the Special Criminal Court, the Government declared a state of emergency in August 1976 (DE: 31/08/76). This led to the passing of the Emergency Powers Act 1976, which granted gardaí the temporary power to detain suspects for up to seven days for offences against the state on the direction of a garda of rank of Chief Superintendent (O'Halpin 1999; Mulcahy 2005). The controversial nature of this Act was reinforced by the IRA's planting of a bomb on the day that the President signed the Bill into law, killing a young garda, Michael Clerkin, and blinding another.

Some of those interviewed expressed the view that the lengthy periods of detention did not make the policing of subversive work any easier:

> A guy can come in and he'll pick a spot on that wall. He'll look at it for seven days and not open his mouth ... He'd just come in and stick to the spot on the

Table 5.1 Use of s.30 arrest powers.

Year	Arrested	Charged
1981	2303	323
1982	2308	256
1983	2334	363
1984	2216	374
1985	1834	366
1986	2387	484

wall and that was it. Wouldn't open his mouth. I've seen it. And every question you ask you have to write it down, no reply. Every question …You've
a guy in there for seven days, and says nothing, you've to write down every
question you ask him. Which is ridiculous … When they were released, that
came from a higher authority. You were told 'hold on. He might break'.

(G17)

While from the garda perspective seven-day detention may not have been particularly useful, advantage was taken of it as much as possible. Levels of confessions
were high, demonstrated by Kilcommins *et al.*'s assertion that up to 80 per cent of
convictions for serious crimes were based on confessions (2004: 209). Statutory
requirements as to treatment of persons in custody were not introduced until
1984 and as we will discuss below, allegations of brutality were commonplace in
interrogations.

The Criminal Law Act 1976 extended garda powers in relation to persons
arrested under s.30 of OASA and failure to provide information such as name and
address became an offence in itself. Recruiting, inviting or inciting others to join
an illegal organisation became an offence under the same legislation and the
punishment for membership of an unlawful organisation was increased to seven
years. The army was given powers of arrest in limited circumstances for the
purpose of delivering the suspect to the gardaí. No legal safeguards applied to a
person while detained by the army. The Criminal Law (Jurisdiction) Act 1976
enabled the prosecution of a person in the Republic for an offence committed in
Northern Ireland. It also amended a range of offences central to the activities of
republicans, including explosives, firearms, burglary and hijacking of vehicles. In
1985 the OASA was amended to enable the freezing of assets of members of
illegal organisations.

Farrell comments that it was 'surprising that such inroads on human and democratic rights could be made with so little protest in a state which is a functioning
democracy with regular changes of government' (1993: 128). These powers
become particularly difficult when the combined effect is considered: enhanced
garda powers without supervision or safeguards followed by a non-jury trial in
which a garda can give evidence of his beliefs. Some of the most controversial
cases in the state such as the cases of Nicky Kelly and Peter Pringle, involving
the murder of a garda and allegations of brutality, were convicted in the Special
Criminal Court and it can certainly be argued that the composition of the courts
was instrumental in securing many of these convictions. Between 1972 and 1980,
1500 people were prosecuted in the Court, two-thirds of whom were convicted
(Salmon 1985: 80). In a report in 1977 Amnesty International, investigating allegations of brutality, found that the Special Criminal Court proved willing to
accept the testimony of a garda over that of an accused person consistently.
One interviewee expressed the view that this court enabled these convictions:
'There was no way they could have convicted any of them if without the
Special Criminal Court … There was no jury. Their evidence would not have got
passed a jury. All the judges wanted was sufficient evidence to convict' (DSG1).

Other participants maintained that the context and circumstances created pressures understood by these courts: 'When you had all these bombings there was such public outrage. There was pressure to get convictions. There was such a balancing act. The courts were sympathetic to their evidence' (DSG1). This reflects the argument made by Brodeur that: 'The secretive aspects of political policing, whether real or fabricated, stem from a partnership among the police, politicians, the courts and, ironically, the victims of aggressive political policing themselves' (1983: 510).

Law was the government's primary vehicle for curtailing the IRA. Added to this was a dramatic increase in garda numbers with substantial recruitment drives in the coming years. In 1970 there had been 6551 gardaí whereas in 1984 this figure had almost doubled to 11,387. This naturally meant a substantial increase in spending on policing, from £23.9 million in 1974 to £233.8 million in 1985 (Brewer *et al.* 1996: 92).

The government's response to intense pressure was to combine a tough legislative response, what Salmon calls 'a formidable arsenal against the IRA' (1985: 79), with highly increased garda numbers. Certainly some of this increase in manpower would have occurred irrespective of the Troubles given rising crime rates in Ireland. Figures relating to C3, Crime and Security Branch, which had responsibility for intelligence on paramilitary groups, suggest that the increase was not directed at improving the policing of the IRA:

> In the initial period of the Troubles, the spiralling escalation of paramilitary activity threatened to swap C3's capacity. In 1970, it opened 55 new intelligence files; in 1971, 89; while in the next two years, the number rocketed to 1595 in 1972 and 1575 in 1973. However, despite this the number of staff members allocated to the analysis, assessment and distribution of intelligence in these files was kept to 14.
>
> (Patterson 2012: 239)

But by the mid-1980s police numbers in Ireland reached levels not seen since the last days of the RIC, when it was for the whole island. Vaughan and Kilcommins' premise is that in Ireland 'two parallel systems of justice emerged, one committed

Table 5.2 Garda recruitment 1970–83.

Year	Number recruited	Year	Number recruited
1970	181	1977	535
1971	192	1978	718
1972	854	1979	302
1973	536	1980	446
1974	510	1981	127
1975	366	1982	983
1976	86	1983	578

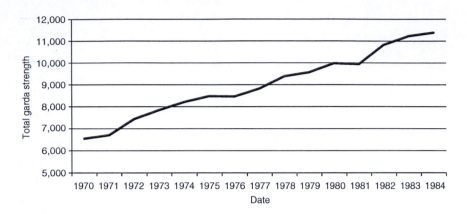

Figure 5.1 Garda strength 1970–84 (DE: 21/10/80, 05/03/85).

to the rule *of* law, the other to the rule *by* law' (2008: 67). Fifteen of those interviewed for this work joined the force after the outbreak of the Troubles, seven between 1972 and 1975, a four-year period in which over 2000 additional gardaí were recruited. By then the first garda had been killed by paramilitaries but this did not generate any hesitation in joining. If anything to young men this enhanced the prospect of excitement.

Criminalising the Troubles

With greater powers of arrest and detention, specifically created offences and more gardaí the potential for intense criminalisation of terrorist efforts was clear. When the Troubles began crime rates in Ireland were exceptionally low, as discussed in Chapter 4. As Figure 5.2 shows, recorded crime grew exceptionally through the 1970s and 1980s.

Between 1967 and 1983, just 16 years, the level of recorded indictable crimes increased fivefold. If the 1983 rate is compared to 1955, the lowest level of crime on record, it increased nine-fold. Some debate has emerged on the contribution of the Troubles to this growth. The Garda Commissioner stated in 1975: 'Violent criminal activity designed to intimidate for political purposes in the border areas has undoubtedly influenced crime trends throughout the whole country. This is particularly noticeable since 1969' (cited in Mulcahy 2002: 281). Influenced certainly, but it would be wrong to suggest that the Conflict was responsible for these dramatic increases in crime levels. Mulcahy (2002) contends that the changes in crime rates reflected a general trend for the whole of Europe:

> Rapid urbanisation, internal migration, a rise in general prosperity levels coupled with a widening gap between rich and poor, all had a profound impact

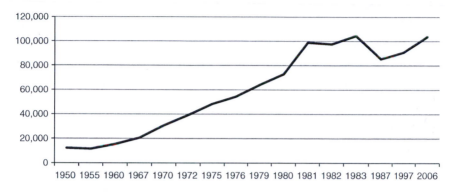

Figure 5.2 Recorded crime rates 1950–2006 (Garda Síochána reports on crime, annual reports).

on the nature of Irish society, and especially on attitudes to, opportunities for and responses to crime.

(Mulcahy 2002: 281)

The garda crime reports can be used to identify and analyse the extent to which paramilitary activity was criminalised during the Troubles. There are a number of specific offences that can be considered: offences under the OASA (including membership of an illegal organisation), firearms and explosives offences, kidnappings, seizing of vehicles (an offence from 1976 on) and armed robberies. In analysing the figures recorded for each of these offences, we cannot say that the numbers all relate to the Troubles. However, without more specific data recorded, we will proceed cautiously.

Between 1981 and 1986 about 2000 people a year were arrested under s.30 but given the low evidential requirements for such arrests these figures do not necessarily relate to actual criminal offences. They primarily reveal garda suspicions and perhaps tactics to disrupt the IRA. Figure 5.3 indicates the levels of offences recorded by the gardaí for offences in the above listed categories between the years 1969 and 1989.

There is a strong growth in recorded paramilitary activity but this cannot simply be taken as evidence of growth in that activity. Legislative changes, for instance, contribute to this: seizing vehicles was not a specific offence prior to the Criminal Law (Jurisdiction) Act 1976. But dominating this graph is the growth in armed robberies. In a period of ten years (1969–79) armed robberies rose from 12 to 228 on an annual basis, rising again dramatically to nearly 700 in the mid-1980s. Convictions were secured in a very small number of cases (changes in recording practices make it difficult to provide conviction statistics for the 1980s).

Patterson reveals the gardaí believed one-third of these were being conducted by paramilitaries, although detection rates were very low, rarely above 15 per cent (2013: 118). According to Salmon (1985: 89) between 1975 and 1978 over

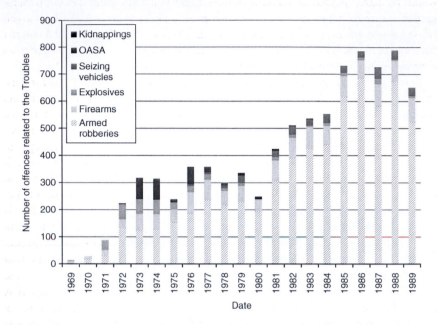

Figure 5.3 Offences related to the Troubles 1969–89 (Garda crime reports).

£4.5 million was taken, much of which was to fund paramilitary efforts. In some of these instances cars had been stolen in Northern Ireland and used for robberies in the Republic, particularly in border towns. The scale was overwhelming at times. G17, stationed in Dundalk, recalled one particular night: 'I was working on my own for eight armed robberies. Probably the same crowd of boys. Every shop they were getting 1500 quid … if that happened in Clonmel the whole force

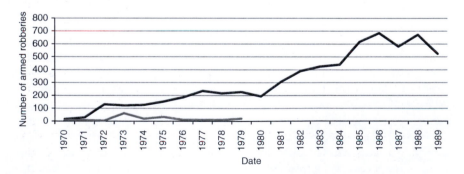

Figure 5.4 Armed robberies, recorded (1970–89) and convicted (1970–9) (Garda annual crime reports).

would be there.' Added to the scale of the work was the attendant danger, particularly for unarmed gardaí. More than half of the gardaí killed during the Troubles died responding to an armed robbery. This was dangerous work, which occurred without warning. While armed robberies primarily occurred in Dublin and the border areas they did occur throughout the country and to all types of establishments.[3]

Garda responses to this type of crime included increased protection for cash transportations and places where explosives were used, continued support and education in crime prevention, and efforts to seize arms and ammunition. Protection work was regularly mentioned by interviewees. I4, for instance, was engaged in round-the-clock protection at the Tynagh silver mines in Loughrea: 'anything to do with explosives at that time would have come under the subheading of high risk facility that had to warrant [protection]'. G7 did similar work at the explosives factory at Enfield. Protection also had to be provided at the courts, in particular the Special Criminal Court. G13 recalled doing protection at a hospital in Dublin following the transfer of a prisoner who was on hunger strike in Portlaoise and being 'pelted with rocks and stone and bottles'. Others were sent on temporary transfers to areas where the IRA were active. SG7 spent four months in County Kerry while the IRA caused trouble as they did not like the number of tourists in the vicinity. SG6 was later sent to Killaloe when the IRA had burned down a school. Any perceived threat received a redirection of garda numbers; boring work, which did not draw on policing skills. As much of this work was so bound up in national security little data exists about the intelligence-gathering side of policing the Troubles, but it appears that the government focus was not on strategic, intelligence-led policing of the IRA.

If armed robberies are removed from Figure 5.3 we can assess recorded offences in the other categories more clearly, as per Figure 5.5.

Most surprising is the relatively rare usage of the OASA by the gardaí. Despite the fact that this included offences such as membership of an illegal organisation

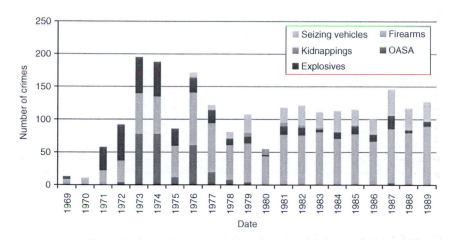

Figure 5.5 Police recorded crime 1969–89 (Garda annual crime reports, 1969–89).

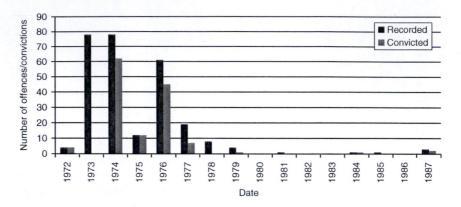

Figure 5.6 Recorded offences and convictions secured under OASA 1972–87 (Garda crime reports).

it was only used, as Figure 5.6 shows, in any substantial way between 1973 and 1977, after which there are never more than ten offences recorded in any year.

Figures 5.7 and 5.8 show that firearm offences were steadily recorded throughout but with limited success in terms of convictions, while explosives offences appear predominantly in the early years of the Troubles.

But it was not just about numeric rises. In addition to British political pressure to subvert the IRA, some of these crimes attracted significant international attention. Kidnappings, for instance, were relatively rare but very high profile. In 1974 Lord and Lady Donoughmore were kidnapped and held for five days before being released in Phoenix Park. On one occasion in Dublin nine hostages were held in a shop during a 12-hour siege (*IT*: 28/11/77). Jennifer Guinness, of the Guinness

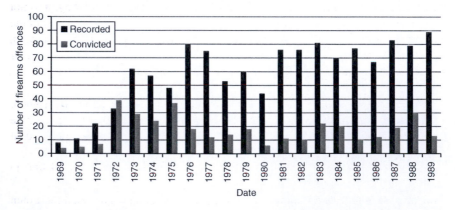

Figure 5.7 Firearms offences, recorded and convicted 1969–89 (Garda annual crime reports).

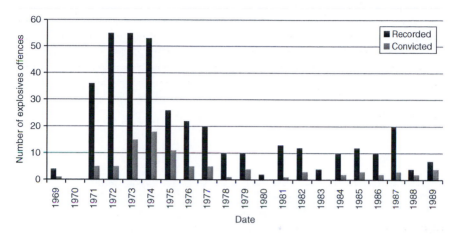

Figure 5.8 Explosives offences, recorded and convicted 1969–89 (Garda annual crime reports).

family, was kidnapped in 1986. In 1975 there was the 36-day kidnapping of Dr Herrema, a Dutch businessman, in an IRA effort to assure the release of three republican prisoners. That Dr Herrema was Dutch meant that this investigation, one of the largest mounted in the state, was broadcast across the world, placing additional pressure on gardaí (Courtney 1996). In the 19 days it took to locate where the hostage was being held allegations were made that investigating gardaí used violence to secure information about his whereabouts.[4] The efforts of the IRA were undermining an Garda Síochána who resorted to more coercive policing methods (Wrong 1995).

The 23-day kidnapping of Don Tidey, a supermarket executive, ended with the death of a trainee garda, Garda Sheehan, and a soldier, Private P. J. Kelly (Courtney 1996). That it was a trainee garda and a member of the army, and not experienced police detectives, who were at the front line of efforts to intercept the kidnappers shows how ill-equipped an Garda Síochána was in such instances, even 14 years after the Troubles had begun. This raised questions as to their capacity in such scenarios and the *Garda Review* conceded:

> We must in honesty admit that events in Ballinamore and Claremorris [where these men were killed] give rise to at least some questioning as to whether we are satisfactorily structured, controlled, directed, trained and equipped to deal appropriately with such situations.
>
> (1984: 1)

This analysis suggests a number of points. If armed robberies are excluded then the numbers of crimes recorded and prosecuted by gardaí are somewhat lower than what might have been expected. There are two related points here: firstly, as indicated above, enhanced powers were not necessarily helpful for this type of policing and secondly, given the discretion involved in policing and how politically directed policing has been in Ireland, if gardaí felt that governments did not want republicans heavily policed then they would not avail of those powers. What is clear is that gardaí were not sufficiently trained or equipped to deal with many of the crimes that the Troubles brought their way. In addition to making these crimes harder to investigate and prosecute this also brings, as we will examine in detail below, danger for the gardaí involved.

Death work

Over the course of the Troubles seven fatal bombs exploded in the Republic, killing civilians. On 1 December 1972 two car bombs exploded in Dublin city centre killing two and injuring 127. Four weeks later two were killed in a bomb blast in Belturbet, County Cavan and a month later a car bomb exploded in Dublin city centre killing one Scottish student. On 17 May 1974, four car bombs exploded, three in Dublin and one in Monaghan, killing 33 and an unborn child. This was the greatest loss of life in any one single day of the Troubles, on either side of the border, and was attributed to loyalist groups (Mullan *et al.* 2001). One employee was killed during an explosion at Dublin Airport in November 1975 and the following month two were killed in an explosion in Dundalk. Early in 1976 one man was killed in a bombing in Castleblayney, County Monaghan. A number of civilians were killed during armed robberies. In August 1979, after the ambushing and killing of 18 British army soldiers at Narrow Water, the British army fired across the border into the Republic and killed a man.

Non-civilians were also killed in Ireland. The British ambassador, Christopher Ewart Biggs, and a British civil servant were killed in 1976. Three years later Lord Mountbatten, a cousin of the Queen's, was killed along with three others. There were also a number of deaths in Ireland of members of paramilitary groups when bombs exploded prematurely. Four members of the RUC were shot and killed while in the Republic.[5] A senator, Billy Fox, and a councillor, Eddie Fullerton, were both murdered.

Mulcahy (2002) determines from Sutton's index of those killed in the conflict that 107 people died in the Republic in incidents directly related to the conflict in Northern Ireland. No records have been maintained as to how many were injured though it is known that hundreds were injured in bombings. There is no consolidated data on how many bombs exploded in the Republic during the Troubles. In the first five months of 1972 alone there were 172 bomb threats recorded by gardaí (DE: 15/6/72). Police responded to, attended and investigated these incidents. The bombings were recalled by participants as particularly harrowing. I5 was 100 yards from the first fatal blast in the Republic, in Dublin in 1972 when two busmen were killed: 'I pulled your man out from under the car, his head blown clean off his shoulders. And I mean clean gone, and this arm here gone … I can still see the 'vadoom' you know.' This was undoubtedly a distressing experience and as the first fatal bombing in the Republic connected to the Troubles chaos naturally ensued. It is indicative of the garda preparedness at the time that I5 was sent to the morgue with the bodies of the two individuals who died that day and was required to sit with them for hours as they were evidence in a murder scene.

Both SI6 and I7 attended the scene of the Belturbet bombing in December 1972. SI6 recounted it as the 'toughest time' he experienced, seeing 'people dead and bits blown off them'. The bomb had blown out the telephone exchange, making communication and policing intensely difficult. Though not specifically trained to deal with bombs, he remembered checking under cars for secondary devices. I7 spoke of how he had been standing five yards from where the bomb went off 20 minutes before the blast but had left to check on a local dance and on his way heard the blast: 'I never heard a bomb or anything before.'

The bomb exploded outside a pub and I7, knowing people in the pub, checked both upstairs and downstairs. This was not something that he should have done as he knew neither what structural damage had been caused nor whether there were secondary devices: 'And it was only afterwards, the next day, when I saw, jeez, was I in there last night? You just, you didn't think … you couldn't say I'm not going in there, wait till the fire brigade comes.' Not only did these individuals not have the training to deal with this situation but there was a lack of experts to call on. It took a half hour at least before support arrived from elsewhere: 'loads of people were coming down, "Sergeant, there's a Northern Ireland car parked up outside our house. There's probably another bomb in that. Will you check it?" … We didn't know if there was a bomb up the road and we didn't have the manpower to go up' (I7). When support arrived their task was difficult as the electricity had gone and they were reliant on torches supplied form a local hardware shop. He remembered no formal forensic investigation of the scene. The police were clearly overwhelmed in this situation.

SG6 was at the scene of the loyalist bombings of Monaghan in 1974, which, occurring minutes after the Dublin bombings, are believed to have been designed to distract gardaí from the border while the culprits escaped back to Northern Ireland. He 'dashed' to the main street arriving to 'a horrible-looking scene. The first thing I saw was a man's head on the street, and carnage everywhere'. There were difficulties getting the emergency services as many had just begun their dinner break and phone calls were coming from Dublin to close the border. He knew all four people who were killed in that bombing. The next three weeks were consumed with taking statements and gathering information. Others, like DG15, spent days doing additional border checkpoints in the wake of the Monaghan bombing. Investigations were hampered by a lack of forensic technology and no prosecutions were ever secured. The McEntee Report (2007) into the investigation of the bombings was critical of how garda investigations were wound down within months and that key documents and pieces of evidence were not retained by gardaí. Rather than a concerted effort to conceal information, these investigations may have been hampered by ineptitude.

In addition to these fatal blasts there were numerous explosions that injured people. In October 1972 Connolly station in Dublin was bombed and four hotels firebombed. The next month a cinema in Dublin was bombed injuring 40 and in 1969 the UVF car-bombed the garda detective bureau in Dublin (*IT*: 28/12/69). Throughout the course of the Troubles there were dozens of incidents involving bombs, car bombs, letter bombs and incendiary devices in Dublin, Limerick, Portlaoise, Galway and along the border. Those who attended the aftermath of the bombings encountered horrific scenes, in dangerous circumstances, and received no support or counselling. In the early years particularly, they often did not have the requisite training or skills to investigate appropriately.

The Troubles also brought what was mentioned by many as the worst part of the job: the death of colleagues.

> The good times block out to a great extent the bad times. Although there were bad times and there were harsh times and there were rough times when some of your colleagues got shot.
>
> (SI5)

> That was the worst part of it. That end of it when people were being killed … and at that stage you had Dick Fallon and there was a few shootings and various things that, then again you were off. You were going in uniform to these garda funerals and that was the sad time of the whole lot of it. But there was no real need for the shooting of them, no more than again blowing the fellas up.
>
> (G16)

Garda Richard Fallon was the first garda killed since 1942 when he attempted to catch a group of armed bank-robbers, members of the republican group Saor Éire, in April 1970, in Dublin. His death had a profound impact on the force; 1000 gardaí, more than one in every seven in the country, attended his funeral. G14 felt compelled to travel from Galway to Dublin for the funeral even though he did not personally know Garda Fallon. Fallon's son described the scene:

> All the way along the route all you could see was a sea of uniforms. Old people were kneeling saying the rosary by the side of the road … I remember we were driving up by O'Connell Street and looking up at the monument and seeing people right up on top of it, and on lampposts, like they do for the Patrick's Day Parade. Everyone assumes that my father was given a state funeral. He wasn't: it just looked like one because so many Gardaí had turned out in force.
>
> (Cited in Walsh 2001: 8)

There were very few members left in the force that had been serving the last time a colleague had died on duty. For close to 30 years the entire organisation had performed its duties without the threat of such violence. The impact of this death was intense:

> The death of Dick Fallon was a watershed. He was a man in uniform. He just got a phone call that a bank was being raided. They just got there as the men

were running out. This incident shook the force to the roots. People were shocked.

(I1)

When that word reached us it stunned the place for days. Like I mean, never in our lifetime, the previous shooting of a guard had been in 1942 or something. And it cast a pile of gloom over the whole force for weeks if not months you know because it hadn't happened for so long.

(SI5)

The fact that he was just a uniformed garda, not Special Branch, made the impact of his death even more profound. He was not involved in a major anti-terrorist operation, he was just a garda who responded to a routine call. Overnight any garda suddenly could face this threat.

You suddenly realise that if the person who committed it only drove three hours it could be you. It was the luck of the draw that you were stationed in Cork.

(G1)

A sea change to us. A massive realisation. You see you think about all these things. You go out in the morning, you go out in the evening, you're working with the community. You never think about the ultimate sanction that would be placed on you by the opposition, for want of a better description, such as happened in the Fallon case. I mean, he was there in a patrol car, doing his normal duties. And furthest from his mind was that he wouldn't be back in the station or back with his family. So that was something. That brought the realisation to all of us at the time. A big shock and a big change.

(G12)

The men who joined in the 1950s and 1960s, joined for a safe, pensionable and varied job. There had in recent years been deaths of members while on duty, usually in traffic collisions, deaths that could have occurred irrespective of their occupation. Fallon, however, died because he was a garda pursuing criminals. His death was violent and purposeful. Henry, who has studied the impact of 'death work' on members of the NYPD, reports that '[s]everal tenured collaborators made the point that other members of their command were psychologically unprepared for the death of their co-worker because no cop had been murdered or grievously injured in their precinct' (2004: 251). This would explain why when asked about low points in their careers most of the interviewees in this study spoke of the death of a colleague, often naming Richard Fallon. To this end the death of Richard Fallon was a signal event (Loader and Sparks 2004), one that altered the course of an Garda Síochána. A signal event has been considered as 'exerting a disproportionate impact upon public beliefs and attitudes when compared with their "objective" consequences' (Innes 2004). Through its creation of a substantiated fear within an Garda Síochána that its members were now, once again, the targets of such violence, the death of Richard Fallon was a signal event altering both public and official discourse on the garda.

The death of Richard Fallon was soon followed by further garda deaths.[6] Inspector Donegan was killed by a booby trap on the border in 1972 (he had, in fact, crossed over into Northern Ireland by a few yards). Garda Reynolds was killed intercepting a bank robbery in Dublin in 1975. The following year Garda Clerkin was killed in Portlaoise, as detailed above, on the day the Emergency Powers Act was signed into law. In July 1980 Garda Byrne and Detective Garda Morley were killed during the pursuit of three armed men who robbed a branch of the Bank of Ireland near Castlerea, Roscommon, taking £46,500. Their funerals in Mayo were 'the largest ever to be seen in Knock' (Courtney 1996: 35). Colm O'Shea, Patrick McCann and Peter Pringle were all charged and convicted of the murder. Murder of a garda was a capital offence in Ireland until 2002 and they were sentenced to death, although this was commuted by the President to 40 years' imprisonment without remission. Pringle's conviction was quashed in 1995 on the basis of contradictory evidence by two of the investigating members (DPP v. Pringle, 16 May 1995). Later that same year Garda James Quaid was killed after attempting to search the van of a suspect following a robbery in Kilkenny (Courtney 1996). Peter Rogers was subsequently sentenced to death for the murder, although again this was later commuted to 40 years' imprisonment (Courtney 1996). Four more gardaí were killed in the next five years, with Garda McCabe's death in 1996 at a post-office raid in County Limerick the final garda death caused by the Troubles.

In all 12 gardaí were killed as a result of the Troubles. Data has unfortunately not been collated either by the force or the GRA on how many gardaí were injured during the Troubles but a newspaper search indicates that at least a further 20 gardaí were shot and injured while more were injured in various scenarios from riots to attacks on stations to explosives injuries. On one occasion a garda had his car hijacked and was ordered to drive a 200lb bomb across the border to a village in Fermanagh, Northern Ireland. Knowing the area he managed to drive the car to a secluded area and raise the alarm before it exploded. The annual crime reports reveal something about attacks on gardaí at the time, though we cannot say that these relate exclusively to the Troubles.

The number of woundings, a more serious attack than an assault, peaked at 31 in 1983. In 1982 the head of the Forensic Science Laboratory, Dr James Donovan, who had been instrumental in the conviction for the killing of Lord Mountbatten, was seriously injured when a bomb was placed under his car. This attempted assassination marked a new departure for those who worked in security services. Calls for gardaí to be armed came quickly, however they did not have the support of the members. The Association of Garda Sergeants and Inspectors (AGSI) declared:

> Arming an Garda Síochána is a simplistic and unsatisfactory solution to a
> highly complex problem. Such a course would create far more problems for

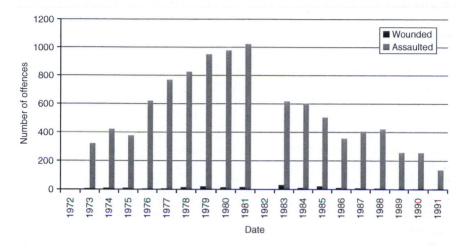

Figure 5.9 Recorded indictable offences for wounding and assaulting gardaí (Garda annual crime reports).

the Force than it might ever solve. The overwhelming confidence and support of the public for the Gardaí might well be placed in jeopardy.

(AGSI, *Horizon*, March 1982, quoted in Allen 1999: 212)

This stance was impressive given the circumstances and the level of threat, and shows the importance members placed on the ideal of the unarmed garda. The *Garda Review* explained that 'the unarmed Guard is as much an expression of our aspirations, a microcosm of our national ideal, as a practical policing device' (1975: 1). Disarming an Garda Síochána had been the defining break from the RIC back in the 1920s.

Public outcry at such deaths was substantial. SG3 explain that the support from the public in the wake of the death of Gerry McCabe was 'absolutely fantastic. People rang in to do anything they could. Supply transport, give their cars. Give everything. It was unreal the support'. An opinion poll in 1982 revealed that 64 per cent of people were in favour of executing those responsible for his death (Walsh 2001). In a political sense it seemed to put an Garda Síochána beyond reproach. Mulcahy has outlined how such deaths were utilised in respect of the RUC:

Official discourse characterizes the force as a long-suffering and heavily victimized organization. The fact that these sacrifices are willingly made, and that officers continue to perform their duties in full knowledge of the danger they face, establishes a moral dimension to their activities and the broader organization. These extreme human costs are used to demand a response from the community, namely support for the RUC.

(Mulcahy 2000: 75)

These sacrifices made by gardaí served to strengthen the symbolic power of the force. As Loader states: 'an idealised force for good is imagined as struggling with, and seeking to contain, an unknown, unpredictable and demonized evil' (1997: 4). This can certainly be evidenced in the Republic. Gardaí were now dying to protect the country from the activities of the IRA. Dissatisfaction with gardaí in previous decades was forgotten, certainly in official discourse. If anything the deaths served to reinforce an Garda Síochána's representation of Irish nationalist sentiment. Just as politicians and cultural revisionists recreated Irish history in the 1920s, in the 1970s the myth emerged that the gardaí had always been held with high esteem in Ireland and had served the country proudly. As Mr L'Estrange TD stated in a law and order debate in 1972:

> We have … much respect for them and we have stood by them ever since they were set up, as an unarmed force, by Cumann na nGaedheal. We have always backed them up and we will continue to back them up.
>
> (DE: 01/1272)

This reconnected policing to the nationalist ideal around which they had been founded and while for other institutions, such as the Catholic Church, this type of discourse was becoming irrelevant, the Troubles made it more relevant than ever for an Garda Síochána. A prime example of this is the comment of Deputy Harney when she prefaced comments on an Garda Síochána by saying:

> Like many Members one is always very wary about being critical of our Garda Síochána. They have a very difficult job to do and many members of the force have tragically lost their lives trying to protect the State and its citizens … It is all too easy for politicians to undermine the Force by criticising constantly what they might and might not do.
>
> (DE: 13/05/87)

Notions of sacrifice and bravery thereby became part of the official discourse of an Garda Síochána. This discourse shielded gardaí from criticism and emerging questions of accountability, as discussed in Chapter 6.

Of course, these deaths and this work had implications for members on a personal level. Many of those interviewed knew some of these men, either having worked with them in different stations or were working with them at the time of their death. SG3 was stationed in Limerick when Gerry McCabe was killed:

> It was very tough. I was in the incident room in Henry Street for that investigation. Very tough. Very traumatic for everybody, for the lads. There were some of them were ashen faced. We'd have conferences there every day. And some of the lads they were just distraught, they couldn't take it. But none of us could … I did those escorts myself several times … So it could have been any of us.

The psychological impact of such 'death work' has been considered by Henry (2004) who considers the impact of death on police officers in comparison to other occupations such as doctors and emergency services, and points out that most other occupations involving 'death work' are given de-sensitising training.

> Police encounters with death, on the other hand, often occur under volatile, objectively dangerous, emotionally charged and highly ambiguous circumstances in which immediate social and psychological supports are absent, and they frequently involve death in its most grotesque and trauma-provoking forms.
>
> (Henry 2004: 16)

This lack of support was noticeable among interviewees. SG1 took early retirement due to post-traumatic stress. While doing security work he and three colleagues were held at gunpoint and despite reporting this to superiors he was given no immediate time off and no support. Henry (2004) similarly found that PTSD and alcoholism can be linked to near-death experiences. Sewell's 1983 seminal study of stressful work-related incidents for police officers placed the 'violent death of a partner in the line of duty' at the top of the list (cited in Ainsworth 2002). The 'nothing can happen to me' illusion held by many police officers is shattered by the death of a colleague.

Brewer (1990b) and Brewer and Magee (1991) analysed how danger impacted on the self-image of members of the RUC, 302 of whom were killed, during the same conflict. The reaction of retired gardaí who spoke of how the deaths affected them, even if they did not know the victim, contrasts greatly with the attitude of RUC officers who were part of Brewer's study. One conversation recounted by Brewer showed that police deaths could be normalised.

> PC1: That's right, in two weeks' time he'll be forgotten about.
> WPC [sic]: Like, I bet there's nobody can remember the name of the last policeman killed. Nobody gives a shit really. We don't know them so it does not affect us like … People will look at this in station tonight and say, 'a full time reservist killed, that's terrible, get the tea on'.
>
> (Brewer 1990b: 668)

In the Republic deaths of gardaí were never normalized in such a way. This difference comes down to the number of such deaths and the experience of such scenarios.

> It was a different situation, it was so common there [in the North] that people just expected it every week that there'd be another one killed … It was a different feeling here, we didn't, in general it wasn't, it didn't feel like it was going to happen that much, because we were an unarmed force and we didn't, we weren't a great threat to anyone. We just went out with two arms, one as

long as the other as you say, and we hadn't a backup service like the forces in the North.

(SG5)

If anything interviewees suggested that they simply tried not to think about it, because concern about such dangers would impact on your ability to perform: 'You wouldn't be thinking. If you did you'd be a nervous wreck. You'd be in the mental hospital if you were thinking of all these things every day. You just get on with it' (G11). Brewer and Magee found that few officers were willing to avail of support and that those who did admit to experiencing stress negated its impact by:

admitting that it is a problem in the Force but denying it is a personal problem; admitting it to be a personal problem but attributing the causes to the organisation and management; confessing that stress once was a personal problem but it is no longer; relating the stress problems of others.

(Brewer and Magee 1991: 179)

This analysis holds true for gardaí as well. Only one garda interviewed talked about the extreme nature of the stress he suffered as a result of the job without trying to negate the extent (SG1). Others told of how colleagues could not cope or spoke of the difficult times in the past tense, implying that they had overcome any impact they had. Some were dismissive of such talk however:

There was a couple of young fellows down there, there was a woman murdered below in the Curragh and they went in and found the body. And they were counselled for about six months after it. We'd say 'hello, you are in the guards. You are supposed to be immune to these, you are supposed to build up a certain resistance to this kind of stuff.'

(I5)

This type of tough, masculine response to the difficulties of policing has been well documented in writings on police sub-culture (Reiner 2000; see Kopel and Friedman 1997 for this phenomenon in South Africa). Malone (1992) has argued that gardaí are unwilling to admit the true extent of the anxiety and fears of their occupation. Instead such feelings fuelled a determination among members to ensure that the IRA did not succeed, which is interesting if it is remembered that over 90 per cent of those who joined an Garda Síochána initially were ex-IRA.

Public-order policing

The Troubles brought protests with political and cross-jurisdictional currents. There were two particularly difficult riots in terms of policing. In 1972, in the aftermath of Bloody Sunday, a demonstration of 20,000 people led to the burning down of the British Embassy in Dublin. Attacks were also made on the offices of seven UK firms in Dublin (*IT*: 02/02/72). A riot followed and gardaí baton charged.

Thirty persons, including gardaí, were injured. In July 1981 14,000 marched in Dublin against the treatment of the hunger strikers in the Maze Prison (the H-Blocks) in Northern Ireland.[7] About 500 protestors became involved in a riot (Salmon 1985: 82) and 1500 gardaí were involved. Only a few had riot gear. Gardaí were attacked with stones and petrol bombs and eventually retaliated with a baton charge. Over 200 members of the public received treatment and allegations abounded of excessive use of force and police brutality (Brewer *et al.* 1996; Salmon 1985). Brewer describes the scene:

> At this moment, An Garda Síochána, according to one eye witness, seemed to have 'gone berserk'. Individuals were batoned to the ground, a German student had his leg broken, a journalist had his notebook taken, groups of people were beaten in corners and doorways of houses where they vainly sought refuge.
>
> (Brewer *et al.* 1996: 100)

The Minister for Justice praised the gardaí for 'restraint and efficiency' (*IT*: 03/02/72). For neither of these events was the garda heavily armed or equipped with riot gear. In Britain by the time of these later protests what has been called the militarisation of the police had occurred, with what Reiner has described as Darth Vader replacing Dixon of Dock Green (Reiner 1992).

This absence of militarisation (Jefferson 1990) may arguably have limited hostility and antagonism. However, that is not to say that was by design. It is difficult to see evidence of the British philosophy of 'wining by appearing to lose' at play. In terms of strategy the then Minister for Justice has stated that while more could have been done to save the Embassy building, like sending in the army, this would most likely have resulted in loss of lives (*IE*: 02/2/12). I5, speaking of the H-Block protests, stated that soldiers joined them on the line and in fact at one point when a protestor began driving a JCB towards the line, the soldier next to him stated that if it came any closer he would shoot the driver given the risk involved. The JCB cut out at that point. We can speculate as to how serious the incident would have become had a soldier shot a protestor. It does seem that it is arguably more fortune than design that these incidents did not become more serious. There was a lack of knowledge involved: G13 was drafted into the Embassy riots while still a trainee in Templemore. For those gardaí involved in the riot it was a terrifying experience.

> The H-Block riots in 1981 were hair-raising. I wouldn't like to be there again and nor would any other guard. They were worse than any world war. There were bricks and mortar being thrown. We weren't prepared at all and lots of Guards were injured that day.
>
> (G5)

> It was frightening, it was a frightening experience … we got into a situation whereby we got a right trouncing for a good half hour and we couldn't move

left or right … That had an effect on me because I think on that particular night we would have had 24 members in the unit and that night at 10 o'clock we paraded for work, only two of us paraded for work. The rest were all hospitalised.

(G8)

Gardaí were not prepared for what they experienced when the H-Block marches turned violent, in the context of a country with a history of low crime rates and control-orientated public-order policing. One interviewee spoke quite honestly about how the situation compounded to inevitably produce violence, as they were not directed otherwise:

We came under sustained attack from bricks and bottles and everything. So this went on for about half an hour or three quarters of an hour. And the next thing, someone had got fed up and charged. So there was every man for himself then … guards beat the living daylights out of them … that day it was just like a free for all, a charge, you just took enough stones and stuff on the head … we had no helmets around that time.

There was this one particular fellow and he was frothing from the mouth, screaming and roaring and bottles flying and bits and all kinds of stuff coming. And no one was doing anything. The next thing some guard – the officers at the back were doing nothing – some guard said 'charge' and of course all the guards in their own minds were all looking at this one fellow. So, when the charge came they all made for this lunatic that was frothing at the mouth. He got an awful beating altogether because there was a build-up of tension and human beings being what they are. He got an horrendous hiding but it was ironic that six of us, if something starts here, like, he is going to get it anyway, if nothing else happens.

(I5)

An Garda Síochána refuted many of the allegations but the *Garda Review* piece on the event concluded: 'Gardaí are not perfect, but they do their best. If some individuals do not maintain the standards of their colleagues, we should not blame the whole force' (Reyolds 1981: 6). This statement represents a position that would be reiterated repeatedly in the coming years. There was no institutional problem in an Garda Síochána. There may be a few bad apples in the force but there is no other, imbedded problem to be addressed. This is not a statement that violence by members will not be tolerated, and that those who participated in such actions will be brought to account. Nor is it a statement acknowledging that the force was not trained or sufficiently resourced to deal with such incidents or that, as established in previous chapters, strong use of force was regularly resorted to in such incidents. Instead a few, unnamed men are blamed and the incident is brushed over as not symptomatic of anything greater.

Working in prisons

Prisons in Ireland during the Troubles were sites of conflict 'with regular riots and pitched battles with prison staff, hunger strikes, escape attempts and the build-up of a well organised group of political prisoners' (Tomlinson 1995: 209). Hunger strikes were commonplace (Rogan 2011: 143). Between 1972 and 1974 there were three successful escapes from Irish prisons, with numerous others attempted. Crime was dramatically rising in this decade meaning that prisons were more crowded and strained than ever before. In 1983 the Chief Prison Officer of Portlaoise Prison was shot and died 18 months later from the injuries suffered. Gardaí were on occasion called to assist in prisons where paramilitary prisoners were detained. Thirteen of those interviewed had spent time in prisons either at Portlaoise, Limerick or Mountjoy.

For one, who had a more senior, organisational role in relation to this, this was important satisfying work:

> When I was a sergeant from '74–'80 in Portlaoise there were a lot of security problems with the prison, escapes, strikes, and an Garda Síochána had to take over. It was a very high-profile place to be. They had a lot of incidents, searches and so on. There were riots in the prison. They were tense situations. They were national and international events. There was plenty of media coverage. We had to get lots of additional personnel. But we feel that we achieved our objective.
>
> (SI2)

This was a managerial perspective, which differed from the experience of those going into the prison. This was more difficult, particularly after the deaths of gardaí began. Working in the prison in such close proximity to members of paramilitary organisations was difficult. But the overriding view was that the work was intensely boring. It could involve being in the prison itself, standing guard on the landing or yard or providing security for the perimeter of the prison, either patrolling in a car or sitting in a centenary box.

> Very, very boring. You were literally in a box for eight hours. And it was just stay there and anything that moved, take it out … it was soul destroying … It was worse actually than being, probably, in the prison. The prisoner had someone to talk to. You were in a box on your own.
>
> (I3)

> Mind-boggling. Just stuck inside a prison all day long sitting on the landing waiting for something to happen.
>
> (G11)

This work did not require members to draw on their policing skills: it was not police work. Furthermore, for men who signed up for a job that is fundamentally diverse and varied sitting in the same room all day was particularly difficult. Those assigned to the prison were not building policing experience and this could shape careers. Hundreds of men could be assigned to Portloaise and surrounding areas simply to service the prison:

> So it formed an awful lot of fellas, both good and bad, naturally because normal policing duties went out the window. 'Specially for fellas who were starting off their careers we'd say that, the same opportunities would not have been there because it was fire-fighting more than anything.
>
> (G7)

The work in the prisons could be tense and violent:

> It would be one of the regrets you'd have. You'd be a young fella and things went on we'll say in searches and that that shouldn't have gone on ... it was fairly grotesque at times, no point saying otherwise ... There were episodes that were fairly severe, that shouldn't have happened.
>
> (G7)

> [V]ery tense, yes, very tense. Some of the landings were, you could literally just touch it with your finger, you know?
>
> (I3)

Given that some continued to do this work for years, particularly as it often attracted overtime payments, it could have an effect on members:

> You'd be better off nearly inside, locked up yourself ... It ended up a lot of fellas, they used to drink a lot and you'd have other fellas then, they usen't spend tuppence, the greed, and they would just do overtime.
>
> (G10)

> Three of them cracked up that way. Ended up in mental hospitals. It was all very degrading. You couldn't bring in a paper. You had to sit in a chair watching these guys. You found ways to get a paper in – down your trousers or folded up in your shoe.
>
> (G4)

As will be explored in relation to policing the border, the potential for trouble or danger was a constant threat. So while G9 spoke of the boredom and feeling 'fundamentally locked up' he also acknowledged that 'it was volatile. You didn't know what was going to happen'.

Such prison work shows once again how gardaí were put in the position of doing work alien to their training and experience. Some were being forced into situations they could not mentally cope within a context where there were no support structures. During the Troubles up to 70 RUC men took their own lives (Ryder 2000). This raises questions for the Republic of Ireland as to whether any gardaí were so affected by their experiences that took their own lives. And how many were traumatised by this work, to the extent mentioned above, that they needed psychiatric help?

In addition to mental anguish there were physical dangers connected to prison work. In 1975 Garda Michael Clerkin, who was stationed in the prison, was killed by a booby trap when he and four other gardaí answered a call about men acting suspiciously at a house.[8] Due to the high-profile nature of the prisoners, being stationed in the vicinity of Portlaoise had the capacity to be dangerous work, yet it was still a quiet town in which everyday policing was mundane. A bifurcation of roles, from garda on the street, just dealing with the low level of crime rates in Ireland to quickly being drawn into paramilitary-related, dangerous activities, was a reality for many police in Ireland at the time. A bifurcation in the nature of policing can also be evidenced if we look at the policing of the border at the time.

Border duty

The border between Ireland and Northern Ireland is some 280 miles in length with over 260 crossing points. The IRA and other republican groups operated on both sides of the border. Crossing the border to further their activities was regular. Patterson states that in 1988 ten of the sixteen most active IRA units were based in the Republic (2013: 198). At times during the Troubles, the IRA directed its activities to towns just inside the northern border, often operating from Irish towns. For instance, Patterson cites that between July and November of 1972 there were 286 security incidents in the vicinity of the border (2012: 243). In addition, loyalist paramilitaries occasionally engaged in activities in the Republic, such as the bombings detailed above. On the other hand, community life in the region did not ascribe to the border, with communities, parishes and sometimes individual farms straddling both sides of the border. A further dimension to the policing of these regions was that it was a substantial political issue as northern activists and politicians accused Ireland of providing a 'safe haven' for republicans (Patterson 2012: 232).

This political context is essential to any analysis of policing the border. We have already discussed how it was not until 1972 that legislative changes were made or that garda numbers were increased, but as we will see the border was already highly active by then with gardaí in the region facing difficult and dangerous scenarios. Garda numbers on the border were relatively low. MacAnthony indicated in 1971 that there were about 400 gardaí and 300 army personnel on the border while he estimated that it would take 9000 men to seal the border (*SI*: 19/12/71). He contended that it was government policy at this point not to increase numbers due to the financial implications, the unpopularity of any intervention perceived as aiding British efforts, the sympathy which some gardaí in the region had for IRA efforts, and the fact that by forcing the British to keep the army at the border it kept the army away from doing work elsewhere in Northern Ireland. Following a change of government, by April 1974 there were 1000 gardaí and 1000 army personnel on the border (Patterson 2013: 72). This accounted for more than 10 per cent of the force.

For gardaí in border regions that took a number of years to get either personnel or powers, there may have raised questions as to how heavily they were expected to police the IRA. Patterson has uncovered a number of revealing statements about Irish government attitudes to border security. Conor Cruise O'Brien stated in 1973 that if Ireland moved more proactively against the IRA 'inevitably members of the Gardaí and Irish would get shot. This would produce an immediate reaction in public opinion ... their reactions would not be to turn against the terrorists but to accuse the government of bungling' (Patterson 2013: 63). Haughey stated in 1982 that he was concerned that if legislation permitting the prosecutions of individuals in the Republic for crimes committed in the North continued to be used it would provoke republicans to 'bring their war to the South' (Patterson 2013: 181). Politically then, there was an unwillingness, or at least a reluctance, to police the IRA too heavily (see Walsh 2011: 305). As we have seen in previous chapters, policing in Ireland has a history of being politically directed and it appears that the Troubles were no different. Cooney, who became Minister for Justice in 1973, asserted in an interview with Patterson that 'the republic rhetoric of Fianna Fáil TDs had made the garda unsure of how their political masters would react to a tough response to such challenges from the IRA' (Patterson 2012: 246). He also mentioned incidents where gardaí had sent files to the Attorney General but no prosecutions resulted, even when there was clear evidence: 'There was astonishment right throughout the ranks of the Garda, and this coloured their attitude to what their response to the IRA should be' (Patterson 2013: 54).

Gardaí received criticism for inaction against the IRA. On one occasion an army officer had been shot on the Northern side and the British had aerial photographs of a garda car just 450 yards from the shooting point (Patterson 2012: 244). The frequency of successful border raids and attacks was also mentioned, including the fact that by May 1974 nine UDR men were killed in Fermanagh, a county that bordered four counties in the Republic. The political context must however be borne in mind. Not only had successive governments not called for a crackdown on the IRA but in 1970 Ministers Haughey and Blaney had to be removed from office after it was revealed that they had attempted to import arms for the IRA. In 1983 the Fianna Fáil government had instructed the Garda Commissioner and the head of Special Branch to tap the phones of journalists at *The Irish Times* due to a belief that information was being used for anti-nationalist purposes. Salmon further refers to an allegation that gardaí were used to transcribe conversations between ministers recorded at the behest of the Minister for Justice (1985: 95).

Of those interviewed for this work 12 men were temporarily transferred to the border and eight served the majority of their career in the border region. In this section we will focus on policing in border areas and how that experience differed extensively from policing in the rest of Ireland.

Tasks on the border

For those who worked on the border matters relating to the Troubles formed a predominant part of their work from the 1970s to the 1990s. Asked to estimate, a typical answer was 'I suppose 60 per cent. I'd say maybe more sometimes … possibly up to 70 per cent when you think of the day-to-day administration it affected as well' (SI5). This was in part a self-fulfilling prophecy as, due to the numbers of gardaí stationed there and the number of checkpoints, ordinary crime was very low. Investigation of paramilitary activity was reserved for Special Branch. Some duties were ongoing including checkpoints, searches for weapons, policing of gatherings and protests, and provision of protection at the border. Specific events in either jurisdiction (murders or bombings) may have increased the intensity of this work. G17, stationed in Dundalk reported that:

> every night the news would come on … something happened in Dundalk. A shooting a bombing, a hijacking … you played it by ear. Nobody could tell you, because nobody had seen it before. You just had to learn yourselves as you went around.
>
> (G17)

Checkpoints were a central part of the policing strategy, enabling stops and searches at border crossing points. In the case of particularly serious incidents orders could be given to 'seal' the border whereby checkpoints would be established at all border crossing points, an enormous task on the 280-mile border and the 260 crossing points (including private roads and tracks).

> The first guard that was shot in Dublin, I was in Belturbet at the time, and we got word that a guard had been shot and we were to keep a look-out for a white Anglia or whatever it was and the border was sealed. Seal the border, that was the answer to every problem … you could be out for 16 to 17 hours.
>
> (I6)

Army support was provided at checkpoints. For instance, in 1975 10,000 joint checkpoints were established between the gardaí and the army, though in the early years there was no radio communication between the two. Checkpoints were not necessarily just on the border. G16 worked at a checkpoint by the cathedral in Monaghan town for years following the bombing there. Checkpoints could be active 24 hours a day irrespective of the weather, some checkpoints not even having a hut. Conditions were poor at a time when technology was only in its infancy.

> There was no shelter. Your own car and you sat into it and you brought the grub with you. I remember the army kept us fed for many's a time. It was only in the latter years that we got hot food at checkpoints … You were out

> for eight hours or sixteen hours at a time and that was a long day. Especially the night. At least during the day you had traffic, but at night…
>
> (DG15)

In addition to the boredom, given the length of shifts, food was regularly mentioned:

> You were dependent on the neighbour, farmer and his wife to come down the road, 'God, you're a long time here. We'll bring you down a sandwich or a piece of bread.' People kept the guards alive in them days out on the border.
>
> (I6)

Given that gardaí were unarmed, usually without radios, there was little that could be done if trouble did arise. Their presence could prevent things from happening, even if they would struggle to effect an arrest or defend themselves if attacked:

> There was a place where we just happened to drive down a lane and just turned a corner and there was a van, and it turned out it had been hijacked … a transit van and it was being resprayed blue. It was obviously being used, going to be used for a bomb … when they saw us coming they just legged it across the border but the paint was still wet on it.
>
> (DG15)

General Order 8 of the IRA directed that members of the Irish security forces were not to be attacked, but that was not always followed and only applied to the IRA. Stumbling across things like this was potentially dangerous:

> I came across this stolen car one night, I stopped the car anyway about one o'clock in the morning. There was two fellas in it and one of them was armed with a handgun. I tried to get him out of the car but he clubbed me in the head with the butt end of the thing … Now I wasn't hurt apart from getting a few stitches here but still it's just that, you'd be that close to…
>
> (SG7)

So policing checkpoints could be dangerous and that was knowledge that men carried with them always:

> You never knew what you were going to come across. You opened a boot of a car, you didn't know what was in it. It could be somebody with a gun or there could be someone in the back that you wouldn't know, would have a gun or that. You were always more wary we'll say than you would be five years previously before things started.
>
> (G16)

Gardaí and army also did mobile patrols of the border. In 1975 the military (for whom statistics are available) sent out over 5400 such patrols with gardaí. In 1979 a Special Garda Task Force was created that permanently patrolled with handguns and Uzi sub-machine guns, though this was disbanded in 1983. Substantial periods of time were spent doing searches, which again was tedious but resulted in significant finds of weapons, which inherently meant disrupting paramilitary activity:

> A lot of searches, searching houses, suspect houses, suspect areas. It's a very big country area around here, very wild area, rough land. Arms are hidden there and explosives hidden there. Searching those all the time. Searching fields upon fields. Hedges and hedges. Houses and suspect houses, went on, continued on and on. That was the main field of our work here.
>
> (SG7)

Searches could, of course, be dangerous. Inspector Sam Donegan died while conducting a search for weapons when he came across a booby trap on a road. He had in fact strayed a few metres across the border and was in Northern Ireland at the time of the explosion.

Both searches and checkpoints, while helping to prevent subversive activity, had negative consequences for community engagement.

> [They thought] we were cooperating with the Brits. 'You are no better than the Brits.' You stop them at the checkpoints. 'You're worse than the Brits', I've heard. Particularly down around the border. 'You're worse than the Brits.' 'In collusion with the Brits.' 'In collusion with the RUC.'
>
> (17)

Certainly in the 1970s there would have been those in the community who would have remembered the RIC and the way in which they were viewed as traitors. Those interviewed appeared somewhat sympathetic, or at least understanding, of this perspective:

> I remember searching houses at the time and you'd get dogs abuse for Maggie's work. Margaret Thatcher, you were doing her work. We got dogs abuse at that stage. People really, people were up in arms. These were fellas that were fighting for their country and they were dying for their country and we were out raiding houses.
>
> (16)

This response inherently made such work difficult and stressful and placed gardaí in a difficult position. This was not helped by the British policy of closing roads crossing the border, adopted as they believed checkpoints were insufficient and that Irish efforts to interrupt IRA activity were ineffective. Following the deaths of two RUC constables on a border-crossing road in 1970, British forces began closing roads by blocking or cratering them. This was a politically contentious issue as it interfered quite directly with community life. The Irish government opposed the cratering of roads but by the summer of 1971 close to 90 had been blocked (Patterson 2012: 236). In what are the most deprived regions of Ireland this intense security and interference with their daily lives was infuriating. Some gardaí attempted to prevent this work. Patterson tells of Paschal McArdle, a sergeant who, in September 1971, drove and kept his vehicle for two hours on a bridge that the army intended to blow up (2012: 239). Locals, often supported by republicans, took action to fill in the roads. Protests and skirmishes were regular. Gardaí were required to provide support while the British forces cratered the roads, in case of attacks from the Irish side:

> [On] a stretch of fifteen miles, there were about four or five roads where one road was opened and closed seven times in a fortnight. You'd spend maybe a couple of days out there. The Brits would come in with their machinery, they'd dig this big crater and they would withdraw and a couple of nights later [Irish people] would be down with their JCBs and fill it in … And you were there protecting them for closing the road. And we had to man the hills anywhere where there was a vantage point where somebody could fire from, we had to cover that.
>
> (I6)

Indeed, any activities by British forces along the border would require garda cover:

> If they wanted men to search places anywhere north of the border we had to go in and cover them this side of, south of the border, to prevent anyone from attacking them on this side … At that time there were a lot of landmines on the border. They'd have the bomb just in the north and a cable coming across … and on this side, they'd be sitting on top of a hedge and they'd have a good view of where their target was. And whenever the police or the army came down they would set off the booby trap.
>
> (SG7)

Gardaí assisting the British forces were unpopular and this and searches were linked to a number of attacks on garda stations. Through the course of the Troubles there were attacks on a number of garda stations, including on one occasion an attack by the DUP member Peter Robinson on Clontibert garda station, for which he was later prosecuted. In 1972 four garda stations were attacked by huge crowds of people. G14 and G16 were present in March 1972 when the station in Monaghan was attacked following the arrest of two people who had fired shots at a road closure protest:

> In the evening they all converged in Monaghan and decided they were going to burn down the station. So they started to petrol bomb us with bottles of

petrol and everything, started coming through the windows. I'll never forget it … you just didn't know what to do … I phoned all the garda stations and in no time at all there was a big contingent of members arrived.

(G14)

The Irish Times reported a crowd of over 2000 people involved in the attack. Baton charges were used to disperse the crowd and one garda was hit by a petrol bomb, which set his coat alight. Earlier that day at a road closure protest 'two live bullets, nearly 60 rubber bullets and about 30 canisters of CS gas were fired by British forces at a crowd of 800' (*IT*: 19/03/72).

SG8 was on duty the day of the attack on Dundalk garda station in September 1972. That morning he had been involved in a search in which explosives were discovered. The destruction of the explosives (a process which damaged SG8's hearing) spurred on a crowd already gathered to protest the detention of republican Liam Fagan on hunger strike in the Curragh. Gardaí in that town were accustomed to protests which paraded through the grounds of the garda station, but the atmosphere on this occasion was palpably different:

All the stones were banging. Ah, it was serious, they attacked us … And then all the windows broke; petrol bombs in. I remember about 20 two-pound bags of sugar, because sugar would burn … I was in there and I got a fire extinguisher and I'll never forget the pain up along my hand because I had to keep my hand up along the front of it and only use it when I had to use it, to spare it. When the bombs came in I could give it a few shots. The bombs and the sugar…

(SG8)

SG8 told of how the attack came in waves:

[A] good friend of mine who is now dead God rest him, he was tough now. And below the stairs he was saying an act of contrition. And I said, 'What are you at?' 'We're gone. We're never going to get out of here. I'm gonna say some prayers.' I said, 'I haven't time for that.' That really shook me.

… then the front door started buckling. It was a double door with a bar across inside. It was coming in six inches, and back out, in six inches and back out … There was a forum on one side for sitting on, they were using that as a battering ram to burst the door. And eventually the door burst open and I was just inside it. And these fellas stood there. He had a five-gallon drum in his hand. And next thing all hell broke loose with the guard's gunfire. I didn't know where it was coming from. It was a friend of mine [name of colleague] in the station, broke into the press, got the gun out, sitting on top of the stairs, and he opened up. Not on him, it was just, blew the fan light over the door. The boys, they dropped the can and ran. There was a five-gallon drum of petrol there. They were going to burn the place and us inside it.

(SG8)

Newspaper reports document that thousands of pounds worth of damage was caused and more than 20 cars in the yard of the station were set alight. On leaving the station the crowd ran through the streets smashing shop windows, setting the courthouse on fire and overturning a fire engine. In order to clear the streets the police engaged in baton charges and the army used CS gas (*IT:* 22/09/72). That event, unsurprisingly, took its toll. SG8 was unable to sleep for some time afterwards. They had to return to work in a burnt-out station and conduct intensive patrols in the following days to prevent a recurrence. SI5 arrived in Dundalk station a month later and it was still 'all burnt. It was a dive'. Gardaí were being expected to simply accept attacks of this nature and continue to work with a community with whom they had had such violent encounters.

From the outbreak of the Troubles many people opted to flee Northern Ireland. The army was engaged to set up refugee camps for these people. On one night alone in August 1971, following the reintroduction of internment in Northern Ireland and the killing of 17 persons in the 48 hours after that, 2825 persons were received at Gormanstown Military Camp, north of Dublin. In the coming months this number rose to 5436 with people housed across eight army refugee centres, the garda training college and local authority accommodation. While many soon returned to the North, significant numbers chose to stay, often in border areas, which created what Patterson refers to as a 'febrile atmosphere' in border towns (2012: 237).

Into this mix were thrown men sent on temporary transfers to do border duty. Single men were required to attend for at least two months. Married men only went on request and stayed for one month. Border transfers attracted overtime payment, which created some appeal: G4 did five transfers and took the view that he earned bonuses and avoided summons work. Normally, transferred men manned checkpoints and patrolled, experiencing the boredom and tough conditions outlined above. There was, however, always the potential for some dramatic occurrence. While those who served on the border long-term may have come to expect the volatile, traumatic and potentially dangerous nature of work on the border, for those gardaí who came to the border for weeks at a time this was removed from their normal policing life. They were now in more regular contact with republican groups who had proven their willingness to kill gardaí. Men were drawn from peaceful rural stations or busy inner-city stations to remote outposts where they could encounter members of paramilitary organisations, guns, and bombs for which they had neither training nor experience: 'It was a different world altogether … from a policing point of view it was a different job completely. Different as chalk and cheese' (I6).

Those men who served 'temporaries' on the border were working in situations opposite to their previous policing experiences. Whether they had served in rural or urban stations they would have been used to a steady stream of work, whereas on the border they could be standing in the cold for hours on end. This duty could then be unexpectedly interrupted by paramilitary behaviour requiring them to respond to and deal with situations for which they had no training. There was no preparation given for this work and when they returned to their stations they were expected to just slip back into the old routine not sure if and when they would be called back to the border. Such disjointed and inconsistent policing work cannot have been good for morale. Nor did these men have local knowledge or understanding of the particular circumstances and so the contribution that they could make was limited:

> As far as the government was concerned it was a man there and if there's a man there that's it. But he wouldn't be as efficient as the man that's there permanently, who has a continuous picture of the whole situation.
>
> (SG6)

Danger

As much of the above discussion has indicated, danger was real for police on the border. Those interviewed related much of the danger to the influx of people from Northern Ireland to the Republic, rather than the residents of border towns. This influx occurred for three reasons: to escape the North (either IRA on the run or families wishing a safer upbringing for their children), to attend protests along the border or further South, or to avail of the less strict licensing laws at the weekend.

> But at weekends then there was a lot of protests. They came down from, groups of them came down from the north to Monaghan ... They were quite nasty. Not the local people, but the Northern element that came down were quite nasty. And they were just looking for trouble ... And they were very abusive as well. They'd call you all the names under the sun and what have you. It was a bad time really. It was hard to take it.
>
> (SG6)

For these gardaí it could lead to quite threatening situations:

> I remember there was a big meeting in Monaghan, they were there from all over one night, and I was the only one on duty in the street, and I was just walking up and down, just looking casual ... The speakers said that the biggest troublemakers this side of the border were garda sergeants. And I was the only member on the street, and I was one of them! And the crowd all turned around and started looking at me, you know, 'What do we do with him?' You know? And I stood my ground. I just stood and passed no remark and kept cool, and was cool as a breeze and I said 'if anything happens now I'm for it'. And they jeered and booed and everything and I just passed quietly. And funnily enough they didn't attack me ... it fizzled out.
>
> (SG6)

SG6 recalled that local community members told him afterwards that they would have helped if anything happened. This animosity was not always initially directed at gardaí. SG7 attended the scene of brawl in Dundalk between people from the North and locals. There were apparently six gardaí but 600 people engaged in this brawl and when SG7 grabbed a man who was attacking a colleague he was hit on the head with a stone resulting in loss of sight in one eye. Again, this incident was put down to the actions of the northern crowd, though unlike in other towns, animosity toward gardaí was greater in Dundalk at a local level and so SG7 could not count on local people for support. For those on temporary transfers this level of animosity toward gardaí would have been unusual.

In addition to concern that particular circumstances could lead to danger there was also a continuing concern for direct attacks. After policing a parade that went through Donegal and preventing people from breaching the instructions issued, SG8 received a warning that he had been discussed by senior republicans in the area and his house would be burned down: 'nothing happened but them sort of things would scare you, with the kids around and everything'. Most dramatically, following the arrest of a man for dealing in stolen goods, DG15's car and house were petrol bombed in November 1972. He and his young family were in the house at the time. A colleague on the same case received a bullet in the post. Weeks later the man he believes did this was arrested for the murder of a garda.

> Took a while to calm down because you always had your ear cocked. Between that happening and him being captured there was a couple of weeks where you were always on tenterhooks. And then there was no counsellors come round the place … I remember the only word of comfort was given to me, was the chief in Monaghan says to me, 'make sure you claim plenty off the insurance'.
>
> (DG15)

He believed this was intimidation for his proactive policing. The effect, of course, was that others would not be proactive in their policing if it involved that level of danger, particularly when support was so limited. I7 made this point:

> Well again the ones who were threatened were the ones who were good. There were a few that were very active all the time or talking the provos, others were, if it happens we'll deal with it but we're not going looking for trouble. Others were, they couldn't be content out but they had to be searching routing around, and they were perceived as a threat, more than a threat. And they would have been the ones that would have maybe would have got threatening phone-calls.

This, of course, created a natural disincentive to engage in serious police work, particularly if there was no political pressure to be proactive in this regard.

There was also the fact that these were people living in an area where paramilitaries were active. As residents of that area they were exposed to danger, but this was heightened by their occupation. SI5, for instance, had his car hijacked one night by men who then recognised that he was a garda. The hijackers resolved the situation by taking another car and having SI5 take its driver into town: 'That was the only incident where I felt threatened really in a way.' His young daughter was in the car:

> She never said a word. That's the only thing, she had a pair of corduroy jeans on her and with the tension on either side she rubbed the cord off and two circles under the jeans on the right hand side.
>
> (S15)

This impact on families of members and the fear they experienced was recognised by many members, such as SG6 who recognised that families feared that the member could be in danger or their home could be targeted. G16 spoke of his wife's concern when hearing on the radio of the attack on Monaghan garda station and not being able to contact him. That fear of the unknown was not the only element of danger that families were exposed to. In Dundalk, a town with a strong republican element there was local animosity towards gardaí. During my interview with SG7 I also met one of his sons who spoke of being targeted as a boy for being the son of a garda, including having bottles thrown at him as he cycled home from school and having derogatory comments made by teachers in the school he attended. This experience bears much more similarity with that of police in Northern Ireland. Some of those who spent substantial parts of their career on the border adopted mindsets similar to those identified by Brewer and Magee in the RUC:

> I mean you could walk into a domestic violence and meet a guy with a shotgun and what happens is that they see you as the infiltrator here and they could turn the gun on you. You don't know.
>
> (G8)

> It was just, it's like any job. People, there are industrial accidents, people get killed. It doesn't stop people going into the construction industry. It never entered my head.
>
> (DG15)

Though this was often the case, the evidence presented above substantiates that the threat was real and the job was dangerous. As mentioned above however, there has been no data maintained on the extent of injuries suffered. Of the eight men interviewed who worked on the border for the majority of their careers, most experienced or felt danger on a regular basis. Little research has been done on the experience of danger and stress within gardaí. Harris (1988) found that nearly half of those with less than 20 years' service found life in the force to be worse than expected. In his study one-quarter of respondents declared that they would not chose police work again. The sources of dissatisfaction mentioned by respondents included border duty and physical unpleasantness such as dealing with bodies. In light of the danger faced and a lack of political pressure it is not surprising if gardaí did not take the initiative to be proactive against paramilitaries.

RUC interaction

A final core factor in border work was the relationship between the gardaí and the RUC. This was pivotal during the conflict for a number of reasons, including the sharing of information to both investigate and prevent paramilitary activities and the prosecution of persons who committed offences in other jurisdictions. Security cooperation was heavily politicised. In the early years there was no sanctioned cooperation but informal relationships developed between counterparts. In 1972 a meeting occurred between the Garda Commissioner and the Chief Constable of the RUC to establish working groups on the sharing of intelligence in relation to explosives (Patterson 2012: 243). In 1974 a summit was held at Baldonnel military airport at which it was decided to create four panels between the police to deal with communications, exchange of information, planning and detection of weapons etc. (Patterson 2013: 83). Legislation enabled the prosecution of persons who committed a crime in the jurisdiction.

I6 talked about how in those early years individuals often established informal links with RUC counterparts:

> [B]ut to start it was, what there would have been was on a one-to-one basis. Like I was a sergeant in A and I knew the sergeant across, my counterpart in the north, and I had a relationship with him. Unofficially I would talk to him and he would talk to me.
>
> (I6)

Before the relationship was enhanced, incursions into the other territories occurred, often to much political clamour. Indeed in September 1971, after a crowd set fire to a British army vehicle that crossed into Irish territory, the Irish government called for a UN observer group to operate in the area (Patterson 2012: 236). I6 admitted crossing the border to talk to the RUC sergeant about a man they were looking for. He stated that he crossed the border while on duty 'umpteen times'. Likewise he encountered British forces crossing over. One night he received a phone call from a woman saying that British soldiers were passing outside her house and 'if my father sees them he'll go spare'. When they drove out they found 12 soldiers walking on patrol. They offered to escort them back to the border though not before the soldiers asked them to pose in a photograph (which they did not do). One incursion in 1976 by members of the SAS led to a prosecution of the men in the Special Criminal Court for possession of firearms with intent to endanger lives. They were convicted of minor offences and fined.

In 1982 a garda, Thomas Nagle, was prosecuted for assault in a Northern Irish town. Nagle happened to be the brother-in-law of the then Minister for Justice Seán Doherty, himself a former garda. The prosecution against Nagle was dropped when the principal witness failed to turn up, having been arrested by the RUC hours previously, giving rise to serious allegations of political interference in cross-border policing. What became known as the Dowra affair had political ramifications for the Minister and stalled the development of more formal relationships between the RUC and the Garda for some time.

The Anglo-Irish Agreement of 1985 specifically called for cooperation between the two forces (Article 9) and from this point on the relationship was greatly enhanced. Formal meetings were held at headquarters once every eight weeks. Border Superintendents held meetings on at least a monthly basis. There were also border Superintendent group meetings held every eight weeks. All of these meetings would alternate in locations between the two jurisdictions (Cory 2003: 2.19). Individual members could and did also organise informal meetings with their counterpart in the other jurisdiction. SG7 commented on how improvements to the radio network significantly enhanced this working relationship. From 1987 meetings with the RUC were regularly scheduled and what SI5 called 'an excellent working relationship' developed. However, the context gave rise to difficulties:

> There was always that tension about going to these meetings about who was responsible for what happened and where do they come from and where do they go back to when it happened ... it went to a political level because Ian Paisley and his boys were out shouting about it about all these people down the south and a haven for terrorists.
>
> (SI5)

Further, this could be dangerous work and SI5 stated that at times when he was having regular meetings with RUC counterparts he began to worry for his safety. This was not without reason. On 20 March 1989 RUC Chief Superintendent Harry Breen and RUC Superintendent Robert Buchanan were shot and killed by the IRA as they travelled home from a meeting with gardaí in Dundalk garda station at which cross-border smuggling was discussed. The Smithwick Tribunal is currently (December 2012) investigating allegations that gardaí leaked information about the meeting to the IRA. This inquiry stems from the work of Judge Cory who, in reviewing all the documents, held there were grounds for a public inquiry. SI Buchanan regularly held such meetings in the Republic and usually travelled the same route in the same car. He did not avail of any security or protection. The precise timing of the attack as well as a statement received by a British agent who infiltrated the IRA gave some credence to the presence of collusion. Justice Cory also considered allegations of collusion between gardaí and the IRA in relation to the murders of Lord Justice and Lady Gibson who were killed crossing the border on 25 April 1987. They had been escorted to the border by gardaí and were killed making their way to meet an RUC escort. Justice Cory held that there was no evidence to support allegations of collusion. The findings of the Smithwick inquiry will undoubtedly contribute greatly to our understanding of cross-border policing. In the main, little is known about this work, falling as it largely does under the rubric of national security over which much secrecy is maintained.

Conclusion

Chapter 4 outlined how policing in the 1960s in Ireland involved little crime and much administrative work. Garda concerns centred on pay and conditions and morale was low as a result. Set against that, the impact of the Troubles was stark. The Troubles exposed how unprepared the force was to deal with anything beyond the peaceful policing experiences of the preceding years. It changed the nature of policing in Ireland, the functions members were expected to perform and the incidents encountered on a daily basis.

An Garda Síochána had not been forced to deal with the subversive tactics of groups like the IRA since the early 1940s. Only those within Special Branch had any relevant training but as the death of men painfully showed, policing the Troubles was not a task performed solely by Special Branch detectives. The force was consumed in this work but did not have the equipment or the skills to deal with the crimes being committed in the country. This was most pointedly witnessed by the killing of a trainee garda in the search for the kidnappers of Don Tidey and in the fact that despite riots in the 1970s none of the gardaí present at the protests for the hunger strikers in July 1981 had received riot training.

The daily routine of their jobs and the functions they had to perform altered substantially. While one garda spoke of dealing with little more than thefts of bicycles in his first few years in the force, gardaí were now dealing with dramatic rises in crime, with a particularly large increase in the number of armed robberies occurring, being sent to the border or to prisons, and responding to incidents where individuals had been killed. Nor was there any geographical pattern to these events, so members in any part of the country could at any point become involved in these incidents. Interviewees told how this work could be boring, exciting, scary or traumatic, and at all times they were expected to deal with whatever happened. As I5 stated, 'the career varied from basically mundane void of nothing happening to explosions, guns off fellows, violence in the H-Block demonstration to tranquil living in Headquarters'.

For all those interviewed the most difficult part of their job was when fellow gardaí were killed in the line of duty. That which had been a peaceful, safe, respected job, no longer was. The reality was that they could be killed in the course of their work, even if not in Special Branch. Not only did they have to deal with this danger, but also with the fact that there were people who were willing to kill them. Their authority and legitimacy was being challenged in a way that this generation had never experienced previously. The effect of this on these men was clear in the interviewees' responses.

Policing along the border was both political and dangerous. The lived experience of the border during the 1970s and 1980s bears a greater resemblance to the accounts documented by Brewer *et al.* of what the RUC experienced. This suggests the creeping nature of conflict across borders. What is particularly important to emerge from this work is that the difficulties experienced by men in these regions have gone largely under-acknowledged in Ireland. The response of government to the challenges of the Troubles – providing additional police powers and greater numbers – were of limited assistance on the border. Indeed, it was suggested that they could in fact hinder work at times. As was seen, surprisingly little use was made of criminal sanctions that were created once the Troubles began. What was lacking, from the perspective of gardaí working on the border, was incentive and direction to police the IRA proactively.

The next chapter will examine how an Garda Síochána responded to these challenges institutionally and what impact the conflict had for the accountability of the force.

Notes

1 In the Irish Republic 12 gardaí lost their lives in the course of duty between 1971 and 1996 as a result of the conflict; 302 RUC officers were killed during the conflict.
2 Deemed to be constitutional in O'Leary v. AG [1993] IR 102, when it was held that though this evidence could be admitted the court could still evaluate it.
3 For a time the gardaí provided quite detailed breakdowns of the data so in 1985, for instance, the crime report indicates that houses, banks, post offices, betting offices, licensed premises, chemists, garages, factories, offices, schools, hotels, petrol stations, shops, railway stations and even a hospital were targeted by armed raiders. In most incidents that year less than £500 was taken.
4 See discussion of the Heavy Gang in Chapter 6.
5 John Doherty was shot in 1973 in Donegal; Stanley Hazelton was shot in 1979 in Monaghan; Samuel McClean was shot in 1987 in Donegal; Harold Keys was shot in 1989 in Donegal.
6 For a complete list see Appendix 3.
7 In 1981 republican prisoners who were held at the H-Blocks, at the Maze prison outside of Belfast, went on hunger strike in an effort to secure political status and to be allowed to wear their own clothes and not prison uniforms. Bobby Sands was the first to die on 5 May 1981. Nine other hunger strikers died that summer (Mulcahy 1995).
8 As mentioned previously, this occurred on the day that the Emergency Powers Act 1976 was signed into law by the President.

6   The Special Branch
and the Troubles

> Of all the functions of the police department none is both so famous and infamous,
> publicised and privy, political and private, so repudiated and protected as that
> function performed by the secret and sibilant section known internationally as
> 'special branch'.
>
> (Breathnach 1974: 157)

The previous chapter focused on the experience of policing the Troubles for most
gardaí. Of course, much of the specialist work relating to the Troubles and subversives in Ireland fell into the domain of the Special Branch. Special Branches of
police forces are divisions tasked with intelligence-gathering in relation to terrorist or subversive crime. Within an Garda Síochána it is the only armed division
and is therefore responsible for state protection, protection of cash in transit,
armed responses, as well as operating the witness protection programme (Walsh
1998; Allen 1999). The nature of the work conducted by such departments within
police forces makes them inherently controversial the world over. They operate
at the far end of the policing spectrum, dealing with those who would seek to
challenge their status and that of the state within which they operate. Working at
these limits, 'ordinary' policing tactics are often ineffective and fail to suppress
the threat (O'Reilly and Ellison 2005). The nature of their work makes maintaining the democratic balance exceptionally difficult. This is heightened in the Irish
context where national security is a function of the police, unlike other countries
where that task is often assigned elsewhere.

The operations of counter-terrorism units and detective units, often referred to
as 'high policing', have been researched in many jurisdictions (Stalker 1988;
Brodeur 1983). The Special Branch in the Royal Ulster Constabulary (RUC)
became particularly notorious, with allegations of abuse of powers and collusion,
in this way but similar debates have emerged over the detective branch in
Canada's Royal Canadian Mounted Police. In the case of the latter, in the 1970s
their application of security measures in the name of the security of the state came
under enormous criticism and led to the establishment of a Royal Commission
(Cameron 1985; Brodeur 1983). In Northern Ireland, John Stalker was appointed
to investigate the killing of six men by the RUC due to concerns that the Special

Branch was operating a 'shoot to kill' policy. Stalker said of his investigations into the RUC:

> The 'career' special branch were the most difficult of people to deal with. They did not seem to understand the responsibilities of others. The internal power they wield within the RUC was a factor we had not at that time measured, but in the course of time we realized it was very pervasive indeed.
>
> (Stalker 1988: 33)

He determined the Special Branch occupied the position of a 'force within a force', stating that he 'had never experienced … such an influence over an entire police force by one small section' (1988: 56). To suggest that the Special Branch is a 'force within a force' is to suggest it operates separate to the rest of the force, that it is seen as distinct and that it has a different code of practice and regulation to other members of the police. One interviewee for this research, who had been in Special Branch, suggested an element of this operated within the gardaí, believing that garda Special Branch applied its own code of accountability (DSG1). There was unwillingness on the part of the Irish government to impose restraints and accountability on the force, and particularly the actions of the Special Branch. As one Minister for Justice stated:

> There is nothing between us and the dark night of terrorism but that Force. While people in this House and people in the media may have freedom to criticise, the Government of the day should not criticise the Garda Síochána. We all know there are mistakes in the operation but it is obscene that the Government and the Ministers should be the first to lead the charge in the criticism of the Garda Síochána.
>
> (Noonan, DE: 10/11/87)

This chapter will consider the Special Branch, their role in policing the Troubles, and the allegations of a Heavy Gang, which emerged at this time. Through examining the existence of this gang it will be argued that violence was institutionalised in the force, a significant finding that means it was embedded and supported within the police force. This was in large part due to the position an Garda Síochána was placed in by the government and failures to pronounce that violence would not be tolerated. Accountability, it shall be seen, was not relevant in the context of the conflict. As before, government was rhetorically supporting the police, not criticising them, but not giving them the resources and practical support required.

Heavy-handed policing

Edmund Garvey, a 'tough cop', became Commissioner in 1975 in the wake of the Herrema kidnapping. He was described in the *Garda Review* as 'a man of action, a man who gets things done, a man who goes straight for target if the target is worth going for' (Brady 1975: 1). He had been recruited to the Taca (see Chapter 3) and had previously been in charge of the Serious Crime Squad, often referred to as the Murder Squad, a division of Special Branch. This background in high policing clearly influenced the operation of an Garda Síochána under his tenure. The strength of the Special Branch doubled but it soon became embroiled in controversy with allegations arising in a number of high-profile cases involving the IRA that Gardaí were using illegal and violent tactics to extract confessions. A former member of the Special Branch explained some of this:

> We did do some illegal bugging. We would have bugged solicitor-client interviews in the station. We solved some really big cases that way. It was especially used if the solicitor was sympathetic to the IRA. The solicitors never knew it had been done but the client would have told them everything. We could secure a conviction that way. There certainly was senior approval; the equipment was supplied wasn't it? In our work, the cases were big. The Commissioner would have been on the phone every hour. Usually the superintendent would know. That was as high as knowledge and approval went.
>
> (DSG1)

This, of course, constitutes sanctioned breaches of suspects' fundamental rights and, as is overtly stated, was sanctioned at the highest level. The men involved may have believed it was justified in light of the suspects they were dealing with, a form of so-called 'noble cause corruption' (Punch 2000). The scale of the threat posed by the IRA and the challenge it posed to legitimate, rights-compliant police investigations justified the use of alternative tactics. However, it must be remembered that much legislation had already been passed by the government which strained the notions of rights and due process. In a liberal democracy such as Ireland decisions as to when rights can be extraordinarily curtailed and limited are not for the police to make. Failure to abide by due process delegitimises the criminal justice system.

The substance of concerns about the behaviour of Special Branch grew and in the late 1970s claims were made of a 'Heavy Gang' existing within the force (O'Halpin 1999; Farrell 1993; Walsh 1998), a body defined by Kilcommins *et al.* as 'a loose affiliation of Gardaí drawn from different sections of the Force and specialising in extracting information under interrogation' (2004: 209). The barrister Paddy McEntee SC coined the phrase in a murder trial (Courtney 1996) but it received public notoriety in February 1977 when *The Irish Times* ran a week-long series of front-page articles 'exposing' the gang, with headlines such as 'Gardaí using North-style brutality in Interrogation Techniques' (14/02/77), 'Beaten by Six Guards' (14/02/77), 'Heavy Gang used New Act to Intensify Pressure on Suspects' (15/02/77), 'Claustrophobia Victim says Gardaí Shut Him in Locker' (16/02/77). It was alleged to be very systematic, with the same names and methods being mentioned in a number of cases. In one case reported, the suspect, Mr Thomas Connors, ended a six-hour interrogation by jumping out the window in a suicide attempt (*IT*: 14/02/77). It was alleged that using seven-day detention under the Emergency Powers Act 1975, gardaí could inflict beatings in the first day or two and the wounds would have healed by the time the suspect was released. Suspects, it was claimed, were also being denied their rights to see solicitors and doctors, thwarting their efforts to verify their allegations. It was countered that subversives were making these allegations to stall the work of gardaí and divert attention from their criminal activity.

The most serious case to which the Heavy Gang has been linked is what Farrell describes as 'the Republic's own version of the Birmingham Six, Guildford Four and Judy Ward miscarriage of justice cases – the Sallins mail train case' (1993: 123). The case is important, not just for exposing violent tactics but also for displaying broader systemic support for such abuses. In March 1976 a postal train travelling from Cork to Dublin was robbed just outside Sallins, County Dublin, with a gang stealing a large sum of money. Nicky Kelly, one of the men convicted of the crime, made allegations of garda brutality during a 43-hour interrogation. In court Kelly gave the following description:

> (Garda A) rammed my head off the locker door. Some of the Brits treatment. Spreadeagled. Jabbed in ribs, slapped in face, legs kicked. Lights switched off. Placed behind door. Spreadeagled. Door pushed in. Collision. Ended up on ground. Once on floor refused to get up. Hair pulled. Hit on back. Frightened more than hurt. Taken upstairs by (Garda A). Smell of drink off him. Corner of cell. Toilet. Grabbed by hair. "Tomorrow — long day". Shoved head five-six times down toilet, didn't wet face. Taken out of cell by (Garda A). To wall — out of sight of cell. Short delay. Knee in groin. Caught in thigh. Spat in face. Back to cell. Five minutes there. (Garda A): 'eventually you'll talk'.
>
> (Garda A) hit (me) back of ears after wrong answers. Telephone ears ten times. (Garda B) slapped in face and arms. (Garda C and Garda D) punched, punched. Fell to ground. (Garda D) hit me with chair — not much force.
>
> On floor, on back, hands stretched backwards. Chair put on palms. (Garda A) sits on chair. Spits on face. Leering. Cried. Frightened. Don't know what they are going to do to me. Very tired, sore, ears ringing, bad headache, stomach sick, afraid of my life. (Garda A) produced blackjack. Beaten by (Garda E) on biceps. Left on table. Black lathe ten inches long, one inch in diameter. Flexible, Swish noise. 'Own up, make statement.' Beaten above the knee...
>
> (Cited by Costello, SE: 23/10/91)

Kelly claimed he feared for his life. His girlfriend was also arrested and gardaí told him that his mother was in hospital having had a heart attack on hearing of his arrest. Kelly signed a confession to end the beatings stating, 'I could not take any more' (McGarry 2006) and this was the sole evidence against him. Four doctors stated the injuries were consistent with the allegations and despite their expert evidence the Special Criminal Court ruled that the injuries were self-inflicted. Kelly's initial trial was unsuccessfully challenged by the defence in the

Supreme Court on the grounds that one of the judges kept falling asleep. The judge in question died during the trial and Kelly was convicted on retrial on the basis of the confession.

Those convicted alongside him, McNally and Breathnach, soon had their convictions overturned due to oppressive questioning but Kelly fled the country. The Provisional IRA released a statement claiming responsibility for the robbery after which McNally and Breathnach successfully appealed. Kelly returned to the country, expecting the same fate, but was imprisoned. Amnesty International and the Irish Council for Civil Liberties became involved in a campaign for his release but an appeal to the Supreme Court failed. They held that the claims of abuse were fabricated. Kelly later went on hunger strike. He was released in July 1984 on humanitarian grounds. Later linguistic analysis showed that the statement on which he been convicted was almost certainly made by at least two people, not one. He was given a Presidential pardon in 1992 and received over £1 million in compensation (McGarry 2006). No inquiry was ever conducted into the case and no gardaí were ever sanctioned. This case illustrates both how the Heavy Gang operated but also the protection they received from the criminal justice system, from judges to ministers, at enormous cost to the state.

The Heavy Gang was believed to be a subset of the Murder Squad, which Commissioner Garvey had previously led. At the time that *The Irish Times* made the allegations, Cooney, the Minister for Justice, dismissed the claims stating that '[i]t is inevitable that sometimes you get one colleague disapproving of another's method of interrogation'. He resisted calls for an inquiry stating that courts could evaluate allegations in individual cases: 'There should not be a star tribunal for the police – they should be neither above nor below the law' (*IT*: 18/02/77).

While it is agreed that they should not be above the law, stating that they should not be below it suggests that he did not believe they should be subject or answerable to the law. It is difficult to understand the concept of accountability underlying this perspective. In terms of the courts' ability to handle such allegations Mr Cooney informed the Dáil that in 1975–6 there had been 58 allegations of assault by gardaí, 22 of which were referred to the DPP by gardaí, 8 of which went to court, none of which resulted in a prosecution (*IT*: 18/02/77). An Garda Síochána took disciplinary action in four cases. This leaves 18 cases which gardaí themselves felt merited referral to the DPP but which did not merit disciplinary action, a standard which is much lower than criminal activity in a system with a lower burden of proof. A lack of garda accountability could be brushed over with confusing statements as to the relationship between the police and the law. The official position remained that the Heavy Gang never existed.

Amnesty International conducted a 'mission' to Ireland in the months after these allegations surfaced and its report to the government was highly critical of an Garda Síochána (Farrell 1993). It investigated 28 cases and concluded that a significant number of people had been ill-treated while in custody:

> Allegations common to every case examined are that the victims were at various times beaten and punched ... knocked or thrown against walls or furniture; kneed in the stomach and kicked. It is also commonly alleged that

victims were pulled or swung by the hair, had their arms twisted behind their backs while they were punched; were spread-eagled against a wall and had their legs kicked apart so that they fell to the ground. In five cases detained persons alleged they were beaten with objects ... In a number of cases suspects allege that they were deprived of sleep, food and drink throughout the interrogation ... There is evidence that the type of interrogation methods described were undertaken in order to induce arrested persons to make incriminating statements or confessions.

(Cited in MacFarlane 1990: 96–7)

Walsh adds:

Particularly significant was Amnesty's finding that the source of the ill-treatment was a group of plain-clothed detectives from the central detective unit in Dublin, who featured in nearly all the cases irrespective of their location throughout the country. This confirmed a widespread public belief that there was a 'Heavy Gang' operating within the Garda Síochána with a brief to get results without any questions being asked about their methods.

(Walsh 1998: 262)

Amnesty International also found a readiness by the courts to accept the evidence of gardaí when allegations of abuse were made, and to reject defence evidence (*IT*: 08/10/77). These findings were dismissed by the General Secretary of the Representative Body for the Guards, Jack Marrinan, who in response stated, 'I am absolutely convinced that it does not happen' (*Garda Review*, 1977). On the other hand he did acknowledge that:

it would be close to a miracle if it transpired that in the face of guns and bullets, in the face of loss of life, serious injury, assassinations, pistol whippings and beatings which Gardaí themselves have had to endure over the past few years, as well as the insults and abusive treatment which they have encountered when dealing with some accused people, and the hardship and misery which they see inflicted by criminals on people that they are appointed to protect, if the odd Guard did not over-react.

(*Garda Review* 1977: 43)

The extremities of the Troubles, he conceded, could provoke inappropriate responses from individual gardaí, but it was not, according to Marrinan, a systematic or institutionalised practice. This is a twist on the bad apples thesis as the circumstances dictate that those men are under threat and therefore not bad.

On the other hand, there is some evidence that supports their existence. Garrett Fitzgerald, then Minister for Foreign Affairs, tells of how two gardaí approached him in the mid-1970s, complaining of the operations of the 'Heavy Gang':

In some pending cases it was believed by some in the Force that confessions had been extracted by improper methods, and Garda morale would be

seriously damaged if these cases went ahead and some Gardaí were persuaded
to perjure themselves in the process.

(Fitzgerald 1991: 313)

He raised these matters with government but the Minister for Justice was unsym-
pathetic, feeling these men should have approached the Commissioner (Courtney
1996). Conor Cruise O'Brien in his autobiography made similar allegations,
referring specifically to the Herrema kidnapping case. A detective in that case
told him:

> One of the gang had been arrested, and we felt sure he knew where Herrema
> was. So this man was transferred under Branch escort from a prison in the
> country to a prison in Dublin, and on the way the car stopped. Then the escort
> started asking him questions and when at first he refused to answer, they beat
> the shit out of him. Then he told them where Herrema was.
>
> (Cited in Dunne and Kerrigan 1984: 236)

The *Garda Review* on the other hand described how 'skilful, time-tested and
methodical police methods led the gardaí to the scene' (December 1975). Derek
Nally, President of the Association of Garda Sergeants and Inspectors in the
1970s, claimed that he approached the then Minister for Justice along with a
number of others to complain about the Heavy Gang (SE: 23/10/91). Cooney has
denied that this ever happened. If Nally's assertions are true, then the Minister for
Justice was informed of this by a garda and failed to act. This would suggest,
at the very least, tacit acceptance by government ministers of such abusive
strategies.

At the same time that the Irish government was attempting to silence these
allegations, it was pursuing a case against the United Kingdom for the use of
brutal interrogation techniques against suspected republican paramilitaries. In
1978 the European Court of Human Rights ruled that these constituted inhuman
and degrading treatment. While Ireland was attempting to secure a finding of
torture against the UK, it was denying serious allegations of brutality at home.
A commission was established under Justice O'Brian to look at safeguards for
persons in custody. The 1978 report made a number of progressive recommendations, including an end to the practice of binging people 'to a garda station "to
help the police with their enquiries"' (O'Brian 1978: para. 46), an independent
complaints procedure, and consideration of the use of videotaping of interrogations (O'Brian 1978: para. 67). Most of the recommendations were not, however,
put into practice.

Mixed reactions were provoked when the Heavy Gang was discussed with
participants. One interviewee became hostile at their mention:

> There was never any such thing as the Heavy Gang. Paddy McEntee was
> the first person to bring this up. He made up the name. The myth of the
> Heavy Gang – t'was a lovely thing to say. McEntee was told to withdraw

the allegations. No one was investigated, no one was charged. You can't say that it's true.

(SG1)

Of the 42 retired gardaí interviewed, three actively denied its existence. Others were more muted in their commentary, denying their involvement but suggesting context must be considered:

> You cannot deal with the allegations of the Heavy Gang in isolation from the type of era we were living in. The Provisional IRA was threatening to take over the North and this was a huge issue in the South. They were a law unto themselves ... There was a very thin blue line between anarchy and democracy in that period.

(AC1)

> It was different times. There was a government or political will, or not a will but a political necessity, to hold the state together. The whole thing was in balance. Now the ordinary guard on the street, he didn't realise it at the time, or the ordinary person on the street. But the politicians knew how close the whole thing was to falling in around their heads ... there was certainly a political will behind some of the things that had to be done in investigations.

(DG15)

This represents the mindset of many members at the time. The IRA, gardaí and politicians believed, was on the verge of taking over the state. In these circumstances such behaviour was the means to an end, and this perspective emanated not from senior gardaí but from politicians.

Thirteen of those interviewed confirmed the existence of the Heavy Gang. DSG1 spoke of how they were a group of about half a dozen Special Branch men who used 'fairly tough tactics'. He also linked the work of the Heavy Gang directly to the Special Criminal Court, where the lack of a jury made the trial more convenient for the police in terms of procedure. Most of those who discussed the Heavy Gang were clearly uncomfortable with its existence:

> There would have been a lot of fear I suppose and the need to get results but, I mean, it's hard to justify anything like that. To my mind, you do something like that, you're no better than the crim ... in fact you're worse than the criminal because you are supposed to know different ... Any ordinary guard would have felt that they shouldn't be resorting to that.

(G16)

Indeed, not only did many not approve of these tactics, but some actively resented Heavy Gang involvement in a local investigation:

> If they came ... and I happened to be Station Orderly I was accountable for everything that was happening with my prisoner. He's my prisoner at the end

of the day. I'm minding him. So you had to be very conscious and make sure that they knew you were very conscious.

(I3)

The Heavy Gang were a heavy gang, no doubt about that. They were heavy, too heavy. Because even when they came down here the odd time, you'd be hoping they wouldn't come down because they were upsetting the normal run of things here. They might go the extra hard on some of them. We didn't approve of them. We didn't like them.

(SG7)

G16 stated that they were 'more bother than they were worth' as the local gardaí would be excluded from cases.

This resonates with the complaints made to Garret Fitzgerald, but the political pressure to be seen to be combatting the IRA meant that 'it was seen on high that these lads were getting results. They didn't seem to mind how they got them, but they got results' (G16). In the year after the government declared a state of emergency, many believed there was some official sanctioning of these actions. Speaking out would clearly not have an impact and gardaí may have believed it would be detrimental to their careers. Instead gardaí learned that despite any dislike for such an approach it was accepted as it got results. The legal framework, implemented by government in the response to the Troubles, enabled such tactics.

Discussing accountability

On the other hand the legal framework of garda accountability militated against investigation of such complaints. At this point there was no external body to receive or examine complaints though Ireland had committed under the Sunningdale agreement of 1973 to establish both a police authority and an independent complaints mechanism (1973: para. 15). Democratic accountability through government and parliament was ineffective. Perceived political interference reached such a level in 1982 that AGSI unsuccessfully called for the creation of a police authority. A number of individuals had attempted civil actions, however in many cases the questionable character of the complainant hindered this approach. Criminal actions were occasionally pursued but did not result in convictions. Complaints, therefore, were processed through an internal system.

One former Special Branch member replied as followed when asked if he ever had any complaints made against him: 'Complaints at that time would not have been taken seriously. This was even more true when it came to the Special Branch. There was an intrigue about them. They were above the law' (DSG1). The operations of the Special Branch appear to have been shielded against rebuke. Yet, if it is accepted that those promoted would have carried with them the lessons learned in their time in Special Branch, then this also indicates that they would not have been overly supportive of complaints procedures, or any other mechanism of accountability.

The existence of a 'Heavy Gang' was vehemently denied by an Garda Síochána. If something is denied in such a way then it cannot be addressed. An Garda Síochána was never formally held to account for the use of force and abuse of detainees' rights, was never forced to admit the existence of the Heavy Gang, and never had to address the permeation of violence through the force. What is more, such claims did not have an impact on the public standing of an Garda Síochána. In an interview with a retired garda, Mulcahy was informed:

> The public were very, very supportive totally supportive right throughout the Troubles, even in the border counties where they would have been inconvenienced more than anywhere else ... I don't think that any of that [Heavy Gang allegations] had any long term impact on our public standing.
>
> (Mulcahy 2002: 289)

A study conducted by Bohan and Yorke in 1987 was revealing, finding that 56.8 per cent of respondents felt 'the police tended to abuse suspects either physically or mentally' and that 40.3 per cent felt the police 'may cover up the facts', suggesting that a large section of the public believed the allegations. At the same time, the study found that 62.4 per cent were either quite satisfied or very satisfied with the force, indicating clearly that while people accepted that such things happened, it did not impact on their confidence in the force. The study also found that 45 per cent believed the media gave the gardaí a hard time, 75 per cent felt the law favoured the criminal over the police, and over 70 per cent believed gardaí did not get enough recognition for risking their lives (1987: 79–81). Clearly, at the time of these allegations, there was a great deal of support for the gardaí.

The calls for accountability and allegations of abuse came from alleged and convicted terrorists who were aiming to subvert the state. They may have been abusing IRA suspects but they were not, as far as people were aware, abusing 'normal', 'decent' citizens of the state. Walsh points out that:

> If this had happened in another jurisdiction such as Northern Ireland, it would have instigated a crisis of confidence in the police force. In Ireland, however, public support for the Gardaí was so widespread and strong, compared with that for subversives, that the government was able to defuse the situation by the appointment of an inquiry into the treatment of persons in Garda custody.
>
> (Walsh 1998: 262)

More than ever, in the context of the Troubles, people believed in the ideal that an Garda Síochána represented. Some developments in terms of accountability occurred at this time with the establishment of the Garda Síochána Complaints Board in 1986, discussed in Chapter 7. This, however, was not an independent investigative body. Even with this body, given the public support for the police, the volume of complaints was undermined by the argument that the body was being used as a delay tactic.

> There were lots of vindictive vexatious complaints that were just being used as a plea bargaining tool by criminals. We found in searches Provisional IRA circulars which instructed that every time someone was arrested they were not to leave the station without making a complaint. This would completely clog up the system but it was part of their duty. They would then turn around in court and bring it up arguing 'he saw fit to make a complaint'.
>
> (CSI1)

Faced with such a challenge to the omnipresent view of the garda as a pillar of the community, it was easier for the public to accept such an argument. In a post-colonial framework those who challenged the Irish state (or were suspected of doing so), in a subversive and violent way, did not enjoy those rights. Their allegations should not be used as the basis for questioning or restricting an Garda Síochána. To reiterate the words of Mary Harney, a leading Irish politician of the time:

> Like many Members one is always very wary about being critical of our Garda Síochána. They have a very difficult job to do and many members of the Force have tragically lost their lives trying to protect the State and its citizens … It is all too easy for politicians to undermine the Force by criticising constantly what they might and might not do.
>
> (DE: 13/05/87)

We have therefore a context in which violence was used in an officially sanctioned manner for which accountability was evaded. McAleese argued in 1987 that a tolerance for violence had spread throughout the force:

> Such evidence as exists raises a prima facie case for the contention that abuse of police powers may be a product of the history, institutionalised structures, limited tools, pressures on, and expectations of, the police and may be much more accepted and widespread than we have been led to believe.
>
> (McAleese 1987: 54)

It is suggested here that violence was not just widespread or tolerated but was institutionalised. Meyer and Rowan indicate that '[i]nstitutional rules function as myths which organizations incorporate, gaining legitimacy, resources, stability, and enhanced survival prospects' (1977: 340). Institutionalisation means it is not simply tolerated but dependent on incorporation and support. Zucker (1977) contends that there are three elements that contribute to the persistence of institutionalised rules within a culture: 'generational uniformity of cultural understandings, maintenance of these understandings, and resistance of these understandings to change' (1977: 276). In addressing these she indicates that they could persist due to the internalisation of the rules in a normative way but prefers the ethnomethodological approach. This approach concerns itself with how individuals experience reality and then project an objective reality. This projection then determines what reality is both for them and other actors. The institutional myths are passed on by one person seeing them as reality, internalising them, and expressing them as reality, thereby encouraging others to experience the myth through the same process. The context within which this occurs can enable this myth to become institutionalised, particularly if it is an organisation in which acts are generally viewed as institutionalised, where other acts can easily be viewed in this light. In a police force this is easy to imagine. A rookie is told he will learn the job from his superiors; he must do what they do. Their actions become internalised as reality by the rookie, who then projects them as reality, leading to their institutionalisation over time.

This explains the transmission of institutionalised values. Maintenance is dependent on control and Zucker states that 'as long as the expected behaviour is in the actor's self-interest, it will be maintained' (1977: 740). Resistance to change occurs as a result of the combination of transmission and maintenance, and is essential to the institutionalisation process.

Analysed from this framework the process of institutionalisation of violence within an Garda Síochána is evident. Previous chapters have argued that use of force has been a perennial feature of policing in Ireland, be it against the IRA, the Blueshirts, the Animal Gangs, the Teddy Boys or through the work of the Riot Squad in Dublin. The attribution of value to violence within a group such as the Heavy Gang could easily lead to transmission within an organisation as institutionalised as a police force. The failure to sanction those who used violence allows for maintenance of the action and the combination creates a resistance to change. Within the context of the Heavy Gang there was support for institutionalisation of violence. In fact, not only was there support for violence but as the analysis in Chapter 5 argued gardaí were not sufficiently directed to police the IRA through legitimate means. The use of coercive methods to secure confessions in high-profile cases enabled convictions in those cases, satisfying political demands, while methods that may have been more effective against the IRA (such as proactive, intelligence-driven policing) were not prioritised, satisfying a political desire not to interrupt the IRA excessively. The political climate created the context from which the Heavy Gang emerged, just as in the 1930s when the gardaí felt they had little other option when it came to the IRA. Violence in response to serious threat had been institutionalised at that point, and the Heavy Gang was in fact a product of generational transmission. These values could easily be maintained and the lack of criticism meant there was no requirement to resist change, as change was not even mooted. In fact, the opposite was the case. The Special Branch produced a disproportionately high number of the upper ranks of an Garda Síochána in that period. Commissioner Garvey, in charge at the time of the emergence of the allegations, had been head of the Special Branch:

> Pat Byrne, the former Commissioner was a Detective Sergeant with me. He promoted every pal he had. The members of the Special Branch were

promoted up and formed a clique ... Eugene Crowley was Chief of Special
Branch and he became Commissioner. There was too much coming from there.
(DSG1)

Courtney, in his book, describes those he worked with in the Special Branch:

> After a period in Clondalkin, I was asked to join the Murder Squad by Chief
> Superintendent Patrick McLaughlin, who later became a Commissioner. In
> the Squad I joined another future Commissioner, Patrick Culligan ... Later
> we were joined by the now Deputy Commissioner John Paul McMahon.
> (Courtney 1996: 124)

Given how much the Troubles had affected policing in Ireland, it was understandably necessary to have people at senior levels with experience of high policing.
However, the questionable manner in which they are said to have operated
suggests that they were not necessarily the right people to be promoted. As one
member said: 'In that work, the Special Branch, there were a lot of cover-ups.
This was natural when dealing with a ruthless organisation. If they were involved
in these they will carry that into other areas of policing' (DSG1). The questionable operation of the promotion system, which lacked transparency, arises here.
Members of cliques were being promoted, but more than this, they were members
of a clique that was responsible for sustained allegations of ill-treatment of
suspects. These values are transmitted and maintained through the higher ranks,
lead to a trickledown effect and institutionalisation. Garvey became the second
Commissioner to be dismissed by government in January 1978. Just as with the
dismissal of O'Duffy in 1932, the government refused to explain its actions,
simply stating that it was important for government to have confidence in the
Commissioner. In addition to the allegations of ill-treatment and fingerprint problems, it seems that the Commissioner had attempted to prosecute five editors of the
Garda Review in the Special Criminal Court, without advising government (*IT*:
20/01/78). Rather than addressing the Heavy Gang allegations the Commissioner
associated with those methods was removed due to his divisive actions.

Conclusion

This chapter has shown how, faced with this threat, members of the Special
Branch who had the most dedicated focus on policing the IRA, resorted to
violence. What was particularly concerning about the allegations recounted in
this chapter was the systematic and sustained nature of the alleged violence.
While the existence of the Heavy Gang has repeatedly been denied by both
government and the force, evidence was gathered in this chapter, including the
views of those interviewed for this research, supporting a conclusion that the
Gang existed. More than this, the scale to which violence became supported and
rewarded through promotion leads to a conclusion that it has become institutionalised within the force, or at least within the Special Branch. In the face of public

allegations, the failure of either internal or democratic accountability to initiate investigations enabled the maintenance and transmission of these values, earning them institutionalised status.

Additionally, there was legal support for these practices. The way in which the powers of the police were expanded in this period via the Offences Against the State Act, the Emergency Powers Act and the use of the Special Criminal Courts, also enabled the use of this approach without rebuke. As the interviewees indicated, these courts were more amenable to the questionable evidence being presented by gardaí. It was not just the policing organisation that endorsed this approach; government, parliament and the judiciary all had a role to play. The public support for the gardaí in spite of an acknowledgment of misconduct, demonstrated in Bohan and Yorke's study, displays the extent to which this permeated.

The lasting impact of this is tied most strongly to the fact that an Garda Síochána was not held to account for these abuses. As an institution, it has never been forced to admit the existence of the Heavy Gang. It continues to deny the abuses of power that took place in the period and this contributes to a culture of denial (Cohen 2000). There were calls from certain quarters for the development of accountability measures. Independent groups such as Amnesty and the ICCL, as well as official bodies such as the O'Brian Commission, made numerous recommendations in this regard. These were however ignored, further entrenching police attitudes to both violence and accountability. As the next chapters will explore, many incidents that occurred in this period have become the focus of lengthy internal investigations and public tribunals in recent years.

7   The end of the century
Policing change

It would be easy in the light of the previous two chapters to create the impression that the Troubles were all-consuming for gardaí in the 1970s, 1980s and 1990s. This, of course, was not the case. Those decades saw Ireland undergo change in all facets of society, changes that impacted on policing in fundamental ways. Most obviously, from a policing perspective, crime rose exponentially between 1969 and 1983, redirecting the function of the police from administrative to crime tasks. Deeply connected to this growth in crime was the spread of drug use and dependence, which posed very particular challenges for policing and community relations.

The economy of the country changed in this period rising from the depths of recession to the boom of the Celtic Tiger. For gardaí this period began optimistically with the adoption of the recommendations of the Conroy Commission, but pay and conditions remained a bone of contention. There was a shift, however, identified through interview data, in members' motivation, which centred on pay like never before. The changing economic position also helped fund technological advances. All of these changes will be considered in this chapter.

The impact of the increasing secularisation of the country, leading to an increasing rights orientation and critical outlook, will also be explored. In this context a number of specific themes will be explored. Firstly, the role of women in the gardaí will be considered. Secondly, the demise of the Catholic Church is examined, as this prompted consideration as to how the gardaí had handled allegations of abuse by the clergy. Finally, the chapter will consider allegations of abuse by gardaí that were made at the time, in particular the Kerry babies case. But this section will also examine how through the 1980s and 1990s, in spite of growing evidence of garda misconduct, little concern was expressed about this. The establishment of the Garda Síochána Complaints Board will be examined to establish that relatively minimal steps were taken toward accountability in the context of expanding police powers. The argument will be made that this unwillingness to question an Garda Síochána was a legacy of post-colonialism, reinforced by the threats of the Troubles.

Rising crime

As explored in Chapter 4, through the 1950s and 1960s reported crime was low and policing was not centred on crime control (Brewer *et al.* 1997). Garda Commissioner

Annual Reports began in 1947 and from then to 1961 just over 15,000 indictable offences a year were recorded. By 1970 the figure had doubled to 30,000, growing rapidly through that decade and hitting 102,000 in 1983 and 1995.[1] Non-indictable crime saw a 180 per cent increase between 1950 and 1998 (Young *et al.* 2001). Property crime accounted for the majority of these offences, with larceny and burglary representing 98 per cent of all indictable crime in 1998, almost half of which occurred in Dublin. The increasing numbers of motor vehicles 'played a central role in shaping crime statistics' in the closing decades of the century, both in terms of theft of vehicles and traffic offences (Young *et al.* 2001: xii). Violence against the person represented just a tiny percentage of offences (2 per cent in 1998) and while levels of homicide rose, it remained rare even at the end of the twentieth century, save for the Dublin and Monaghan bombings in 1974. The number of sexual offences recorded rose from under 400 in the late 1980s to over 1000 per annum. This is most likely due to increased reporting – often of offences that occurred many years previously – rather than increased offending. Since 1960 the amount of crime recorded as having been committed by juveniles has been falling, with less than 15 per cent being attributed to young people in the 1990s.

Numerous participants cited the rise in crime rates as the biggest change in policing in their time in the force. It naturally meant that greater portions of their time were dedicated to responding to reports of crime, investigating crime and attending court when prosecutions were undertaken. This change meant that policing in Ireland was not about the administrative tasks or engagement with the community; it was about crime fighting (Manning 1977). This change was not perceived by all participants as a negative development. SI7, who joined in 1969, took the view that '[t]here's nothing as boring as being in the guards with nothing to do or no crime'. These changes brought a certain thrill to the job:

> I used to love the weekends. I wouldn't take Saturday off. I used to go out in the car … and you'd be getting calls. There'd be rows and there'd be suspicious activity here and there. It's very exciting … You're anxious maybe to get some criminals actually committing a serious crime and you'll get him and you'll arrest him and charge him and it's exciting.
>
> (SI7)

It was only at this time that many aspects of a police culture documented by scholars such as Banton (1964), Cain (1973) and Reiner (2000), such as a thirst for action or a sense of mission, began to appear in Irish policing. Numerous interviewees told stories of particular crimes they investigated that stood out in their careers, cases they had solved by applying some canny thinking or questioning skills. These were their high points. The excitement was linked to the greater challenge posed and other social changes could intersect with this. For instance, as one garda pointed out, the enhanced road network meant more transient criminals who were impossible to identify:

> You'd go to a burglary and you only had to look around and you'd a good idea who done it … From the time the road to Dublin improved … it was only

a very simple thing for Mr and his friends from Tallaght or Dundalk or wher-
ever to hop in a car and drive. It was only an hour. Do a couple of burglaries.

(G12)

Criminals were not the only ones availing of cars more. Other participants stated
that the demise of beat policing in favour of cars and fire-brigade policing, as well
as specialist units in the 1980s, meant that knowledge of local people, key to
investigation, was lost.

All the different crime units, they took away from the person on the beat. The
thing I'll say about the older guards before me, no matter where you went
in Dublin, up Thomas Street or anywhere around the city centre, they knew
everyone. That's something the guards lost in the '80s. They weren't in touch
with the people maybe as much as they probably should.

(G13)

This lack of community-based knowledge was cited by many participants, echo-
ing what had occurred in England 20 years previously. This was not just about
the use of cars however. This was connected to the rise in crime, which diverted
garda time from the administrative roles that had created so much knowledge of
the community. As explored in Chapter 4, that knowledge had created fear of
gardaí and so its decline may have created space for the public to be less deferential to the police.

Mulcahy (2002: 281) attributes the rise in crime rates to 'processes of urbanisation and industrialisation, higher levels of prosperity, as well as changes in family
structures and in the public's general attitudes towards authority and hitherto
widely-respected institutions'. Changing societal attitudes also meant that sexual
offences and domestic violence were reported to the police more. For interviewees, however, the arrival of drugs was the undoubted cause. Drug offences appear
in the Annual Crime Reports for the first time in 1970. In 1979 there were just
five heroin charges. In 1981 there were 177 charges. From 1989 to 1998 recorded
misuse of drug offences more than tripled. In 1999 proceedings were instigated
against more than 7000 individuals for misuse of drugs.

The growth in drug use was related to both changes in the economy and
increased mobility through the EEC/EU, and had a significant impact for crime
rates more broadly. Charleton states that '[f]rom 1973 over a period of 18 years
robbery has increased in levels of commission by more than four times and
burglary by almost six times. The cause of this is drug abuse' (1995: 221). One
study suggests that heroin addicts were responsible for two-thirds of all indictable
crime in Dublin (Keogh 1997). The peaks of the heroin epidemics certainly coin-
cide with the peaks of crime rates in 1983 and 1995. Heroin use had exploded in
inner-city Dublin in the early 1980s and Dean *et al.* (1983) found that almost
10 per cent of 15- to 24-year-olds surveyed in a northern inner-city community
had taken heroin at least once a day in the previous year.

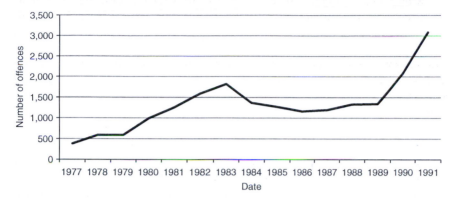

Figure 7.1 Offences recorded under the Misuse of Drugs Acts 1977 and 1984, 1977–91.

Participants in Dublin spontaneously raised the arrival of drugs in the 1980s as one of the biggest changes to policing. For those who served in other parts of the country this effect was not felt until the 1990s, but all agreed that it was with drugs that 'the viciousness crept into the scene' (DSI3). That scene developed a particularly sinister slant in the mid-1990s when the drug market in Ireland became more organised and gangs emerged. Gangs brought a growth in lethal weapons, which previously did not circulate in Ireland beyond paramilitary organisations (Campbell 2010): 'We went from the sawn-off shot gun in the '50s and '60s to the machine guns and glocks and rifles in the '90s and the '00s' (SI5). I5 linked it directly to freedom of movement across Europe, 'particularly when the Eastern European countries broke up, you know like Yugoslavia and places like that, they had lots of arms to sell' (I5). This was connected to increased fatalities linked to drugs. Gang feuds led to eight deaths in 1996. That year also saw the assassination of Veronica Guerin, a journalist who had been investigating a criminal gang in Dublin: 'There was a feeling up to then, that organised gangs wouldn't kill a reporter or wouldn't kill a guard but after that the rule books seemed to have changed' (SI5). This perception of danger exists, despite the fact that organised gangs had not killed a garda. The belief created by the Troubles that policing in Ireland was a dangerous occupation was nevertheless reinforced.

The force was largely caught unprepared when it came to drugs. Neither the training nor the legislation was sufficient. The controlling relationship of the Department of Justice was cited as having a stymieing effect:

> I remember there was a specific video on drug enforcement you could get from the Canadian authorities, Canadian Police Service. This training video cost £120 at the time. Now we couldn't get consent from the Department of

Justice to purchase it … that's the only time that I saw those kind of things, you didn't get what you felt you needed.

(SI6)

This inability to tackle drugs proactively had disastrous effects for community relations, particularly when the destructive effects of the heroin epidemic were felt in Dublin. In 1983 an action group called Concerned Parents Against Drugs (CPAD) was formed, an organisation that felt the gardaí were not policing drugs sufficiently and who intended to take action against drug pushers. Lyder states that their approach 'was characterised by wide scale breaking of the law in the sense that scores of forced evictions took place across the city. These were decided upon at mass public meetings and, generally, carried out by the local community' (2005: 288). CPAD argued that the police strategy was to contain the drugs problem within certain communities, rather than eradicate it. The gardaí countered that there was little they could do with outdated legislation (McCullagh 1996: 168). Many members of CPAD maintained that they were stopped, searched and detained by hostile gardaí (*IT*: 17/06/96). It was counter-alleged that these groups were dominated by republicans, though many feel this influence was overstated with the intention of diverting attention from their claims (McCullagh 1988). A serious breakdown in police-community relations occurred. Commissioner Wren stated in 1982: 'The gardaí are not wanted in some areas of Dublin, and a potential exists for the sort of breakdown between the police and the public which led to last year's urban riots in Britain' (*IT*: 31/12/82).

It was within this context that the first discussions of community policing emerged; however, for too long they remained discussions. A Community Relations Office was created in 1978, into which the juvenile liaison scheme was subsumed. A circular from Headquarters in 1980 stated that 'since the distinctive role of the force is the prevention and detection of crime, the wholehearted support of the community at large is vital' (cited in Feehan 2010: 17). Three years later, at the same time as CPAD emerged, a further circular proposed that a nomi-nated garda patrol particular areas and also discussed the continuing role that community policing had to play: 'It should never be looked upon as an emer-gency measure to take the pressure off the gardaí during stressful situations involving public criticism. It is neither a whitewash for incompetence nor an attempt to appease minority groups.'

Actions however were somewhat limited on this front, with no concerted effort to create a dialogue with the communities being devastated by drug abuse. Anti-drug activists assaulted and killed a drug pusher, Josie Dwyer, in 1996. Twelve men were prosecuted in relation to Mr Dwyer's death, a number of whom were acquitted after it was alleged that gardaí had falsified confessions.[2] Not only had gardaí failed to engage with the communities to prevent such an escalation, but when it did escalate it seems it was investigated inappropriately. It was only after this death, and that of Veronica Guerin in the same year, that action was taken. In the next 18 months four pieces of legislation were passed to deal with drugs, intro-ducing the Criminal Assets Bureau and seven-day detention for drug-trafficking offences (Ryan 1997). Much of what was done here was to apply the powers usually reserved for subversives to drug traffickers (Vaughan and Kilcommins 2008; Campbell 2006). Steps were also taken to work with communities. In 1999 the Dublin North Inner City Community Policing Forum (CPF) was created, which finally created a space for direct communication between the police and the community (Connolly 2002; Feehan 2010). Despite a stated commitment to community policing in the early 1980s, no concerted action in this regard was taken for nearly 20 years. The impact of this is undoubtedly profound for those communities that see themselves as under-policed when crimes such as drug dealing occur, and over-policed when they attempt to self-police.

Unsurprisingly, this growth in crime led to legislative changes and enhanced police powers. The Criminal Justice Act 1984 gave gardaí power to arrest without charge for the first time and regulated attendant powers to search, photograph and take samples. The drug-trafficking legislation also created incursions in the right to silence. Connolly warned that:

> while there is no evidence that the introduction of the enhanced police powers will have any obvious impact on crime, there is a strong likelihood that these powers will be abused and that this abuse will further undermine relations between the police and the community,
>
> (Connolly 1998: 183)

The Act attempted to address such concerns by introducing safeguards for suspects, including the custody record, recording of interviews and regulations for treatment in custody (Ryan 2000). This was influenced by the O'Brian Report (1978), which examined the treatment of persons in custody. The requirement to maintain a custody record was mentioned by some interviewees as representing a noteworthy change (DSG4). According to G8, changes to detention and interrogation took time to adjust to, as gardaí felt that they could no longer approach interviews in the relaxed way that they had previously. The advantages soon became apparent however:

> Lads got very comfortable with it after a while and actually they wouldn't actually carry out an interview unless it was on camera because they saw the advantage of it protecting them. We had one great case there where one particular high-profile criminal was arrested in Limerick. Going into the interview room, he wasn't two minutes in the interview room and he got up and he broke one of our lad's jaw with a box inside in the interview room. That was all recorded on camera and he got five years for it, and not one of our lads raised a finger. We just walked in, handcuffed him and took him out and it was all shown on camera, which was brilliant and I think that in itself reinforced the benefit of it.
>
> (G8)

SG3 felt that while it was important, it created a lot of work for gardaí. Members had to be trained and someone had to be assigned to act as custody sergeant. G16 stated that criminals became well-versed in their rights, in itself a 'problem'.

The rise in crime in Ireland in the 1970s both brought changes and exposed problems. Policing was for the first time primarily about crime-fighting, which brought excitement and danger but also meant that police were no longer engaged in the activities that had produced strong knowledge of communities. Gardaí were slow to adapt and engage in other forms of interaction with the community. The development of community policing forums in Dublin was notably slow given the scale of the community relations crisis which emerged.

Economic change

A shift in economic policy in the 1970s toward foreign direct investment and membership of the EU saw Ireland finally break from its economic dependence on the UK (Bradley 2000; Daly 1981, O'Grada 1997). This culminated in the 'Celtic Tiger' of the 1990s, which brought unprecedented economic development to the country. Between 1987 and 1993, Irish GDP rose by 36 per cent, compared to 13 per cent for Europe as a whole, and unemployment dropped to 4.5 per cent (O'Grada 1997). However, before this bore fruit, the 1970s and 1980s were particularly difficult economic periods. Unemployment hit 17 per cent. Over 70,000 people emigrated in 1989 and for the first time in Ireland this affected skilled workers as well as unskilled: 30 per cent of people with a university degree left the country. The economic state of the country had numerous effects for policing. There is a link to the rise in the property crime rates and drug consumption. On the face of it spending on the force rose dramatically during this period, from £23.9 million (punts) in 1974 to £224 million in 1984. Brewer *et al.* point out, however, that during this period the percentage of the Department of Justice's budget spent on policing fell, while it rose for prisons, and that in fact 'governments of both parties have spent much less on the Garda Síochána than its needs require despite promises made by politicians, especially when in opposition' (1996: 92). Much of this spending was generated by increased numbers and the security situation. In this section both the conditions of policing and the technological changes in this period will be considered.

Conditions

The implementation of the Conroy recommendations created much hope for gardaí in relation to pay and conditions. For a time most gardaí received substantial overtime payments on top of their wages. However the reality of the cost of the recommendations for government quickly became clear: with the garda working week limited to 42 hours, increasing crime and security concerns and more garda wages to pay, the payment of overtime soon exceeded budgets. Rather than stating that they could not afford this, the government cited garda morale as the reason for a reduction in overtime:

> A serious temptation was being placed in the way of some members to undertake and subsequently claim payment for overtime in circumstances which I

shall content myself to describe as questionable ... It is the considered view of the Garda authorities that excessive overtime, especially when it is, as it must be, very uneven in its incident is a menace to good morale in the force and that it must be got rid of with all possible speed.

(DE: 04/11/71)

Gardaí quickly adjusted to the enhanced wages that overtime payments brought and members began to compete for overtime. Financial rewards replaced a great deal of the vocational elements of the job. Practical examples of this were pointed to as SG5 remembered an occasion when he needed men to respond to a call about a break-in:

> And I went up and I saw four of them playing cards you see ... And I said, 'Put your jackets on and follow me quick'. So, I went to the front door, expecting four men to come out after me. Nothing. I was a Sergeant then, they were guards. And I went back in to the table and they were still playing cards. And I said, 'Did you hear what I said?' And one of them had the courage to say, 'We are on our break.'

(SG5)

This is a very significant point in the history of an Garda Síochána. All the founding members of the force had retired. This was a new generation of members, with a new attitude to their work, which was being redefined by the growth in crime and the Troubles. For the first time members, albeit briefly, experienced payment for the additional hours they worked. As stated by G8 'if overtime is coming in the morale is high because the lads are able to go out'. Money was tied to satisfaction and morale in a stronger way than ever before.

Increased pay exposed the dichotomous position whereby,

> [o]n the one hand, one encounters what might be described as a secular disposition towards the Job and its rewards, one whose basic orientation runs *this is a demanding, sometimes dangerous job for which we ought to be properly paid* ... On the other hand we find among officers a wistful sense of loss that the job has come to be apprehended in these terms, as if it has somehow been sullied, it's cultural worth devalued, by its association with (too much money). On this view, *non-pecuniary notions to do with honour, obligation, duty and sacrifice are central both to being a police officer, and to the proper relationship between policing and the social.*

(Loader and Mulcahy 2003: 189–90; emphasis in original)

Interestingly, for those gardaí who had joined prior to Conroy, this altruistic, non-pecuniary outlook seems to have developed on the job. As outlined in Chapter 4, for most people who joined an Garda Síochána up until the 1980s, it was a largely economic choice not based on altruistic principles. It was the only viable alternative to emigration. For interviewees who joined after 1970 Conroy did not impact on reasons for joining. It was still an alternative to emigration (I3, DG15, G10), which attracted a stable pension (G3, G10 and G17), although two interviewees mentioned that it was a career option (SI5 and G5), which may indicate some progression in how the job was viewed. A suggestion that men joined the gardaí out of some sense of honour or obligation, viewing it as a worthy profession even in poor conditions, is a myth. And this is in spite of the fact that a number of these people joined during the recruitment campaigns prompted by the Troubles:

> I had no intentions of joining until I saw a sign displayed outside of my own garda station one day. Myself and another man, Henry Byrne, who was unfortunately killed with Morley back in 1980, the two of us were working together and we decided we'd have a go … It was just something that was there and there wasn't an awful lot back then.
>
> (I3)

This contrasts directly with Loader and Mulcahy's finding that in England the respectability of the position, rather than the salary, made it an attractive career (2003: 184). It does, however, fit with Reiner's findings that people often join for instrumental reasons (1978: 159). Harris (1988) reviewed the personnel files of all garda recruits from 1966 and 1986. Only 13 per cent cited pay as a reason for joining and just 17 per cent felt it had good career prospects (1988: 184). Varied and interesting work was the most commonly cited reason (64 per cent) followed by security (41 per cent). Thirty per cent stated that it had been a lifelong ambition. Vocation is very much a secondary reason for joining the gardaí. The percentage of recruits who had finished secondary-level schooling doubled in that period, rising from 30 to 60 per cent. Whilst education is valuable in policing, Harris argued that such a reduction and under-representation of unskilled and working-class members would impact negatively on community relations (1988: 45). Worryingly, Harris found that almost half of those who had joined in the previous 20 years found that life in the gardaí was worse than expected. A quarter said they would not join the force again and 40 per cent of those who had joined in the 1980s had thought seriously about resigning. While there was great variety and interest in the job, pay, conditions and supervision were all rated poorly. Indeed, dissatisfaction with management was the most frequently cited reason among members who were unhappy or had considered resigning (1988: 201). All of this negativity was higher among those who worked in border areas. More than two-thirds felt the promotion system did not operate fairly and a similar number felt that favouritism influenced promotion. Harris also found that the vast majority of those he surveyed viewed law enforcement as the most important aspect of their job. The reality was that two-thirds of their work was dedicated to service provision or crime prevention, and just one-sixth to law enforcement (1988: 210).

Morale was clearly very low during this period. By 1979 gardaí were once again agitating for further pay increases and a commission was established to explore the issue under Professor Louden Ryan. In 1988 at the annual conference of the GRA a motion was proposed condemning the role of the Department of

Justice and garda management in restoring and maintaining morale. The following year the *Garda Review* reported that there was an average of nearly 1400 assaults on gardaí and that this level was 'very alarming' (1989: May: 14). As Brewer *et al.* stated: 'it has been a common complaint that successive governments have been long on promises but short on action when it comes to the legal and organisational reforms that the guards feel they need' (1996: 104).

Some advancements were made in training during this period, both for recruits and those in senior positions. The Garda Síochána College was opened in 1981 (Moran 1983) and provided training for the ranks of inspector and above, delivering for the first time internal management and leadership training. A committee was established in 1985 to review garda training (Walsh 1985). The length of training was extended from 18 to 42 weeks. Recruits became known as student gardaí in 1989 and the College was accredited to provide higher education, at first a diploma and later a BA in Police Studies. The focus of training moved from drill and learning laws by rote to a more practical orientation, which was divided into phases, including two placement phases in garda stations. It was only in this that some of the colonial aspects of training were removed.

In the mid-1990s the country entered the boom period of the Celtic Tiger and members felt that garda pay should be enhanced in light of the condition of the public finances. There were significant disputes within the representative organisations as to how this should be approached, leading to a highly acrimonious and public split within the GRA in 1994. For a time three separate representative bodies, including the Garda Federation, existed for the rank of garda. The government intervened in an effort to resolve the dispute, passing legislation that permitted just one representative body at each rank. A call for a commission to be established on pay was rejected. A proposal from government of a 7 per cent increase was rejected in April 1998. In perhaps the most serious display of garda dissatisfaction since the Kildare Mutiny, 82 per cent of members at the rank of garda, supported by the GRA, were struck down by 'Blue Flu' and phoned in sick on 1 May 1998 (DE: 14/05/98). Commissioner Byrne called it 'a black day for the force'. The public response was not sympathetic: *The Irish Times* wrote, in the aftermath, that '[t]he psychological contract between the nation and the force has been broken' (07/07/98). Even those who participated were demoralised by the events. G8 felt that it 'was for nothing' while G7 outlined how difficult a period it was:

> The Blue Flu was a fierce dilemma for a lot of us. I suppose you'd be very conscious of the position you hold and you'd be afraid that would get eroded. And we were demeaned I think, we lost a little in the Blue Flu and there are people that will throw it back.
>
> (G7)

A former GRA executive member described it was one of the greatest mistakes ever made by the GRA: 'It was wrong because it gave the signal that the gardaí could cheat. They could pretend to be sick and still draw pay' (G2).

A further notable change is this period was creeping managerialism. In the mid-1990s the government had developed a Strategic Management Initiative (SMI) across the public sector. As part of this process a Steering Group was appoint to consider SMI issues for an Garda Síochána, which reported in 1997, making recommendations in relation to the organisation, operations, financing, performance and accountability of the force. This report led to the creation of a number of additional bodies including a Bottom Up Review Group (BURG), supported by an implementation group. Additionally, a Garda SMI Implementation Group was established to oversee the implementation of the 1997 report. This wave of bodies and discussions of reform saw the rhetoric of managerialism play an important role in Irish policing. Jones and Newburn have described managerialism as one 'of the most significant changes in policing in the last 20 years or so … one that could fundamentally subvert the nature of policing as a collectively purchased public service should it be taken to the extreme' (2002: 135).

Technology

Chapter 5 outlined early efforts to develop police technology, which focused on transport and communications. The 1970s and 1980s saw a continued development in these areas though at a slow pace. One experience that displays both the impact of technology and the slow progress in Ireland is G13's work in the emergency services centre in Dublin Castle from 1976 to 1996. When he was first posted there it comprised one small room in which four gardaí worked. They used a switchboard-operated telephone, had radio contact with gardaí and documented everything on paper:

> Every call you got you documented it on a bit of paper, signed off on it. Put it in a box in the middle of the table and every 24 hours then all taken out, tidied up, bundled like that, put away in a special room somewhere.

Every stolen car would be logged by hand in a book and the registration details of all located cars had to be cross-checked by hand. When the first computer was installed in the late 1970s it was dedicated to stolen cars:

> It was the job you didn't want for the day … if you were put on that duty for the day you were just there for the whole day. The whole country, imagine, ringing up to see if this car was stolen.

Phone calls were not recorded until the early 1980s and the computerisation of all work did not commence until the end of that decade: 'Up to that we were struggling with paper. We were still bundling the paper mountain up to that.' This was in spite of the fact that he had witnessed a growth in calls from 700 to 800 a day to 2000 a day. At the time of computerisation staffing grew to 25 people, all gardaí, in a task that could arguably have been performed by civilians. It was at times difficult work. G13 recalled the 'traumatic' night of the fire at the Stardust disco on Valentine's night, 1981, which killed 48 people:

> We were talking to a girl on the phone in the Stardust about two minutes before the fire went off. Her bag had been stolen and she was ringing would we get someone to come out. She was on the phone and the next thing she said 'hold on'. We never heard from her again. I would say it was at that time the fire started … We never heard her again. But it was just amazing that we'd just had a call from there and we sent a few units there and the first unit that arrived was told we had a problem and we had.

He spoke of how that tragedy required the implementation of the city's disaster plan, which had been written in 1969 (DE: 12/12/72) for the first time:

> We wouldn't have been familiar with what it was until that night. It was the first time it was put into action. It mightn't have worked too well but that was for; a lot of people who were in the book had retired or gone somewhere else. They never updated the book. After that they got it updated.

This suggests that both planning and training were needs-driven rather than proactive.

Computerisation of police work and networking of garda information was attempted through the late 1980s and early 1990s, culminating in the introduction of the PULSE (Police Using Leading Systems Efficiently) computer system in 1999. This system contains information on recorded crimes, traffic management, progression of criminal cases, firearms and driver licences, insurance and character vetting. It was an expensive system (€61 million) to which only larger stations had access. In spite of the promised increases in efficiency to policing there was resistance initially from gardaí to the system (RTE: 23/11/99). Interviewees expressed conflicting views about PULSE. G7 considered it 'a necessary evil' and complained that while it enabled you to check things immediately it also meant that 'discretionary powers go out the window' as all actions have to be recorded on the system. For 'summary offences, you could do deals before whereas now you can't'. G10 similarly felt:

> Discretion has gone now because at that time you went to an incident, you took out your notebook and wrote down the details. If you wanted to do something about it, it was up to you to do, to come back and do up your files. But now, when you go to an incident you must put that onto PULSE. That's now a public record.
>
> (G10)

More than anything, this displays a defensive attitude to what could be considered a form of accountability. The fact that their notes on the PULSE system could be accessed by others created fear and resentment. SI4 contextualised the problems by stating that most gardaí did not have computer experience and were now inputting their own data, a process which, at least initially, took a great deal of time and was not always accurate: 'you could have ten incidents on the one street but ten different spellings' (G11). Gardaí, rather than civilians, were employed to input old data. G13 spent close to two years inputting bags of back-dated data. All of this did, of course, create resistance to technology:

> They wouldn't touch it. 'That machine is watching me', kinda thing ... The older fellas were very anti-IT, anti-computers. They were so used to writing everything long hand in pen, that anything technological was taboo.
>
> (G13)

Forensics and DNA, on the other hand, were cited by many as areas of immense progress, bringing a 'sea change' to criminal investigation (SG5): 'no matter how they [criminals] try, they will always leave something'. SG7 felt that the impact could be overstated as criminals kept apace with developments: 'when they got back to a house the first thing they would do was wash and clean themselves. Get rid of any residue, firearms residue off their hands'. The Morris Tribunal, considered in Chapter 8, showed however that when it came to a road traffic collision appropriate forensic preservation and examination was not conducted at the scene. Numerous recommendations had to be made relating to crime scene preservation.

Secularisation and democratisation

In the 1970s Irish society began to have a greater conception of individual rights. Since 1965 the concept of personal rights had been significantly expanded by the Supreme Court (Ryan v. AG). *The Late Late Show* generated discussions about topics such as contraception and divorce, and membership of the EEC exposed citizens to ideas from elsewhere. Society, just as societies elsewhere, began to slowly consider the rights of others and question those institutions that attempted to control individual behaviour. This section will consider changing attitudes towards women and the Church, followed by an examination of the extent to which Irish society became questioning of the garda institution.

Women in the gardaí

Women in the police have been universally found to experience resistance to entry, differential deployment, impediments to career progression and sexual harassment (Martin 1980; Heidenshon 1992; Silvestri 2003). Irish culture works to make this more explicit. Dooley states that: 'Women's citizenship, as it is ideologically framed in the Constitution, is a case study of gender-differentiated and "second-class citizenship"' (1998: 112). On paper it would certainly seem that some progress has been made. The gender breakdown of members is not provided in annual statistics of the force, but from a variety of sources the following numbers can be gathered (see Table 7.1).

There are three structural factors that contributed to the rise in the number of female gardaí in the 1980s. Firstly, the marriage ban, which meant that women had to resign on marriage and that married women could not join, was lifted in 1973. Secondly, equal pay was finally achieved in 1985. An Garda Síochána was excluded from the Anti-Discrimination Pay Act 1974 until a number of women threatened to challenge this position and Ireland was directed by the EC to amend this (EC Directive, S.I. 331/1985). Thirdly, the rapid expansion of the size of the force in the 1970s and 1980s meant that there was greater recruitment to the force more broadly. The growth in numbers of women must therefore be considered in terms of the growth in the force as a whole.

The total strength of the force stood at 10,023 in 1995, with females occupying 764 positions, or 7.6 per cent. There was just one female superintendent, five inspectors and 49 sergeants, putting women in just 2.4 per cent of positions above the rank of garda, a figure which rose to just under 6 per cent in 1999 (*Garda Review* 2004). So while numbers increased women were still largely invisible and absent from the management of the force. Other structural changes included the dropping of the term ban-gharda in 1991 and the removal of the requirement to wear skirts and heels, both of which were physically impeding and differentiating. There were sound-bites of a managerial effort to move toward equality. Since 1995 the gardaí have participated in the European NOW programme (New Opportunities for Women). In 1998 Garda HQ issued the following statement on equality:

> An Garda Síochána is committed to and supports equality of opportunity in employment regardless of gender, creed, colour or marital status. It is the policy of the Commissioner that the principles and practices of equality of opportunity should apply to the recruitment, placement, selection, career development and all other conditions of service of members of An Garda

Table 7.1 Numbers of women in an Garda Síochána 1969–2004.

Year	Females	Total	% of total
1969	23	6,500	0.35%
1978	35	9,387	0.37%
1980	97	9,982	0.97%
1985	328	11,349	2.89%
1995	764	10,023	7.62%
1999	1,093	11,458	9.53%
2004	1,943	12,210	15.91%
2009	3,375	14,603	23.11%

Source: Allen 1999; DE: 09/03/72, 12/12/74, 21/02/78, 29/01/85, 03/03/95, 10/03/99; *Garda Review*, August 2004.

Síochána, and to ensure that no member of An Garda Síochána or job applicant receives less favourable treatment on the ground of gender, creed, colour or marital status.

This is not just a numbers game however. In the course of this research one female retired garda (G6) was interviewed. She joined having worked as a clerical officer for the force and repeatedly experienced differential deployment:

> We had to fight for our place on the job ... The sergeant was inclined to put us on office duty, particularly in my case, as I had that experience. I would say 'no' but they liked to put you as station orderly, 'put the little crater in, it's cold outside' ... You had to fight for it.
> Back over the years, the girls, in my day they wouldn't drive a patrol car. Oh if I wanted to do that they would feel there would be favouritism. But you would be discriminated against. Car courses were unheard of for women.
>
> (G6)

Brown's comparative study of women in the gardaí, RUC, Scottish, English and Welsh police (2000) found that in 1996, 42 per cent of female members in the gardaí were performing support roles, compared to 14, 19 and 6 per cent in the other countries respectively. A belief that women were unsuitable for certain tasks appears to have persisted longer in the gardaí. The McAleese Report on the Magdalene Laundries mentions that escorting women to the Laundries was identified as a suitable task for female members (2013: 306). G6 certainly experienced this attitude: 'There was the attitude with some of the lads, "What good is she? You'll only be minding her. She can't deal with a row".' (G6).

A number of the male participants expressed similar opinions during interviews:

> There are too many women in the job. A woman in a police car is at a disadvantage when dealing with things. They need a degree of strength. If you are with them you end up minding them more than anything. I've seen police cars with two women. It's a mad scene. If they get into a violent situation they are in trouble. There is no room for women at the fore-front.
>
> (G4)

> If there was row you didn't send them out for the row. They were picked for typing duties and dealing with children ... You're always worried, you go outside and you have a female with you. It's probably the male thing in you, you feel you have to protect her.
>
> (I3)

> There's too many women now and they're not, it's not a job for women. And it's hard if you're out with a girl and maybe she's not adept at looking after herself ... now you're just thinking, 'Jesus, do I have to look after her first?'
>
> (SI4)

Both these comments and those of G8 correspond with what has been found elsewhere, that policing is one of the most gendered of professions (Young 1991; Martin 1989). Brown states that differential deployment of women was due to a combination of both paternalism and protectionism (2000: 97), though the above quotes express a degree of frustration at enforced protectionism that might hint at a more basic degree of misogyny. Heidenshon has said that 'much research on women in policing is basically how women cope with policemen rather than with policing' (1992: 84).

In addition to the immediate difficulties and frustrations that differential deployment creates for women, it has a substantial impact on promotion. G6 experienced this: 'if there's ten men and one woman why should she get it? Men felt they didn't do the same work'. Women were structurally barred from doing the same work as men, which then justified a belief that they were not suitable for promotion. They did not have the range of experiences and knowledge deemed necessary for promotion (Jones 1986; Martin and Jurik 1986). Maternity issues also became central to promotion applications:

> I remember one girl who was asked [in a promotion interview], 'how will you manage your children?' … The attitude of management was that all women are a nuisance, pregnant, no good to me. They would resent the fact that they'd go on maternity leave.
>
> (G6)

Indeed, in 1985 a female unmarried member who became pregnant by a garda recruit had disciplinary charges brought against her for discreditable conduct. Jack Marrinan, head of the GRA at the time, stated:

> We certainly would not encourage our female members to think that this is a normal condition for them to get into, out of wedlock. We would expect our ban gharda to be moral in every way and we would not think that their morals are necessarily their own private business.
>
> (*IT*: 06/02/85)

Flynn, in a review published in the *Garda Review* (2000), found that women believed that there was a restrictive quota operating on female promotions: at that point no woman had reached a senior rank. This would, of course, generate concerns that any promotions of females were at least influenced by tokenism, which is not only problematic in itself but also creates what Kanter (1977) has described as 'token dynamics' whereby the 'token' feels pressure to perform at a higher level to justify their position.

While women in the force felt excluded from many tasks and disadvantaged in terms of promotion, male members begrudged efforts made to address child-rearing responsibilities. G8 stated that men 'felt that they were getting the easy jobs because the few that was in it, if a vacancy came up [for office or 9–5 roles], and more particularly I suppose where it's prevalent is that if women get pregnant'.

Women returning from pregnancy requested 9–5 shifts, which precluded men from access to that working pattern. The impact of having a family was raised by a number of participants: 'when the babies come on it isn't easy to be getting up in the morning. They all want handy numbers' (G11). These statements suggest a number of determinative factors. Firstly, within the Irish context it was taken for granted that the childrearing responsibilities lay with the mother: G8 was married to a garda and she took an office job after they had children. Secondly, absent from these discussions is a recognition that if women were largely excluded from progression there may have been little incentive to battle both work and societal structures and pressures to continue an ordinary shift pattern.

There were societal pressures that affected female gardaí more so than women in other professions. It was not just gardaí that had such views of female gardaí. G6 described how '[w]e had problems with male members' wives who didn't want their husbands out with ban ghardaí'. And when she was first sent to a country station where they had not seen female members before, '[p]eople nearly crashed cars when they saw you. They couldn't get over it. Men chatted you up' (G6). The difficulties of inclusion and acceptance were present in the general public, as well as in the station. The admission of women to the force challenged very strongly held opinions on the place of women in Irish society. The difficulties experienced when women were first admitted were documented in Chapter 4, but even 40 years on, at the end of the twentieth century, they had achieved neither parity nor acceptance in the force. The views of participants in this research were informed not only by the patriarchal nature of the state and the authoritative position of the gardaí, but also the strong Catholic hold over the country until more recent times. All of this is problematic for many reasons. Not only does it constitute discrimination for women within the force but it also prevents the much-needed deconstruction of misogynist homogeneity. If these views are unchallenged, the pervading sexism could well affect the way in which certain crimes, such as sexual offences and domestic violence, are responded to. Evidence of this will be presented in other parts of this chapter.

The role of the Church

Inglis comments that 'one of the first impressions of the country that marks it out as different from other Western societies is that the Church is a strong and active force in everyday life' (1998: 1). This position developed during the nineteenth century through the Church's association with the nationalist movement: in the mid-nineteenth century mass attendance was 35 per cent but by the end of the century it had risen to 90 per cent.[3] Coulter explains the importance of religion in colonial nations: 'it has often been a badge of separateness from the occupier, offering a sense of moral superiority in the midst of social inferiority and transcendental salvation where there was no sign of a temporal one' (1993: 9). Catholicism had been a central site of British intolerance and so a freedom to worship in the Church was a core part of the post-colonial project in Ireland. As O'Toole describes:

> The groundwork laid down in the nineteenth century was the basis for the Church's triumph in independent Ireland. Once there was an Irish state, it became the effective arbiter of social legislation, having a ban on divorce inserted into the Constitution, encouraging the introduction of draconian censorship of books and films, delaying the legalisation of artificial contraception until 1979, retaining largely unquestioned control over schools and hospitals funded by the taxpayer, resisting the slow development of a welfare state.
>
> (1998: 70)

The 1920s through to the 1950s were the peak of the Church's hold in Ireland, both in terms of devotion and influence over the state (Inglis 1998). The ideological power of the Church was reinforced through its control of institutions such as education, social welfare and health as well as its strong influence on other institutions such as the gardaí. That power was of a nature that was self-perpetuating. As Inglis stated, '[t]he dominance of "the simple faith" meant that many Irish Catholics did not develop an intellectual interest in, or critical attitude towards, their religion' (1998: 2).

Indeed, this power, wielded directly through sermons and confession, performed a strong policing function in society, controlling people's behaviour. It inculcated an uncritical deference to authority, which was subsequently awarded to other institutions such as the gardaí. The early part of the 1960s was a turning point in terms of dedication to religion, a change usually considered to relate to change in the Church on a global level. The Second Vatican Council, a meeting of all bishops of the Church from 1962 to 1965, to discuss matters of doctrine and practice, made significant departures on a theological level. But it was the practical changes, such as allowing Mass to be conducted in the vernacular and removing the requirement to eat fish on Friday, which had the greatest impact for Catholics in Ireland (Inglis 1998). The Church became less dogmatic and more inclusive, allowing for a relaxation in the lives of Catholics.

The arrival of television in 1961 with its topical programmes such as the *Late, Late Show*, an Irish talk show which discussed issues such as sex, contraception and divorce, as well as more liberal American programmes, was a huge instrument in social change and modernisation (Tovey and Share 2000). For the first time certain matters were openly discussed on national television. This growing critical outlook was tempered for a time by the visit of Pope John Paul II to Ireland in 1979. A third of the population turned out to hear him say Mass in Phoenix Park, Dublin (Inglis 1998). This required a substantial policing presence. For a number of the participants that duty was a high point in their career, despite the fact that it involved long shifts, with little to do and limited food provided. The country was united in its religious belief. The tide turned relatively quickly, however, as the movement for the legalisation of contraception grew in the late

1970s, followed by a campaign to decriminalise homosexuality. The 1990s saw bitter and divisive debates on abortion and divorce in which religious arguments were dominant. The 1990s also saw the revelations of clerical sexual abuse in Ireland, which weakened the Church's position (Inglis 1998). An opinion poll conducted in 1995 showed that 42 per cent of people had lost some respect for the Church as a result of these cases (Inglis 1998: 219). Still further, the scale of abuse suffered by children and young people in Church-run reformatories and industrial schools, such as the Magdalene Laundries, has been exposed of late (McAleese 2013). These realities have been exposed in part due to Irish society at last developing a willingness to question authority and develop a more open approach to sexuality, in particular homosexuality (Tovey and Share 2003). This willingness to question can also be connected to Ireland experiencing the effects of globalisation, the EU, an improved economy and the stronger sense of rights associated with secularisation. As Loader and Mulcahy outline, '[t]he effects of improved educational achievement; the coming to the fore of discourses of equality, rights and citizenship (not least around questions of gender, ethnicity, sexuality, disability); and the heightened expectations attached to the "quality of life"' (2001: 19) are all features of a more democratised society.

However, Ireland is now attempting to address the effects of the failure to question authority and to understand not just the abuse but the revictimisation caused through avoidance and silence. In relation to each of the social issues over which Church policy prevailed, the Church was not the sole actor. It was gardaí who prosecuted those who sought to sell or distribute condoms or other contraceptives and those who practised homosexuality. It was gardaí that sought to prevent a 13-year-old-girl who had been impregnated by a rapist from travelling to England when they became aware that her parents intended for her to have an abortion, leading to a hugely controversial Supreme Court decision and referendum on abortion (the X-case). In those incidents the police interfered with matters in the private domain, on the stated belief that it was in the public interest. Religious beliefs also determined that at times gardaí would *not* interfere in private matters. Gardaí, like other police forces, were very slow to respond to domestic abuse. Harris' survey of gardaí found that they classified responding to domestic disputes as service provision rather than law enforcement, and 30 per cent of his respondents felt it was a task that should be performed by another agency; 56 per cent rated it their least liked duty (Harris 1988: 185). Casey (1989) found that victims of domestic violence were dissatisfied with their treatment by gardaí.

Perhaps most disturbing of all is the garda role in relation to the clerical abuse of children. It was gardaí who delivered children, young people and pregnant women to the schools where abuse was systematic. Indeed for many, the gardaí were the gateway to the system to which they were consigned due to poverty or criminal offending. More than most, through this role, gardaí witnessed first-hand the conditions in these schools and did nothing. Such failures to protect the vulnerable are also apparent in relation to clerical abuse in non-residential settings. The Ferns Report (2005) identified 100 allegations against 21 priests in one diocese in a 40-year period. The report concluded that nothing was done despite complaints of sexual abuse of children being made to gardaí in the 1970s and 1980s. No record exists of these early complaints: gardaí did not even document that such complaints had been made: 'This unsatisfactory approach may have been due to … reluctance on the part of members of An Garda Síochána to investigate allegations of wrongdoing by members of the Catholic clergy' (Ferns Inquiry 2005: Executive Summary).

A number of such cases have since come before the courts. In *PC* ([1999] 2 IR 25), when a young girl told her friends in 1988 that she had been abused, one friend told her father, a sergeant. He took no action, despite the seriousness of the allegation. In *NP* ([2005] IEHC 33), a young boy made a complaint to gardaí in 1984. The sergeant involved, now Chief Superintendent, took statements and organised a physical examination of the victim but took no further action. Not only this, but the Chief Superintendent refused to testify, leading Justice Quirke to comment:

> The deafening silence so created gives rise to a conclusion in simple terms. The complaint and the resultant investigation was allowed to lie dormant. Nothing whatsoever was done by or on behalf of the prosecuting authorities to progress it between June 1984 and April 2000.

The result of this inaction was that by the time the victim had the courage to complain again, the court felt that a prosecution could not fairly be taken. Rather than enforcing the law, the garda response in this case made it impossible to prosecute an abuser. This type of revictimisation is alarming and raises questions as to how many individuals may have been deterred from pursuing their case by garda inaction. In *SA* ([2005] IEHC 262), despite a complaint being made to police in 1996, a statement was not taken from the defendant for 16 months.

Most recently, the McAleese Report on the Magdalene Laundries begins to recount the garda role in this abusive system, which continued to receive women until the mid-1990s. As discussed in Chapter 4 gardaí were involved both in directly referring women to the Laundries and in transferring women there from court and prisons, often for minor infractions of the law, homelessness or as a refuge of sorts. A memo written by the Department of Justice in 1971, cited in the McAleese Report, presents the view that referral to a laundry was an alternative to arrest and prosecution. Not only is the involvement of the criminal justice system in this exploitative treatment of women confirmed but this memo also reveals the broad spectrum of female activities (including running away from home or vagrancy) classed as deviant and criminal in the 1970s (2013: 318). The question also arises as to garda knowledge of treatment of women within the Laundries. This is not directly discussed by the report though some comments are relevant. While some gardaí interviewed by the committee expressed the view that the Laundries were a shelter or refuge for these women, one garda is quoted as having seen the laundry room and recognised that it was 'a tough working environment in a room full of steam' (2013: 322).

The failure of an Garda Síochána to defend the rights of those vulnerable persons abused by the Church was an unacceptable derivation from duty. In part, it is an indication of the power of the Church and the unwillingness of gardaí to question or be critical of that institution. As has been stated a number of times in this book, political influences have repeatedly over-ridden objective policing in Ireland and for many decades religion and politics were inseparable. It is also a statement as to how the functions of the police were (self) defined and (self) selected. Uncertainty abounded in terms of what fell within the garda remit, with the concepts of public and private shielded and invaded in inconsistent ways. Violent or sexual abuse, whether in the private home or in the Church, was beyond the grasp of the gardaí, yet matters of sexuality, contraception and perceived sexual deviance between consenting adults were public matters, ripe for criminalisation. Never was this more evident than in the investigation into the deaths of two babies in Kerry in 1984. At a time when the decline of the Church in England and Wales detracted from the ability of the police 'to stand as the embodiment of a common moral and political community' (Loader and Mulcahy 2003: 16) garda action was to stand as the definition of Irish morality.

The Kerry babies case

The death of a baby in the south-west of the country in 1984 was to test the status of the gardaí. On 14 April the body of a newborn baby was found on a beach in County Kerry. He had been stabbed several times, prompting the involvement of the murder squad of an Garda Síochána.[4] When Joanne Hayes admitted herself to hospital two weeks later having recently given birth, but with no baby, the doctors alerted the gardaí (Inglis 2003; O'Mahony 2002b). Joanne Hayes and four members of her family were arrested.

The previous year Joanne had had a baby by a local married man and soon became pregnant again (McCafferty 1985). On arrest Joanne told the interview-ing members that the baby had died at birth at home on the farm and she had buried him in a field but they did not follow this up. Within hours she and four members of her family had signed confessions to the effect that Joanne had killed the baby and that members of her family conspired to throw it into the sea in Dingle. Gardaí later searched the field on the farm and discovered the body of a second baby. When blood tests showed these babies had different fathers, the investigating gardaí pursued the theory that Joanna became pregnant in a short space of time by two different men. Medically known as the exceptionally rare process of superfecundation, this implied Joanne gave birth to two babies and was responsible for both deaths (Inglis 2003). Charges of murder against Joanne were sustained on this basis for five months, until the office of the DPP directed that all charges be dropped (O'Mahony 2002b).

When it became publically known that the family had made such detailed, false confessions a tribunal of inquiry was established to be chaired by Justice Lynch. The Lynch Tribunal's investigation into the 'Kerry babies case' began just eight months after the false confession was made by Joanne Hayes and her family.

The Tribunal reported to the government in October 1985. The report cleared gardaí of all allegations of physical abuse and serious wrongdoing. McAleese describes how this report,

> painted a picture of inept and bungled investigative procedures, stubborn re-
> fusal to reassess assumptions even in the face of clear evidence and clear use
> of the practice of bringing people into garda stations without making it clear
> to them that they were there voluntarily and were free to go.
>
> (McAleese 1987: 63).

Even in light of such evidence the Tribunal would not go so far as to condemn the behaviour of gardaí. The report vilified Ms Hayes, the single woman in rural Ireland who became pregnant twice by a married man. Her transgressions contravened the teachings of the Church, they challenged the traditional role of women in Irish society, and they represented a threat to all decent Irish men:

> Women like Joanne Hayes consequently became infamous, exotic, scape-
> goats, because they were a threat not only to the traditional Catholic concep-
> tion of sexuality, women and mothers, but to a patriarchal order centred on
> the sexual oppression of women.
>
> (Inglis 2003: 226)

During the Tribunal hearings the male lawyers and judge questioned Ms Hayes in detail about her menstrual cycle and her sexual encounters with the father of her child. When she broke down on the stand she was required to give evidence while sedated (McCafferty 1985: 104). The failure of the Tribunal to acknowledge the misconduct on the part of gardaí enabled it to hold to its version of the story and thereby deny any wrongdoing. Indeed, the central question of how this family could deliver such similar false confessions was never answered by Justice Lynch. As with the Heavy Gang allegations, an Garda Síochána managed to displace attention from its behaviour to that of the victim, whom it portrayed as blameworthy.

This case was not the only allegation of abuse of police powers to emerge at this time. That same year saw a prosecution for manslaughter of a detective for the death in custody two years previously of Peter Matthews in a garda station. Mr Matthews voluntarily attended the station on suspicion of stealing from an old man. Within three hours of arriving at the station he had died. Both he and his pregnant wife were strip-searched. Mr Matthews had suffered a heart attack earlier that year, of which the gardaí had been advised. A brutal, sustained assault precipitated the heart attack that killed him. Five gardaí are believed to have been involved in the assault. Another was heard to say in the day room, 'I love to hear them roaring'. Two members admitted in court that they deliberately falsified statements in the ensuing investigation (*II*: 19/10/84). Despite the medical evidence that assaults were perpetrated against Mr Matthews while he was in garda custody and the various testimony of witnesses, the imprecise nature of that testimony lead to the manslaughter charges being withdrawn. A jury found the accused garda not guilty of assault (*IT*: 20/10/84). One account stated that this was due to the skilled barristers (*Magill*: 01/11/84), but there may also have been an unwillingness on the part of the jury to convict a garda. Three of the gardaí involved were subsequently dismissed from the force, on the same day that Garda HQ received the internal report into the Kerry babies case (*IT*: 01/12/84). Between 1975 and 1983, 23 persons died in garda custody, a disturbingly high number, which has received limited attention despite the inherent implication of serious wrongdoing.

The Kerry babies case convinced the government of the need for an independent mechanism for investigating complaints, although only for procedural reasons (Walsh 1998). It was not believed that the behaviour of an Garda Síochána was problematic or that a tough stance on accountability was required, more that the existing procedures were inappropriate. The introduction of the Garda Síochána Complaints Board the year after the Tribunal reported was not a condemnation of police behaviour, or a statement of what would not be tolerated. It was simply a new way of doing things that would appear to be more open, more transparent. This is apparent in the debates on the Bill, where the Minister for Justice stressed the need to protect gardaí from vexatious claims as much as the need to assist the public:

> An effective independent complaints procedure would be established to safe-guard both the public and the garda, who are often the subject of false allegations ... Any system that would separate the Commissioner from involvement in the investigation and adjudication of complaints against members of his force would seriously undermine his authority and have adverse effects on the maintenance of discipline and morale.
>
> (DE: 28/01/86)

The new body was tasked not with conducting independent investigations but with reviewing investigations conducted by gardaí and making recommendations on what action the Commissioner should take. Rather than the opposition suggesting that the government was not going far enough, one TD stated:

> Many gardaí feel genuinely hurt that they, and their profession, should be held in such low esteem by the Government that they can no longer be trusted, can no longer be accorded the same rights and respect as all other public servants – not to mention the criminals. At a time when gardaí are under siege from all sides the least they could have hoped for was that their own Minister for Justice would not add to the cacophony of abuse, but would instead do something to boost flagging morale ... How more accountable are they going to have to become before the Government is satisfied?
>
> (DE: 20/03/86)

The political attitude at the time was that to ask for accountability of the gardaí, at whatever level, was to question and undermine an institution which had served successive governments loyally. It is into this context that the Complaints Board was introduced.

The accountability of an Garda Síochána

The Garda Síochána Complaints Board (GSCB) was established under the Garda Síochána (Complaints) Act 1986. The Act laid down the system for dealing with complaints against members of an Garda Síochána and lasted until May 2007. The Act was reactive in nature and did not address the central issues that had been revealed through the various cases (Walsh 1998). There was no objective assessment of the role and importance of an independent complaints procedure in a democratic system of policing. Walsh has described how:

> [c]learly, the government did not approach the issue from the broad perspective of how a complaints procedure might assist in the general task of calling the police to account. On the contrary, it confined itself to the task of producing a procedure which could be used by a citizen to call individual members to account for the manner in which they had exercised their powers or behaved in certain limited situations.
>
> (Walsh 1998: 263)

At the time of the introduction of the GSCB, it had the widespread support of gardaí, although there was some effort to ensure that a member of the GRA be on the board (*Garda Review*, 1984). The Board had a chairman and eight members, all appointed by government, one of whom had to be a high-ranking garda. Some members anticipated its establishment as a positive development:

> The internal system was so strict that when ultimately legislation was being introduced a significant body of gardaí felt that all discipline should be dealt with by that board. It would provide a fairer shake, not necessarily easier.
>
> (G2)

Not only does this indicate the problems with the internal structures and garda frustration but it also shows how out of touch the political rhetoric, evidenced in the opposition statement above, was with the reality of policing in Ireland.

Complaints could be received by the Board or any garda station and had to relate either to an offence under the disciplinary code or a criminal offence. There was a sixth-month time limit and if the member concerned had retired or resigned it was excluded. If an internal inquiry had been established the complaint would not be investigated separately. A member of an Garda Síochána, not below the rank of superintendent, conducted the investigation (s.6), with the board maintaining a supervisory role. If this investigation suggested a serious breach a tribunal was established to determine whether there had been a breach. This tribunal included a senior garda of the rank of chief superintendent in addition to two members of the board. The decision of the tribunal was a majority one and they determined the action to be taken if a breach was established, with possible responses ranging from dismissal to caution (s.9). If the conduct constituted a criminal offence it was referred to the DPP.

If the board felt at any time that it was in the public interest to do so, they could instigate an independent investigation, although the Act stated this should only occur in exceptional circumstances. The reality was that for resource reasons the board was invariably unable to supervise investigations, let alone conduct them independently. In 1989 the board, less than three years old, announced that 'for over a year now the Board has not been in a position to discharge its obligation to supervise investigations' and the inability to do this meant that 'it became no more than a rubbery stamp providing the appearance, but not the reality, of an independent inquiry ... a dangerous charade' (*IT:* 16/12/89). The fact that complaints were investigated by serving gardaí sparked criticism that it was just the police investigating the police. Walsh explains that:

> Initially its performance was hampered by inadequate resources, but it soon became apparent that the Board's problems were more deep-rooted. Public criticism focused primarily on the use of members of the Garda Síochána to carry out the investigations in virtually all cases ... These concerns were fuelled by an incredibly low rate of complainant success and an exceptionally high rate of complaints being found to be inadmissible.
>
> (Walsh 2004: 2)

This system had limited claim to legitimacy, making it even less likely that complaints would come forward. These flaws were not only apparent to the public. Gardaí, too, were defensive and dissatisfied. Interviewees tended to take one of two perspectives. Either they felt that the call for independent investigations was misplaced:

> [P]eople in the press and the media got the wrong end of it. They were on about guards investigating guards. The wrong perception goes out that we will be easy on our own. We were far from easy on people. The vast majority were without any real evidence of anything.
>
> (SI2)

Or they recognised that independent investigation was appropriate but felt the remit of the board was too broad:

> It is totally abused as a system ... Sean Hurley [the chairperson] had no control. The participants would dictate what happened. There were lots of vindictive, vexatious complaints that were just being used as a plea bargaining tool by criminals.
>
> (CSI1)

Over time, gardaí continued to complain about the breadth of the system, with the GSCB annual report being greeted each year by the GRA focusing on the number of vexatious or inadmissible complaints (*Garda Review* 1998: 25). This rather ineffective method of accountability was introduced two years after police powers had been substantially expanded by the Criminal Justice Act 1984. While that legislation included some safeguards for persons in custody, these had a limited effect: even in 2005 electronic recording of interviews was not in effect in all garda stations (DE: 12/10/05). The powers of the gardaí were being expanded with limited safeguards and no independent complaints mechanism.

Chan (1999) maintains that there are 'competing meanings' of accountability when discussing the police: (i) controlling the police and (ii) demanding explanations for behaviour and actions. Brogden *et al.* (1988) refer to this distinction as 'prospective control' versus 'retrospective accounting'. The retrospective element is often the focus of policy discussions on accountability, but importance of control to accountability is explicitly sated by Lustgarten in his seminal work *The Governance of the Police* (1986). For Reiner and Spencer, controlling police actions was 'the fundamental problem' (1993: 170). Even the title of Jefferson and Grimshaw's book, *Controlling the Constable* (1984), indicates the centrality of control. They believe that 'accountability concerns the institutional arrangements designed to ensure the obligations of the police are upheld' (1984: 10). Explanations for behaviour have a limited function in this model, as resort to them means that attempts to control the police have failed.

Complaints procedures, civil actions and democratic accountability can provide 'retrospective accounting – requiring police to offer legally acceptable justifications for their operations after they have been undertaken' (Brogden *et al.* 1988: 152). They do not, however, control police actions and any effective system of accountability needs to combine both controlling and explanatory mechanisms. In Ireland at this point the policy focus was on the explanatory side. Control was hierarchical and political. Comparatively, at this time police in England were controlled through a tripartite system of power, being divided between the Chief Constable, the Home Office and the Police Authority. The Authority ensured that neither the police nor the politicians had too much control. Her Majesty's Inspectorate of Constabulary (HMIC) conducts inspections on individual forces but also engages in reviews of policing themes to establish how particular issues are address. The Irish system could only consider individual complaints and cases, preventing an institutional analysis of the problems of police misconduct.

Since 1978 the Association for Garda Sergeants and Inspectors has called for a police authority and submitted formal proposals to this end in 1981. In the election the following year, Fine Gael and Labour committed to the establishment of an authority, as they did again in 2002, but when they were elected this failed to materialise. Other commentators have agreed, including Brewer *et al.* who maintain that 'it would cut the umbilical cord that currently ties the Garda Síochána to government' (1996: 107). That umbilical cord, which has been evidenced elsewhere in this book, was also prominent in a clear connection between tenure of the Commissioner role and the government of the day. Commissioners Garvey (1975–8), McLoughlin (1978–83) and Wren (1983–7) all left their post within months of a change of government.[5] Policing was politicised, poorly controlled and immune from the identification of institutionalised problems.

There is reason to believe that there were institutionalised problems within an Garda Síochána at this time. Beyond those cases discussed in Chapter 6 concerning convictions in the Special Criminal Court, a number of people have been wrongfully convicted of 'ordinary' crimes in the last two decades. Each case displays gardaí using unacceptable methods to secure a conviction, a lack of oversight of investigative procedures and of controlling accountability mechanisms. A prosecution against Damien Marsh for the murder of an English tourist in 1994 had to be dropped as the confession on which the case relied could not be located and the two investigating gardaí gave contradictory evidence in court (O'Mahony 1996). Vincent Connell's conviction for murder was quashed in April 1995 for oppressive interrogation methods when he had been denied access to a solicitor (People v. O'Connell [1995]). And two years later, Dean Lyons, a homeless heroin addict, made a detailed, seemingly accurate confession to two murders and was held for nine months, despite the fact that another man had also made a confession to these murders (O'Cuiv, DE: 30/05/01). A commission to investigate the case was set up and although it was acknowledged that proper interrogation procedures were not followed, an Garda Síochána escaped serious criticism (Birmingham 2006). The O'Brian Report of 1978 had called for lawyers to be present during interrogations and the 1990 Martin Report on Certain Aspects of Criminal Procedure called for recording of interviews. Both recommendations were largely ignored. It was only after these cases that it became a requirement to record interviews with a person suspected of a serious offence (the Electronic Recording of Interviews Regulations 1997). Even then it was limited to particular offences.[6]

The handling and disclosure of evidence has also been problematic. In 1996 a murder trial collapsed on the sixth day when it became apparent that the gardaí had not disclosed inconsistencies in the statement of a key witness. Justice Barr concluded that:

> Superintendent Brennan and his team have consciously and deliberately resorted to a policy the objective of which, as the officers must well have known and appreciated, was to deprive the accused of his constitutional right to a fair trial in accordance with law. Such conduct by police officers under the direction of a high ranking person is as saddening as it is reprehensible ... The mendacious conduct of Superintendent Brennan and other police officers have grievously undermined the integrity and legality of the criminal process in this case.
>
> (DPP v. Flannery, 25/06/96)

Responding to a question in the Dáil, the Minister for Justice, Mr John O'Donoghue, informed the House that an internal investigation had been conducted and that 'no action was warranted in respect of any of the members of An Garda Síochána involved' (DE: 20/03/02). It is difficult to reconcile the statements of the judge with a finding that no disciplinary action was warranted. Paul Ward, a member of a leading Dublin criminal gang, was convicted in the Special Criminal Court for the murder of Veronica Guerin on the basis of super-grass testimony. In that case, the court rejected a confession due to oppressive garda interrogation methods (DPP v. Ward, 27/11/98). After the Court of Criminal Appeal overturned the conviction the Garda Commissioner stated:

> These things happen. The judges and the courts make their decision and we respect those decisions and go on and continue our policing operations ... At the end of the day we do our best in gathering the evidence. It's put before the courts and they make the decision and we respect their decision and carry on with our business after that.
>
> *(IE:* 23/02/02)

The Commissioner was able to suggest that an Garda Síochána had done its best, when this was clearly not the case. A garda was later convicted of leaking information to the criminal gang involved in Guerin's death (*II:* 04/04/98).

The conviction of Frank Shortt, a Donegal publican, was declared a miscar-riage of justice after the court found that gardaí had fabricated the evidence. The gardaí involved were found to have perjured themselves at his trial. The Supreme Court awarded him €4.5 million in damages (Shortt v. Commissioner of an Garda Síochána and Ors [2007] IESC 9). Describing this case as 'a stain of the darkest dye on the otherwise generally fine tradition of the institution of An Garda Síochána', Chief Justice Murray stressed that:

> this affair cannot be bracketed as a couple of bad apples in the proverbial barrel. The misconduct penetrated the system of law enforcement too deeply and persisted over too long a period to be discounted in such a fashion ... The cavalier manner in which those two members set about concocting evidence and subsequently persisted in trying to cover up their misdeeds, not entirely out of sight of other Garda members, displayed a worrying confi-dence on their part that they could get away with it.

It was determined by the court that 'the conduct of the Garda officers involved set at nought core constitutional rights of the plaintiff to due process and a fair trial'.

These cases establish that the courts have identified significant problems with both garda interrogation and the gathering and use of evidence. Oversight by superiors was insufficient and these issues could not simply be dismissed as a few bad apples. Previous chapters have suggested that violence has been an embed-ded policing tactic and reports from international bodies have continually high-lighted the problem. Amnesty International made such a report in 1984. The European Committee for the Prevention of Torture found significant ill-treatment in its visits in 1993 and 1998. During the 1993 visit, eight stations were visited and allegations of ill-treatment were repeatedly made. One Cork station delayed the Committee in gaining access to places of detention. One detainee was

examined by ECPT doctors and had marks and injuries consistent with the allegations made while the custody record confirmed that he was uninjured at the time
of arrest. During a visit to one station the following 'non-standard issue weapons'
were found in drawers:

> various home-made wooden batons (quite unlike ordinary police truncheons)
> and a variety of real and replica guns (e.g. two sawn-off shotguns, a pipe
> pistol, a bolt gun, a replica of a Beretta 9mm pistol) several hunting knives,
> and a short, leather-covered metal cosh.
>
> (ECPT 1995: 15)

It was concluded that persons in custody in Dublin 'run a not inconsiderable risk
of being physically ill-treated'. Following a query from the Committee, the
government stated in its response that between 1991 and 1993 that 88 civil
actions had been initiated against the force, 42 of which centred on allegations
of assault. It is difficult to find data on civil actions taken against the gardaí for
much of this time, but the following amounts of payments in damages were
stated in the Dáil (DE: 27/11/02): 1997: £864,313.74; 1998: £1,220,198.70 and
1999: £1,517,844.93.[7] A review of *The Irish Times* through these decades also
finds repeated reports of garda use of baton charges, whether against students
(*IT*: 01/02/75), attendees of a pop concert (23/04/75), an Irish Civil Rights
Association protest (29/08/77), following a car chase (25/03/80), following a
GAA match in Cork (23/07/84), a crowd of youths in Dublin (01/07/85), against
anti-drug protestors (01/04/87) or after a World Cup football match (27/06/90).
On Halloween night 1995, riots erupted in Gallanstown, Dublin, believed to
have been orchestrated by drug dealers. Hundreds of youths clashed and a garda
baton charge was ordered. Even if the riot was organised by drug dealers the end
result was to alienate the excluded young people further from gardaí (Saris and
Bartley 1999).

During the 1998 ECPT visit particular reference was made to allegations of
ill-treatment in Henry Street garda station in Limerick in the aftermath of the
death of Garda Gerry McCabe, who had worked in that station. Medical records
were consistent with those allegations. Further allegations were made by detainees when the ECPT visited stations. In both reports the Committee recommended
that a lawyer be present during interrogation and that the system for examining
complaints against the police should be reviewed.

The above incidents, when taken together, provide evidence of serious misconduct within an Garda Síochána: use of oppressive questioning techniques,
perjury, failure to disclose evidence, mistreatment of vulnerable witnesses,
assault, excessive use of force, failure to care for detainees and harassment. These
are just the high-profile cases which make the headlines. While there are a variety
of factors that contribute to people's trust and confidence in the police, dependent
on personal experience, expectations and knowledge, it is not unreasonable to
expect that such events would at least generate a more questioning perspective
towards the police. In the English context, it has been argued that there has been

a 'desacrilization' of the police (Reiner 1992). Loader and Mulcahy through their study have curtailed this somewhat, suggesting that:

> English policing has not in the latter half of the twentieth century travelled speedily along a one-way path toward desacrilization but has, rather, come to be encircled by an uneasy, conflicting mix of profane and sacred dispositions.
> (Loader and Mulcahy 2003: 303)

In the twentieth century there was limited analysis of attitudes towards the police in Ireland. The first traceable study of public attitudes towards the gardaí was conducted between 1972 and 1973 by MacGréil, a priest and lecturer in sociology (*Garda Review*, 1976); 2311 people over the age of 21 were surveyed on how close individuals were willing to get to members of the gardaí.

The result was a resounding expression of trust in the Irish police with the vast majority willing to accept gardaí as members of their family. There was no statistically significant difference for sex, marital status, education or occupation of respondents, with just minor fluctuations for older or Protestant participants. MacGréil concluded that there was 'amazing consistency' across all categories. These results are not surprising given that crime was low, the Troubles had begun, Richard Fallon had been killed, and the allegations of the Heavy Gang had not yet been made. On the other hand, as we saw in previous chapters, in some sections of the community, particularly in inner-city Dublin, relations between the community and the gardaí were poor. There was however no indication of this in these statistics. A study the following decade, however, noted a difference between communities. While the overall finding was that 86 per cent had either a great deal or quite a lot of confidence in the gardaí (Fogarty *et al.* 1984) this dropped dramatically for unemployed persons, just 67 per cent of whom expressed confidence.

Bohan and Yorke's study (1987), conducted in the wake of many allegations, the spiralling crime rate and the conflict over the drugs epidemic in Dublin, is one of the most revealing in terms of Irish conceptualisations of policing. Nearly two-thirds of respondents felt 'the police tended to abuse suspects, either physically or mentally', suggesting that allegations penetrated on some level. Furthermore, 40 per cent felt the police 'may cover up facts in court'. This would seem to

Table 7.2 Acceptance of gardaí (MacGreil 1976).

Extent of acceptance of gardaí	Percentage
Welcome into family	85.5%
Have as a friend	8.1%
Have as a neighbour	4.0%
Have as a co-worker	0.6%
Welcome as a citizen	1.4%
Have as a visitor	0.2%
Debar or deport	0.3%

indicate low levels of confidence in an Garda Síochána, but the same study found that two-thirds were either quite satisfied or very satisfied with the force, although this fell to just over half for working-class people. While people accepted that gardaí abused their powers, this did not translate into a lack of confidence. It may be that the public believed that the abuse was directed towards suspects of crime relating to the Troubles and so was justified in the circumstances. It may be that in the face of growing crime, people felt the police needed to be supported. In this vein, the majority of people believed the law favoured the criminal and that gardaí did not get enough recognition for risking their lives.

There is just one final study from this period. In the mid-1990s Hardiman and Whelan (1994) documented public confidence in an Garda Síochána to be at 85 per cent, compared to a European average of 65 per cent. They did at the same time find that unemployed people were 'substantially less likely to have confidence in the police' (1994: 129).

These various studies indicate that despite acknowledgment that police abused their powers, the public, generally speaking, had unusually high levels of confidence in the gardaí. A number of explanations can be suggested. Firstly, those directly affected by garda misconduct, in as much as is known about such people by way of the media, can be dismissed as connected with the IRA or other paramilitary groups, women who deviate from acceptable social conduct, those suffering from mental ill-health or vulnerable in some other way such as their age. As far as the general public is concerned 'ordinary' or innocent people are not being affected by the mistreatment or misconduct of gardaí. As long as personal experience is positive the experience of those 'others' can be dismissed in some way. Alternatively, it may be that people dismiss these incidents as being the fault of a small number of bad apples, and not indicative of a larger, institutionalised problem. The reality is that this ignores the extent of the allegations and the fact that individuals can only abuse their powers in this way through failings in control and supervision. A final possible explanation is that political rhetoric on the bravery and dedication of the force inculcated a social unwillingness to criticise the force, founded in no small way on the post-colonial nature of the state.

Conclusion: enter Morris

When considered in combination with Chapter 5, the closing decades of the twentieth century were in some ways exceptionally challenging. The difficulties of the Troubles, combined with a dramatic increase in crime and the burgeoning threat of organised crime, meant that what it meant to be a garda was entirely different to what it had been in the 1960s. Gone was the easy way of life where time was spent getting to know the community. Now the job was crime-orientated and attracted a sufficient degree of threat to merit concern. Technology and training were slow to keep up and appear to have been introduced to gardaí in a manner that was perceived as threatening. Conroy had brought a fixation with money, which pay deals failed to satisfy. Indeed, while many concerns with conditions appear to have been resolved post-Conroy, pay continued as a concern leading to a split within the main representative body. The Blue Flu of 1998 not only displayed the depths of low morale but damaged relations with the community and within the organisation. It is disappointing for all concerned that this happened during Ireland's most successful economic period.

The growth of crime and increasing use of cars left gardaí without the local knowledge that had been a cornerstone of Irish policing. This knowledge had previously been assumed, stemming from their authoritative position in the community. The lack of familiarity with communities left gardaí exposed when communities protested, as in Dublin during the heroin epidemic.

The Church in this period experienced a substantial fall in public attachment, partially linked to child sex abuse scandals. Whelan suggests that the decline of the Catholic Church can be linked to the decline in acceptance of that decolonising and post-colonial vision of Ireland:

> This artificially constructed identity – Roman Catholic, not Protestant, rural not urban, Celtic not Anglo-Saxon, agrarian not industrial, religious not secular – was imposed in the name of tradition … However, like its colonial predecessor, it too was a lightly incised inscription which dissolved rapidly through the internationalization of capital, the impact of global communications, rapid social transformations, the creation of an extensive underclass and shifting gender roles. Over time, this hollow edifice was crumbling for the knocker's ball which hit it full frontal in the 1970s … The shallow construction of inert Irishness offered little resistance.
>
> (Whelan 2003: 96)

This national image, constructed in the 1880s through the nationalist movement, could not withstand the pressures of late modernity and the collapse of the authority of institutions like the Church can be linked to this. The gardaí escaped the demolition ball for one reason: the Northern Irish conflict. Just as other institutions were falling apart, gardaí were being asked to defend the nation, all that had been built up over the previous 50 years. Ireland had at that point established itself as a state reflected in its membership of the EU. The gardaí, that body of individuals that had worked hard to be 'Irish in thought and action', were defending the state from subversives, and they were supported by the public in that endeavour. In the very moment when the nationalist image fell apart in general, the gardaí were reasserting their nationalism, risking and losing their lives for the Irish state, thereby retaining the confidence and authority that had been based on such imagery.

This view was not entirely justified. There was plentiful evidence of unacceptable conduct and breaches of power and authority by an Garda Síochána. There was use of oppressive questioning techniques, lying in court, failure to disclose evidence, mistreatment of vulnerable witnesses, assault, excessive use of force, failure to care for detainees and harassment. This list indicates serious disregard for police practice, disciplinary codes and the rights of members of the public.

In Chapter 6 it was argued that the use of force had become institutionalised. It was a constant feature in this period and led to substantial civil action payments, the only operable form of accountability. However the gardaí were not called to account. While the government responded to the Kerry babies case by introducing the GSCB, this was not an effective complaints mechanism. It was not independent and it was not sufficiently resourced. Further, it was shown above that members of the opposition were critical of the government for introducing this mechanism in the first place, suggesting it placed unfair demands on the police and indicated a lack of trust. Nor did any of this evidence impact on public confidence in the force. Various surveys continued to find that a substantial majority of the public expressed confidence, at a higher rate than other countries in Europe. It was in this context that the events that would be subject of the Morris Tribunal came to light.

Notes

1 That said, comparative to other Western states the Irish crime rate is low. The crime rate per capita is a quarter of that for England and Wales (www.crimestatistics.org.uk). Further, this solely represents officially recorded crime. The Central Statistics Office National Household Survey 1998 suggested that for many offences garda figures recorded less than half of all offences.

2 Indeed the two gardaí who claimed that a confession had been made were involved in securing a false confession from Frank McBrearty, examined in the Morris Tribunal and considered in Chapter 8.

3 Tovey and Share (2000) relate this upsurge in religious belief to the Famine, providing the following reasons: decline of the landless class where the folk religion prevailed, nationalist movement which cemented Ireland and Catholicism, urbanisation leading to rationalisation of Irish society, rapid social change which encouraged religious belief, increased civilisation of Europe, 'gentling' of Irish society and the growth of moral discipline, centralisation of churches made them more efficient, a means of disciplining and controlling the working population.

4 The division from which the Heavy Gang was said to have been drawn.

5 For a full list of Commissioners of an Garda Síochána see Appendix 5.

6 Namely, offences under s.4 of the Criminal Justice Act 1984, s.30 of the Offences Against the State Act 1939, and s.2 of the Criminal Justice (Drug Trafficking) Act 1996.

7 For a table of payments in civil actions against an Garda Síochána from 1997 to 2007 see Appendix 6.

8   The twenty-first century
Scandal, austerity, reform and managerialism

As the twenty-first century began Ireland was buoyant from the Celtic Tiger. This meant significant investment in policing. The Garda Training College became a third-level institution and student garda could now proceed to secure a degree in police science. A research unit was established in the College, which began to produce reports on matters such as public confidence in the garda. A new radio communications system was implemented in addition to PULSE, the new computer network discussed in Chapter 7. Other enhancements included Automatic Number Plate Recognition, automated fingerprint systems, a ballistics identification systems and the Garda National Immigration Bureau information systems. The government committed to increasing garda numbers to 14,000 for the first time. On the other hand, while crime rates had fallen in the late 1990s to 73,000 in 2000 they had since risen, reaching 106,000 in 2002. The daily prison population increased by one-third. Drugs took hold far beyond Dublin, stretching into rural areas. Organised crime, or 'gangland' crime, became problematic with related feuds and killings in Dublin and Limerick in particular.

The signing of the Good Friday Agreement in 1998, two years after the death of Gerry McCabe, brought a significant reduction in the commitments required in policing the border. The IRA and other republican groups became less active although they continued to be a focus of policing. The Agreement itself required Ireland to commit to enhance human rights provisions in policing and to create a more independent method of handling complaints against the police.

So as Ireland faced the twenty-first century policing was facing an unusual position: the country looked set for peace and prosperity, the force had evaded crisis on numerous occasions, public and political confidence was high and while gardaí bemoaned their pay and most likely resented the new managerialism and reform prospects, accountability was limited. Yet in October 1996 the death of a man on a roadside in Donegal was to lead to an investigation that would bring scandal and crisis on an unprecedented scale. Just as the force began to adjust to the reality of criticism and accountability, the Irish economy collapsed. The recession would have stark implications for the gardaí. This chapter will examine the changes that the twenty-first century brought, looking first at the work of the Morris Tribunal, then at the efforts to embed human rights, the reforms implemented in the wake of the Tribunal and the impact of austerity.

Barron's death and political attention

Mr Richard Barron was found injured on a roadside outside the town of Raphoe, County Donegal on 14 October 1996 and died shortly after arriving at hospital. As would be detailed in the findings of a tribunal, gardaí failed to attend the scene promptly, failed to preserve or examine the scene and failed to request an autopsy by the state pathologist among other things. The police soon decided that Mr Barron had been murdered, without any supporting evidence. The suspects and their families were detained in December, and one of the suspected men, Mr Frank McBrearty Jr, made a false confession to murder. An autopsy in 2001 would confirm that he was killed by hit-and-run, not murdered.

Concerns as to this investigation emerged internally within months and were expressed by Garda Headquarters to the Minister for Justice, Nora Owen, in February 1997.[1] Early in 1999 an internal investigation was established under Assistant Commissioner Carty. While investigating the allegations relating to Mr Barron, the estranged wife of a garda came forward and told the investigation that her husband had stored explosive materials on their property. Within months the media knew that Carty was also investigating allegations that gardaí had planted hoax bombs (*IT*: 16/04/99). In spite of these investigations gardaí continued to pursue 160 summonses against the McBreartys for breaches of liquor licences. Media and political attention grew (*IT*: 20/11/99). By the middle of 2000, when half a dozen civil actions were pending before the courts, Deputy Howlin of the Labour Party presented to the Dáil prima facie evidence of activities including the framing of individuals for murder, the harassment of the McBrearty family, the withdrawal of summons against them, and details of arms and explosives which had been hidden by gardaí (DE: 21/06/00). The media were speculating as to 'the possible existence of wrongful convictions or miscarriages of justice in Donegal, assaults and intimidation of civilians by officers and the use of Garda informers who allegedly made false allegations' (*IT*: 22/06/00). Concerns spread beyond Donegal to places where the members at the centre of allegations had previously been stationed. In Limerick a murder trial was adjourned until the completion of the McBrearty investigations as some of the same gardaí were involved (*IT*: 12/07/00).

The Garda Commissioner received the Carty Report at the end of July 2000 and announced five transfers (*IT*: 27/07/00). Calls for the publication of the report and the establishment of a tribunal were ignored. The accountability mechanisms were being stretched to their limits: in October 2000 the Minister confirmed that six civil actions had been initiated, the DPP was considering criminal proceedings, the Commissioner was considering disciplinary action, two further internal investigations were proceeding and the Garda Síochána Complaints Board was dealing with complaints. No sanctions had been imposed on any members. In November 2000 the conviction of a publican in Donegal was overturned by the Court of Criminal Appeal. Frank Shortt had been convicted after some of the same gardaí raided his premises and found controlled drugs. The Minister maintained the line that a tribunal could not be established due to the conflict with ongoing criminal and civil proceedings.

In the autumn of 2001 a state autopsy was finally performed on Mr Barron showing conclusively that his death had been caused by a hit-and-run accident. Still the government stalled, opting to have all the papers reviewed by a barrister to determine what course of action to take: this was the first action proposed by government on the matter. Deputy Shatter replied, 'Another investigation of papers behind closed doors will be wholly inadequate in addressing the real concerns about policing, which is a fundamental branch of the administration of the State' (DE: 13/11/01). The editorial in *The Irish Times* the following day described the move as 'a limp response, to a most serious situation. It has the hall-marks of political window-dressing, aimed at creating the impression of action while buying time before a general election … This is a smokescreen' (*IT*: 14/11/01). A private member's bill proposing a tribunal was defeated by just one vote (73 to 72), one of the tightest votes in the history of the Dáil and the closest faced by that government.

The media seized the issue. *Prime Time*, a leading investigative current affairs programme, had its first in-depth consideration of the allegations. The *Sunday Tribune* described the events as 'Sinister, Ruthless, Malicious' and called for 'a Garda force we can believe in' (25/11/01). *The Sunday Business Post* alleged that garda corruption was 'a national blight' (02/12/01). Vincent Browne of *The Irish Times* dedicated his weekly column to quoting the allegations made by Deputy Higgins in the Dáil that week (05/12/01). That leading Irish broadsheets, traditionally supportive of the force, were using such critical language in the reports is indicative of the seriousness of the situation.

The review by a barrister took just six weeks and reported in January 2002 that the only viable action was to establish a tribunal. In February, the government announced the establishment of the tribunal, chaired by Justice Morris, formerly of the High Court. Legislation was introduced to prevent a clash between the civil and criminal proceedings, giving powers to exclude the public from proceedings if it might prejudice criminal proceedings (the Tribunals of Inquiry (Evidence) (Amendment) Act 2002). The terms of reference of the tribunal were to investigate a number of very specific allegations arising from the Donegal division but did not include the case of Frank Shortt and excluded the Department of Justice from the remit of the tribunal. It was the first time in Ireland that a tribunal was not tasked with examining the work of the parent department.

From mid-2000 a tribunal appears to have been necessary and yet the government delayed for another 18 months. Not only did that delay compound the experience of all of those alleging victimisation at the hands of gardaí and exacerbate the stress of any gardaí concerned, but it detracts from confidence in the justice system for the public as a whole. The government clearly hoped to avoid this tribunal, perhaps for financial reasons, but possibly also due to a desire not to aggravate gardaí. Establishing the tribunal flies in the face of the rhetoric of support and gratitude, which dominated political discourse on policing.

The Morris Tribunal

Justice Frederick Morris opened the tribunal in July 2002 and in the next six years sat for 686 days of hearings. Between June 2004 and October 2008, eight reports

were published totalling over 4000 pages. The findings of the tribunal are exceptionally critical of the gardaí, in itself unusual. They document corruption, abuse
of power and negligence from management, evidencing a disregard for procedure
at every turn and a belief that this could be done with impunity (Conway 2010).

Examining allegations that gardaí were involved in the planting of explosives
finds in Donegal Justice Morris held that two members, Garda McMahon and
Inspector Lennon, pretended that a local woman Adrienne McGlinchey was an
IRA informer. To ensure her credibility as an informer Garda McMahon supplied
her with bullets, tripods, rockets, balaclavas, angle grinders and so on. The tribunal connected her to six discoveries on both sides of the border between 1993 and
1994, all recorded as IRA bomb and weapon finds. The men involved were highly
praised for each of the finds, which were not properly investigated or reported to
headquarters. Numerous other members were found to be at fault in this regard.
Senior members should have uncovered the charade. When a number of junior
members attempted to express concern about the supposed informer they were
ignored. When asked why he failed to speak out, one garda stated 'you don't hang
your own' (I/13.124). McMahon and Lennon presented 'a tissue of lies' in
evidence to the tribunal.

> The Tribunal has reluctantly been forced to come to the conclusion that there
> was corruption among a small number of individuals within the Donegal di-
> vision but it has also been compelled to find that this situation could not have
> flourished and gone unchecked had the leadership of the Donegal division not
> behaved negligently and slothfully.
>
> (I/1.40)

The second report focused on the investigation into the death of Mr Barron.
A central problem with the investigation was that gardaí did not attend the scene
before Mr Barron was removed by the ambulance. Justice Morris found that the
on-duty garda had left the station to consume alcohol in a public house with
another garda, in breach of disciplinary regulations. The gardaí in the next closest
town refused to respond until they had finished meal-break. By the time they
arrived at the scene Mr Barron had been removed by the ambulance. No forensic
examination of the scene was conducted and the only notebook in which a
description had been made could not be located for the tribunal. The state pathologist was not requested to conduct an autopsy.

After rumours of murder circulated at the deceased's wake, gardaí coerced an
informant to provide a statement, which they then doctored, which stated that two
men were seen leaving the scene. Hoax phone calls, made from the home of a
garda, attempted to lure one man into admitting involvement. Within seven
weeks three men were arrested on suspicion of murder. The tribunal found that
the immediate response in the investigation was a 'catalogue of errors' and 'is
indicative of the general undermining of morale within an Garda Síochána'
(II/3.615). The response of superiors was 'shockingly inadequate and dilatory'.
Where disciplinary action should have been taken, 'the matter was swept under

the carpet'. Appropriate investigative avenues were not pursued as tunnel vision took over.

In total, 13 individuals were arrested during this investigation, many of the arrests being unlawful. In a separate report Justice Morris stressed the potential 'catastrophic injustice' of wrongful arrest and abuse in custody,

> That unhealthy focus or tunnel vision in the course of the Barron investiga-
> tion led to manufactured evidence, wrongful arrests and completely improper
> behaviour by Gardaí towards prisoners in their custody. It cheapened the pre-
> sumption of innocence and undermined the truthful resolution of a very tragic
> case. It dominated the lives and struck at the reputation of two families … it
> did serious damage to the reputation of An Garda Síochána and its integrity
> and professionalism. It contributed towards social division in the town of
> Raphoe.
>
> (VI/1.89)

Consistently throughout interviews of all these detentions gardaí verbally abused detainees, showed them autopsy photos of Mr Barron, failed to take proper notes and disregarded legislative safeguards. So distressing was one woman's experi-ence that she was hospitalised within weeks for mental illness. On another occa-sion gardaí listened in on a detainee's phone call with his solicitor. Frank McBrearty eventually 'crumbled' and signed a false confession. During a further interview Mr McBreaty Jr became highly distressed, banged his head against a wall and lay down on the ground. Instead of being aided, he was called names while the incident was videotaped. His father became ill during a search and was hospitalised for a week. Despite medical advice that he was not fit for interview, he was arrested and interrogated on release from hospital. Within 24 hours he was readmitted to hospital.

The tribunal found that Sergeant John White and an informer conspired to produce evidence that would lead to prosecution of the McBreartys for breaches of liquor licences. When it came to the investigation and prosecution of these offences Justice Morris said that the behaviour of gardaí involved 'was scandal-ous and calculated to undermine the integrity and fairness of the trial at which it was given. It was disgraceful conduct. I am shocked' (III/2.110). False docu-ments were then provided by gardaí to increase the informant's expenses claims. Justice Morris found that these actions constituted harassment of the McBreartys.

In an unrelated event Sergeant White was found to have planted a crude bomb to a telecommunications mast, which was at the centre of protests, for the purpose of enabling arrests under the Offences Against the State Act. A separate module determined that Sergeant White planted a gun at a travellers' encampment, which he then found during a search for which the warrant procedure had been circum-vented. No file was created about the possession of a gun and the individuals were arrested for the purpose of investigating another offence. Others later corruptly attempted to shift the blame for this onto a deceased member. 'Proper discipline has been lost from An Garda Síochána', was Justice Morris' conclusion (V/6.05).

Justice Morris also determined that the GSCB was systemically incapable of handling the 61 complaints received concerning the above events. Justice Morris found that the investigating garda met with the 'Blue Wall of Garda denial ... [and] was being fed a particular line by many of the Gardaí' (VII/12.54–6). The investigating garda admitted that at times he simply did not believe that gardaí would have done what was alleged.

It would be easy to review these findings and determine that there were a number of unsuitable members who did a number of appalling acts. Certainly there were a number of rotten apples operating in the Donegal division, however, Justice Morris stresses at length that this was just as much about negligent management and supervision. Poor promotions and bullying played a significant role.

> The sorry sequence of events ... is an appalling reflection on the standards of integrity, efficiency, management, discipline and trust between the various members and ranks of the Garda Síochána ... Gardaí looked to protect their own interests. The truth was to be buried. The public interest was of no concern.
>
> (I/3.179)

The behaviour detailed by Justice Morris breached most aspects of the disciplinary code of conduct: discreditable conduct; misconduct towards a member; disobedience of orders; falsehood or prevarication; neglect of duty; breach of confidence; corrupt or improper practice; abuse of authority; misuse of garda property; drinking on duty without good or sufficient cause; criminal conduct; failure to cooperate with disciplinary investigations; and accessory to a breach of discipline. This was not a case of one or two acts of misconduct; it was systemic and compounded. Furthermore, Justice Morris saw no reason why it happened in Donegal and not anywhere else:

> Of the Gardaí serving in Donegal it cannot be said that they are unrepresentative or an aberration from the generality. All of them were trained as Gardaí and served under a uniform structure of administration and discipline that is standardised.
>
> (V/6.02)

That said, proximity to the border certainly played a role in how this lack of discipline manifested itself in Donegal. Punch warns of 'danger zones' in policing which are by their very nature vulnerable to corruption (2000: 319). He includes drugs, vice, undercover work, informant-handling and licensing, a list which overlaps with much of what occurred in Donegal. This, combined with the work of Chapter 5 which highlighted that the political context of this work could give the gardaí something of a carte blanche, explains how the border context could be abused in this way.

Particularly striking throughout the reports of the tribunal is the predominance of a blue wall of silence whereby members lied to internal inquiries and the tribunal in an effort to protect themselves and each other. Undoubtedly, a member of the police who becomes aware of corrupt or unlawful activities is in a difficult position. To come forward almost certainly guarantees alienation and ostracisation, and their position may become untenable (Moran 2005: 66; Westmarland 2001: 523). Not coming forward will most likely mean the continuance of the behaviour (Knapp 1973). Both options are problematic for the officer, for as Kleinig describes: 'It brings into conflict two strong commitments: on the one hand, the professional (and personal) commitment to integrity; and on the other hand, the institutional or fraternal commitment to loyalty. Both of these may be felt as moral requirements' (cited in Newburn 1999: 613). But there are two aspects that make this particularly worrying. The first is that even when the tribunal was sitting in public, members continued to lie. The second is the role of the GRA in protecting those who refused to tell the truth: Justice Morris was forced to find that 'members of the Garda Representative Association set out to destroy an investigation ordered by the Garda Commissioner' (I/12.110).

These issues of management, internal discipline and the wall of silence indicate not just procedural problems, which abounded, but a more fundamental concern of culture, which can be so difficult to combat (Chan 1996). Most disconcertingly there is limited evidence in the aftermath that the garda institution wished to change. The Commissioner issued statements following the publication of each of the reports as did the representative bodies. He initially focused on very particular findings as matters of concern, rather than the broader picture revealed by reports. In relation to later reports he rejected some of the findings and stated that immense change had occurred within the organisation.

> While I would accept from reading the reports that some people were clearly in breach of discipline I also say that we have over 12,500 sworn officers around the country and it is not unusual in an organisation of that size that there are some people who do not comply with the discipline regulations and who are sometimes in breach of the criminal code. I am not saying it was completely confined to Donegal. We have experienced it in different parts of the country, but I want to emphasise that it is not a major problem. It is not a major problem throughout the country.
>
> (*Garda Review*, September 2006)

After the report on the mistreatment of detainees the Commissioner apologised to victims of garda misconduct, though stressed that it was only a small number of men who abused their powers. The GRA, on the other hand, expressed serious concerns at the treatment of Sergeant White: 'no citizen of the country would have their rights tramped on in this fashion' and reiterated that White had not been found guilty in the criminal trial (*Daily Mail*, 18/08/06). The GRA felt that rank-and-file gardaí were being scapegoated when failures lay with senior management, and rejected the findings accordingly. There was further talk of how these events were now ten years old yet the force was being tarnished by them.

For all of this, however, the findings of the tribunal do not appear to have adversely affected stated public confidence in the institution. In 2002 the gardaí began conducting and commissioning surveys of public attitudes. These were conducted and published every year for seven years. While the number of people stating that they are very satisfied with the force has dropped slightly, in each year more than 80 per cent expressed satisfaction with the service. The number of persons stating that they are very dissatisfied has remained consistently low. Even if the Morris Reports led to a slight reduction, stated confidence remains very high.

The sampling frame for this study is the electoral register and so persons under the age of 18, or who have not registered, are not included – people who may have a more negative view of gardaí. Before analysing these figures a number of methodological caveats must be highlighted. Additionally, the electoral register is not updated very frequently, raising further questions as to its robustness (Bryman 2004). In the final two years there were some methodological improvements to the survey, with a change from telephone interviews to face to face, and with an enlarged sample size of 10,000 (Kennedy and Browne 2006), but there are still concerns as to how representative the survey is, with the current sampling frame.

What these figures indicate, if they are broadly accepted, is that scandals and concerns do not impact on the public's confidence in the force. As one interview showed, following immediately from a discussion of the Morris Tribunal, which centred on events in Donegal:

> The force is 80 years old and there have been 5 or 6 issues that have arisen that the public were taken aback at. Last year a study was done on public confidence. Which county was placed second in the country? Cork and Mayo had about 85/86 per cent confidence. Donegal was in second position.
>
> (CSI1)

These levels of confidence may be for a number of reasons. Firstly, the media coverage of the tribunal presented the events as so extreme and so unusual that it would be possible to dismiss them as the action of rotten apples, rather than symptomatic of a wider, institutionalised problem (Conway 2010). The general

Table 8.1 Public satisfaction with an Garda Síochána, 2002–08 (Garda Public Attitude Surveys, 2002–08).

	Very satisfied	Satisfied	Dissatisfied	Very dissatisfied
2002	17	69	11	2
2003	17	64	15	4
2004	15	69	11	4
2005	16	67	14	3
2006	13	67	16	4
2007	14	67	16	3
2008	11	70	14	5

public can maintain the view that in the norm police treat people fairly according to what Tyler and Sunshine (2003) call the procedural justice model of confidence. However, in Chapter 5 we saw that even in the 1980s people recognised that the police abused their powers, there are an average of over 2000 complaints annually to GSOC and from 2002 to 2008 over €37 million was paid in compensation from civil actions against the gardaí. So it is difficult to suggest that this perspective is operating in Ireland. During this period the Garda Síochána Complaints Board received an average of 1000 complaints a year, over half of which related to either unlawful arrest or assault. The European Committee for the Prevention of Torture made further visits in 2002 and 2006. The latter report expressed concern at continuing allegations of ill-treatment. They encountered four particular cases where their doctors verified existing injuries were consistent with the ill-treatment alleged, with injuries including fractures and thrombophlebitis (ECPT 2007: 13). The Committee also expressed serious concern at allegations that judges tended to dismiss, or deem irrelevant, claims of ill-treatment. There was, therefore, evidence that could counter any belief that garda treated people fairly. While some of this may have been under-reported and therefore not penetrated public consciousness, the Morris Tribunal received substantial coverage. I have, however, argued elsewhere (Conway 2010) that the media coverage enabled an acceptance of the bad apples thesis.

Secondly, it may be that while people have knowledge that some people are treated badly by the gardaí they do not feel that this will happen to them personally. An instrumental approach to confidence is adopted (Sunshine and Tyler 2003): for many people in Ireland having their passport form signed is their main contact with the police, and even for victims of crime the gardaí maintain a detection rate of over 40 per cent (Ionann 2004: 11). This may override knowledge of abuses or corruption. However, for this instrumental approach to explain expressed levels of confidence it would require that less than 20 per cent of the population have negative interactions with the police. A third perspective is the expressive model outlined by Jackson and Bradford (2009). In this perspective public satisfaction is a barometer of sentiment around social solidarity. It's not about fear of crime, but concern as to the perceived erosion of community morality. This approach relies on consensus views on morality and solidarity. Ilan (2007) analysed interactions between the gardaí and inner-city young people and found that this model did not explain the nature of dissatisfaction with the police.

It is submitted that there may be a further factor at play, which the dominant Anglo-American literature has not addressed. It is possible that post-colonialism and the political control of policing in Ireland have shaped discourses and attitudes towards the police. The argument has been made in previous chapters that transition and lingering attitudes led to wholesale support for the gardaí to the point that criticising the institution was perceived as an attack on those defending independent Ireland. This became a dominant narrative in the 1930s and was revived in the 1970s and 1980s by the impact of the Troubles. It is suggested that this may still play a factor, at least to the extent that some people express satisfaction with the institution as a whole, irrespective of any procedural or instrumental reasons for thinking otherwise. In this way there may be a conflation of concepts between confidence in and aspirational support for the police, and not even the findings of the Morris Tribunal can disrupt this. The discourse of confidence in the police is predisposed to accept a rotten apples thesis. We will now consider how this limited the scale of reforms implemented in the wake of Morris, though first we will briefly turn attention to the burgeoning human rights environment of policing.

The human rights era

At the same time that the Morris Reports were being published, and reform being contemplated, an audit of human rights in the force was published. The centrality of human rights to policing has received increasing attention since the mid-1990s (Neyroud and Beckley 2001; Crawshaw and Holstrom 2006). In 1997 the Council of Europe began a three-year programme on Policing and Human Rights. Two years later an Garda Síochána established a Human Rights Office and a working group to look at human rights implementation. In 2003 the ECHR was incorporated into Irish law through the European Convention on Human Rights Act 2003. Part of the working group's programme involved commissioning an audit of human rights in the force, which was published in 2004 by Ionann Management Consultants. The audit combined information from reports, interviews, surveys and focus groups with senior management, uniformed and civilian staff as well as community groups.

A number of the external bodies who engaged with this review expressed concerns for respect for human rights in the exercise of a range of specific police powers including arrest, interrogation, detention, public order, use of force, accountability, training, firearms, racist incidents and working with asylum seekers and immigrants. The audit found that 'the structures for and resources devoted to human rights work are weak' (Ionann 2004: 26). The researchers attempted to assess whether a human rights culture was present in the organisation, and found that many gardaí felt that common sense and existing regulations made sufficient provision for human rights. However, actual knowledge of human rights and the role it played in particular policing situations was very limited. On the one hand, a garda declaration on human rights had passively been distributed and few had read it. Understanding of the ECHR and its relevance to policing was vague. It was seen as distant and removed from police work. On the other hand, many rank-and-file members felt that leadership was not committed to human rights and it was often 'lip service or covering their backs' (2004: 48). An inability to speak out against abuses was also documented: 'If you take action, you are alienated from everyone. Like Serpico' (2004: 52). The view was also expressed that when abuses occurred management 'hung some members out to dry' (2004: 72).

A focus of the report was the policing of diversity. Amnesty International (Irish section) (2001) found that a quarter of racist incidents experienced by minorities were at the hands of gardaí and over half of black Irish people experienced discrimination from immigration gardaí, felt that gardaí did not take racists incidents seriously, and that they would not be welcomed as gardaí. Specific problems that were identified by community groups included working with travellers, particularly the treatment of allegations of domestic violence, working with young people who are often 'terrified' of gardaí, interaction with black communities, particularly Nigerians, and immigration work. While the Ionann Audit found some sensitivity to the difficulties involved in diversity policing, some police participants expressed racist views to the researchers.

The report also looked at the gardaí as a human rights employer. Structural barriers to diverse recruitment were identified. Bullying was regularly reported by members, and female gardaí expressed ongoing concerns as to equality and a belief that complaints about sexual harassment would impact upon career prospects. The report made numerous recommendations as to what reforms were necessary to enhance the progression and embedding of human rights within the organisation, and expressed the belief that a fully independent police authority could enhance transparency and accountability. These findings were published in 2004 just as the debate as to reforming policing began in earnest.

The nature of reform

Before the Morris Tribunal was even established reform of policing had become inevitable, if nothing else due to commitments under the Good Friday Agreement. The heads of a bill were published in July 2003 and the Bill itself was published a year later, at the same time as the first Morris Report and the Ionann Audit. The findings and recommendations of both reports however were barely mentioned in the parliamentary debates on the legislation. A proposal to delay passing the legislation and establish a commission to review an Garda Síochána was dismissed. Instead, in the final stages of the debate, a large number of amendments were hastily made following publication of the second Morris Report. Out of 300 amendments proposed, including some of significant changes to oversight of the gardaí, just 42 were discussed in the Dáil.

The Act, which came into force in July 2005, was heralded by the Minister as 'the most profound piece of legislation relating to an Garda Síochána in the history of the State' (DE: 29/11/06). It addresses a wide range of issues including internal affairs, whistleblowing, the relationship between Garda HQ and the Department, citizen complaints, public consultation and financial accountability. It makes an Garda Síochána a police service, rather than a force, and provides the first statutory definition of its functions:

> a) preserving peace and public order, (b) protecting life and property, (c) vindicating the human rights of each individual, (d) protecting the security of the State, (e) preventing crime, (f) bringing criminals to justice, including by detecting and investigating crime, and (g) regulating and controlling road traffic and improving road safety.

Two of these functions are of particular importance: human rights take a prominent role while State security remains within the remit of the service.

Both the disciplinary codes and the process of investigation have been reformed by the Act and secondary legislation. A new disciplinary offence of failing to account when questioned is created under the Act, meriting dismissal. The Commissioner is empowered to summarily dismiss members under the rank of inspector where 'due to the conduct, retention would undermine public confidence' in the service and dismissal is necessary to maintain confidence. In 2007 changes were made to the disciplinary regulations. The composition of the Disciplinary Board was altered to include one independent member (of three), nominated by the Minister. It remains the case that a member can avoid disciplinary proceedings by resigning. In accordance with the Act a code of ethics has been published and a Professional Standards Unit was established in January 2006 with a staff of 20, which has conducted examinations of dozens of Garda Districts and Garda Headquarter Units. This body is further complemented by the independent Garda Inspectorate, tasked with inspecting or inquiring into any particular aspects of the operation and administration of an Garda Síochána and reporting to the Minister on these matters, advising him on best practice. To date this body has conducted reviews of management, barricade incidents, roads policing, missing persons, resource allocation and responding to child sexual abuse.

The Act calls for a whistleblowers' charter, which was introduced in 2008, and a confidential recipient was appointed to whom gardaí could confidentially, not anonymously, report information. New promotion regulations made the promotions board two-thirds civilian to address allegations that the system was cliquish. The admissions requirements were altered with both the Irish language requirements and the citizenship requirements eased in an effort to break down the homogeneity of the service, which Justice Morris felt created an 'us and them' mentality. However, a ban on recruitment, in place since 2009, has meant that this has had little effect as yet. In 2008, just 2.2 per cent of new recruits were from an ethnic minority background, despite an aim of 5 per cent.[2]

A Garda Reserve, a voluntary body whose purpose is to conduct patrols and engage in crime prevention activities, is provided for by the Act. Members of the Reserve are permitted to have the same powers as gardaí, however by ministerial order these were initially limited. In June 2012 however it was clear that they were being used to supplement falling numbers of gardaí, with reservists now constituting almost 10 per cent of the service.[3] Members of the Reserve have been provided with increased powers for public-order offences and vehicle seizures as well as training for domestic violence, child protection and conflict resolution (*IT*: 21/06/12). Efforts to enhance dialogue with the community have been made under the Act through the creation of Joint Policing Committees. Throughout the country these should serve as forums for consultation, discussion and producing recommendations on policing matters with the community.

A number of provisions in the Act target the relationship between Garda management and the Department of Justice. The Act requires the Commissioner to account fully to the government and the Minister on any aspect of their functions, including providing any documents or records requested. It can be assumed that this power was inserted as a result of the government's inability to secure a copy of the Carty Report from Garda HQ despite repeated requests. No limitations or conditions are laid down for the exercise of this power. The Commissioner is also required to provide the Attorney General with any documents relating to ongoing legal proceedings. This is the first time that the government has been given powers to demand police documents. As Walsh has stated, 'while there may be situations in which it would be legitimate and proper to place such a power in the hands of government, it must be acknowledged that, in the absence of express limitations, it can also be used for more sinister reasons' (2009: 371). The Minister is also given the power to issue directives to the Commissioner concerning *any* matter relating to policing and the Garda Commission shall comply. This has the potential to undermine the Commissioner's operational control of the service. The Minister is also given the power to appoint an individual to inquire into any aspect of the administration, practice or procedure of an Garda Síochána where public concern arises. This all combines to give the Minister and the Department much greater control over the police than previously was the case. Despite numerous reports and recommendations to introduce an independent element, such as a police authority, governance of the police has been centralised and politicised even further.

In terms of accountability, however, the Act purported to do what had long been called for. It replaced the Garda Complaints Board with a new independent body, the Garda Síochána Ombudsman Commission (the Commission). The Commission, which became operational in May 2007, is a three-person body, with Commissioners appointed by the government. Complaints are made directly to the Commission or to the gardaí, who must pass them on to the Commission. There is a six-month time limit and complaints must relate to either criminal offences or breaches of discipline, a requirement that has resulted in a high inadmissibility rate. On paper the range of methods for handling complaints is flexible and much more independent than before. Admissible complaints can be handled by informal resolution or mediation, be investigated by gardaí, with the option of Commission supervision, or the Commission may conduct its own, independent investigation. Commission investigations take different forms dependent on whether (s.98) or not (s.95) the allegation appears to involve a criminal offence. Where the complaint appears to involve an offence the investigating officer has all the powers, immunities, privileges and duties of a garda, including entry, search, seizure, arrest, charge, summons, taking samples, detention and questioning.

The Commission conducts investigations in any case where death or serious harm to a person has occurred pursuant to garda operations (s.102[1]). Without complaint, the Commission may instigate an investigation if it appears a member has committed an offence or behaved in a manner meriting disciplinary proceedings. The Commission is permitted a further power to conduct an investigation into the practices, policies and procedures of the service. The aim of this provision is to allow intervention in a problematic area, either before complaints are made or where complaints indicate a systemic problem, rather than focusing on individual incidents (s.102[4]). The permission of the Minister is required for such 'public-interest' investigations.

Table 8.2 below reviews the handling of complaints up until the end of November 2011.[4] It shows clearly that where the Commission has discretion (i.e. outside of s.102 investigations) it is only conducting independent investigations when complaints appear to involve an offence. Over 40 per cent of complaints are still investigated by gardaí, most without Commission supervision.

This is disappointing. While the framework was created for independent investigations of complaints, this occurs in less than half of all cases. Further, the Minister has declined permission on occasion for s.102 public-interest investigations.

The Garda Síochána Act, through the wide range of reforms and initiatives introduced, certainly changes the context of policing in Ireland. On paper, the accountability mechanisms are stronger, though a discernible trend towards centralisation of power and increased control by government is evident in a number of provisions. The introduction of Joint Policing Committees and a Whistleblowers' Charter are welcomed but their efficacy, particularly that of the committees, is to open to how individual areas choose to implement the regulations. The Inspectorate is proving an active body that can provide useful and realistic research and recommendations for the service. As has been outlined, however, the Ombudsman Commission, one of the defining features of the Act, has not become the independent body it could have been under the provisions and many investigations continue to be conducted by gardaí.

Some recommendations made by Justice Morris in relation to the use of informants, treatment of persons in custody, the role of the Member in Charge, the use of the PEACE interrogation method, changes to the caution, mention of suspensions in the disciplinary regulations, and the issuing of search warrants have largely been ignored. Despite recognition by Justice Morris, the SMI Report and a subsequent Garda Inspectorate report, failures of management, particularly in terms of clear delineation of roles and responsibility as well as the appropriate training and promotion have not been addressed. Indeed, as we will see, the recession has brought some retrograde steps in this regard.

Reform of culture emerges from the various reports as a pressing need. Culture cannot be reformed through legislation and regulations alone. It is a difficult process, which often necessitates a 'reforming chief'. Punch identifies the

Table 8.2 GSOC handling of complaints, 2007–November 2011.

Method	2007	2008	2009	2010	2011 (Nov)	Total
IR	228	136	215	172	268	1,019 (13.4%)
s.94 unsupervised	312	638	519	728	512	2,709 (35.5%)
s.94 supervised	28	175	125	73	37	438 (5.7%)
s.95	–	2	30	23	25	80 (1%)
s.98	384	641	559	632	497	2,713 (35.5%)
102(1)	247	129	103	103	82	664 (8.7%)
102(4)	1	2	2	–	1	6
Total	1,200	1,723	1,553	1,731	1,422	**7,629**

following characteristics of reform chiefs through analysis of these processes in London and New York:

> Both displayed steely determination in tackling the organisation and its deviants; they displayed courageous leadership, demanded accountability from senior officers, put resources into personnel and altering the opportunity structure and above all showed ruthlessness in ridding the organisation of bent cops.
>
> (Punch 2009: 192)

Such reforming leadership, which makes high demands of a police service in a period of change, has been largely absent from an Garda Síochána. A great deal of the reform work has been delegated in a way that distances the Commissioner from it. There have not been dramatic statements of change or strict sanctioning of those who were found by Justice Morris to have engaged in misconduct. By March 2008, four members had been dismissed, 14 had either resigned or retired thus avoiding disciplinary action, one was on long-term sick leave, one was transferred, one was issued with a letter of advice and no action was taken in two cases. Instead of a determination to purge the service of 'bent cops' there has been an effort to reassure the public that the majority of gardaí are honest, decent members.

In addition to the statutory reforms an internal reform process was also undertaken. This was consumed by a discourse of managerialism and performance indicators, not moral or ethical values, nor a return to core, fundamental policing basics. In 2008, 22 change projects were in progress and a Deputy Commissioner for Strategy and Change Management was appointed. Working groups were established in relation to each of the 14 areas of concern identified from the Morris Tribunal Reports. The reports from these groups either imply that the statutory reforms will remedy the issues or technical rather than cultural responses are proposed. For instance, the working group considering the relationship with the Department of Justice discussed communications and suggested that a better email system was required. Given the fundamental flaws identified by Justice Morris, and the descriptions provided in the Dáil of the stilted relations between the two, it seems naive to propose that improved computer systems will improve the relationship.

Equally unaddressed is the issue of police use of force, which has been a dominant theme throughout this book. A number of other contentious incidents occurred around the time of these reports relating to the use of force. In April 2000, John Carty, a 29-year-old with a depressive illness, was killed by members of the Emergency Response Unit (ERU) at Abbeylara, Longford. His death followed a protracted barricade incident during which time he fired more than 30 shots, some towards the gardaí. Questions were raised as to why the ERU and not local police responded, and how the scene was managed. This came after the killings by the ERU of John Morris, a member of the INLA, during an attempted robbery in 1997, and Ronan MacLochlainn, a dissident republican, during an attempted robbery in 1998. The Barr Tribunal (2006) established to examine the events at Abbeylara identified 'crucial failures' in the handling of the situation, a lack of experience of those in command, and a lack of non-lethal weapons such as stun-guns. Nevertheless, the report was relatively sympathetic to those members at the scene given the unusual circumstances, declining to state whether the result would have differed had the gardaí acted more appropriately. A subsequent Garda Inspectorate review of barricade incidents evidenced 73 such incidents between 2000 and 2006. Twelve of these involved a firearm; another 15 involved another form of weapon. Justice Barr's view that these were unusual and difficult circumstances for the gardaí involved seems misplaced.

Lethal force was again used in May 2005 when two men were shot dead by gardaí as they tried to raid a post office in Lusk, County Dublin. Amnesty International and the Irish Council for Civil Liberties unsuccessfully called for an inquiry to be established into the events. Other incidents generating concerns as to the use of force have included the May Day protests in Dublin in 2002, after which seven gardaí were prosecuted and one convicted, and ongoing rural protests at the construction of a refinery by Shell in the west of Ireland since 2000 (Siggins 2010). Both scenarios raise questions as to how public-order incidents are policed in Ireland. The volume of police assigned to the peaceful protests at the Corrib Gas Project has been striking, as has the prosecution of protesters, but not Shell, for breaches of the law. A review of the policing of the dispute by Front Line Defenders in 2009 (Barrington 2009) concluded that there were grounds to be concerned about the protection of human rights. Front Line Defenders were particular troubled by the fact that the Garda Ombudsman Commission was denied permission from the Minister for Justice to conduct a public interest investigation into the dispute. This decision by the Minister in relation to a dispute that has economic and commercial ramifications raises questions as to whether both policing and police accountability are being politicised.

Concerns have also been raised in relation to the deaths in or following custody of Brian Rossiter, Terrence Wheelock and John Maloney. The Hartnett Inquiry examined the death of 14-year-old Brian Rossiter who was found in his cell in a coma the morning after he had been arrested in September 2002 on suspicion of public-order offences. The Hartnett Report found that, while unlawfully detained, he was not assaulted during the detention. The custody record was not accurately maintained and the investigation into his death was not properly conducted. Campaigns to have the deaths of Terrence Wheelock and John Maloney re-examined have not led to fresh investigations. While it can be hoped that the accountability vacuum will be filled in such cases by the Ombudsman Commissioner this will not address concerns that use of force is an institutional problem.

The political rhetoric on policing in Ireland has, nevertheless, remained constant. In November 2006, following the publication of further Morris Tribunal Reports, as well as the Abbeylara inquiries, arguably a time of crisis of legitimacy for the service, the Minister for Justice stated, 'I and members of the public still retain full confidence in the Garda Síochána as an organisation. Its members are in the front line in the fight against crime and deserve our full support' (DE: 29/11/06). A discussion of the final Morris Tribunal Reports was held in the Dáil in October 2008. The Minister informed the House:

> It is now an organisation that is more open to the outside. It has a new pro-
> fessionalism in its management development and selection systems. It is
> prepared as never before to perform its functions effectively, efficiently and
> fairly in responding to the needs of local communities. Thanks in large mea-
> sure to the findings and recommendations of the Morris Tribunal, we now
> have a system of oversight in place to ensure, as far as humanly possible, that
> the abuses uncovered by the tribunal do not recur.
>
> (DE: 22/10/08)

It will take time to assess the impact of the reforms and whether they will be accepted by serving gardaí. Reforming police is notoriously difficult (Brogden *et al.* 1988; Punch 1985; Prenzler 2002). Chan (1997) argues that police reform, particularly where any reform of culture is required, is an exceptionally complex process. It requires acknowledgment of the role of the police officer as an actor with influence over three elements: the structural conditions of policing, the cultural knowledge within the service, and the police practice that occurs as a product. To have the greatest chance of taking effect reform has to address the conditions of policing, the culture of policing, the nature of officers who take action and the practice which results. The culture of policing, for Chan, is not a static body of characteristics but a fluid source of knowledge adapted by newer officers to their situations. Reform should not be limited to rule-tightening or police training, but requires changes to the social and legal structures of policing as well as the knowledge of officers of policing. Chan warns 'change is traumatic, it has to be directed and continuous, people must be willing to change and, finally, planned change is difficult to achieve, especially where it is imposed by one group on another' (1997: 237).

Applying Chan's analysis to the Irish reform process, there have been some structural changes and minor attempts, through diversity training primarily, to alter the cultural knowledge of serving officers. Increased professionalism and managerialism may involve greater recognition of the police as an actor in this process. However, the reform has largely been limited to rule-tightening and training, with little effort directed towards reforming the social structures. The only changes to the relationship with the Department have been to centralise this relationship further. Despite calls from organisations and some political parties the idea of a police authority has repeatedly been rejected by the Minister for Justice on the grounds that, 'Dáil Éireann is Ireland's police authority and accountability through the Minister and the Commissioner is the most appropri-ate mechanism for democratic oversight of a modern police and security service' (DE: 29/11/06). This directly contradicts the research of Walsh (1998) on the failings, either through unwillingness or inability, of Dáil Éireann to hold the police to account.

Policing Ireland after Morris

By the end of the tribunal the organisation was in a state of flux like never before. Policing in Ireland had been battered by years of scathing tribunal reports and negative media headlines, on a scale never before seen. There can be little doubt that the Morris Tribunal had negative consequences for morale within an Garda Síochána. For many dedicated gardaí it was difficult to believe what had happened. Those interviewees who had previously worked on the border were astounded, particularly in relation to the hoax IRA bomb finds. In DG15's experience there was a clear procedure to be followed in such cases. Further, if gardaí wanted to make a weapons find it did not take much police work to find one along the border. Participants described what happened in Donegal as 'despicable' (G16), a 'cancer' that was contagious (DSG4) and the 'blackest chapter in the history of the gardaí' (G5) while I1 stated that it 'defies fiction'. SG3 talked of the effect it had on garda morale: 'I know it has been thrown at people, "ah sure, you're the same as Donegal".' The scale of the investigation also impacted on morale, with the view expressed that it was somewhat unfair:

> No matter who you are or what you are, you don't do everything 100 per cent all the time. It was that kind of forensic examination of what you were doing. You're going to get caught out some time or another, which happened in Morris.
>
> (SI6)

While some discussed the events in terms of a few bad apples, some not only acknowledged the role of management in this but in fact found this the more shocking aspect of the tribunal's findings:

> They have been really and truly acting disgracefully, beyond their powers. Because they had no scruples … there were people that were unworthy of being in any organisation … They should have been rooted out earlier but the danger then is if you have the wrong people given responsibility they'll mess up before there's time to control.
>
> (G12)

> It's not hard to understand the one or two lads that did something wrong but it's hard to understand how it was kinda under cover for so long, that it didn't break much earlier than it did.
>
> (SI4)

All interviewees had retired by the time the Morris Tribunal had completed its work. It would be worrying if serving members similarly felt that management had failed and that they, resultantly, had to bear the repercussions. In a national police service members are aware that they could work with any chief superintendent in the future. Further, the public recognition during the tribunal of problems with admission and promotions, as well as the identification in the Ionann Audit of bullying and discrimination, has publicly aired grievances that were long internal. Good leadership through this period is essential if these sentiments are not to overpower policing. Chan found that the speed of change in post-scandal reform can 'create an atmosphere of paranoia and distrust' (1996: 196). One consequence she noted was the ability of inappropriate members to prosper in this new climate by telling management what they wanted to hear. Another consequence, well documented, is resistance to change and reform (Reiner 2000). Certainly in the initial reform stages there was some resistance from gardaí towards the work of the Ombudsman Commission (*II*: 20/05/07). Some interviewees felt that while these events were shocking, the service would bounce back. SI7 believed morale would not be damaged long-term, stating that the misconduct was limited to a core number of men in Donegal, a difficult district at the best of time. I5 expressed the view that the adaptability of the police would see the service recover in a matter of months. For this to happen, however, either leadership would have to be exceptional or the bad apples thesis would have to be internalised.

The unfortunate reality however was that rather than having an opportunity to be adaptable the service soon found itself facing a substantial crisis, which affected every member even more directly. Just as the tribunal completed its work, Ireland entered a recession leading to cuts in public expenditure. The police, like other members of the public service, had new taxes and levies imposed, resulting in up to 20 per cent cuts in take-home pay. Recruitment was frozen in 2009 and remains that way in late 2012. Promotions were stalled. Retirements surged as older members feared the impact of the new taxes and levies on pensions. Between 1997 and 2005 annual retirement numbers averaged at around 340 a year but over 700 retired in 2009. The EU-IMF 2010 bailout of Ireland required a reduction in garda numbers to 13,000 by 2014. Retirements and a recruitment freeze are being relied upon to deliver this. In the meantime recruitment to the unpaid reserve continues and now comprises over 10 per cent of the service. However, the combination of retirements and promotion freezes left serious gaps in senior positions. In February 2012 there were 61 vacancies among senior ranks: five assistant commissioners, eight chief superintendents and 48 superintendents. Through 2012 many of these were filled but for a period of time the service was without leadership at these levels, and this at a time when strong leadership was needed to lead the service through the reforms.

Protests have been multifaceted. A billboard campaign was launched with graphic images of the violent injuries which gardaí suffer on the job. In February 2009, 2000 gardaí marched in protest on the day that the imposition of a pension levy was passed by government. The cuts, however, continued. In 2009 the McCarthy Report on Public Service and Expenditure Programmes, a report to suggest cuts across government spending, made a number of recommendations on saving money in an Garda Síochána. It recommended that half of the country's 702 garda stations could be closed and suggested that gardaí no longer conduct passport checks at border points. Interestingly, the Ionann Audit on human rights had also recommended that their role in immigration be reconsidered as it brought gardaí into conflict with communities (2004: 76). In December 2011, 39 garda stations were closed and 10 more began working on reduced hours. In December 2012 the Minister announced that 100 stations would close in 2013. In addition 28 districts were being revised into 14 as part of what the Minister called 'the most radical restructuring of the policing system since the foundation of the State' (*IT*: 05/12/12). A number of allowances have been terminated and the replacement of garda vehicles has been slowed down. In more recent years there has been a resurgence in the use of horses, bicycles and foot patrols (I1). I2 was quite actively involved in the push to get more gardaí out on bicycles, which offer greater flexibility and access in urban areas. In 2007 garda overtime surpassed €134 million, but the budget has been reduced to €54 million for 2012. Many of these proposed changes are being considered and implemented as part of a garda strategic review called GRACE (Garda Response to A Changing Environment).

In June 2011 the Justice Vote group conducted a review of expenditure and proposed a range of cuts. These included suspension of financial support for additional training such as the Garda Executive Leadership Programme or the undertaking of a BSc in Police Management. Given that garda management and leadership has repeatedly been identified as in need of advancement this is disappointing. More than a quarter of detectives had weapons rescinded (at a saving of over €1000 per weapon) and units such as Air Support and Traffic had cuts imposed. It was also proposed that charges be introduced for a range of services such as producing fingerprints for non-crime purposes, garda certificates of good character, traffic collision reports, and other non-public duties. It should be noted, however, that unlike the experience of austerity in England and Wales the suggestions have not yet been made to privatise certain policing functions (Brodgen and Ellison 2012).

Writing in 2009, before the full extent of the recession had become clear, Walsh expressed concerns about the implementation of both Morris and Ionann reforms:

> Some important issues have not been seriously addressed at all; and, four years after the implementation of the Ionann human rights audit, many of the key Garda initiatives to implement its recommendations have still not been brought to fruition ... There is a particular concern with the Garda response to several important recommendations from the Inspectorate. In too many of them the Garda response has been to refer to a draft policy (contents unspecified) under consideration, or that the recommendations will be considered by a committee which has or is about to be established. This can too easily translate into a strategy of offering appearance over substance.
>
> (Walsh 2009: 765)

It is not difficult to imagine that in the context of cutbacks and reduced numbers less resources will be devoted to exploring these initiatives further. Walsh further contextualises this argument by pointing to the 'relentless' expansion of police powers in Ireland in recent years. This has been primarily related to the growth in organised crime since 1996, which has been part of a resurgence in crime rates more broadly, and the death of Veronica Guerin.

Organised crime, however, has created a particular fear, as it has been associated with, in the Irish context, a large number of deaths, on occasion of civilians. One politician claimed in 2008 that 'there were 106 incidents involving grenades, pipe bombs and other explosive devices, an increase of 340 per cent in 12 months' (DE: 03/07/09). It has been estimated that 17 out of 50 murders committed in the state in 2008 were gangland killings, which would mean that organised crime was responsible for over one-third of murders in the country. Official figures reveal that between 2008 and 2009 offences involving discharge of a firearm had risen by 49 per cent (Central Statistics Office 2009). Deputy Bruton claimed in 2009 that since the death of Veronica Guerin in 1996 there have been 146 gangland killings (Bruton 11/05/09), whereas between 1972 and 1991 only two killings could be attributed to gangland feuds (Dooley 1995: 16). All of this culminated in 2009 in the passing or introducing of six pieces of legislation to combat organised crime: the Criminal Justice Surveillance Act, the Money Laundering and Terrorist Finance Bill, the Communications (Retention of Data) Bill, the Criminal Procedure Bill, the Criminal Justice (Miscellaneous Provisions) Act and the Criminal Justice (Amendment) Act. This package has alarming consequences for human rights and civil liberties (Conway and Mulqueen 2009), particularly in the context of the limited impact of the above reforms on the culture of Irish policing, which has a longstanding attachment to abuse of rights.

On 25 January 2013 Detective Garda Aidan Donohue was killed by a single gunshot to the head as he was providing security to a cash-in-transit vehicle at a credit union in Dundalk. This was the first murder of a garda since the killing of Gerry McCabe in 1996. Others have been killed since 1996: Sergeant Andrew Callanan died in 1999 attempting to aid a man who walked into a garda station, poured petrol on himself and set it alight; Garda Michael Padden and Garda Tony Tighe were killed in April 2002 when a car involved in a robbery struck their patrol car. Detective Garda Donohue's death is, however, the first murder of a garda in 17 years. Members will no doubt be feeling anger, fear and sadness, as

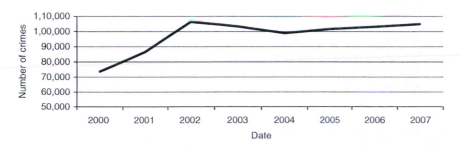

Figure 8.1 Indictable crime in Ireland 2000–7.

explored in Chapter 5, realising again the possibility of danger that attaches to their jobs. Certainly these killings indicate that danger in Irish policing did not end with the Peace Process. The GRA have stated that on average two members a day, or 800 a year, are assaulted. In Chapter 5 it was seen that between 1973 and 1991 that this number of assaults was only exceeded in four years. The year 2012 alone saw the payment of over €6.7 million in compensation to 121 gardaí assaulted or injured in the line of work; €13.4 million has been paid in compensation since 2000. The Assaults on Emergency Workers Bill 2012, currently before Parliament, proposes a minimum of five years' imprisonment for such assaults.

The twenty-first century has thus far been difficult for gardaí. A substantial reform package has been introduced but the impact of the recession has detracted from the leadership and support needed to see them through that process. While recruitment has now stalled, the years preceding the recession saw large numbers being recruited. Those who joined at this time represent yet another shift in the demographics of the service. The total strength of the service in 2009 was 14,412 and women held 23.4 per cent of all positions. Assistant Commissioner Clancy became the first woman to be appointed to such a senior post in 2003 and in 2011 Noirin O'Sullivan became the first female Deputy Commissioner. That said, of 19 senior management positions, Deputy Commissioner O'Sullivan is currently the only female office holder. Sheridan (2009) found that gender impacts on career progression in the service in a number of ways. Women still struggle to gain experience in specialist units, key to promotion. The increase in female recruits did appear to have reduced male opposition to female members but work-life balance still posed obstacles.

Since the mid-1990s emigration from Ireland became the option of the educated, not the necessity of the poor. Joining was no longer a means of avoiding emigration. Recruits were more affluent, better educated and chose the gardaí as a prosperous and rewarding career alternative. Beagley-Imhoff's study indicates that respondents joined for the most part for job security (55.9 per cent) and also due to family influence (32.4 per cent) (2000: 30).

Those interviewed in the current research acknowledged that the younger generation of gardaí had different motivations for joining. They felt that this was not necessarily positive:

> One of the biggest changes now is that young people leave school and go to college or university for three or four years. They get a diploma or a degree and enter at 21/22 ... It's a different generation of officers. They have been in different atmospheres, which are liberal, free-thinking and they are able to do their own thing.
>
> (G1)

> It's a different type of Guard now. Most have third-level education. Most have never worked before. We all worked before joining An Garda Síochána. Often we had been to England. We had a better understanding of people and

their problems. Now they are all competing for promotion and when it doesn't happen they get disinterested.

(DSG1)

If they are correct in this assessment then it is easy to see that the recession, the freezing of promotion and the pay cuts would have particularly negative consequences for these younger gardaí.

Conclusion

The path to the Morris Tribunal established yet again the failings of garda accountability mechanisms. Internal reports have not been published and so it is impossible to state how effective they were. The Complaints Board could not cope. The Dáil could not operate in its democratic accountability function as it had not received the internal reports. A tribunal, an expensive, lengthy and extraordinary measure, was the only option remaining. Government, however, stalled and delayed, exacerbating the experience of both the victims of garda misconduct and gardaí who stood accused, who deserved swift resolution of the matter. Justice Morris was uniquely critical of the gardaí and his meticulous examination exposed the truth of misconduct and corruption in Donegal. This pervaded all aspects of the exercise of garda powers but, most importantly, he unequivocally determined that this was not about a few bad apples. Senior management was negligent and should have prevented the situation. At times they were complicit. It should be remembered that Justice Morris was not permitted to examine the role of Garda Headquarters or the Department and so their involvement could not be explored.

The silver lining of a scandal is that it can generate the motivation and energy for reform, to rectify the damage done to the service's relationship with the public (Newburn 1999). Scandal-driven police reform, however, is needs-driven and is likely to only address those aspects that have caused greatest public alarm (Sherman 1978). Scandals prompt knee-jerk reactions, with short-term goals of instant improvement (Punch 2000). The calls for change come before the problem is fully understood. But the reality is that corruption is invariably so ingrained and interwoven with police subculture that it cannot be transformed overnight (Newburn 1999). Much of this was evident after the Morris Tribunal. An immense reform project was commenced within an Garda Síochána but little attention was paid to the findings of the Morris Tribunal nor was any attempt made to think more broadly about what may be wrong with policing in Ireland. A large number of necessary changes were made and innovations such as the Garda Inspectorate and the Joint Policing Committees are particularly welcome. However, one of the most fundamental issues with the gardaí, the political control and influence, which Justice Morris referred to, has been strengthened (Conway and Walsh 2011). This is alarming given the way in which political control over the service has been exercised in the past. Further, the managerialist approach to the reform process internally is unlikely to address the cultural issues such as the blue wall of silence, which Justice Morris encountered, or the gap in commitment to human rights found by both Ionann (2004) and Walsh (2009). The changes to the accountability mechanisms have been particularly disappointing and it must be concluded that the semblance but not the reality of independence has now been created (Conway 2009; Walsh 2009b).

At the same time as pointing to these concerns, the undermining effect of the tribunal and attendant publicity on garda morale must be acknowledged. That this and the unsettling reform process were followed immediately by a recession has made the past five years difficult for members. Cognisance needs to be taken of what gardaí have endured if positive reforms are to be embedded and further misconduct avoided. Justice Morris stated: 'Ultimately the gradual erosion of discipline within an Garda Síochána is a developing a situation that will, sooner or later, lead to disaster' (2004, I/13.102). Nearly ten years on, it seems that the experience of policing Ireland has only become more difficult while the reforms have been insufficient to prevent a recurrence.

Notes

1 It was not until November 2001 that the government revealed that they had been made aware at this point (DE: 21/11/01).
2 It may not be simply about admissions requirements however. In 2007 a Sikh member of the reserve force sought and was denied permission to wear his turban while on duty (*II*: 24/08/07).
3 In December 2011 there were 800 reservists; in June 2012 there were 918 with a further 225 in training.
4 Up until November 2011 the Commission published monthly statistics, which included the breakdown of how complaints were handled. This has not been published since, nor was this data included in the 2011 Annual Report.

Conclusion
Appreciating the colonial legacy

This book has examined policing in Ireland, predominantly in the twentieth century. An over-riding theme has been that policing in independent Ireland has been simultaneously colonial and post-colonial. The influence of colonialism, it has been argued, continues to be felt. The design of the Civic Guard in 1922 retained the core structure of the RIC: an armed, national, centralised force directly accountable to politicians and widespread on the ground. There were practical, contextual reasons for retaining these features. This was the only form of policing that had been experienced in Ireland, added to the fact that the crisis nature of the country in 1922 directed attention away from in-depth planning. However, it has also been suggested that Michael Collins may have desired to replicate certain features of the RIC, in particular its level of local knowledge. There were alternative systems operating nearby, which could have provided models for a different approach. Indeed, the DMP operated effectively in quite a different format.

At the same time that these structural features were retained, numerous highly visible changes were made to differentiate the Civic Guard from the RIC: a new name, a new uniform, new personnel and less of them. This was essentially a rebranding, presenting the same force in different packaging. There were just two deviations. Firstly, the mutiny in Kildare over the role of former RIC men in the force led a fearful government to disarm the force, not out of principle, but from a need for a trustworthy, reliable police force. Secondly, the strength of the force grew quickly: it still appeared smaller than the RIC but this was mitigated through an acknowledgement of partition. Comparisons that recognise that the Civic Guard policed a smaller population and landmass reveal that before too long the new force had reached a strength comparable to that of the RIC.

The features of the RIC that stemmed from the concerns of a colonial power, which focused on controlling the population and preventing uprising, remained at the core of the Civic Guard. These features largely remain today. An Garda Síochána is a national police service, which is heavily centralised and directly accountable to the Minister for Justice. It has traditionally performed many functions far beyond crime-fighting, such as gathering census or agricultural data and signing passport forms. Governance of an Garda Síochána is achieved solely through political mechanisms. While other countries adopt varying mechanisms to introduce an independent and democratic aspect to police governance, in Ireland to this day it remains entirely centralised. Walsh (1998) clearly established that this was not an effective method of overseeing the exercise of considerable police powers which engage a range of fundamental human rights. Not only does it detract from the democratic nature of policing (Patten 1999: 22) but evidence abounds that this relationship has enabled overt political involvement in policing: from the instructions of how to police the IRA in the 1930s (Chapter 3) or in the 1970s and 1980s (Chapter 5), the dismissal of Commissioners, the tapping of journalists' telephones (Chapter 5), the recording of ministerial phone conversations (Chapter 5), the policing of the Corrib gas project (Chapter 8) to the use of the promotion systems (Chapter 4). Rather than remedying this lacuna in police governance, the recent legislative reforms of the 2005 Act entrench political power over policing in the statute books (Conway and Walsh 2011), giving government powers to demand information and issue directives on any matter of policing. The politicisation and centralisation of the police has been further embedded. Through these various ways policing in Ireland remains, in part, colonial.

Simultaneously, policing in Ireland is also post-colonial. In the introduction I explored the contention that politicisation and centralisation are common features of post-colonial states. The process of retaining features of the preceding system, as just described, is common. This can be due to the somewhat shaky nature of the emerging state and a perceived need to ensure control and stability. The analysis presented in this book has shown that post-colonialism can have other, corrosive effects. The rebranding of policing that occurred in the 1920s, combined with a determination, pursued zealously under the leadership of Commissioner O'Duffy, that the gardaí would be the embodiment of the nationalist ideals for which Irish people had fought, placed the gardaí at the forefront of what might be called Ireland's post-colonial project. Members of an Garda Síochána were pioneers, sportsmen, devout Catholics, Irish speakers and educated. These were values that had been suppressed under British rule but which would be celebrated and promoted in independent Ireland (Whelan 2003). These efforts are evident in the earliest days of the force and in time they contributed to engendering an intense national pride and confidence in the police.

In the early decades, however, the force encountered difficulties in gaining acceptance in communities. Those that opposed the Treaty that created the new Irish Free State, close to half of the public, challenged the legitimacy of the police force. As government attempted to steer the country through the wounds of the bitter civil war, an Garda Síochána was pulled into a political tug-of-war, directed to crack down on the IRA while Cosgrave was at the political helm, directed to ease off when de Valera came to power. The dismissal of O'Duffy as Commissioner for political reasons and the subsequent requirement to police the Blueshirts, whom O'Duffy led, could have pushed gardaí to the point of revolt. Significantly, it did not. Brady (2000) suggests that this is due to a learned loyalty to principles of democratic policing. However, much more likely is apathy to the politics of the day and an economic need to stay in employment. The events of

1932–5 are defining in Irish policing. When gardaí did not revolt or refuse to obey de Valera's orders, they secured political support from all parties, in rhetoric at least. Since this time, the main political parties in Ireland have eagerly spoken of their support for the gardaí, shouting loudly of how the gardaí have *always* performed their duties with pride and heroism and making significant promises of support. A mythology emerged of the heroic garda. From this moment, the discourse (but not the reality) of policing in Ireland became that which O'Duffy had attempted to create, an institution of which the nation could be proud, fundamentally different to its predecessor.

This discourse of difference prevails. In August 2012 two retired gardaí sought to commemorate the Royal Irish Constabulary at Glasnevin cemetery, the same place where republican heroes such as Michael Collins are buried and remembered. This provoked a flurry of consternation, letters to newspapers and media commentary from those who viewed the RIC as traitors. An Garda Síochána refused to sanction the memorial. Such was the scale of public disquiet that gardaí were stationed at the cemetery on duty on the day of the memorial. The comments provoked were surprising, mostly for the intensity of feeling still present 90 years after the fact. One reader on *the Irish Times* website stated: 'Commemorate those brave members who disobeyed the orders of their British masters and helped the revolutionary struggle. Let the memory of the rest, Britain's useful idiots, be consigned to the dustbin of history' (*IT*: 24/08/12). What is most significant is not the abundant hatred for the RIC, but the appositional pride in the gardaí also expressed. One reader questioned whether the gardaí were not in fact built on the DMP rather than the RIC and another stated: 'Maybe the Guards in Donegal and other places, that were exposed for corruption owe much to the RIC but the majority of professional, capable and honest guards certainly do not.' The controversy caused by this commemoration shows that the relationship between the RIC and an Garda Síochána continues to impact upon views of policing in Ireland. The rebranding was effective in convincing the public that policing was different, despite the fact that in core structural ways an Garda Síochána is a replication of the RIC. Combined with weak governance and the aforementioned political commitment this prevented any questioning of the police. Policing in Ireland, therefore, is both colonial and post-colonial.

The impact of all of this has been to engender high levels of public confidence in the gardaí. The police are an Irish institution of which people are proud. Levels of satisfaction that would be the envy of other European states have been expressed in Ireland and not even grave scandals shake this position. This is not without good cause. Crime in Ireland, even in more recent decades, is low, with few people subjected to serious violent crimes. Detection rates are high, particularly for violent crimes. For many people their only interactions with gardaí are when they have their passport forms signed, at public events such as GAA matches or music concerts, or when they are involved in a traffic collision that must be reported for insurance purposes. Many people have positive interactions with the police and believe that they perform their function well.

Of course, support for and commitment to institutions and authority has been somewhat of a defining feature of independent Ireland. The Catholic Church, politicians, lawyers and doctors can all attest to this (Inglis 1998). Critical and questioning attitudes were somewhat absent in Ireland until the late 1960s and early 1970s. The arrival of television, joining the EU, the end of de Valera's leadership and the development of constitutional rights planted the seed of questioning and challenging in the Irish public (Tovey and Share 2000). The authority of these institutions began to wane. However, right at this time the Troubles began, which may have prompted a more questioning attitude to how the gardaí policed Irish society. For the first time in 30 years, gardaí lost their lives in defending the country. Civilians feared bombings, deaths of civilians and for the stability of the state. The combined effect of this fear and respect for gardaí was to shield the force, to place them beyond questioning and criticism. A 'sacred canopy' was built over gardaí (Manning 1977: 5), obscuring the reality of policing.

One curious point however in relation to attitudes to the police is the fact that in any study conducted the majority of expressed reasons for joining the gardaí are instrumental (join or emigrate, pension, steady salary) rather than normative. Few of those interviewed for this study or Harris's work (1988) stated that they wished to be a police officer, that it was an ambition, that they looked up to the local garda. Further work would need to be done to explore this more fully, but on the face of it there are grounds to question whether, as much as they express confidence in the force, people cannot bring themselves to want, or at least say that they want, to be a garda. Joining the police in a post-colonial country is something done out of necessity rather than desire.

We have then a position where in fundamental ways the gardaí embody much of the RIC yet are perceived by the public to be wholly different, Irish and independent. The service has achieved political and public acceptance on the basis of this, it seems. The sacrifices made over the decades by gardaí have led to a position whereby politicians and the public are slow to question the gardaí. As Walsh (1998) has so clearly demonstrated, even in the face of disconcerting evidence, politicians in Ireland have vied to show their dedication to, and support for, the force. Ministers for Justice have stated that it is not for government to lead the criticism of the force and, most bizarrely, that the gardaí should neither be above nor below the law. Holding the service to account is a task in which, save in the most extreme cases, unpatriotic people engage. And so it has only been in the most extreme circumstances that an Garda Síochána has been held to account. This did not happen when allegations of a Heavy Gang abounded and it did not happen in any meaningful way in numerous cases where individuals died in garda custody. Where structures have been put in place to achieve accountability they have been minimal versions of what could have been done. Even now, under the Garda Síochána Ombudsman Commission, only cases involving criminal allegations are independently investigated. The vast majority of complaints against the police continue to be investigated by gardaí. Governance of the police is political and centralised, while accountability lacks effective independence.

It might be argued (though this author would disagree) that a strong system of accountability is only important if gardaí are abusing their powers and engaging in misconduct. A dominant perspective, informed by post-colonial attitudes, has been that this is not the case, that misconduct is not systemic in Irish policing. Politicians and garda leadership alike have contended that whatever problems do exist relate to a number of bad apples, not to the institution as a whole. The 'rotten apples' thesis is based on the assumption 'that unlawful activity by police is a manifestation of personal moral weakness, a symptom of personality defects, or a result of recruitment of individuals unqualified for police work' (Stoddard 1968: 201). The blame for corrupt activities rests solely therefore with individuals rather than the service as a whole. It has been relied upon in many jurisdictions at different points in time. Ellison and Smyth (2000: 193) point to the comments of the Chief Constable of the Royal Ulster Constabulary (RUC) in 1993. He stated: 'I am absolutely satisfied that collusion is neither widespread nor institutionalised. From time to time, however, there will be some bad apples in every barrel.'

Policing scholarship warns us that this is an inaccurate and unhelpful analysis, which can distract us from the true nature of police misconduct. Newburn (1999) shows that any time it has been relied upon, usually by police unions, the evidence suggests otherwise. The Knapp Commission, which was investigating widespread, institutionalised corruption in the New York Police Department (NYPD), found that:

> According to this theory, which bordered on official Department doctrine, any policeman found to be corrupt must promptly be denounced as a rotten apple in an otherwise clean barrel. It must never be admitted that this individual corruption may be symptomatic of underlying disease…
>
> The rotten-apple doctrine has in many ways been a basic obstacle to meaningful reform. To begin with it reinforced and gave respectability to the code of silence … A high command unwilling to acknowledge that the problem of corruption is extensive cannot very well argue that drastic changes are necessary to deal with the problem.
>
> (Knapp Commission 1973: 6–7)

Whether it is through ignoring it, tolerating it or even encouraging it, there are organisational origins of police misconduct. It is never simply down to a few rotten apples. Lundman (1980) goes so far as to say that individual officers are marginal to organisations. As Patrick Murphy, the NYPD Commissioner at the time, explained, '[t]he task of corruption control is to examine the barrel, not just the apples – the organisation, not just the individuals in it – because corrupt police are made, not born' (cited in Barker and Carter 1986: 10). If reform proceeds on the basis of the bad apples thesis then it will take an individualistic and not an organisational form. Such an inappropriately targeted response is set to fail because it does not acknowledge that at the very least the organisation operates with ineffective supervision. On the other hand, through scapegoating, the 'rotten apples' approach can be a convenient and distracting cover-up for embedded, institutional problems. Is there evidence that indicates embedded or institutionalised problems within an Garda Síochána? Should Irish society be more concerned about misconduct and abuse of powers by gardaí? Four areas have emerged as predominant in this work, which should generate such concerns: use of force, interrogations, the Special Branch and promotions. These, however, are symptomatic of a culture that pervades policing.

Most obviously, this book has evidenced that violence and unnecessary use of force have been continual features of Irish policing. They have been used on the streets against the IRA, the Animal Gangs, the Teddy boys, students, protestors, revellers, the Dublin Unemployed Association, Concerned Parents Against Drugs, the May Day and Corrib Gas protestors and in garda stations against suspects and witnesses, by the Heavy Gang, whose existence was confirmed by participants in this research, and more generally as documented by the European Committee for the Prevention of Torture. Use of force is a commonly resorted to response in Irish policing. Often it is directed at those who challenge the political order, persons who lack the political power, credibility or collectivity to challenge this. Use of force can be a legitimate police response if the threat faced by gardaí in the immediate circumstances justifies a violent response. It has, however, been argued, most especially in Chapters 4 and 7, that often violence has been used when there was no immediate threat. Violence has been used to control rather than defend. In Chapter 6 it was argued that the problem is no longer that gardaí use force in circumstances in which it may not be legitimate with some regularity. Through a failure to sanction its use and, in fact, the praising and rewarding of results secured on the back of such violence, it has in fact been endorsed and institutionalised. Some of those interviewed for this research expressed disapproval of the methods adopted by the Heavy Gang but knew that those who were part of that gang were promoted to senior levels.

Interrogation methods are another area that has consistently generated concerns. Many high-profile convictions have been overturned on the basis of oppressive interrogation methods. Police powers in relation to the length of detention and incursions on the right to silence have been regularly expanded while at the same time the state was slow to require mandatory recording of interviews. Even now such recording is only required in relation to serious offences, and not for any witness interviews. The impact of this was vividly documented by the Morris Tribunal where people who should not have been arrested had their rights repeatedly violated, were called names, were shown autopsy photographs of a person they knew, were threatened with the removal of their children, had their hair pulled and the lights flicked on and off to disorientate them. The safeguards in existence, most noticeably the custody sergeant, failed to protect these individuals. In spite of these findings, when the institution objected to a new approach to interrogation recommended by Justice Morris, it was not implemented.

The role of Special Branch hangs like a cloud over many of these allegations. This unit is the only armed division within the service and its work engages the most secrecy, gathering intelligence and investigating the operations of those who challenge the state. Special branches the world over are notorious (Brodeur 1983) but a peculiar feature of the Irish policing system is that it also conducts all national security work, work often performed by a separate organisation in other countries. Most disconcerting is that this location of national security within the police has justified the non-disclosure of much information, on the basis that these matters relate to national security. It has formed the basis for arguments that neither governance nor accountability can be different to how it is, because only the Minister can receive all the information about policing.

Time and again criticisms have been made of the promotions system within the gardaí, that it operates on the basis of favouritism rather than skill and aptitude. Participants in this research expressed frustrated views with the promotion system. The result has been the promotion of inappropriate people who were unskilled and unable to supervise or control gardaí. Justice Morris argued that the gardaí was 'losing its character as a disciplined force', that members felt free to lie to superiors and do as they wished, an issue exacerbated, if not caused, by promotion of unsuitable members.

These features indicate that a culture exists within Irish policing that promotes violence, disregards rights, views certain groups with suspicion and isolates gardaí from society. The work of Ionann (2004) and Walsh (2009) examining human rights in an Garda Síochána supports such conclusions in relation to police culture. Justice Morris felt that the homogenous nature of the force, which comprises predominantly white, Irish males, reinforced that outlook. He called for greater recruitment of minorities to challenge dominant perspectives and encourage broader thinking within the force. In relation to this, this book has documented the difficult experiences of women within the gardaí. While women in police generally experience discrimination and harassment, Brown's (2000) study showed that women in the gardaí had in some respects a more difficult time than they did in British police forces. Promotion and progression are particularly problematic.

This study has also revealed however that while political support for the gardaí has been expressed publically and vocally, the garda experience of that support has differed. This work documents, for the first time, the experience of policing Ireland during the latter half of the twentieth century, through oral history interviews. The most striking finding to emerge from these interviews is that there has been a continuing failure to address the basic needs of the gardaí. For decades they were required to live in substandard conditions, with next to no time off and for quite poor pay. Training was outmoded, continuing to centre on skills like drill, which were relics of the colonial system. Uniforms were heavy and unsuitable. Communications systems and efficient transport were practically non-existent. Gardaí regularly complained via the representative bodies to no avail. Denied the right to strike or vote, the Macushla Ballroom Affair in 1961 was perhaps as stark action as could be taken. Even then, while political expressions of support abounded, it did not achieve the primary goal of improved pay and conditions. Through the 1950s and 1960s claims made for improved conditions were sidestepped and ignored, treatment that was disastrous for morale. It took another decade for change to come when the government eventually accepted the recommendations of the Conroy Commission. In many ways Conroy revolutionised work in the force, introducing a 42-hour working week, overtime payments and an end to requirements to live in the station. These changes, however, were not properly implemented by government. Chapter 7 documented that gardaí quickly became fixated on the financial benefits. Had government and senior gardaí managed this better these changes could have improved conditions for gardaí without transforming attitudes to work in this negative way. Had reform not been left so late, such dramatic shifts and stark changes may not have been required.

Pay has continued to be a source of immense dissatisfaction within the service, along with other aspects of working conditions, transfers, promotions and training. While politicians have clamoured to express their support for the service this has not translated into support for the practical, everyday requirements of the organisation. Instead the government have satisfied itself with not criticising the service as its method of support. The dangers of this approach are abundant. The lower garda morale is, due to failures to address issues core to gardaí, the greater the likelihood of misconduct, which prompts politicians to express their support for the gardaí. The Northern Ireland Troubles brought this into sharp relief. Largely unacknowledged have been the difficulties faced by gardaí at this time, particularly on the border. Certainly the state has acknowledged the fact that a dozen gardaí were killed by paramilitaries and that other gardaí have risked their lives in service to the country. Chapter 5, however, documented in honest and disturbing detail the hardships brought by the Troubles on an everyday basis, particularly in border areas. Danger and fear became a part of policing in a way that this generation of members had never known. These experiences were exacerbated, if not directly caused, by the approach of successive governments to the policing of the Troubles. Garda numbers were increased, new powers created and more actions criminalised, but this approach had limited effect in preventing the dangers faced. What was needed was clear direction on how to police the IRA and technology to assist that work. Instead, when it came to the border, men were sent to checkpoint duty with no weapons, no communications and no clear desire to intercept the IRA. Those that were proactive about policing the IRA were personally attacked, to which the official response was 'make sure you claim on the insurance'. Nothing was done to compensate the fact that in 1970s Ireland policing became a dangerous occupation in a way that had not been seen for some time.

There is a highly dangerous combination at play here. Policing in Ireland is politically influenced, if not directed. Commissioners have regularly risen and fallen with governments, which must create an inclination to do political bidding. In particular, others in society, such as the public, the opposition or an influential civil society, are not clamouring for change in policing. Garda misconduct, such as the Heavy Gang, appears to have not only been condoned at high levels within the force, but by officials in the Department of Justice. Gardaí did not receive the support that they called for, mostly for economic reasons, and morale within the force has reached low depths with alarming regularity. The 1990s saw the near disintegration of the representative body for gardaí and the Blue Flu. The last five years have seen worries about the impact of the recession, stalled recruitment and promotions and waning technology. At the same time a dedication to new managerialism seems to have pervaded the service with a staunch commitment to outcomes, change management and performance indicators. The Morris Tribunal provided a blueprint for reform, although based on just one division and particular investigations. Nevertheless, it established how wrong things could go. Justice Morris warned that without significant reform further disasters could occur. As was detailed in Chapter 8 many of the reforms of that tribunal have not been implemented and in recent months Justice Morris' prophecies appear to be coming true. At the time of writing a scandal appears to be on the brink of emerging over the abuse of the PULSE system to erase penalty points for driving offences on a large scale. Further, the GSOC Report on the use of Kieran Boylan as an informant has not yet been published, though media coverage suggests that due to a failure to implement Morris' recommendations on informants serious drug trafficking was permitted to continue and a number of miscarriages of justice may have occurred (*II*: 13/12/12).

There are serious problems embedded in an Garda Síochána, largely due to the government's controlling influence over policing. A number of things need to happen urgently to remedy this. Ideally a commission on policing would be held to ascertain fully and honestly, in a way that can restore the confidence of excluded communities, the positive and negative aspects of Irish policing. Academics and social scientists should be engaged in research of a sort not seen in Ireland, but prolific elsewhere, to ground that work. Transparent access should be given to government documents on policing. Unfortunately this, in all likelihood, will not happen, if for economic reasons as much as anything else.

Without this there is still action that can be taken. Changes should be made to the systems of accountability to ensure that most complaints are independently investigated while both the promotions and transfer systems also need further reform. Most importantly and immediately an independent police authority should be created. Calls for this have been made time and again since the creation of the gardaí in the 1920s. This would insert an independent element into the governance of policing, controlling how powers are used and money is spent. The UK equivalents appoint the chief constables (equivalent of the Garda Commissioners), hold them to account for the management of the police, ensure dialogue with the communities, draft policing plans as well as set the budget. The authorities are made up of councillors and independent community members so an Irish equivalent could include TDs as well as other independents (perhaps members of NGOs, business organisations, senior teachers, community activists and academics). The government role in policing would be limited therefore to setting national policing objectives, facilitating training, promoting the efficiency of the force, primarily through financial provision, approving the appointment of the Commissioner and seeking his dismissal. This division of labour and separation of powers would provide a thoroughly needed disaggregation of politics and policing, ensuring both the police's operational independence but also strong democratic governance (Lustgarten 1986). It would represent a seismic shift in Irish policing on a scale that will be scary for many politicians to contemplate. This is however a system which works, which was endorsed by the Patten Commission and which would enable many of the problems identified above to be addressed in an unbiased, non-partisan way. Without this separation an Garda Síochána is consigned to failure: it is a colonially structured service attempting to operate in a democratic state. It is brimming with members eager to do their best but who are structurally constrained from so doing.

As much as it is essential for Ireland to address these ills, those from countries that have emerged from colonialism or engaged in other processes of transition should read this history cautiously. This book documents clearly how the legacy of colonialism can survive and impact on policing for decades. It can corrode morale and the practice of policing whilst also distorting social conceptions of and attitudes to policing. While the reasons for this occurring in Ireland are understandable, a failure to recognise emerging centralisation and politicisation could prove fatal to the development of democratic policing.

Appendix 1: Methodology

Research design

This study began within the confines of a narrower PhD that sought to analyse the development and progression of the concept of accountability within the Irish police. Criminology was at the point quite nascent in Ireland and no academic study had been conducted involving empirical work with members of the police force. Quite quickly the decision was made to interview retired gardaí for two reasons: firstly, access to serving gardaí is very difficult to secure (indeed, this researcher is unaware of any study of serving gardaí by someone external to the organisation) and secondly, many of the historical writings on the gardaí covered the early decades of the force's history. Little had been done to analyse the period 1960–90. Retired gardaí could provide information on that period.

Prior to interviews, in-depth analysis was conducted of existing histories and texts on an Garda Síochána, Dáil Debates, the *Garda Review* as well as its predecessor *Iris na Ghardaí*, legislation, official policing documents, newspapers and a number of memoirs written by gardaí. The approach was based on the principle that with this information gathered, interviews could focus on personal accounts, interpretations and lived experiences (Grele 1998). The operation of the 30-year rule in Ireland means that many official documents relating to the latter part of the twentieth century have not as yet been released.

While Payne and Payne (2005) suggest that one of the advantages of documentary analysis is the ease of access, some problems were encountered to that end. Many of these documents are not widely available though there is a well-stocked library in the Garda Museum in Dublin Castle. On planning a second visit to the Garda Museum entry was refused until authorisation from the Garda Press Office was secured, despite this being a public library. The Press Office readily contacted the Museum and access was granted.

Sampling

As is now outlined it was not possible within this project to be selective as to the sample. There were no set gatekeepers to retired police officers who could help identify subjects and secure access (Noaks and Wincup 2004). Without gatekeepers

I was largely reliant on contacts and using a snowballing method whereby one participant would suggest another and so on. The research was conducted in two waves, with greater success in terms of access in the second wave.

Access: Wave 1

A notable feature in wave 1 was the difficulty in securing access. The first interviews were secured through personal contacts and snowballing, whereby interviewees pointed me toward other interviewees, followed. A letter was published in the Retired Garda Association Newsletter to no avail. Notices were placed on a number of online forums with general interests in Ireland and Irish history, though this did not prove fruitful. Making contact with the Irish branch of the International Policing Association secured a further contact. Most successfully, family, friends and colleagues were bothered for contacts and suggestions. Fourteen interviews were conducted in Wave 1, in five different counties.

The difficulties in securing access at this stage are attributed to two factors. Firstly, facilitating research is not something which an Garda Síochána has been called upon to do regularly and, as this book attests, there is a culture of secrecy in Irish policing. For this reason there may have been hesitancy in participating. Secondly, many of these interviews were conducted around the time of the publication of the early Morris Tribunal Reports. Given how critical these reports were of gardaí, it may have been that there was an unwillingness to be interviewed in that period of time.

Access: Wave 2

The second effort to secure participants was more successful. By this point in time the Retired Garda Association had grown in prominence and acquired premises in Dublin. A visit there proved exceptionally valuable, as they kindly

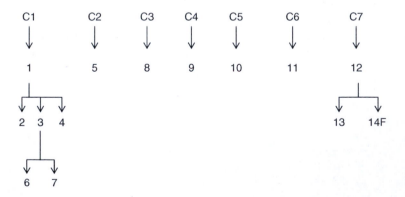

Figure A1 Source of interviews, Wave 1 (C = contact, F = female).

distributed my request across the country. A large number of participants, particularly in the border area, were accessed in this way. Colleagues and students also assisted in providing access to contacts.

Data collection

An interview schedule was drafted (Appendix 4) and ethical approval secured from the Ethics Committee at Queen's University Belfast. Interviews were conducted in two phases. The first phase, which included 14 interviews, was conducted between 2004 and 2006. The second phase in 2010, supported by the British Academy, comprised a further 28 interviews, providing a total of 42 in-depth interviews. These 42 interviews included a diverse range of ranks: 17 gardaí, 8 sergeants, 7 inspectors, 7 superintendents, 1 chief superintendent and 2 assistant commissioners. Commissioner was the only rank not represented. The youngest participant was 48 years of age, the eldest was 75. Most participants were in their 50s or 60s. The interviews were conducted in ten different counties in all four provinces of Ireland. There was a mix of urban and rural experiences, as well as a strong mix of rank-and-file and management perspectives. The shortest of these interviews was 0.6 hours, the longest 3.5 hours, with an average of 1.5 hours. They were conducted in a place of the participant's choosing, mostly in the interviewee's home or in a neutral place. Four took places in cafes, which may have had a stultifying effect on what was said.

Just one female was interviewed. Efforts could have been made to be put in touch with more female subjects but it was decided that this would distort the

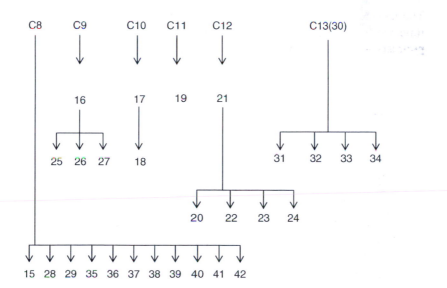

Figure A2 Source of interviews, Wave 2.

findings and it was determined that for the period in question this was in fact representative. The size of this sample cannot be representative of all retired gardaí or all experiences within the Irish police. However, the depth of interviews, the range of ranks and the geographical spread does provide sufficient data which can be analysed to understand the experience of policing Ireland in this time.

As the interviews took place all over the country research trips were organised with interviews grouped geographically. Wave 2 comprised three dedicated research trips of about five days in length, which could cover thousands of miles. One such trip involved driving over 600 miles between seven different interview locations. Up to ten interviews could be done in those five days, though there were often three interviews in one day. This required a great deal of coordination (and map reading!) on my part, but thankfully interviewees were flexible in accommodating my organisational difficulties.

Arranging the interviews generally involved three to four phone calls: the first explaining the nature of the project and sounding out a willingness to participate; the second arranging a date and time; and a final phone call confirming the interview the week it was due to take place. A fourth was occasionally required when map-reading skills failed. In most instances the participant had already discussed the project with the contact who provided their details in the first place. As a result of this, I found that many participants had considered in advance what the discussion would focus on ('I thought you might ask me that' was said on more than one occasion) and had often revisited photographs, official documents and magazines. Some had a range of these items spread on a table when I arrived. One even took me to his shed to show me the original garda bicycle, which he had reclaimed some years ago.

Interviews generally began with me explaining further the nature of the project, the intended outputs and reiterating both anonymity and that subjects could decline to answer any questions at any time. Any questions about the project were clarified and they often enquired as to my background, my qualifications and where I was from in the country. Refreshments were usually provided by the participants. The nature of the questions (see interview schedule, Appendix 4) put them at ease quickly and a rapport was quickly established. Often this might be through discussion of the contact, particularly if this was through a friend or a family member. At times this related to the seemingly inbuilt desire among Irish people to 'place' each other. At one interview, which was independently secured, the participant was being quite guarded in the interview until, after an hour, he realised that he knew my father. Suddenly the interview was transformed and he became exceptionally helpful. He began speaking more freely about the issues we had been discussing and provided me with a selection of literature he had collected over the years. On two occasions since he has posted me material related to my research and put me in contact with other interviewees.

Recording the information

Wave 1 of the interviews were recorded by way of field notes due to an unwillingness on the part of participants to be tape-recorded. That some interviewees may be uncomfortable with the audio-recording of interviews is well documented in qualitative research literature. Arskey and Knight point out that 'the idea of taping might increase nervousness or dissuade frankness' (1999: 105). As to why these interview subjects were unwilling, to varying degrees interviewing suspects was a significant part of the job of police and the recording of suspect interviews had long been resisted by police in Ireland. They may not have desired a permanent, attributable record of the interview (Rubin and Rubin 1995; Rapley 2004). It should, of course, be stated that confidentiality had been promised and they had been assured the tapes would be destroyed following transcription. Another factor may have been the climate of tribunals and civil claims (two interviews took place on the day of the publication of the second Morris Tribunal Report). It is easy to imagine that retired members would have concerns that what they said in an interview could be used to put a further negative slant on the force. A final point relates more specifically to content. A number of those interviewed detailed specific cases they had worked on, often relating to the IRA. In the openness of the lengthy discussions a number of interviewees spoke of misconduct in specific cases that they, understandably, did not want to be attributable.

Instead of interview transcripts, field notes were made during interviews. Notes were then typed up immediately in an effort to remember as much as possible, including what had not been possible to note (Lofland and Lofland 1984; Sanjek 1990). These typed notes took the form of an interview diary including notes of what was asked, why that was asked, and additional notes on the interviewee's demeanour – laughter, sarcasm, being defensive (Sanjek 1990). In the end, while it may have been preferable to tape-record the interviews, it was still possible to record rich, qualitative data, as is, I hope, evidenced throughout the book.

The participants in Wave 2 however, consented to recording, which brought numerous advantages, including a more detailed and accurate record of the interview, more verbatim references, and enabled me to focus more on what they were saying and tailor follow-up questions. On the other hand, participants may have spoken more freely in the absence of the recording device and certainly some of the more surprising comments, such as membership of the Heavy Gang, were made when the recorder was not used. Minichiello *et al.* warn that the researcher 'may find that [it] inhibits interaction' (1995: 99). All data was then transcribed, coded and analysed using NVivo software.

Reflexive observations on interviewing gardaí

While there were some comments made relating to my comparative youth, perhaps the greatest subjective impact I noted in the course of the research was my gender. The difficulties faced by women interviewing elite men, and police officers in particular, are well documented (McEvoy 2006; Gill and Maclean 2002; Horn 1997). Horn (1997: 299) describes how women interviewing the police are likely to be viewed in the traditional female role. There may be advantages and disadvantages to this:

> The 'traditional woman' tends to be seen as harmless and unthreatening, and slightly incompetent. Beliefs in women's 'harmlessness' may allow them

access to areas which are barred to male researchers ... she also gives the impression of someone who must be protected ... a female researcher will be sheltered from the more unpleasant aspects of police work and the more unpleasant attitudes and beliefs held by police officers.

(Horn 1997: 300)

In this research a number of incidents would indicate that gender did have an impact, both positively and negatively. It certainly altered behaviour. For one, each man apologised if they cursed (Sarikakis 2003). In one particular interview, with the eldest subject, my gender clearly tainted his responses. He had served for a long time in the Special Branch, a division of an Garda Síochána I was keen to explore in great depth; however he spent over 25 minutes discussing when he was assigned to protective duty with Jackie Kennedy. I very much felt at the time, and still do, that he would have spent a lot less time on that if I were male. Equally, it could be argued that it was how I acted as a result of my gender awareness that affected his approach to me. Maclean, in her doctoral research, found that because of her age, gender and student status 'it fitted appropriate roles to be in a deferential, listening and learning mode' (2002: 3.2). This rings true for me, and I must accept that I may well have assumed such a role, which may have promoted such a focus.

At the same time I did hear what I believe to have been uncensored, graphic stories of serious incidents in the careers of those interviewed, suggesting gender did not have the impact I feared. Many men expressed highly negative attitudes towards female gardaí, with some commenting that their presence on the street was inappropriate, that they would be incapable of looking after themselves and how they themselves had spent much time 'looking after' such women. I had certainly not expected such views to be expressed to me, as a woman. Further, I was surprised at times by the willingness to discuss wrongdoing, which may perhaps relate to a perception of me as 'harmless'.

Another factor that became abundantly clear through these interviews was that these were effectively professional interviewers. This was particularly true with those who had reached more senior positions. I recognised the application of interviewing techniques to me, ones that I had been trained in during research methods courses. This was particularly true of the use of silence, which I recognised was being used at times by participants. A quizzical look, without a word, would prompt me to rephrase my questions, giving them a greater understanding of my meaning and more time to think. This is, however, not something that I feel altered the responses in any way. Indeed, I happily explained any question further if a participant asked me to do so.

Reliability of the data

Memory is often cited as detracting from the reliability of the oral history interview data. In the current research this did not appear to be a substantive problem.

The majority of interviewees were in their fifties or sixties and so did not have any particular memory difficulties. Many had, prior to the interview, reviewed any literature they had and such prior preparation would no doubt have aided recollection. Finally, and this is a purely subjectively perceived point, the interviewees for this research were entirely engaged with the subject matter. They did not appear to have any difficulty at all in remembering their time in an Garda Síochána. For instance, when asked the opening question, 'when did you join the gardaí?' the exact date was invariably rattled off.

There is a potential problem of how respondents present their history – do they glorify or deny their involvement in certain events? There is no evidence of glorification in the accounts obtained in the present research – some spoke modestly of cases they were proud of, or smiled at the recollection, but a sincere sense that the highs and lows were all part of the job was experienced. However, it seemed (subjectively perceived) that there was some degree of denial present in many interviews, most particularly in relation to the use of force. It was expected going into every interview that interviewees would claim that abuses of force did not occur. This was not the case. Some spoke frankly about times they had done so. Others spoke with acceptance of how it happened in the past, but how it was all different now. A significant number, however, denied entirely that this ever occurred, calling it a conspiracy on the part of the IRA who were always at the centre of such claims.

As the interviews sought to document the lived experience of policing, the focus was not on the accuracy of the information. It was however often possible to triangulate the data gathered. For instance, when gardaí told of the attack on the Dundalk garda station it was possible to verify through numerous different newspaper accounts that they had not over-estimated crowd sizes or sensationalised the sequence of events. Such triangulation enabled me to focus on understanding the impact of those incidents for gardaí as individuals and for the organisation as a whole.

Ethical concerns

Initially the ethical considerations of the research seemed limited, as police would not be considered particularly vulnerable research participants. All were retired so there were no potential repercussions professionally for them as participants. As the interviews began however, and some participants made unexpected admissions, some ethical concerns arose. One interviewee provided significant detail in relation to the operations of the Heavy Gang, referring to particular cases and investigations. Given that officially the existence of the Heavy Gang was still denied this was significant information. This generated a dilemma as to whether this abuse should be reported. Such ethical concerns have been experienced by other police researchers. Manning (1977) considers the impact that reporting brutality can have for the continuation of the research. In the case at hand, given the length of time that had passed and the fact that I had not witnessed the misconduct it was decided that there was little I could do.

In conclusion, the oral history method used for this research provided an invaluable insight into a very difficult period of policing in Ireland. Participants discussed issues that previously had not been explored in the literature, particularly in relation to the impact of the Troubles. Such information could not have been accessed through other means. Those interviewed were forthcoming and actively participated in the process, producing what was deemed to be reliable data.

Appendix 2: Guide to interviewees

The following are the abbreviations that are used in the text for those interviewed. They are identified by way of the highest rank they achieved in the force. The numbers refer to the order in which they were interviewed.

G1: Garda 1
G2: Garda 2
G3: Garda 3 etc.
SG1: Sergeant 1
SG2: Sergeant 2 etc.
DSG: Detective Sergeant
I1: Inspector 1
I2: Inspector 2 etc.
SI1: Superintendent 1
SI2: Superintendent 2
CSI1: Chief Superintendent 1
AC1: Assistant Commissioner 1
AC2: Assistant Commissioner 2

Appendix 3: Gardaí killed in the line of duty since 1922

14/11/1922 **Garda Henry Phelan** killed by IRA in Mullinahone, Co. Tipperary.

03/12/1923 **Sergeant James Woods** killed during an armed raid on Scartgalen Station.

29/01/1924 **Garda Patrick O'Halloran** was shot while trying to arrest two bank raiders in Co. Wicklow.

07/05/1924 **Sergeant Thomas Griffin** was killed while trying to arrest an armed criminal in Co. Tipperary.

19/10/1924 **Garda John Murrin** was shot with Sergeant Griffin while trying to arrest an armed criminal in Co. Tipperary.

28/12/1925 **Garda Thomas Dowling** was ambushed and killed in Co. Clare as a response to his enforcement of the distillation laws.

14/11/1926 **Sergeant James Fitzsimmons** was killed in Cork City when an armed gang attacked the garda station he was in.

16/11/1926 **Garda Hugh Ward** was killed in Co. Tipperary in the same series of attacks on stations as Sergeant Fitzsimmons.

11/06/1929 **Garda Timothy O'Sullivan** was killed in a booby-trap bomb in Co. Clare.

21/03/1931 **Superintendent John Curtain** was ambushed outside his home in Co. Tipperary.

04/01/1940 **Garda John Roche** was killed while arresting a wanted man in Cork City.

17/08/1940 **Sergeant Patrick McKeown** was killed while arresting a wanted man in Dublin.

16/08/1940 **Garda Richard Hyland** was killed with Sergeant McKeown in Dublin.

09/09/1942 **Sergeant Denis O'Brien** was ambushed outside his home in Co. Dublin.

01/10/1942 **Garda Micheal Walsh** was shot in Cavan while arresting a wanted man.

24/10/1942 **Garda George Mordant** was shot in Dublin while arresting a wanted man.

3/04/1970 **Garda Richard Fallon** shot when trying to intercept a bank raid committed by the Republic group Saor Eire in Dublin.

8/06/1972 **Garda Inspector Samuel Donegan** killed in a booby-trap explosion on the border. It is unknown who is responsible.

11/09/1975 **Garda Michael Reynolds** was shot when he, off duty, intercepted three people who had just committed armed robbery in Raheny, Dublin. A couple, who had met at a Sinn Fein meeting, were convicted for his death.

15/10/1976 **Garda Michael Clerkin** died during an explosion at a house in Portlaoise after a call was made stating there was suspicious activity at the house. No one has been charged with his murder although it is widely believed that members of the Provisional IRA are responsible.

07/07/1980 **Detective Garda John Morley** and **Garda Henry Byrne** were both shot in Co. Mayo when they followed a car full of men who had just committed armed robbery at a nearby bank. Three men were convicted of the murder, one was a suspected member of the IRA and the other two were believed to be members of the Irish Republican Socialist Party.

13/10/1980 **Detective Garda James Quaid** was shot by a member of the Provisional IRA when he asked to search his van following an armed robbery in Wexford. Peter Rogers was later convicted for his death and released from prison in 1998 under the Good Friday Agreement.

20/02/1982 **Garda Patrick Gerard Reynolds** was shot when he and three others investigated a call that men were acting suspiciously at a block of flats in Tallaght Dublin. Sixteen years later a member of the INLA was tried for the murder but the case fell on the issue of identification.

16/12/1983 **Recruit Garda Gary Sheehan** was shot along with Private Patrick Kelly by members of the Provisional IRA who were attempting to escape after the hostage-taking of Don Tidey in Leitrim.

10/08/1984 **Detective Garda Frank Hand** was shot while performing protective duty for a post-office delivery van that contained over £200,000 at the town of Drumree north of Dublin. Four members of the Provisional IRA were convicted of charges relating to his death, two for murder.

27/06/1985 **Garda Sergeant Patrick Morrissey** was shot dead at point-blank range having pursued armed raiders in Co. Louth. Two men, members of the INLA, were convicted of his murder.

18/05/1995 **Sergeant Paul Reid** was killed while performing peacekeeping duties for the UN in Sarajevo.

7/06/1996 **Detective Garda Gerry McCabe** was shot while performing security duties for cash deliveries in Limerick. Five members of the Provisional IRA were convicted for the murder.

20/07/1999 **Sergeant Andrew Callanan** died from injuries sustained after a man walked into Tallaght garda station and set fire to a can of petrol which he was carrying. The man in question was saved by Sergeant Callanan's actions.

25/01/2013 **Detective Garda Adrian Donohue** was shot dead while performing security duties for cash deliveries in Dundalk.

Appendix 4: Interview schedule

Personal service history:

- When did you join the force?
- Why?
- Had you worked before?
- How long were you a member?
- What was your position?
- Where were you stationed?
- Why did you leave?
- What stands out for you as the high points, both for you as an officer and for the force as a whole in the time that you were a member?
- And the low points?
- What were the most substantial changes you noticed during your time in an Garda Síochána?

Internal Legitimacy:

- How did you view an Garda Síochána before you joined?
- Did your own view of an Garda Síochána change over the years?
- At particular low points were efforts made to boost internal confidence?

External legitimacy:

- How do you think you were perceived by the public generally?
- How much of a concern was this?
- It would seem like the public have always had very high levels of confidence in an Garda Síochána, much more than is generally seen in other jurisdictions. Do you think there was any particular reason for this?

Accountability:

- Was 'accountability' an issue when you joined?
- How were problems dealt with at the time?

- When do you think it did become any issue?
- How do you think the force responded to calls for increased accountability in the 1970s/1980s?
- Did you ever have any contact with accountability mechanism like the Garda Complaints Board? What was your view of it?

Appendix 5: Commissioners of an Garda Síochána

- Michael Staines TD, February–September 1922
- Eoin O'Duffy, September 1922–February 1933
- Eamon Broy, February 1933–June 1938
- Michael Kinnane, June 1938–July 1952
- Daniel Costigan, July 1952–February 1965
- William P. Quinn, February 1965–March 1967
- Patrick Carroll BL, March 1967–September 1968
- Micheal Wymes, September 1968–January 1973
- Patrick Malone, January 1973–September 1975
- Edward Garvey, September 1975–January 1978
- Patrick McLoughlin, January 1978–January 1983
- Lawrence Wren, February 1983–November 1987
- Eamon Doherty, November 1987–December 1988
- Eugene Crowley, December 1988–January 1991
- Patrick J. Culligan MSc, January 1991–July 1996
- Patrick Bryne, July 1996–July 2003
- Noel Conroy, July 2003–November 2007
- Fachtna Murphy, November 2007–December 2010
- Martin Callinan, December 2010

Appendix 6: Payments in civil actions against an Garda Síochána, 1997–2007

Year (Total)	Payment	Assault (€)	Unlawful arrest (€)	Other (€)
1997	Award	NIL	NIL	NIL
(€864,313.74)	Settlement	43,171.09	104,753.39	316,535.37
	Costs	32,281.23	101,863.06	264,709.60
	Total	**76,452.32**	**206,616.45**	**581,244.97**
1998	Award	25,394.76	NIL	143,018.22
(€1,220,198.70)	Settlement	179,033.07	140,940.93	119,699.00
	Costs	45,755.21	78,016.14	488,341.38
	Total	**250,183.04**	**218,957.06**	**751,058.60**
1999	Award	NIL	NIL	NIL
(€1,517,844.93)	Settlement	86,342.19	49,329.32	826,446.37
	Costs	197,984.54	131,883.24	225,859.27
	Total	**284,326.73**	**181,212.56**	**1,052,305.64**
2000	Award	32,708.45	NIL	NIL
(€874,915.35)	Settlement	204,523.06	79,612.58	248,977.86
	Costs	89,425.90	183,518.56	36,148.94
	Total	**326,657.41**	**263,131.14**	**285,126.80**
2001	Award	1,904.61	20,950.68	22,220.42
(€1,619,746.83)	Settlement	123,164.59	33,965.49	162,782.25
	Costs	244,665.35	123,199.41	886,894.03
	Total	**369,734.55**	**178,115.58**	**1,071,896.70**
2002	Award	1,270 (1)	3,809.21(1)	56,500 (2)
(€1,240,388.40)	Settlement	166,924.48 (6)	106,835.58 (10)	185,078.82 (11)
	Costs	230,769.67	148,714.19	340,486.45
	Total	**398,964.15**	**259,358.98**	**582,065.27**
2003	Award	11,000 (1)	10,000 (2)	4,870 (2)
(€1,276,127.55)	Settlement	75,000 (4)	303,011 (5)	112,814.84 (4)
	Costs	145,561.70	71,794.28	542,075.73
	Total	**231,561.70**	**384,805.28**	**659,760.57**
2004	Award	15,000 (1)	NIL	3,215.06 (1)
(€938,799.09)	Settlement	198,697.48 (5)	73,007 (5)	50,500 (3)
	Costs	231,646.62	100,019.36	266,713.57
	Total	**445,344.10**	**173,026.36**	**320,428.63**
2005	Award	1,000 (1)	2,025,321 (8)	85,125 (2)
(€4,870,233.53)	Settlement	130,250 (7)	1,569,114 (9)	58,000(2)

	Costs	137,447.90 (10)	658,508.78 (10)	205,446.85 (15)
	Total	**268,697.90**	**4,252,943.78**	**348,591.85**
2006	Award	18,076.32 (1)	41,443.80 (3)	NIL
(€1,951,984.94) provisional	Settlement	386,200.00 (17)	622,000 (15)	606,500.00 (8)
	Costs	187,797.28 (11)	60,983.61 (10)	28,983.93 (3)
	Total	**592,073.60**	**724,427.41**	635,483.93
2007 as at 30/03/07	Award	72,500.00(1)	NIL	70,000.00 (1)
(€513,297.28)	Settlement	126,500.00(3)	8,500.00 (2)	75,000.00 (3)
	Costs	53,514.55 (3)	57,432.04 (3)	49850.69 (5)
	Total	**252,514.55**	**65,932.04**	194,850.69
€16,887,850.30		**3,496,510.05**	**6,908,526.64**	**6,482,813.65**

Bibliography

Ainsworth, P. B. (2002) *Psychology and Policing*, Cullompton, Devon: Willan.

Alderson, J. (1979) *Policing Freedom: A Commentary on the Dilemmas of Policing in Western Democracies,* Estover: MacDonald and Evans.

Allen, G. (1999) *The Garda Síochána: Policing Independent Ireland 1922–82,* Dublin: Gill & MacMillan.

Amnesty International (1977) *Report of Amnesty International Mission to Ireland* (28 November–6 December 1977).

Amnesty International: Irish Section (2001) *Racism in Ireland: A Summary of Research,* Dublin: Amnesty International.

Anderson, M. and Bort, E. (1999) *The Irish Border: History, Politics and Culture,* Liverpool: Liverpool University Press.

Anderson, D. and Killingray, D. (1991) *Policing the Empire: Government, Authority and Control, 1830–1940,* Manchester: Manchester University Press.

An Garda Síochána and Irish Council for Civil Liberties (2006) *The European Convention on Human Rights Act 2003: A Short Guide,* Dublin

Arskey, H. and Knight, P. T. (1999) *Interviewing for Social Scientists,* London: Sage.

Ashcroft, B. Griffiths, G. and Tiffin, H. (1989) *Key Concepts in Postcolonial Studies,* London: Routledge.

Baldwin, R. and Kinsey, R. (1982) *Police Powers and Politics,* London: Quartet Books.

Banton, M. (1964) *Policeman in the Community*, London: Tavistock.

Barker, D. and Carter, D. L. (1986) *Police Deviance,* Ohio: Anderson Publishing Company.

Barr, J. (2006) *The Tribunal of Inquiry into the Facts and Circumstances Surrounding the Fatal Shooting of John Carthy at Abbeylara, Co. Longford on 20th April 2000,* Dublin: The Stationery Office.

Barrington, B. (2009) *Breakdown in Trust: A Report on the Corrib Gas Dispute,* Dublin: Front Line.

Bartlett, T. (1991) 'What Is my Nation?: Themes in Irish History 1550–1850' in T. Bartlett, C. Curtin, R. O'Dwyer and G. O'Tuathaigh (eds), *Irish Studies: A General Introduction,* Dublin: Gill & MacMillan, p. 44.

Bayley, D. H. (1983) 'Accountability and Control of the Police: Lessons from Britain' in T. Bennett (ed.), *The Future of Policing: Papers Presented to 15th Cropwood Round Table Conference, December 1982,* Cambridge: Cambridge University Press.

Bayley, D. H. (1996) 'Control of the Police' in D. H. Bayley (ed.), *Patterns of Policing: A Comparative International Analysis,* New Brunswick: Rutgers University Press.

Bayley, D. H. (1998) *What Works in Policing,* Oxford: Oxford University Press.

Bayley, D. and Shearing, C. (1996) 'The Future of Policing', *Law and Society Review,* 30: 585–606.

Beagley-Imhoff, D. (2000) *Effects of Stress on the Garda Síochána: Willingness to Access Counselling*, Unpublished Master's thesis, Trinity College Dublin.

Beaumont, C. (1997) 'Women, Citizenship and Catholicism in the Irish Free State, 1922–1948', *Women's History Review*, 6(4): 563–85.

Beetham, D. (1991) *The Legitimation of Power,* London: Macmillan.

Bennett, R. (1959) *The Black and Tans*, London: Hulton.

Bew, P. and Gillespie, G. (1999) *Northern Ireland: A Chronology of the Troubles 1968–1999*, Dublin: Gill & Macmillan.

Bew, P., Gibbon, P. and Patterson, H. (2002) *Northern Ireland 1921–2001: Political Forces and Social Classes*, London: Serif.

Birmingham, G. (2006) *Report of the Commission of Investigation (Dean Lyons Case)*, Dublin: The Stationery Office.

Bittner, E. (1974) *Florence Nightingale in Pursuit of Willie Sutton: A Theory of Police Work*, Boston: Northeastern University Press.

Bittner, E. (1990) *Aspects of Police Work*, Boston: Northeastern University Press.

Boed, R. (1999) 'An Evaluation of the Legality and Efficacy of Lustration as a Tool of Transitional Justice', *Columbia Journal of Transnational Law,* 37: 357–402.

Bohan, P. and Yorke, D. (1987) 'Law Enforcement Marketing: Perceptions of a Police Force', *Irish Marketing Review*, 2: 72–86.

Bonner, K. (2004) *Garda SMI Implementation Group Final Report*, Dublin: The Stationery Office.

Bowden, T. (1977) *The Breakdown of Public Security: The Case of Ireland 1916–1921 and Palestine 1936–1939*, London: Sage.

Bowyer Bell, J. (1997) *The Secret Army: The IRA*, Third Edition, Dublin: Transaction Publishing.

Boyce, D. (1982) *Nationalism in Ireland*, Third Edition, London: Routledge.

Boyce, D. G. and O'Day, A. (1996) *The Making of Modern Irish History: Revisionism and the Revisionist Controversy,* London: Routledge.

Boyle, K. (1972) 'Police In Ireland Before the Union: I', *The Irish Jurist,* 7: 115–37.

Boyle, K. (1973a) 'Police in Ireland Before the Union: II', *The Irish Jurist,* 8: 90–116.

Boyle, K. (1973b) 'Police In Ireland Before the Union: III', *The Irish Jurist,* 8: 322–38.

Bradford, B., Jackson, J. and Stanko, E. (2009) 'Contact and Confidence: Revisiting the Impact of Public Encounters with the Police', *Policing and Society*, 19(1): 20–46.

Bradford, B., Stanko, E. and Jackson, J. (2009) 'Using Research to Inform Policy: The Role of Public Attitude Surveys in Understanding Public Confidence and Police Contact', *Policing*, 3(2): 139–48.

Bradley, J. (2000) 'The Irish Economy in Comparative Perspective' in B. Nolan, P. O'Connell and C. Whelan (eds), *Bust to Boom: The Irish Experience of Growth and Inequality*, Dublin: Institute of Public Administration.

Brady, C. (1974) *Guardians of the Peace*, First Edition, Dublin: Prendeville Publishing Limited.

Brady, C. (1975) 'Editorial', *Garda Review*, 3(8): 1.

Brady, C. (2000) *Guardians of the Peace,* Second Edition, Dublin: Prendeville Publishing Limited.

Breathnach, S. (1974) *The Irish Police: From Earliest Times to Present Day,* Dublin: Anvil Books.

Breathnach, S. (2004) *Crime and Punishment in Twentieth Century Ireland*, Florida: Universal Publishers.

Brewer J. (1990a) *The Royal Irish Constabulary: An Oral History,* Belfast: Institute of Irish Studies.

Brewer, J. D. (1990b) 'Talking About Danger: The RUC and the Paramilitary Threat', *Sociology,* 24(4): 657–74.

Brewer, J. and Magee, K. (1991) *Inside the RUC,* Oxford: Oxford University Press.

Brewer, J. D., Guelke, A., Hume, I., Moxon-Browne, E. and Wilford, R. (1996) *The Police, Public Order and the State: Policing in Great Britain, Northern Ireland, the Irish Republic, the USA, Israel, South Africa and China,* Second Edition, Basingstoke: Macmillan.

Brewer, J. D., Lockhart, B. and Rodgers, P. (1997) *Crime in Ireland 1945–1995: Here Be Dragons*, Oxford: Clarendon Studies in Criminology.

Brodeur, J. P. (1983) 'High Policing and Low Policing: Remarks About the Policing of Political Activities', *Social Problems,* 30(5): 507–20.

Brodeur, J. P. (2005) 'Trotsky in Blue: Permanent Policing Reform', *The Australian and New Zealand Journal of Criminology*, 38(2): 254–67.

Brogden, M. (1987) 'The Emergence of the Police: The Colonial Dimension', *British Journal of Criminology*, 27(1): 4–14.

Brogden M. (1991) *On the Mersey Beat: Policing Liverpool Between the Wars,* Oxford: Oxford University Press.

Brogden, M. and Shearing, C. (1993) *Policing for a New South Africa,* London: Routledge.

Brodgen, M. and Ellison, G. (2012) *Policing in an Age of Austerity: A Postcolonial Perspective*, London: Routledge.

Brogden, M., Jefferson, T. and Walklate, S. (1988) *Introducing Police Work,* Boston: Unwin Hyman.

Brown, J. (1997) 'Equal Opportunities and the Police in England and Wales: Past, Present and Future Opportunities' in P. Francis, P. Davies and V. Jupp (eds), *Policing Futures*, London: Macmillan.

Brown, J. (2000) 'Discriminatory Experiences of Women Police. A Comparison of Officers Serving in England and Wales, Scotland, Northern Ireland and the Republic of Ireland', *International Journal of the Sociology of Law,* 28: 91–111.

Brown, T. (1995) *Ireland: A Social and Cultural History 1922–1985,* London: Fontana.

Browne, C. (2008) *Garda Public Attitudes Survey 2008*, Templemore: Garda Research Unit.

Bryman, A. (2004) *Social Research Methods,* Second Edition, Oxford: Oxford University Press.

Burton, F. and Carlen, P. (1979) *Official Discourse,* London: Routledge.

Byrne, E. (2012) *Political Corruption in Ireland 1922–2010: A Crooked Harp?*, Manchester: Manchester University Press.

Byrne, R. and McCutcheon, P. (2004) *The Irish Legal System*, Fourth Edition, Dublin: Tottel Publishing.

Cain, M. (1973) *Society and the Policeman's Role*, London: Routledge.

Caldwell, J. (2004) 'Women in the Gardaí', *Garda Review*, 32(6–7): 14–16.

Cameron, I. (1985) 'Commission of Inquiry Concerning Certain Activities of the Royal Canadian Mounted Police. Second Report: "Freedom, Security and the Law"', *The Modern Law Review*, 48(2): 201–11.

Campbell, C. (1994) *Emergency Law In Ireland 1918–1925,* Oxford: Clarendon Press.

Campbell, L. (2006) 'Decline of Due Process in the Irish Justice System: Beyond the Culture of Control?', *Hibernian Law Journal*, 125–58.

Campbell, L. (2010) 'Responding to Gun Crime in Ireland', *British Journal of Criminology*, 50(3): 414–34.

Canny, N. (2001) *Making Ireland British: 1580–1650,* Oxford: Oxford University Press.

Capoccia, G. (2001) 'Repression, Incorporation, Lustration and Education: How Democracies React to Their Enemies. Towards a Theoretical Framework for the Comparative Analysis of Defence of Democracy', ECPR Joint Sessions of Workshops, Grenoble, 6–11 April.

Caroll C. and King, P. (eds) (2003) *Ireland and Postcolonial Theory*, Cork: Cork University Press.

Casey, M. (1989) *Domestic Violence: The Women's Perspective*, Dublin: UCD Press.

Chan, J. (1996) 'Changing Police Culture', *British Journal of Criminology,* 36(1): 109–34.

Chan, J. (1997) *Changing Police Culture: Policing in a Multicultural Society,* Cambridge: Cambridge University Press.

Chan, J. (1999) 'Governing Police Practice: Limits of the New Accountability', *British Journal of Sociology,* 50(2): 251–70.

Chan, J. (2007) 'Making Sense of Police Reforms', *Theoretical Criminology,* 11: 323–45.

Charleton, P. (1995) 'Drugs and Crime: Making the Connection: A Discussion Paper', *Irish Criminal Law Journal*, 5(2): 220–40.

Clancy, C. (2009) 'Fifty Years Later: Women in Policing', *Communique*, 22–8.

Clancy, P. (1995) *Irish Society: Sociological Perspectives,* Dublin: Institute of Public Administration.

Cleary, J. (2007) *Outrageous Fortune: Capital and Culture in Modern Ireland,* Second Edition, Dublin: Field Day Publications.

Cockcroft, T. (2005) 'Using Oral History to Investigate Police Culture', *Qualitative Research,* 5(3): 365–84.

Cohen, S. (2000) *States of Denial: Knowing About Atrocities and Suffering*, Cambridge: Polity Press.

Cole, B. (1999) 'Post-Colonial Systems' in R. Mawby (ed.), *Policing Across the World: Issues for the 21st Century*, New York: UCL Press, pp. 88–108.

Commission of Inquiry into the Actions of Canadian Officials in Relation to Maher Arar (2006) *A New Review Mechanism for the RCMP's National Security Activities*. Ottawa: Commission of Inquiry.

Connolly, C. (1999) 'Postcolonial Ireland: Posing the Question', *European Journal of English Studies,* 3(3): 255–61.

Connolly, J. (1998) 'From Colonial Policing to Community Policing', *Irish Criminal Law Journal*, 8: 165–95.

Connolly, J. (2002) 'Policing Ireland: Past Present and Future' in P. O'Mahony (ed.), *Criminal Justice in Ireland*, Dublin: IPA.

Conroy, J. C. (1970) *Report on Remuneration and Conditions of Service,* Dublin: The Stationery Office.

Conway, V. (2004) 'Garda Síochána: Garda Síochána Ombudsman Commission', *Irish Law Times,* 22: 157–62.

Conway, V. (2005) 'An Garda Síochána Act 2005 – Breaking Down the Thick Blue Wall?', *Irish Law Times,* 24: 368–72.

Conway, V. (2008) 'Lost in Translation: Ireland and the Patten Report', *Northern Ireland Law Quarterly,* 54(4): 411–28.

Conway, V. (2009) 'A Sheep in Wolf's Clothing? Evaluating the Impact of the Garda Síochána Ombudsman Commission', *Irish Jurist,* 43: 109–30.

Conway, V. (2010) *The Blue Wall of Silence: The Morris Tribunal and Police Accountability in Ireland,* Dublin: Irish Academic Press.

Conway, V. and Mulqueen, M. (2009) 'The 2009 Anti-Gangland Package: Ireland's New Security Blanket?', *Irish Criminal Law Journal,* 19(4): 106–13.

Conway, V. and Walsh, D. (2011) 'Recent Developments in Police Governance and Accountability in Ireland', *Crime Law and Social Change,* 55(2–3): 241–57.

Cook, T. (2004) 'Under Pressure', *Garda Review,* 32: 21–4.

Cory, P. (2003) *Cory Collusion Inquiry Report: Chief Superintendent Breen and Superintendent Buchanan,* Dublin: Department of Justice.

Coulter, C. (1993) *The Hidden Tradition: Feminism, Women and Nationalism in Ireland,* Cork: Cork University Press.

Coulter, C. and Coleman, S. (eds.) (2003) *The End of Irish History,* Manchester: Manchester University Press.

Coulter, W. (1996) 'Accuracy in Oral History Interviewing' in D. K. Dunaway and W. K. Baum (eds.), *Oral History: An Interdisciplinary Anthology,* Second Edition, Nashville: AAHSL Book Series.

Courtney, J. (1996) *It Was Murder!* Dublin: Blackwater Press.

Crawshaw, R and Holstrom, L. (2006) *Essential Cases on Human Rights for the Police,* Antwerp: M. Nijoff.

Cunningham, G. (2009) *Chaos and Conspiracy: The Framing of the McBrearty Family,* Dublin: Gill & MacMillan.

Curtis, R. (1871) *The History of the Royal Irish Constabulary,* London: McGlahan and Gill, reproduced by BiblioBazaar.

Daly, M. E. (1981) *A Social and Economic History of Ireland Since 1800,* Dublin: The Educational Company.

Dantzker, M. (1997) *Contemporary Policing: Personnel, Issues and Trends,* New York: Butterworth.

Davidson, A. J. (2003) *Kidnapped: True Stories of Twelve Irish Hostages,* Dublin: Gill & MacMillan.

Davis, F. (2006) *The History and Development of the Special Criminal Court, 1922–2005,* Dublin: Four Courts Press.

Day, P. and Klein, R. (1987) *Accountabilities: Five Public Services,* London: Tavistock.

Dean, G., Bradshaw, J. and Lavelle, P. (1983) 'The Opiate Epidemic in Dublin 1979–1983', *Irish Medical Journal,* 78: 107–10.

DeMaria, W. (1997) 'The British Whistleblower Protection Bill: A Shield Too Small?', *Crime, Law and Social Change,* 27: 139–63.

Devitt, D. (1997) *Never Bet: A Garda Remembers and Reflects,* Dublin: Premier Publications.

Dixon, D. (2004) 'Police Governance and Official Inquiry' in G. Gilligan and J. Pratt (eds), *Crime, Truth and Justice,* Collompton, Devon: Willan.

Dooley, D. (1998) 'Gendered Citizenship in the Irish Constitution' in T. Murphy and P. M. Twomey (eds), *Ireland's Evolving Constitution,* Oxford: Hart.

Dooley, E. (1995) *Homicide in Ireland 1972–1991,* Dublin: The Stationery Office.

Doyle, T. (1997) *Peaks and Valleys: The Ups and Downs of a Young Garda,* Dublin: TJD Publications.

Dunne, D. and Kerrigan, G. (1984) *Round Up the Usual Suspects,* Dublin: Magill.

ECPT (European Committee for the Prevention of Torture) (1993) *Report to the Government of Ireland on the Visit Carried out by the European Committee for the Prevention of Torture and Inhumane or Degrading Treatment or Punishment (CPT)*, Strasbourg. Available at http://www.cpt.coe.int/documents/irl/1996-23-inf-eng.pdf (accessed 5 April 2012).

ECPT (European Committee for the Prevention of Torture) (1998), *Report to the Government of Ireland on the Visit to Ireland Carried out by the European Committee for the Prevention of Torture and Inhumane or Degrading Treatment or Punishment (CPT)*, Strasbourg. Available at http://www.cpt.coe.int/documents/irl/2000-08-inf-eng.htm (accessed 5 April 2012).

ECPT (European Committee for the Prevention of Torture) (2002) *Report to the Government of Ireland on the Visit to Ireland carried out by the European Committee for the Prevention of Torture and Inhumane or Degrading Treatment or Punishment (CPT)*, Strasbourg. Available at http://www.cpt.coe.int/documents/irl/2003-36-inf-eng.htm (accessed 5 April 2012).

ECPT (European Committee for the Prevention of Torture) (2007) *Report to the Government of Ireland on the Visit to Ireland 2–13 October 2006 carried out by the European Committee for the Prevention of Torture and Inhumane or Degrading Treatment or Punishment (CPT)*, Strasbourg, Available at http://www.cpt.coe.int/documents/irl/2007-40-inf-eng.htm (accessed 10 January 2012).

Ellison, G. (2007) 'Police Reform, Political Transition, and Conflict Resolution in Northern Ireland', *Police Quarterly,* 10: 243–69.

Ellison, G. and Smyth, J. (2000) *The Crowned Harp: Policing Northern Ireland*, London: Pluto Press.

Ellison, G. and Mulcahy, A. (2001) 'Policing and Social Conflict in Northern Ireland', *Policing and Society,* 11: 243–58.

Emsley, C. (1996) *Crime and Society in England 1750–1900*, Second Edition, Harlow: Pearson, Education.

English, R. (2004) *Armed Struggle: A History of the IRA*, Oxford: Pan Macmillan.

Farrell, M. (1993) 'Anti-terrorism and Ireland: The Experience of the Irish Republic' in T. Bunyan (ed.), *Statewatching the New Europe*, London: Statewatch.

Fedorowich, E. (1996) 'The Problems of Disbandment: The Royal Irish Constabulary and Imperial Migration, 1919–1929', *Irish Historical Studies*, 117: 88–110.

Feehan, M. (2010) *Community Participation in the Development of Local Policing Policy and Practice: The Community Policing Forum Model of Engagement*, Unpublished DGov thesis, Queen's University Belfast.

Ferns Inquiry (2005) *The Ferns Report*, Dublin: Government Publications.

Ferriter, D. (2005) *The Transformation of Ireland, 1900–2000*, London: Profile Books.

Ferriter, D. (2009) *Occasions of Sin: Sex and Society in Modern Ireland*, London: Profile Books.

Ferriter, D. (2012) *Ambiguous Republic: Ireland in the 1970s*, London: Profile Books.

Fine Gael and Labour, (2006) *Policing Our Communities: An Agreed Agenda on Garda Reform*. Available at http://www.finegael.ie/news/documents/Policing%20Our%20Communities%20Doc%20%20Cover.pdf (accessed 22 November 2006).

Finnane, M. (1990) 'Police Corruption and Police Reform: The Fitzgerald Inquiry in Queensland, Australia', *Policing and Society*, 1(2): 159–71.

Fitzgerald, G. (1991) *All in a Life: An Autobiography,* Dublin: Gill & MacMillan.

Fitzgerald, M., Hough, M., Joseph, I. and Qureshi, T. (2002) *Policing for London*, Cullompton, Devon: Willan.

Fitzgerald, T. P. (2008) 'The Morris Tribunal of Inquiry and the Garda Síochána', *Communique*, 3–31.

Fogarty, M., Ryan, L. and Lee, J. (1984) *Irish Values and Attitudes*, Dublin: Dominican Publications.

Garda Commissioner (2009) *S.23 Garda Síochána Act Three Year Review Report*, Dublin: Garda Commissioner.

Garda Inspectorate (2007a) *Report on Senior Management Structures in the Garda Síochána*, Dublin: Garda Inspectorate.

Garda Inspectorate (2007b) *Review of Practices and Procedures for Barricade Incidents*, Dublin: Garda Inspectorate.

Garda Representative Association (1970) *Submissions to Commission on Garda Pay and Conditions of Service*, Dubin: Garda Representative Association.

Garda Research Unit (2002) *Garda Public Attitudes Survey 2002*, Templemore: Garda Research Unit.

Garda Síochána Complaints Board (2002) *Annual Report*. Dublin: The Stationery Office

Garda Síochána Complaints Board (2003) *Annual Report*. Dublin: The Stationery Office

Garda Síochána Complaints Board (2004) *Annual Report*. Dublin: The Stationery Office

Garda Síochána Complaints Board (2005) *Annual Report*. Dublin: The Stationery Office

Garda Síochána Complaints Board (2006) *Annual Report*. Dublin: The Stationery Office

Garda Síochána Inspectorate (2007) *Review of Garda Síochána Practices and Procedures for Barricade Incidents*, Dublin: The Stationery Office.

Garda Síochána Ombudsman Commission (2006) *Annual Report,* Dublin: Garda Síochána Ombudsman Commission.

Garda Síochána Ombudsman Commission (2008a) *Annual Report 2008,* Dublin: Garda Síochána Ombudsman Commission.

Garda Síochána Ombudsman Commission (2008b) *Biannual Report on the Effectiveness of the Ombudsman Commission*, Dublin: Garda Síochána Ombudsman Commission.

Garnham, N. (1996) *The Courts, Crime and the Criminal Law in Ireland 1692–1760*, Dublin: Irish Academic Press.

Garvin, T. (1996) *1922: The Birth of Irish Democracy*, Dublin: Gill & MacMillan.

Gethins, M. (2010) *Catholic Police Officers in Northern Ireland: Voices out of Silence*, Manchester: Manchester University Press.

Ghandi, L. (1998) *Postcolonial Theory*, New York: Colombia University Press.

Gill, F. and Maclean, C. (2002) 'Knowing Your Place: Gender and Reflexivity in Two Ethnographies', *Sociological Research Online*, 7(2).

Ginnell, L. (1917) *The Brehon Laws: A Legal Handbook*, London: Unwin.

Goldsmith, A. (2005) 'Police Reform and the Problem of Trust', *Theoretical Criminology,* 9(4): 443–70.

Goldstein, H. (1975) *Police Corruption: A Perspective on its Nature and Control*, Washington: Police Foundation.

Government of Ireland (2002) *Response of the Government of Ireland to the Report of the European Committee for the Prevention of Torture and Inhumane or Degrading Treatment or Punishment (CPT) on its Visit to Ireland,* Dublin: The Stationery Office.

Government of Ireland (2007) *Response of the Government of Ireland to the Report of the European Committee for the Prevention of Torture and Inhumane or Degrading Treatment or Punishment (CPT) on its Visit to Ireland from 2nd to the 13th October, 2006,* Dublin: The Stationery Office.

Graef, R. (1989) *Talking Blues: The Police in Their Own Words,* London: Collins Harvill.

Graham, C. (2001) 'Liminal Spaces: Post Colonialism and Post-nationalism' in C. Graham (ed.), *Deconstructing Ireland: Identity, Theory, Culture,* Edinburgh: Edinburgh University Press.

Grattan, H. (1822) *The Speeches of Henry Grattan*, Dublin: Longman.

Grele, R. (1998) 'Movement Without Aim: Methodological and Theoretical Problems in Oral History' in R. Perks and A. Thomson (eds), *The Oral History Reader*, London: Routledge.

Haberfeld, M. and Cerrah, I. (2007) *Comparative Policing: The Struggle for Democratization*, London: Sage.

Habermas, J. (1975) *Legitimation Crisis,* Boston: Beacon Press.

Hall, S., Critcher, C., Jefferson, T., Clarke, J. and Roberts, B. (1978) *Policing the Crisis: Mugging, the State and Law and Order*, London: Macmillan.

Hamilton, C. (2007) *The Presumption of Innocence in Irish Criminal Law*, Dublin: Irish Academic Press.

Hardiman, N. and Whelan, C. T. (1994) 'Politics and Democratic Values' in C. T. Whelan (ed.), *Values and Social Change in Ireland*, Dublin: Gill & MacMillan.

Harris, W. C. (1988) *Policing in Ireland: The Role of the Garda*, Unpublished dissertation, University College Cork.

Hartnett, H. (2008) *Inquiry Pursuant to the Dublin Police Act 1924 as Amended by the Police Force Amalgamation Act 1925,* Dublin: Government Publications Office.

Hawkins, R. (1966) 'Dublin Castle and the RIC (1916–1922)' in T. Desmond Williams (ed.), *The Irish Struggle 1916–1926*, London: Routledge.

Hayes, M. (2007) *Report of the Garda Síochána Act 2005 Implementation Review Group*, Dublin: Department of Justice, Equality and Law Reform.

Heidenshon, F. (1992) *Women in Control? The Role of Women in Law Enforcement,* Oxford: Oxford University Press.

Hennelly, R. (2007) *Abbeylara: The Tragic Shooting of John Carthy*, Dublin: The O'Brien Press.

Hennessey, T. (1997) *A History of Northern Ireland 1920–1996*, Dublin: Gill & MacMillan.

Henry, B. (1994) *Dublin Hanged: Crime, Law Enforcement and Punishment in Eighteenth Century Dublin,* Dublin: Irish Academic Press.

Henry, V. (2004) *Death Work: Police, Trauma, and the Psychology of Survival*, Oxford: Oxford University Press.

Herbert, S. (2006) 'Tangled Up in Blue: Conflicting Paths to Police Legitimacy', *Theoretical Criminology*, 10(4): 481–504.

Herlihy, J. (1997) *The Royal Irish Constabulary: A Short History and Genealogical Guide,* Dublin: Four Courts Press.

Herlihy, J. (2001) *The Dublin Metropolitan Police: A Short History and Genealogical Guide*, Dublin: Four Courts Press.

Hicks, J. and Allen, G. (1999) *A Century of Change: Trends in UK Statistics Since 1900,* House of Commons, Research Paper 99/111.

Home Office (2012) *Police Service Strength England and Wales: 31 March 2012,* London: HMSO.

Horn, R. (1997) 'Not "One of the Boys": Women Researching the Police', *Journal of Gender Studies*, 6(3): 297–308.

Howe, S. (2000) *Ireland and Empire,* Oxford: Oxford University Press.

Hutchinson, J. (1994) 'Ethnicity and Modern Nations', *Ethnic and Racial Studies,* 23(4): 651–69.

Ilan, J. (2007) *Still Playing the Game: An Ethnography of Young People, Crime and Juvenile Justice in the Inner-City Dublin Community*, Unpublished PhD thesis, Dublin: DIT.

Independent Commission for Policing in Northern Ireland (1998) *A New Beginning: Policing in Northern Ireland (The Patten Report)*, Belfast: HMSO.

Independent Police Complaints Commission (2007) *Police Complaints Statistics for England and Wales 2007*, London: IPCC.

Inglis, T. (1998) *Moral Monopoly: The Rise and Fall of the Catholic Church in Modern Ireland*, Dublin: University College Dublin Press.

Inglis, T. (2003) *Truth, Power and Lies: Irish Society and The Case of the Kerry Babies*, Dublin: University College Dublin Press.

Innes, M. (2004) 'Signal Crimes and Signal Disorders: Notes on Deviance as Communicative Action', *British Journal of Sociology*, 55(3): 335–55.

Ionann Management Consultants (2004) *An Garda Síochána: Human Rights Audit*, Dublin: Ionann.

Irish Human Rights Commission (2002) *A Proposal for a New Garda Complaints System*, Dublin: Irish Human Rights Commission.

Ivkovic, S. and Haberfield, M. (2000) 'Transformation from Militia to Police in Croatia and Poland: A Comparative Perspective', *Policing: An International Journal of Police Strategies and Management*, 23(2): 194–217.

Jackson, J. and Sunshine, J. (2007) 'Public Confidence in Policing: A Neo-Durkheimian Perspective', *British Journal of Criminology*, 47: 213–33.

Jackson, J. and Bradford, B. (2009) 'Crime, Policing and Social Order: On the Expressive Nature of Public Confidence in Policing', *British Journal of Sociology*, 60(3): 493–521.

Jefferson, T. (1990) *The Case Against Paramilitary Policing*, Buckingham: Open University Press.

Jefferson, T. and Grimshaw, R. (1984) *Controlling the Constable*, London: Muller/Cobden Trust.

Joint Committee on Justice, Equality, Defence and Women's Rights (2002) *Interim Report of Committee on the Garda Investigation of the Shooting of Mr. John Carthy at Abbeylara on 20th April, 2000*, Dublin: The Stationery Office.

Jones, S. (1986) *Policewomen and Equality*, London: Macmillan.

Jones, T. (2003) 'The Governance and Accountability of Policing' in T. Newburn (ed.), *Handbook of Policing*, Collompton, Devon: Willan.

Jones, T. and Newburn, T. (2002) 'The Transformation of Policing? Understanding Current Trends in Policing Systems', *British Journal of Criminology*, 42: 129–46.

Jones, T., Newburn, T. and Smith, D. J. (1994) *Democracy and Policing*, London: Policy Studies Institute.

Jones, T., Newburn, T. and Smith, D. J. (1996) 'Policing and the Idea of Democracy', *British Journal of Criminology*, 36(2): 183–98.

Kadar, A. (ed.) (2001) *Police in Transition: Essays on Police Forces in Transition Countries*, Budapest: CEU Press.

Kanter, R. S. (1977) *Men and Women of the Corporation*, New York: Basic Books.

Kearns, K. C. (2006) *Dublin Tenement Life: An Oral History*, Dublin: Gill & MacMillan.

Kelly, F. (1988) *A Guide to Early Irish Law*, Dublin: Dublin Institute for Advanced Studies.

Kempa, M. (2007) 'Tracing the Diffusion of Police Governance Models from the British Isles and Back Again: Some Directions for Democratic Reform in Troubled Times', *Police Research and Practice*, 8(2): 107–23.

Kennedy, L. (1992/1993) 'Modern Ireland: Post-Colonial Society or Post-Colonial Pretensions?' *Irish Review,* 13: 107–21.

Kennedy, L. (1996) *Colonialism, Religion and Nationalism in Ireland,* Belfast: Institute for Irish Studies.

Kennedy, P. and Browne, C. (2006) *Garda Public Attitudes Survey 2006,* Templemore: Garda Research Unit.

Kennedy, P. and Browne, C. (2007) *Garda Public Attitudes Survey 2007,* Templemore: Garda Research Unit.

Keogh, E. (1997) *Illicit Drug Use and Related Criminal Activity in the Dublin Metropolitan Area,* Dublin: An Garda Síochána.

Kerrigan, G. and Brennan, P. (1999) *This Great Little Nation: The A–Z of Irish Scandals and Controversies,* Dublin: Gill & MacMillan.

Kertesz, I. and Szikinger, I. (2000) 'Changing Patterns of Culture and its Organisation of the Police in a Society of Transition – Case Study: Hungary', *European Journal on Criminal Policy and Research,* 8(3): 271–300.

Kilcommins, S. (1998) 'Context and Contingency in the Historical Penal Process: The Revision of Revisionist Analysis Using the Twelve Judges' Notebooks As One Tool of Analysis', *Holdsworth Law Review,* 19(1): 1–54.

Kilcommins, S., O'Donnell, I., O'Sullivan, E. and Vaughan, B. (2004) *Crime, Punishment and the Search for Order in Ireland,* Dublin: Irish Academic Press.

Kinsey, R., Lea, J. and Young, J. (1986) 'Discretion and Accountability: Proposals for a New Police Authority' in R. Kinsey, J. Lea, and J. Young (eds), *Losing the Fight Against Crime,* London: Blackwell.

Kirby, P., Gibbons, L. and Cronin, M. (eds) (2002) *Reinventing Ireland: Culture, Society and Global Economy,* London: Pluto Press.

Kissane, B. (2005) *The Politics of the Irish Civil War,* Oxford: Oxford University Press.

Kleinig, J. (1996) *The Ethics of Policing,* Cambridge: Cambridge University Press.

Kleinig, J. (2005) 'Gratuities and Corruption' in T. Newburn (ed.), *Policing: Key Readings,* Collompton, Devon: Willan.

Klockars, C. (2005) 'The Dirty Harry Problem' in T. Newburn (ed.), *Policing: Key Readings,* Collompton, Devon: Willan Publishing.

Knapp Commission, (1973) *The Knapp Commission Report on Police Corruption,* New York: Braziller Publishing.

Kopel, H. and Friedman, M. (1997) 'Post-traumatic Symptoms in South African Police Exposed to Violence', *Journal of Traumatic Stress,* 10(2): 307–17.

Kritz, N. J. (1996) 'Accountability for International Crime and Serious Violations of Fundamental Human Rights: Coming to Terms with Atrocities: A Review of Accountability Mechanisms For Mass Violations of Human Rights', *Law and Contemporary Problems,* 59(4): 127–53.

Labour Party (2000) *Proposals for Legislation for A Garda Authority and Garda Ombudsman,* Dublin: Labour Party.

Leahy, T. (1996) *Memoirs of a Garda Superintendent,* Dublin: Hero Press.

Lee, J. (1991) *Ireland 1912–1985,* Cambridge: Cambridge University Press.

Lloyd, D. (2001) 'Regarding Ireland in a Postcolonial Frame', *Cultural Studies,* 15(1): 12–32.

Loader, I. (1997) 'Policing and the Social: Questions of Symbolic Power', *British Journal of Sociology,* 48(1): 1–18.

Loader, I. and Mulcahy, A. (2001a) 'The Power of Legitimate Naming: Part I – Chief Constables as Social Commentators in Post-War England', *British Journal of Criminology,* 41(1): 41–55.

Loader, I. and Mulcahy, A. (2001b) 'The Power of Legitimate Naming: Part II – Making Sense of the Elite Police Voice', *British Journal of Criminology,* 41: 252–65.

Loader, I. and Mulcahy, A. (2003) *Policing and the Condition of England: Memory, Politics and Culture,* Oxford: Oxford University Press.

Loader, I. and Sparks, R. (2004) 'For an Historical Sociology of Crime Policy in England and Wales since 1968', *Critical Review of International and Political Philosophy,* 7: 5–32.

Lofland, J. and Lofland, L. H. (1984) *Analyzing Social Settings: A Guide to Qualitative Observation and Analysis,* California: Wadsworth Publishing.

Loftus, L. (2009) *Police Culture in a Changing World,* Oxford: Oxford University Press.

Logue, P. (ed.) (1999) *The Border: Personal Reflections from Ireland, North and South,* Dublin: Oak Tree Press.

Lowe, W. J. (1994) 'Policing Famine Ireland', *Éire-Ireland,* xxix(4): 47–67.

Lowe, W. J. (2002) 'The War Against the RIC 1919–1921', *Eire: Ireland,* 37(3): 79.

Lundman, R. (1980) *Police and Policing: An Introduction,* London: Holt, Reinhart and Winston.

Lustgarten, L. (1986) *The Governance of the Police,* London: Sweet & Maxwell.

Lyder, A. (2005) *Pushers Out: The Inside Story of Dublin's Anti-Drugs Movement,* Victoria: Trafford Publishing.

Lynch, K. (1985) *Report of the Tribunal of Inquiry into the 'Kerry Babies Case',* Dublin: The Stationery Office.

Lyons, F. S. L. (1979) *Culture and Anarchy in Ireland 1890–1939,* Oxford: Clarendon Press.

McAleese, M. (1987) 'Police and People' in W. Duncan (ed.), *Law and Social Policy: Some Current Problems in Irish Law,* Dublin: Dublin University Law Journal, pp. 45–64.

McAleese, M. (2013) *Report of the Inter-Departmental Committee to Establish the facts of State Involvement with the Magdalen Laundries,* Dublin: The Stationery Office.

McCafferty, N. (1985) *A Woman to Blame: The Kerry Babies Case,* Dublin: Attic Press.

McCarthy, B. (2012) *The Civic Guard Mutiny,* Cork: Mercier Press.

McCullagh, C. (1983) 'Police Powers and the Problem of Crime in Ireland: Some Implications for International Research', *Administration,* 31(4): 412–23.

McCullagh, C. (1996) *Crime in Ireland: A Sociological Introduction,* Cork: Cork University Press.

McCullagh, C. (1988) 'Is the Force Still With Us? The State of the Garda Síochána', Presentation on Conference on Policing, University College Cork, April 1988.

McEldowney, J. (1991) 'Policing and the Administration of Justice in Nineteenth-Century Ireland' in C. Emsley and B. Weinberger, (eds.), *Policing Western Europe: Politics, Professionalism, and Public Order, 1850–1940,* London: Greenwood Press.

McEntee, P. (2007) *Commission of Investigation into the Dublin and Monaghan Bombings 1974,* Dublin: The Stationery Office.

McEvoy, J. (2006) 'Elite Interviewing in a Divided Society: Lessons from Northern Ireland', *Politics,* 26(3): 184–91.

MacFarlane, L. J. (1990) *Human Rights: Realities and Possibilities,* Dublin: Macmillan.

McGarry, F. (2005) *Eoin O'Duffy: A Self-Made Man,* Oxford: OUP.

McGarry, J. and O'Leary, B. (1995) *Explaining Northern Ireland: Broken Images,* Oxford: Wiley Blackwell.

McGarry, P. (2006) *While Justice Slept: Nicky Kelly and the Sallins Mail Train Robbery,* Dublin: Liffey Press.

McGlinchey, K. (2005) *Charades: Adrienne McGlinchey and the Donegal Gardaí*, Dublin: Gill & MacMillan.

McKittrick, D. and McVea, D. (2000) *Making Sense of the Troubles*, Belfast: Blackstaff Press.

McNiffe, L. (1997) *A History of the Garda Síochána,* Dublin: Wolfhound Press.

Maguire, M. and Corbett, C. (1991) *A Study of the Police Complaints System,* London: HMSO.

Malcolm, E. (2005) *The Irish Policeman 1822–1922: A Life*, Dublin: Four Courts Press.

Malone, E. (1992) Stress in the Garda Síochána, available at www.irlgov.ie/garda/history/history1.htm (accessed 1 October 2003).

Manning, M. (2006) *The Blueshirts*, Dublin: Gill & MacMillan.

Manning, P. K. (1977) *Police Work: The Social Organisation of Policing,* Boston: MIT Press.

Manning, P. K. (2005) 'The Study of Policing', *Police Quarterly,* 8: 23–43.

Manning, P. K. (2012) 'Trust and Accountability in Ireland: The Case of an Garda Síochána', *Policing and Society*, 22(3): 346–61.

Marshall, G. (1978) *Police Accountability Revisited,* London: Macmillan.

Martin, C. (1996) 'The Impact of Equal Opportunities Policies on the Day-to-Day Experiences of Women Police Constables', *British Journal of Criminology,* 63(4): 510–28.

Martin, S. E. (1980) *'Breaking and Entering': Policewomen on Patrol*, Berkeley: University of California Press.

Martin, S. E. (1989) 'Women on the Move? A Report on the Status of Women in Policing', *Women in Criminal Justice*, 1(1): 21–40.

Martin, S. E. and Jurik, N. C. (1986) *Doing Justice, Doing Gender: Women in Law and Criminal Justice Occupations*, Thousand Oaks: Sage.

Mawby, R. (2001) 'The Impact of Transition: A Comparison of Post-Communist Societies with Earlier "Societies in Transition"' in A. Kadar (ed.), *Police in Transition: Essays on Police Forces in Transition Countries,* Budapest: CEU Press, pp. 19–38.

Mawby, R. (2002) *Policing Images: Policing, Communication and Legitimacy*, Collompton, Devon: Willan.

Meyer, J. and Rowan, B. (1977) 'Institutionalised Organisation: Formal Structure as Myth and Ceremony', *The American Journal of Sociology*, 83(2): 340–63.

Miceli, M. P. (2004) 'Whistle-Blowing Research and the Insider: Lessons Learned and Yet to Be Learned', *Journal of Management Inquiry*, 13(4): 364–66.

Miller, J. (2003) *Police Corruption in England and Wales: An Assessment of Current Evidence*, London: HMSO.

Minichiello, V., Aroni, R., Timewell, E. and Alexander, L. (1995) *In-Depth Interviewing: Principles, Techniques, Analysis*, Second Edition, Sydney: Addison, Wesley, Longman.

Mollen Commission, (1994) *Report of the Commission to Investigate Allegations of Corruption and the Anti-Corruption Procedures of the Police Department,* New York.

Moloney, E. (2002) *A Secret History of the IRA*, London: Penguin.

Moore, L. (1990) 'Policing and Change in Northern Ireland: The Centrality of Human Rights', *Fordham International Law Journal*, 22: 1577–607.

Moran, J. P. (1983) 'Garda Síochána College – An Overview', *Police Studies*, 6(2): 39–43.

Moran, J. (2005) 'Blue Walls, Grey Area and Cleanups: Issues in the Control of Police Corruption in England and Wales', *Crime, Law and Social Change*, 43: 57–79.

Morgan, R. (1989) '"Policing by Consent": Legitimating the Doctrine' in R. Morgan and D. J. Smith, (eds), *Coming to Terms with Policing: Perspectives on Policy*, London: Routledge.

Morgan, R. and Newburn, T. (eds) (1997) *The Future of Policing*, Oxford: Oxford University Press.

Morris, F. (2004) *Report of the Tribunal of Inquiry set up Pursuant to the Tribunal of Inquiry (Evidence) Acts 1921–2003 into certain Gardaí in the Donegal Division: Term of Reference (e): Report on Explosives 'Finds' in Donegal*, Dublin: The Stationery Office.

Morris, F. (2005) *Report of the Tribunal of Inquiry set up Pursuant to the Tribunal of Inquiry (Evidence) Acts 1921–2003 into certain Gardaí in the Donegal Division: Term of Reference (a) and (b): Report of the Investigation into the Death of Richard Barron and Extortion Calls to Michael and Charlotte Peoples*, Dublin: The Stationery Office.

Morris, F. (2006a) *Report of the Tribunal of Inquiry set up Pursuant to the Tribunal of Inquiry (Evidence) Acts 1921–2003 into certain Gardaí in the Donegal Division: Term of Reference (d): Report on the Circumstances Surrounding the Arrest and Detention of Mark McConnell on 1st October 1998 and Michael Peoples on 6th May 1999*, Dublin: The Stationery Office.

Morris, F. (2006b) *Report of the Tribunal of Inquiry set up Pursuant to the Tribunal of Inquiry (Evidence) Acts 1921–2003 into certain Gardaí in the Donegal Division: Term of Reference (g): Report on the Garda Investigation of an Arson Attack on Property Situated on the Site of the Telecommunications Mast at Ardara, Co. Donegal in October and November of 1996*, Dublin: The Stationery Office.

Morris, F. (2006c) *Report of the Tribunal of Inquiry set up Pursuant to the Tribunal of Inquiry (Evidence) Acts 1921–2003 into certain Gardaí in the Donegal Division: Term of Reference (i): Report on the Arrest and Detention of Seven Persons at Burnfoot, Co. Donegal on 23rd May 1998 and the Investigation Relating to Same*, Dublin: The Stationery Office.

Morris, F. (2008a) *Report of the Tribunal of Inquiry Set up Pursuant to the Tribunal of Inquiry (Evidence) Acts 1921–2003 into certain Gardaí in the Donegal Division: Terms of Reference b, d and f: Report on the Detention of 'Suspects' Following the Death of the late Richard Barron on 14th October 1996 and Related Detentions and Issues*, Dublin: The Stationery Office.

Morris, F. (2008b) *Report of the Tribunal of Inquiry Set up Pursuant to the Tribunal of Inquiry (Evidence) Acts 1921–2003 into certain Gardaí in the Donegal Division: Report on Allegations of Harassment of the McBrearty Family of Raphoe (Term of Reference (c)) and Report into the Effectiveness of the Garda Síochána Complaints Board Inquiry (Term of Reference (j))*, Dublin: The Stationery Office.

Morris, F. (2008c) *Report of the Tribunal of Inquiry Set up Pursuant to the Tribunal of Inquiry (Evidence) Acts 1921–2003 into certain Gardaí in the Donegal Division: Term of Reference (h): Report into Allegations Contained in Documents Received by Deputy Jim Higgins and Information Received by Deputy Brendan Howlin that Two Senior Members of an Garda Síochána May have Acted with Impropriety*, Dublin: The Stationery Office.

Morris, M. H. (1996) 'Accountability For International Crime and Serious Violations of Human Rights: International Guidelines Against Impunity: Facilitating Accountability', *Law and Contemporary Problems*, 59(4): 29–40.

Morton, J. (1993) *Bent Coppers*, London: Warner Books.

Muir, W. K. (1977) *Police: Streetcorner Politicians*, Chicago: Chicago University Press.

Mulcahy, A. (2000) 'Policing History: The Official Discourse and Organisational Memory of the Royal Ulster Constabulary', *British Journal of Criminology*, 40: 68–87.

Mulcahy, A. (2002) 'The Impact of the Northern "Troubles" on Criminal Justice in the Irish Republic' in P. O'Mahony, *Criminal Justice in Ireland*, Dublin: IPA, pp. 275–85.

Mulcahy, A. (2005) 'The "Other" Lessons from Ireland? Policing, Political Violence and Policy Transfer', *European Journal of Criminology,* 2(2): 185–209.

Mulcahy, A. (2006) *Policing Northern Ireland: Conflict, Legitimacy and Reform,* Cullompton, Devon: Willan.

Mulcahy, A. (2008) 'Policing, Community and Social Change in Ireland' in J. Shapland (ed.), *Justice, Community and Civil Society: A Contested Terrain,* Cullompton, Devon: Willan.

Mulcahy, A. (2012) 'Alright in their Own Place: Policing and the Spatial Regulation of Irish Travellers', *Criminology and Criminal Justice,* 12(3): 307–27.

Mullan, D. (2000) *The Dublin and Monaghan Bombings: The Truth, The Questions and the Victim's Stories,* Dublin: Wolfhound Press.

Mullan, D., Scally, J. and Urwin, M. (2001) *The Dublin and Monaghan Bombing,* Dublin: Wolfhound.

Murphy, Y. (2009) *Commission of Investigation into Catholic Archdiocese of Dublin,* Dublin: The Stationery Office.

Near, J. P. and Jensen, T. C. (1983) 'The Whistleblowing Process: Retaliation and Perceived Effectiveness', *Work and Occupations,* 10(1): 3–28.

Near, J. P. and Miceli, M. P. (1984) 'Organizational Dissidence: The Case of Whistle-Blowing', *Journal of Business Ethics,* 4: 1–16.

Neary, B. (1985) *Lugs: The Life and Times of Garda Jim Brannigan,* Dublin: Lenhar Publications.

Nevins, A. (1996) 'Oral History: How and Why It Was Born' in D. K. Dunaway and W. K. Baum (eds.), *Oral History: An Interdisciplinary Anthology,* London: Altamira Press.

Newburn, T. (1999) 'Understanding and Preventing Police Corruption: Lessons from the Literature', *Police Research Series,* Paper 110, London: HMSO.

Newburn, T. and Jones, T. (1996) 'Police Accountability' in W. Saulsburdy, J. Mott and T. Newburn (eds), *Themes in Contemporary Policing,* London: Policy Studies Institute.

Neyroud, P. and Beckley, A. (2001) *Policing, Ethics and Human Rights,* Cullompton, Devon: Willan.

Ni Aolain, F. and Campbell, C. (2005) 'The Paradox of Transition in Conflicted Democracies', *Human Rights Quarterly,* 27(1): 172–213.

Nixon, C. and Reynolds, C. (1996) 'Producing Change in Police Organisations: The Story of New South Wales Police Service', in D. Chappel and P. Wilson (eds), *Australian Policing: Contemporary Issues,* Second Edition, Sydney: Butterworths.

Noaks, L. and Wincup, E. (2004) *Criminological Research: Understanding Qualitative Methods,* London: Sage.

O'Brian, B. (1978) *Report of the Committee to Recommend Certain Safeguards for Persons in Custody and for Members of An Garda Síochána,* Dublin: The Stationery Office.

O'Duffy, E. (1929) 'History of an Garda Síochána', *Garda Review,* 331–35.

O'Dwyer, K., Kennedy, P. and Ryan, W. (2005) *Garda Public Attitudes Survey 2005,* Templemore: An Garda Síochána.

O'Grada, C. (1997) *A Rocky Road: The Irish Economy Since the 1920s,* Manchester: Manchester University Press.

O'Halpin, E. (1999) *Defending Ireland: The Irish State and its Enemies since 1922,* Oxford: Oxford University Press.

O'Mahony, P. (1996) *Criminal Chaos: Seven Crises in Irish Criminal Justice,* Dublin: Round Hall.

O'Mahony, P. (1997) 'The Ethics of Police Interrogation and the Garda Síochána', *Irish Criminal Law Journal,* 4(1): 129–40.

O'Mahony, P. (2000) 'Crime in the Republic of Ireland: A Suitable Case for Social Analysis', *Irish Journal of Sociology,* 10: 3–26.

O'Mahony, P. (2002a) 'Policing Ireland: Past, Present and Future' in P. O'Mahony (ed.), *Criminal Justice in Ireland,* Dublin: Institute of Public Administration.

O'Mahony, P. (2002b) 'The Psychology of Police Interrogation: The Kerry Babies Case' in P. O'Mahony (ed.), *Criminal Justice in Ireland,* Dublin: Institute of Public Administration.

O'Reilly, C. and Ellison, G. (2005) 'Eye Spy Private High: Reconceptualizing High Policing Theory', *British Journal of Criminology,* 46(1): 641–60.

O'Sullivan, D. (1999) *The Irish Constabularies 1822–1922: A Century of Policing in Ireland,* Dublin: Dufour Editions.

O'Sullivan, E. and O'Donnell, I. (2001) 'Why is Crime Decreasing?', *Irish Criminal Law Journal,* 11(1): 2–11.

O'Sullivan, E. and O'Donnell, I. (2007) 'Coercive confinement in the Republic of Ireland: The waning of a culture of control', *Punishment & Society,* 9(1): 27–48.

O'Toole, F. (1998) *The Lie of the Land: Irish Identities,* London: Verso.

O'Toole, K. (2007) *Report of the Garda Síochána Inspectorate: Policing in Ireland Looking Forward,* Dublin: The Stationery Office.

Palmer, S. (1988) *Police and Protest in England and Ireland,* Cambridge: Cambridge University Press.

Patten, C. (1999) *The Report of the Independent Commission on Policing for Northern Ireland,* London: HMSO.

Patterson, H. (2012) 'The Border Security Problem and Anglo-Irish Relations 1970–73' *Contemporary British History,* 26(2): 231–51.

Patterson, H. (2013) *Ireland's Violent Frontier: The Border and Anglo-Irish Relations During the Troubles,* London: Palgrave Macmillan.

Payne, G. and Payne, J. (2004) *Key Concepts in Social Research,* London: Sage.

Philips, D. (1980) 'A New Engine of Power and Authority: The Institutionalization of Law-Enforcement in England 1780–1830' in V. A. C. Gatrell, B. Lenman and G. Parker (eds), *Crime and the Law: The Social History of Crime in Western Europe since 1500,* London: Europa Press.

Prager, J. (1986) *Building Democracy in Ireland: Political Order and Cultural Integration in a Newly Independent Nation,* Cambridge: Cambridge University Press.

Prenzler, T. (2000) 'Civilian Oversight of Police: A Test of Capture Theory', *British Journal of Criminology,* 40: 659–74.

Prenzler, T. and Ransley, J. (eds) (2002) *Police Reform: Building Integrity,* Sydney: Federation Press.

Prenzler, T. and Ronken, C. (2001) 'Models of Police Oversight: A Critique', *Policing and Society,* 11(2): 151–80.

Punch, M. (1985) *Conduct Unbecoming: The Social Construction of Police Deviance and Control,* London: Tavistock Publications.

Punch, M. (1994) 'Rotten Barrels: Systemic Origins of Corruption' in E. W. Kolthoff (ed.), *Strategienn voor corruptie-beheersing bij de polie,* Gouda Quint: Arnhem.

Punch, M. (2000) 'Police Corruption and its Prevention', *European Journal on Criminal Policing and Research,* 8(3): 301–24.

Punch, M. (2004) 'Police Crime: Pathways into Police Deviance', British Society of Criminology Conference 2004, University of Portsmouth, 6–9 July 2004.

Punch, M. (2009) *Police Corruption: Exploring Police Deviance and Crime*, Cullompton, Devon: Willan.

Rapley, T. J. (2004) 'The Art(fullness) of Open Ended Interviewing: Some Considerations on Analysing Interviews', *Qualitative Research*, 1(3): 303–23.

Reid, K. (2002) 'Current Developments in Police Accountability', *Journal of Criminal Law*, 66: 172–95.

Reiner, R. (1978) *The Blue-Coated Worker*, London: Cambridge University Press.

Reiner, R. (1992) 'Policing a Postmodern Society', *The Modern Law Review*, 55(6): 761–81.

Reiner, R. (2000) *The Politics of the Police*, Third Edition, Oxford: Oxford University Press.

Reiner, R. and Spencer, S. (1993) *Accountable Policing: Effectiveness, Empowerment and Equity*, London: IPPR.

Representative Body for Guards (1969) *Submissions to Commission on Garda Pay and Conditions*. Dublin: Representative Body for Guards.

Reuss-Ianni, E. (1983) *Two Cultures of Policing: Street Cops and Management Cops*, New Brunswick: Transaction Publishers.

Reyolds, G. (1981) 'Riot Victims', *Garda Review*, July: 6.

Roebuck, J. B. and Barker, T. (1974) 'A Typology of Police Corruption', *Social Problems*, 21: 423–37.

Rogan, M. (2011) *Prison Policy in Ireland: Politics, Penal-Welfarism and Political Imprisonment*, London: Routledge.

Rolston, B. and Scraton, P. (2005) 'In Full Glare of English Politics: Ireland, Inquiries and the British State', *The British Journal of Criminology*, 45: 547–64.

Rowe, M. (2004) *Policing Race and Racism*, Collompton, Devon: Willan.

RSA (Road Safety Authority) (2010) *Deaths and Injuries on Irish Roads*, Dublin: RSA.

Rubin, H. J. and Rubin, L. S. (1995) *Qualitative Interviewing: The Art of Hearing Data*, Thousand Oaks, CA: Sage.

Ryan, A. (1997) 'The Criminal Justice (Drug Trafficking) Act 1996: Decline and Fall of the Right to Silence?', *Irish Criminal Law Journal*, 7(1): 22–38.

Ryan, A. (2000) 'Arrest and Detention: A Review of the Law', *Irish Criminal Law Journal*, 10(1): 2–11.

Ryan, W. J. L. (1979) *Report of Garda Síochána Committee of Inquiry*. Dublin: The Stationery Office.

Ryder, C. (2000) *The RUC 1922–2000: A Force Under Fire*, London: Arrow.

Salmon, T. C. (1985) 'The Case of Ireland' in J. Roach and J. Thomaneck (eds), *Police and Public Order in Europe*, London: Croom Helm.

Sanjek, R. (ed.) (1990) *Fieldnotes: The Makings of Anthropology*, New York: Cornell University Press.

Sarikakis, K. (2003) 'A Feminist in Brussels (and Glasgow, Berlin, Dusseldorf...): Self-Configuration in Research into European Union Politics', *The European Journal of Feminist Studies*, 10(4): 423–41.

Saris, A. J. and Bartley, B. (1999) 'Social Exclusion and Cherry Orchard: A Hidden Side of Suburban Dublin', in A. MacLaran and J. Killen (eds), *Dublin: Contemporary Trends for the 21st Century*, Dublin: GSI Publications, pp. 81–92.

Sarma, K. (2003) *Garda Public Attitudes Survey 2003*, Templemore: Garda Research Unit.

Sarma, K. and O'Dwyer, K. (2004) *Garda Public Attitudes Survey 2004*, Templemore: Garda Research Unit.

Scarman, B. (1981) *Report on the Disturbances in Brixton 10th to 13th April 1981*, London: HMSO.

Schabas, W. (2001) *Introduction to the International Criminal Court*, Cambridge: Cambridge University Press.

Scraton, P. (1985) *The State of the Police: Is Law and Order Out of Control?* London: Pluto Press.

Scraton, P. (ed.) (1987) *Law, Order and the Authoritarian State: Readings in Critical Criminology*, Milton Keynes: Open University Press.

Seneviratne, M. (2004) '"Policing the Police in the United Kingdom", *Policing and Society,* 14(4): 329–47.

Shearing, C. (1981) *Organizational Police Deviance*, Toronto: Butterworths.

Sheills, D. (1991) 'The Politics of Policing: Ireland 1919–1923' in C. Emsley and B. Weinberger (eds), *Policing Western Europe: Politics, Professionalism, and Public Order, 1850–1940*, London: Greenwood Press.

Shephard, C. (2009) 'Women's Organisations and the Campaign for Women Police in Ireland, 1925–1958: A Liberalisation of Irish Social Policy?', *Irish Historical Studies*, xxxvi(144): 564–80.

Sheptycki, J. (2002) 'Accountability Across the Policing Field: Towards a General Cartography of Accountability for Post-Modern Policing', *Policing and Society,* 12(4): 323–38.

Sheridan, G. (2009) *Does Gender Impact on Career Progression in the Garda Síochána?*, Unpublished Masters thesis, Dublin: DIT.

Sherman, L. (1974) *Police Corruption: A Sociological Perspective,* New York: Anchor Press.

Sherman, L. (1977) 'Police Corruption Control: Environmental Context versus Organizational Policy' in D. Bayley (ed.) *Police and Society*, London: Sage.

Sherman, L. (1978) *Scandal and Reform: Controlling Police Corruption,* California: University of California Press.

Siggins, L. (2010) *Once Upon a Time in the West: The Corrib Gas Controversy*, Dublin: Transworld Ireland.

Silvestri, M. (2003) *Women in Charge: Policing, Gender and Leadership*, Cullompton, Devon: Willan.

Skolnick, J. (2002) 'Corruption and the Blue Code of Silence', *Police Practice and Research,* 3(1): 7–19.

Skolnick, J. and Fyfe, J. (1993) *Above the Law: Police and the Excessive Use of Force,* Detroit: Free Press.

Smith, D. and Gray, J. (1985) *Police and People in London*, London: Policy Studies Institute.

Smith, G. (2004) 'Rethinking Police Complaints', *British Journal of Criminology,* 44: 15–33.

Smyth, J. (2002) 'Symbolic Power and Police Legitimacy: The Royal Ulster Constabulary', *Crime, Law and Social Change*, 38(3): 295–310.

Spencer, S. (1985) *Called to Account: The Case for Police Accountability in England and Wales*, London: National Council for Civil Liberties.

Stalker, J. (1988) *Stalker*, London: Harrap.

Starr, L. (1996) 'Oral History' in D. K. Dunaawy and W. K. Baum (eds), *Oral History: An Interdisciplinary Anthology*, Second Edition, London: AltaMira Press.

Steering Group on the Efficiency and Effectiveness of an Garda Síochána (1997) *Report of the Steering Group on the Efficiency and Effectiveness of an Garda Síochána*, Dublin: The Stationery Office.

Stoddard, E. (1968) 'The Informal Code of Police Deviance: A Group Approach to "Blue Coat Crime"', *Journal of Criminal Law, Criminology and Police Science*, 59(2): 201–13.

Sunshine, J. and Tyler, T. R. (2003) 'The Role of Procedural Justice and Legitimacy in Shaping Public Support for Policing', *Law and Society Review*, 37: 555–89.

Tomlinson, M. (1995) 'Imprisoned Ireland' in M. Ryan, J. Sim and V. Ruggiero (eds), *Western European Penal Systems: A Critical Anatomy*, London: Sage.

Tovey, H. and Share, P. (2000) *A Sociology of Ireland*, Dublin: Gill & MacMillan.

Townsend, C. (1992) 'Policing Insurgency in Ireland, 1914–23' in D. Anderson and D. Killingray (eds), *Policing and Decolonisation*, Manchester: Manchester University Press.

Townsend, C. (1999) *Ireland: The Twentieth Century*, London: Hodder Arnold.

Twomey, P. (1998) 'Freedom of Expression – Talking About "the Troubles"' in T. Murphy and P. Twomey (eds), *Ireland's Evolving Constitution 1937–1997, Collected Essays*, Oxford: Hart.

Van Maanen, J. (1978) 'Kinsmen in Response: Occupational Perspectives of Patrolmen', in P. K. Manning and J. Van Maanen (eds.), *Policing: A View from the Street*, Santa Monica: Goodyear Publishing.

Van Maanen, J. (1982) 'Fieldwork on the beat' in J. Van Maanen, J. M. Dabbs and R. R. Faulkner, *Varieties of Qualitative Research*, Beverly Hills, CA: Sage, pp. 103–15.

Vaughan, B. (2004) 'Accounting for Diversity of Policing in Ireland', *Irish Journal of Sociology*, 13(1): 51–72.

Vaughan, B. (2005) 'A New System of Police Accountability', *Irish Criminal Law Journal*, 15(3): 18–22.

Vaughan, B. (2006) 'Reforms to Policing North and South', *Irish Criminal Law Journal*, 16(2): 17–20.

Vaughan, B. and Kilcommins, S. (2007) 'The Europeanization of Human Rights: An Obstacle to Authoritarian Policing in Ireland?', *European Journal of Criminology*, 4: 437–60.

Vaughan, B. and Kilcommins, S. (2008) *Terrorism, Rights and the Rule of Law: Negotiating Justice in Ireland*, Cullompton, Devon: Willan.

Waddington, T. (1987) 'Towards Paramilitarism? Dilemmas in the Policing of Public Order', *British Journal of Criminology*, 27: 37–46.

Walsh, D. (1998) *The Irish Police: A Legal and Constitutional Perspective*, Roundhall: Sweet and Maxwell.

Walsh, D. (2000) *Bloody Sunday and the Rule of Law in Northern Ireland*, London: Macmillan.

Walsh, D. (2004) 'The Proposed Garda Complaints Procedure: A Critique', *Irish Criminal Law Journal*, 14(4): 2–26.

Walsh, D. (2009a) 'Twenty Years of Handling Police Complaints in Ireland: A Critical Assessment of the Supervisory Board Model', *Legal Studies*, 29(2): 305–37.

Walsh, D. (2009b) *Human Rights and Policing in Ireland: Law, Policy and Practice*, Dublin: Clarus Press.

Walsh, D. (2011) 'Police Cooperation Across the Irish Border: Familiarity Breeding Contempt for Transparency and Accountability', *Journal of Law and Society*, 38(2): 301–30.

Walsh, D. and Conway, V. (2011) 'Police Governance and Accountability: An Overview of Current Issues' *Crime Law and Social Change*, 55(2–3): 61–86.

Walsh, L. (2001) *The Final Beat: Gardaí Killed in the Line of Duty*, Dublin: Gill & MacMillan.

Walsh, T. (1985) *Garda Training Committee Report on Garda Probationer Training*, Dublin: Stationary Office.

Weinberger, B. (1995) *The Best Police in the World: An Oral History of English Policing from the 1930s to 1960s*, London: Scholar Press.

Weitzer, R. (1985) 'Policing a Divided Society: Obstacles to Normalization in Northern Ireland', *Social Problems,* 33(1): 41–55.

Weitzer, R. (1986) 'Accountability and Complaints Against the Police in Northern Ireland', *Police Studies International Review of Police Deviance,* 9: 99–114.

Westmarland, L. (2001) 'Blowing the Whistle of Police Violence', *British Journal of Criminology,* 41(3): 523–35.

Westmarland, L. (2005) 'Police Ethics and Integrity: Breaking the Blue Code of Silence', *Policing and Society,* 15(2): 145–65.

Whelan, K. (2003) 'Between Filiation and Affiliation: The Politics of Postcolonial Memory' in C. Carroll and P. King (eds), *Ireland and Postcolonial Theory*, Illinois: University of Notre Dame Press.

White, J. (2000) 'The Confessional State - Police Interrogation in the Irish Republic: Part I', *Irish Criminal Law Journal,* 10(1): 17–20.

White, J. (2000) 'The Confessional State – Police Interrogation in the Irish Republic: Part II', *Irish Criminal Law Journal,* 10(2): 2–6.

Whyte, J. H. (1980) *Church and State in Modern Ireland 1923–1979,* Second Edition, Dublin: Gill & Macmillan.

Wrong, D. (1995) *Power: Its Forms, Bases and Uses*, New Jersey: Transaction Publishers.

Young, M. (ed.) (1991) *An Inside Job: Policing and Police Culture in Britain*, Oxford: Clarendon Press.

Young, P., O'Donnell, I. and Clare, E. (2001) *Crime in Ireland: Trends and Patterns, 1950–1998*, Dublin: University College Dublin Press.

Zucker, L. (1977) 'The Role of Institutionalisation in Cultural Perspectives', *American Sociological Review*, 42(5): 726–43.

Oireachtas Debates
Dáil Eireann Debates (DE)
Seanad Eireann Debates (SE)

Newspapers
The Irish Times (IT)
The Irish Independent (II)
The Cork Examiner
The Irish Examiner (IE)
Sunday Business Post
The Belfast Telegraph
The London Times
The Evening Herald
The Irish Press (IP)
Sunday Independent (SI)

Radio
Radio Telefis Eireann (RTE)

Index

abuse of powers 41, 148, 151, 173, 182, 183, 188, 191, 193, 213, 214; *see also* Royal Ulster Constabulary
accommodation: *see* stations
allowances 21, 35, 36, 56, 204
Amnesty International 102, 142, 143, 151, 179, 194, 200
Anglo-Irish Agreement 135
Anglo-Irish Treaty 5, 20, 23, 26–32, 37, 38, 46, 47, 51, 61, 98, 210
Animal Gang 61, 149, 214
army 11, 12, 13, 50, 53, 125
Attorney General 47, 48, 52, 124, 197
Auxiliaries 21, 22, 29
armed 12, 21, 53, 63, 138; *see also* Emergency Response Unit, Special Armed Unit
armed robbery 99, 100, 105–7, 112, 136
Association of Garda Sergeants and Inspectors 114, 144, 177
asylum seekers 194

Barr Tribunal 200
Barracks: *see* Royal Irish Constabulary
Barron, Richard 186–9
Barry, Kevin 20
Baton: round 20, 99; charge 50, 52–53, 55, 61, 63, 72, 89–90, 119, 129, 130, 180; *see also* use of force
B-Specials 98, 99
bad apples: *see* rotten apples thesis
barricade incidents 196, 199, 200
beat policing 15–16, 60, 62–3, 86, 154, 196, 204
Black and Tans 21–3, 29, 31
Bloody Sunday (1920) 22
Bloody Sunday (1972) 99, 118
'blue flu' 161, 183, 217
blue wall of silence 190–1, 208

Blueshirts 1, 7, 34, 46, 50–4, 56, 63, 66, 85, 149, 210
bombings: 7, 52, 57, 99, 114, 212; Dublin 110, 153; Monaghan 153; World War Two 58; hoax finds 8, 186, 188, 189, 202; *see also* functions (death work)
border: checkpoint 7, 55, 111, 125–7, 130, 216; communications 216; danger 126, 131–6; deaths of members 127; IRA campaign 57, 93–5, 101, 123; IRA raid 124; patrol 130; policing the 7, 99, 100, 123–5, 185, 216; political policing 123–4, 135–6; protection work 125; public attitude 127, 131–3; public order 125, 128–32; refugees 130; RUC interaction 7, 134–6; Special Garda Task Force 127; station attack 128–30; strength 123–4; tasks 125–31; transfer 75, 124, 130, 132; training 130; weapons search 7, 125, 127–8
Brehon Laws 9–10
broadcast ban 101
Broy, Eamon 49, 56
Broy Harriers 51, 54
bullying 190, 195, 203

Carroll, Patrick 77
Carty Report 197
Catholic Church 5, 8, 93, 116, 152, 168–72, 212: clerical sexual abuse 170, 183; public attitudes 170
Celtic Tiger 5, 152, 158, 161, 185
Checkpoint: *see* border
child sexual abuse 152, 170–1, 196: Ferns Report 93, 170–1: garda role 170–2; Murphy Report 93; political influence 172; unrecorded complaints 171; *see also* Catholic Church
Civic Guard 27, 29–31, 38, 41, 53–4, 209